SUBMARINE WARFARE

Today and Tomorrow

Submarine Warfare

Today and Tomorrow

Captain John E. Moore
Commander Richard Compton-Hall

ADLER&ADLER

Published in the United States in 1987 by
Adler & Adler, Publishers, Inc.
4550 Montgomery Avenue
Bethesda, Maryland 20814

Originally published in Great Britain by
Michael Joseph Ltd.

Library of Congress Cataloging-in-Publication Data

Moore, John Evelyn.
  Submarine warfare.
  Includes index.
  1. Submarine warfare. 2. Anti-submarine warfare.
I. Compton-Hall, Richard. II. Title.
V210.M66 1987   359.9   86–7912
ISBN 0–917561–21–X

Printed in the United States of America
First U.S. Edition

Contents

List of Illustrations

HMS *Turbulent*, the second of six (possible seven) 5,208-ton (dived) 'Trafalgar' class SSNs commissioned on 28 April 1984.

A Soviet 'Victor I' class 5,300-ton SSN.

A Soviet 'Victor II' SSN.

HMS *Trafalgar* (SSN), with the Ops Officer at the computerized Action Information (AIO) and fire control system.

HMS *Sovereign* (SSN) at the North Pole.

HMS *Conqueror* (SSN) returning to the Faslane base.

USS *William H. Bates* (ex-*Redfish* SSN-680) with DSRV I *Avalon* embarked.

One of the two Soviet 'India' class rescue submarines carrying two DSRVs.

Between pages 204 and 205

A Soviet Mod 'Golf 1' (ex-SSB).

Anti-submarine netlaying during the Second World War.

USS *Perch* (APSS-313), converted into a troop-carrier in about 1948.

A Barr & Stroud CK34 search periscope.

Captain Third Rank Fisanovich about to tuck into some suckling pig.

HMS *E-51*, taken in 1917.

HMS *Resolution* (SSBN) carrying out basin trials at Rosyth after a refit in October 1984.

Senior Political Officer E. V. Gusarov reading out political information in the Soviet *D-3* during the Great Patriotic War.

Rapid reloading gear in HMS *Resolution*.

A Soviet 'Whiskey' SSK.

A Soviet 'Kilo' SSK.

The Dutch *Walrus*, launched 28 October 1985.

The West German *U-26*, one of eighteen 'Type 206' diesel-electric SSKs commissioned between 1973 and 1975.

A drawing of HMS *Upholder*, the first of the new Royal Navy 'Type 2400' SSKs, hoped to be commissioned in late 1987.

A Soviet 'Tango' 3,000/3,900-ton SSK.

HMCS *Onandaga*, first commissioned on 22 June 1967.

One of Australia's six 'Oberon' class SSKs surfacing.

Between pages 252 and 253

A Spearfish being prepared for sea trials in Scotland.

Foreword

To General of the Army P. I. Ivashutin, Head of the Chief Intelligence Directorate of the Soviet General Staff (GRU)

Although it is the custom in your armed services to keep Western books of reference under lock and key, presumably to prevent the true state of other nations' forces becoming common knowledge in the USSR, this volume should not cause you any such problems. All that is published here is readily obtainable in open literature, not a little of it from your own country. Perhaps by reading it some of your officers might achieve that condition of objectivity which your authorities consider to be lacking in many Western commentators.

To the general (non-submariner) reader

The customary views about those who serve in submarines vary from an assumption of lunacy to that of extraordinary heroism. Neither is remotely true as a generality – submarine services have known their lunatics and their heroes no more and no less than other branches of the armed forces. Those who serve in submarines are particularly fortunate in their close association with the sea and with each other; but they are ordinary people with similar reactions and similar problems to the remainder of their fellows. As a result there are frequent differences of approach to, and analyses of, the many aspects of submarine operations. No two submarines are run in exactly the same way, but the basic principles are immutable. It is how these principles are applied, the emphasis which is placed on one rather than another, that brings out the wholly admirable, competitive variations in approach which are essential in any successful squadron, flotilla or fleet.

In this book two submarine authors offer their individual views on the very wide range of subjects which are included under the broad heading of 'submarine operations'. Each chapter is attributed to a single author and is the result of many years of international experience in a highly professional service. A great deal has been written elsewhere on the subject of submarines – much of it, unfortunately, highly coloured and inaccurate. We have tried to present as accurate a picture of the whole as the use of unclassified material permits; and we have interpreted that material in a way which we believe to be sensible. If, as typical submariners, our viewpoints occasionally diverge, we ask your indulgence.

To submariners

Well, it will be something fresh to argue about . . .

1

Inner Space Today

Submarines are the most powerful and versatile, the most secure and least detectable of all naval units; they are also, tonne for tonne, the most expensive. Although the US Navy is still attack-carrier orientated for seaborne striking power, submarines dominate naval strategy today, and the strength, or the weakness, of a navy is directly related to its underwater warfare capability. The Soviets have no doubt that, tailored for specific tasks, submarines are the main and growing source of offensive power at sea, as well as being a prime means of defence. Accordingly, they have built a massive submarine fleet, and it is still expanding and improving in quality.

Submarines underpin decisions relating to defence in diverse areas, not all of which are linked to classical naval strategy, because nowadays they threaten territories, and hence populations, as well as seaborne assets. They have a marked effect on diplomacy and foreign policies; and their potential has to be reckoned against their price when trying to balance national budgets. Meanwhile, they are proliferating everywhere: even the small navies, formerly little interested in an underwater capability, are turning their thoughts downwards.

It could innocently be assumed, therefore, that underwater warfare is well and widely understood. Unfortunately, this is not the case. There is no area of political decision-making in which it is more urgent and vital to determine the facts and discard the abundant fictions. If nothing else were to be served by establishing the truth, taxpayers deserve to know what they are getting for their money and why social services and other public benefits suffer for the sake of submarines. Should submarine defence proposals be supported, or modified, or opposed? Do gains underwater outweigh sacrifices on the surface and ashore? Should underwater nuclear deterrent forces take priority over land-based strategic missiles and air-dropped weapons? Or are the land and air divisions of the nuclear deterrent no longer truly viable?

In attempting to provide a framework within which questions like these can be answered, this book looks closely at submarines today and over the next four decades. The period is not chosen arbitrarily: at present, research into a new undersea system will generally mature in ten or a dozen years and ultimately produce hardware that will only come to the end of its useful life forty years or more hence. Naturally, it is very desirable to find short cuts – and it is believed that these can be found – but, at the very least, the time lag, whether shortened or not, has to be recognised so that government treasuries can be convinced of the need for plans which look beyond the near horizon to a quite distant future. A proposed system which fulfils only the requirements of today will assuredly be inadequate tomorrow.

The USSR has its own notorious methods of leapfrogging foreign technology with the able assistance of GRU-paid agents and western businessmen motivated by greed and blinded by KGB disinformation. We can scarcely hope to emulate these procedures which have resulted in Soviet threats below the surface moving very fast in every sense – although it might be possible to use the intelligence which Western agencies garner, from various sources, rather more constructively for our own purposes. But, if there is a real will to tackle inefficiencies and cooperate sensibly and economically within the NATO alliance, it should surely be possible, even for a navy with strictly limited resources, to shift research, development and production into higher gear.

Western efforts will have to be speeded up considerably if we are to keep pace with Soviet developments underwater or, better, regain the technological initiative in this most crucial of all potential battlefields.

The authors, although both vintage submariners, do not intend to imply that submarines are the only threat or the only answer to a threat. They cannot be considered without regard to other forces, any more than they can be isolated from the real world which governs their application; but a thorough understanding of underwater warfare is the keel on which to build a reasoned concept of maritime defences. It needs to be laid now, before ignorance of the realities brings closer the chances of a watery Armageddon. The future of mankind may very well be decided in the depths of inner space long before men seriously engage in trekking to the stars or warring outside the earth's atmosphere.

Submariners themselves do not use romantic language; they would not describe their role or environment so melodramatically. Drama is something they studiously avoid. Nor are they prone to philosophical reflections – they are not apt to regard themselves as arbiters of human destiny. Nevertheless, that description is not too wide of the mark: the place for decisive action is, and will be, under the sea.

*

To start setting the scene, it is worth repeating that salt water covers seventy-one per cent of the world's surface. Much of this vast area has yet to be explored, let alone exploited. A hundred coastal states are keenly interested in the riches – chiefly oil, manganese, cobalt, nickel, copper and fish – which the sea, seabed and subsoil have to offer. Two thirds of the interested parties are unable or unwilling to police their inshore territorial waters, and they certainly cannot protect economic zones up to 200 miles from the coast. Beyond that limit, it will be hard for any country to safeguard rights it may acquire over continental margins or on the seabed in deep waters. The United Nations Law of the Sea Conference Agreement (to which the UK has not so far been a signatory) attempts to effect control; but these unguarded areas present an open invitation to trespass. Elsewhere, confined waters are ideal places for harassment, where any nation's shipping may fall victim to squabbles in which it has no direct interest. The utilisation of seabed resources will be a factor in future economic strengths, and is consequently an important and contentious item on the UN agenda. Furthermore, those countries who depend upon mercantile traffic, and have a navy to support it, are naturally determined to retain their ability to use the sea, while any nation, if it has the means, prefers to ensure its security by conducting its defence at a distance from its own territory.

Hidden from view, two or three hundred submarines of various nationalities are constantly at sea – most of them fully armed and instantly ready to fire a variety of devastating weapons if ordered to do so – in deep ocean areas, beneath the northern icecap, and probably sometimes hard up against (or, in the Soviet case, illicitly across) maritime boundaries, where surface vessels and aircraft cannot operate without blatant provocation.

There is, therefore, intense concealed activity in the sea by many and varied players and systems: strategic-deterrent submarines and attack-type boats endeavouring to locate and trail them; submarines of all types deploying, patrolling, listening, watching and waiting for action; submerged intelligence gatherers; midget intruders; oceanographical and oceanological vehicles; pipe-line and cable layers with attendant mini-subs; minelayers and minehunters; oil rigs and mining installations; and fixed ground acoustic surveillance arrays.

Interactions between these players are inevitable – to the point of physical collisions, which can, and do, occur – especially during surveillance operations. (Intelligence-related matters are not, incidentally, open for discussion, and we have no intention of making guesses about them in this book.) There are no fences in the sea, no signs warning poachers, trespassers and peeping-toms to keep off. It does not require an out-and-out pessimist to predict that conflicting ambitions underwater will result in situations which are liable to become more and more volatile as aggressors develop their means and gain confidence in their abilities. In short, while the nuclear balance between the superpowers may, so long as it lasts, prevent a third global catastrophe, underwater warfare at some level must be considered a distinct possibility. All the ingredients for conflict are there and confrontation is all the more likely because, in theory anyway, this form of warfare can be contained within the extensive bounds of inner space.

Submarine skirmishing would seriously damage economies: underwater warfare on any scale, even if it did not erupt into a nuclear exchange between the superpowers, would paralyse all but the more or less self-sufficient nations – and there are only two of those, the USA and the USSR. For the UK, ninety-five per cent of all trade goes by sea and shipping is constrained by key focal areas – such as the Suez Canal, the Red Sea, the Gulf of Oman and the Cape of Good Hope. All of these can all too easily be blocked off in times of underwater conflict.

It would be a mistake to think that the major navies alone can provoke a crisis leading to actual underwater confrontation. While the Western press focusses its attention on Soviet monsters like the *Typhoon* (apparently, when submerged, displacing more than some aircraft carriers), small and medium-sized navies are entirely capable of mounting attacks with modest or pocket-sized submersibles against assets anywhere in the world. It was, after all, only lack of continuation training and misuse of torpedoes – against clear German advice not to fire from deep – that prevented the 1,285-ton Argentinian *San Luis* from robbing the British Task Force of valuable ships during two approaches in the Falklands War of 1982. As it was, Rear Admiral Woodward, the Task Force Commander, was forced to take unwelcome anti-submarine warfare (ASW) measures which were bound to compromise, to some extent, defences against air and missile attacks.

Specific submarine policies cannot be meaningfully discussed unless the basic concept of war in general is first agreed. For this purpose, war may be defined as an organised group using violence to achieve an objective.[1]

In maritime warfare an organised group could be no more than a team of political extremists engaged in sabotage at sea. More usually, of course, it is a large nation with a recognised central government. An alternative but omnipresent possibility is that the organised group could be the relatively small surrogate of a major power.

Violence at sea may occur at levels ranging from acts of terrorism and piracy, through conventional or nuclear warfare in ocean areas, to nuclear bombardment of whole territories. Today, violence is often no more than potential, but defences have to be mounted against it as if it were actual. That is where the money goes – without the satisfaction of being able, physically, to cut the threat down.

The objective of past warmongers has sometimes been hard to predict. It has often been expansion, with an eye to a particular resource or the acquisition of a land mass offering several resources, including coastal waters. More recently it has been the setting up of a subservient government. Or it may involve a claim – genuine or not – for national security. To complicate matters, an objective may not be clearly expressed and it may not be rational – at least to the Western way of thinking: the Libyan Colonel Gaddafi's actions are a prime example.

The Soviet Union's objective, on the other hand, is crystal clear and has in no way deviated since Lenin first stated it more than eighty years ago. It remains the substitution of a system, the so-called Marxist-Leninist system, for society over the entire planet – an unspeakably dreary prospect whether one's politics are left, right or centre. Personalities, the form of leadership at any one time, Madame Gorbachev's Paris couture and her husband's best-selling literary peace efforts are purely incidental. They involve only a change of approach, not a change of aim: the greatest danger to the West is to think that Gorbachev and his colleagues attended some Russian equivalent of an English public school for gentlemen.

How a maritime warlike confrontation is manifested will depend upon the level of intensity decided upon by the organised group that determines to secure its objective. It is assumed that NATO ministries of defence mean what their name implies – that is, they are truly concerned only with national and allied defence and are not bent on expansion or aggression – even if the defence of a superpower may involve it in conflicts arising in and threats to friendly states. In spite of some less than dove-like voices in the Pentagon, this seems to be a fair assumption. There can be no such confidence in the intentions of certain other governments and organised groups outside NATO and other Western alliances. And things change: who would have thought, forty years ago, that Germany and Japan would become allies with America and that both countries would go to the top of the industrial league? Who would have thought that Britain would send a fleet 8,000 miles to do battle with Argentina? One might conceivably have guessed that France would opt out of the NATO integrated military structure at some point; but who else might decide to take an independent or neutral stand? No shifts are entirely beyond the bounds of possibility if we look up to forty years ahead – with one exception: it is not believable, for good practical reasons that will be discussed later, that the United States will divorce itself from Europe in general and the United Kingdom in particular.

Amongst the nuclear nations, with the possible exception of the enigmatic Chinese who will be addressed separately, the indications are that only the Soviet Union might seek to achieve its objectives by means of major warfare at sea, and by submarine warfare specifically. Minor – and very troublesome – submarine operations are quite likely to be mounted by lesser powers but, without question, the Soviet Union poses the principal threat, and will continue to do so. If (a big 'if' at present) the free world can deal with that, it can cope with others.

The Soviet Navy is explicit about using nuclear weapons if it comes to a fight, although this is clearly an option and not a commitment. Nuclear warfare cannot be considered outside the context of war in general: nuclear weapons are an extension of a war-fighting capability. Soviet submarines are intended (along, presumably, with such surface forces as survive) to fight a prolonged war in a nuclear environment, and submarines are uniquely able to do just that. The belief that a nuclear war would be short is no longer held to be tenable: this is evidently appreciated both in the Kremlin and in the White House, from where President Reagan has called on US forces to prepare to win a nuclear war when, not long ago, it was agreed on all sides that there could be no winners – only losers.

It is, at first sight, an unsettling change of attitude because it casts considerable doubt on the theory of nuclear deterrence – and we will be examining the realism, or lack of it, behind this shift later in the book. But does it make any difference to the real world today and tomorrow? That depends upon opinion in the Kremlin, and there, as in reality everywhere else, it is inconceivable that the Politburo is at present contemplating a global nuclear exchange as a serious choice. There is not much point in devising ways by which one's forces can escape annihilation if they have no homeland to return to. Furthermore, to quote NATO's Military Committee (Planning Document MC299), the Soviet Union has put in motion measures which will lead in fifteen years (that is in the year 2000), to the capabilities they deem necessary for launching a major conventional attack on NATO, without necessarily taking the risk of escalation by NATO or of giving it time for full prior reinforcement – either of which could prejudice success. At first sight this contradicts Soviet tactical nuclear doctrine, but the Soviet Navy is flexible: the Kremlin can confidently be expected to keep all options open. It must, by the way, have occurred to the Kremlin that – if such a thing were possible – a European war involving nuclear weaponry (much, on the Allied side, being American) would probably leave the United States in a dominant position.

Whether the Soviet Union will embark on a conventional venture when ready is debatable, but Soviet submarines are clearly involved to a great degree in preparation for it, while still retaining a tactical as well as a strategic nuclear capability. The Soviets will certainly maintain a large number of well-defended submerged ballistic missiles, probably as many cruise missiles, and a substantial fleet of purpose-built submarines whose principal task (not accomplished to date) will continue to be the seeking out, tracking and, if thought necessary, the destruction of Western ballistic-missile submarines.

In the meantime, Soviet disinformation is directed at driving a wedge between the United States and Europe. In that respect it is predictable that, while continuing to encourage and support anti-nuclear lobbies in the West, Soviet propaganda will doubtless put it about that the American people will not be willing to help Europe when, as a result of the Strategic Defence Initiative, the United States is sheltered from all but twenty per cent of the ballistic missiles directed against the North American continent. If a cynic believes that the USA would indeed return, for this reason, to a policy of isolation, it should be pointed out that, before counting cruise weapons, the one in five missiles which SDI could not destroy in space would kill fifty million Americans and bring the American way of life to an end for five centuries – and even the most optimistic SDI supporters are beginning to concede that the ratio of missiles getting through will in practice be much higher.

Moreover, like it or not, America is an island: she needs allies to extend her defences and keep the Soviet Union at arm's length. The US Navy is quite unable to provide enough ships to keep open the sea lines of communication (SLOCs) which are so highly valued, as well as meet fleet requirements in the Pacific and Indian Oceans, without allied help. And American forces cannot possibly, by themselves, patrol the whole vast area of inner space. Nor, come to that, can the entire NATO alliance; but Europe's geographical proximity to the Soviet Union enables European navies, small though they are by comparison, to guard the Soviet exit lanes and choke points with less than one third the number of ships and submarines that the US Navy would need, and could not spare, to patrol the same waters.

A ship or submarine sailing from Norfolk, Virginia, at a realistic deployment speed of twenty knots takes six days and five hours to reach a position off Reykjavik in Iceland; sailing from the Clyde base in Scotland the same distance can be covered in one day and sixteen hours. The speed of reaction at a base which is relatively close to the enemy is also faster because a sudden threat will generally be detected and evaluated that much earlier.

America cannot opt out of the NATO alliance unless she is also prepared to dispense with overseas interests and other obligations and, more importantly, sacrifice defence in depth and at a distance. Yet even the USA's huge reserves are not enough to ensure the security of the entire non-Communist world. The fruitless and tragic war in Vietnam conclusively pointed to the truth of that. It would therefore seem sensible for America to limit her military peace-keeping objectives geographically and adopt a strategy of manoeuvre. It may be that the Soviet administration has come to a similar conclusion with regard to its own objective from a purely military standpoint.

Although theoretically committed to expansion of the Soviet system through struggle, Russia is paranoid about the possibility of yet another armed invasion of the Motherland: defence – real defence rather than disguised aggression – is a genuine concern. Looking out over the world from the Kremlin's towers with Russian eyes, the USSR is surrounded by enemies. We would deny that in the West; but that is how it appears on a Soviet map. These are China and Japan to the south and east; the United States to the east and west; Western Europe at the very borders of the Soviet Bloc; and a number of unreliable countries to the south. What, then, is the best means of defending the USSR at sea?

Reverting to a basic principle, the Soviet Union must seek to conduct its defence at a distance; and highly mobile underwater defences are convenient because if a Soviet administration suddenly wanted to convert defence to war and launch an offensive, a number of boats would already be on station. Submarines, besides being deployable far afield without the enemy knowing where they are or what they are doing, are extraordinarily flexible: they can accommodate themselves to a radical alteration of orders, moving swiftly in, ready to attack, or quietly backing off, at the drop of a hat. Nobody will notice activities in inner space in the way that aircraft carriers certainly are noticed when they thunder off to land marines or prepare to fly off aircraft. Submarines are ideal tools for the flexible approach which the Soviets have adopted of creating and seizing opportunities, taking, then relinquishing the offensive, changing course and even swerving quite violently, without ever losing sight of the objective.

The security of the USSR may well be considered to depend on further expansion, and this will not be restrained by international treaties.

A display of physical or moral weakness by the West will be exploited, preferably by subversion and other non-military methods; but if the objective is barricaded and it appears that the barrier can only be breached by warlike means, then confrontation must be accepted. No matter how hard the democracies seek to reach 'mutual agreements' these will only last so long as it suits the Kremlin's plan.

Expansion to provide buffer zones, with established military bases, between the Soviet Union and the democracies is highly desirable, and the map points to Scandinavia for the next venture. Weakness is evident there, as demonstrated by the reluctance to take strong action against the Soviet submarines and midget submersibles which have been inordinately active in Scandinavian national waters over recent years. Neutralisation would seem to be the immediate aim, with occupation a distinct possibility in the not too distant future.

On the southern borders, Afghanistan is occupied (although the Russian troops must wish it had been the subject of a bloodless coup), while Iran, Greece, Syria and Iraq bid fair to being steadily absorbed into the Soviet Bloc. On the other hand, Turkey, with powerful West German support, is resisting Soviet influences and is likely to hold out.

China and Japan are, for the Soviet Union, a different sort of problem – and a worrying one at that. It is a fair bet that Russia will endeavour to neutralise both giants without precipitating full-scale war, and there has been a lot of Soviet submarine activity in the western Pacific to suggest clandestine preparations. In 1985 the Soviets started to devote an exceptional amount of internal and external propaganda to opposing American–Japanese military co-operation.

The Soviet administration is currently making moves which are principally concerned with preventing the United States from interfering with affairs outside the Americas. For both superpowers, submarines are the least expensive and most effective way of preventing or deterring interference without unduly raising the level of tension (which presently passes for peace), while constituting a kind of 'fleet in being'.

Turning to assets on and in the sea, supposing that the Soviet Union does decide to embark on military ventures – possibly persuading surrogate forces to undertake the dirty work for her – what has to be protected from such submerged marauders?

The most important asset for Britain, and almost as important for continental Europe, is merchant shipping – seldom sailing nowadays under the Red Ensign – on which commercial trading and life itself depends, just as it always has done, and which is also the only way of bringing in substantial reinforcements from across the Atlantic. The merchant traffic flow is crucial to Europe, and indeed the world as a whole is now more dependent on maritime trade than ever before. Although Britain herself has lost much of her share of shipping, the tonnage of the world's merchant fleets increased from 137 to 419 million tonnes between 1964 and 1984, and it is still growing, with an exceptional number of vessels flying the Hammer and Sickle. There is nothing in the foreseeable future that will replace this prime means of transport, with its great capacity and low cost per tonne-kilometre.

Merchant ships are exceedingly vulnerable to the depredations of submarines, and attackers do not have to be modern or nuclear to sink these attractive and easy targets. Nor will it necessarily be obvious, to the point of proof, if sinkings suddenly occur, who the predators are.

Mysterious predators

This happened during the Spanish Civil War, when Soviet ships were amongst the victims. Europe had split and taken sides after the war erupted on 18 July 1936.

The Germans and Italians supported the fascist military rebels under Franco, while the USSR backed the Spanish Republican government – sending, over a period of about eighteen months, some thirty or forty ships each month to Spain, carrying supplies ranging from food, clothing and medicine to arms, tanks and aircraft. Moscow also inspired the International Brigade, made up of volunteers from around the world. German and Italian vessels delivered similar materials to the rebels.

Towards the end of 1936 and throughout most of 1937, 'unidentified' submarines attacked Soviet and neutral merchantmen in the coastal waters of Spain, in the Western Mediterranean, and as far east as the Aegean Sea.[2] Three Soviet ships and some thirty-five neutral vessels of British, Greek, Danish and other nationalities were torpedoed and sunk. It was guessed that Italian submarines were responsible, but that could not be proved and they were not brought to book. In fact, two of the Italian boats were formally transferred to

Franco as the *General Mola* and *General Sanjunjo*. They were apparently crewed by Spanish nationalists, but it is difficult to believe that Spanish commanding officers and men, inexperienced in these foreign boats, were responsible for many of the sinkings. It was, however, a shrewd move by Italy to shift the blame.

The British government, with the most powerful navy in the world, dithered and took no positive action to protect either its own ships or those of its friends. Too late, in September 1937, the British reinforced the Mediterranean Fleet and, at the same time, France called a meeting of all the Mediterranean powers, including Italy, at Nyon in Switzerland. The outcome of this meeting was what became known as the Nyon arrangement – an 'International Agreement for Collective Measures against Piratical Attack in the Mediterranean by Submarines'.[3]

Various measures were introduced and it was agreed that any submarine found attacking shipping, or even suspected of such an attack if found in the vicinity of a torpedoed ship, should be destroyed. The attacks ceased, but the damage was done: Spain's foreign trade had withered and Russia had become fearful for its merchant fleet.

Mine warfare can also be anonymous, and submarines are excellent minelayers. Although most, if not all, of the 190 mines laid in the Gulf of Suez and Red Sea between July and September 1984 were rolled off the Libyan Ro-Ro ferry *Ghat*, the evidence points to them being of the Soviet type. However they were not, apparently, built to full Soviet specifications. Examination of at least one recovered mine suggests that the charges were much reduced – an interesting reflection on Soviet lack of confidence in Libyan discretion, which was justified by the fact that the first and fifteenth victims were Russian ships! Seventeen ships were damaged; the naval crewmen of the *Ghat* were duly decorated; and Colonel Gaddafi telexed Iran to tell Khomeni that he was 'pleased and content with the work accomplished in the Red Sea'. Presumably he would have been even happier if the ships had actually been sunk – which they probably would have been by full charges.

Libya has six Soviet-built 'Foxtrot' class submarines, each capable of embarking about two dozen mines (in addition to a full salvo of torpedoes), and a substantial quantity (with full charges?) is maintained at the Tripoli base. The Libyan Navy also includes two Yugoslav 'Mala'-class, two-man midget submersibles which can carry limpet mines.

Experience shows that it takes twelve years for a navy to create an efficient submarine attack force from scratch. Covert operations like minelaying, not involving action with anti-submarine warfare (ASW) units, are all it can be expected to manage with confidence any earlier. Libyan submariners should by just about now (1986) be arriving at a state of training where they might reasonably embark on torpedo attacks.

A very damaging type of piracy by the submarines of minor underwater navies is readily conceivable. The unwillingness of merchant crews to sail in dangerous waters and the high cost of war insurance could, by itself, be of value to an aggressor. Attrition by submarine *Guerre de Course*, or the mere threat of it, is an inexpensive way of weakening a maritime power or drawing naval units away from other areas.

Far below the surface inner space contains untold wealth in seabed and subsoil assets. Soon, oil and metallic ore will be brought up from great depths as well as from offshore installations and, within the next few decades, floating power stations could be established to harness the sea's energy. These massive investments will be highly vulnerable to submarine attack. Meanwhile, communication cables on the sea bottom can be tapped by mini-submersibles or preparations can be made for cutting them in the event of open confrontation: Soviet Spetsnaz forces have two special units trained for these operations.

Military assets on the surface of the sea are obvious – too obvious in fact. The Soviet Navy responded to the threat posed by the nuclear-armed US Navy Strike Fleet, with its carrier-borne, nuclear-armed aircraft, from the 1950s onwards by rapidly constructing submarines to deal with it. It is true that aircraft carriers make splendid submarine targets and can now be tracked by satellites so their position is likely to be known for much of the time; but if detection leads to attack the carriers can withstand a great deal of punishment.

With a large-scale and sometimes anonymous menace lurking beneath the waves, it would seem very advisable to understand what makes submarines tick, what their capabilities really are, and how submariners go about their business.

Besides widespread misconceptions it is not generally appreciated that underwater warfare, which can take so many forms, is liable to affect the life of each and every citizen. The danger of nuclear bombardment is recognised, but the effect on a civilian population of cutting supply lines has been forgotten since the last war. There are also financial and political considerations which touch us all. The price of a modern submarine is high enough, even if the enormous cost of extensive shore support facilities is not normally mentioned; but the political clout and bargaining power that submarines confer on a country which has the right number and the right type for its purpose is seldom, if ever, pointed out. And there is the rub. What is truly cost-effective for this or that navy?

The answer to that all-important question is confused and bedevilled, in the West anyway, by scanty knowledge at the highest political levels of a submarine's value; by a refusal to recognise its unique security; by parochial and internecine battles within the armed services; by a tendency for submariners to exaggerate their present needs while not looking far enough ahead to the future; by a lack of continuity amongst governmental and naval decision-makers; by misemployed and under-used intelligence about potential enemies; by a predilection for giving priority to the vehicle over the weapon system which it ought to embody; by a common inability to process paperwork quickly and justify operational requirements quantitatively at the design stage; and sometimes, in Britain, France and Germany, by overmuch regard for the export market at the expense of realistic requirements at home.

There are therefore many obstacles to be overcome long before a submarine goes into action, and they are by no means all of the enemy's making. There are bound to be grey areas in any kind of war planning – and inner space is not well illuminated. But if the clutter of muddled thinking can be cleared out of the way so that the facts can be examined dispassionately, it would be a great deal easier to make an educated guess at the few genuinely unknown quantities that remain, and to calculate the course that ought to be steered. There will be little chance of gaining much-needed public and political support, amidst belt-tightening economies, for the necessary hulls and systems if misconceptions persist.

It may be as well to correct a few popular mistaken ideas at this point, by way of an overture, before endeavouring to put the whole record straight:

A nuclear power plant cannot turn itself accidentally into an atomic bomb.

An attack-class nuclear submarine (SSN) is not to be confused with a nuclear ballistic-missile-firing submarine (SSBN). A diesel or nuclear submarine armed with cruise missiles (SSG or SSGN), although a relation of the first two types, is something different again.

Nuclear missiles cannot be unleashed irresponsibly or by mistake.

A diesel-electric submarine (SSK) is not outdated or redundant, although it does have limitations.

Nuclear submarines are not necessarily noisy.

A large submarine may look impressive, but size is not, for its own sake, a desirable attribute.

Torpedoes do not always hit.

Weapon trials in peace do not, historically, prove that weapons will work in war as hoped.

Sophistication and complexity, however exciting, are not to be preferred to simplicity and reliability.

If a navy is credited with a hundred submarines it does not mean that a hundred are at sea or ready for sea. During the Second World War, Admiral Doenitz managed, at best, to keep sixty-four per cent of his U-boats operational.

If one type of submarine suits one navy it may not suit another.

Because a Russian – Admiral Gorshkov, for example, lately head of the Soviet Navy – says something about his submarine force it cannot be assumed that it is the truth, the whole truth and nothing but the truth. The Soviet Navy is not apt to reveal its inmost thoughts. Nor is the attributed name necessarily that of the real author; every book and article is a carefully worded political document.

The Soviet submarine force has never demonstrated effectiveness in war.

Submariners do not suffer from claustrophobia.

There are, naturally, aspects of submarining which must always remain secret and be confined to those who need to know. But it is absurd that the primary question is seldom asked: why does any navy have submarines in the first place? There is no single answer to that question, because every nation has – or should have – its own reasons: the type or types it selects, if it is decided that submarines are necessary, will be peculiar to its own needs and to the mentality of its navy. Whether the equations are worked through to arrive at logical cost-effective conclusions is another question. Due regard ought to be paid, of course, to the needs and contributions of an alliance (NATO for example) but in practice it is not.

The general ignorance about submarines has, from the start, been due partly to submariners themselves. They grew up, as a race apart, at the beginning of the century amidst unpopularity and disdain. In Great Britain submarines were 'underwater, underhand and damned un-English'; submarining was 'no occupation for a gentleman'; and in America the expression 'pig boats', originally signifying that they porpoised up and down like sea-pigs (the mariner's name for porpoises), took on an unintended but more literal connotation.

Then, when U-boats commenced their first onslaught against shipping in 1914, underwater warfare came to be viewed with varying degrees of repugnance, although skilful handling of the press on the Allied side ensured that German U-boat men were cowardly and cruel while Allied submariners were uniformly heroic and humane. The dogma was to be proclaimed again in 1939. This extraordinary distinction spawned by propaganda – admittedly an essential weapon of war – still persists quite widely amongst the former Allies. But efforts in the 1950s to designate Soviet submarines as U-boats and regard them in the same dastardly light have met with scant success – perhaps because Russian submariners have not evidenced the ruthless professionalism for which the Germans were grudgingly respected.

Over the years, especially in Britain, submariners tended to withdraw into private navies of their own, and for long were reluctant to discuss their trade openly with their opposite numbers on the surface or in the air. Add the essential secrecy surrounding submarine operations to an almost Masonic kind of attitude towards outsiders, and a mystical jargon of words and gestures, and it is not surprising that so few people outside submarine clans have become intimately acquainted with their affairs.

All kinds of misconceived beliefs about submarines are, therefore, nothing new. They have always been rife: too many inappropriate designs and frequent failure to employ submarines correctly have followed, and proved disastrous. Three examples will illustrate the point.

The good the bad and the ugly

The excellent anti-submarine British R-class boats of 1917 could make sixteen knots submerged and were thirty years ahead of their time. They were scrapped immediately after the war (they looked too unorthodox) in favour of a few monstrosities (which came to grief) and some singularly pedestrian designs, all with a maximum dived speed of around eight knots.

Steam-driven K-boats were foisted on the RN Submarine Service as fleet submarines for work with the Grand Fleet in 1916–18. They had (to quote a submarine commanding officer) 'the speed of a destroyer, but the turning circle of a battleship and the bridge-control facilities of a picket boat'. Seventeen were built; there were sixteen major accidents and eight disasters. Only one torpedo salvo was fired at the enemy: it missed.

Large lumbering minelayers were sent to impossibly restricted waters (HMS *Seal* for example, consequently captured by the Germans in 1940)[4] or inadvisedly employed as torpedo-attack boats (USS *Argonaut* for example, lost in 1943).[5]

*

During the critical years leading up to the Second World War the German U-boat arm, under Admiral Doenitz, knew clearly what its strategy demanded; but Hitler and the Naval High Command continued to evade the unassailable logic which Doenitz advanced for a fleet of 300 boats and there were only forty-six ready for action on 3 September 1939 – a paucity occasioned by (possibly deliberate) misunderstanding amongst surface admirals and the Luftwaffe that arguably lost Nazi Germany the war.

Between the wars, other submarine navies muddled along with little or no idea of where they were going, or why. The United States had few submariner admirals and the Royal Navy's submarine branch was not represented at the Admiralty Board. There was, within all the submarine services, a scattering of good ideas with a few enthusiasts to promote them. But realistic criticism was emphatically not encouraged, as witness the reception accorded to a thoughtful and constructively critical paper, classified 'Secret', prepared by Engineer Captain George Villar RN on the staff of Rear Admiral (Submarines).

The foreword read:

It has been apparent to many Submarine and other Officers that the new construction submarines built and delivered since the [1914–18] war are not nearly as well thought out as they should have been.

It is also apparent that the E class type of hull, although for its day it was the best in the world, is no longer suitable for modern requirements.

The attached booklet gives reasons, arguments and a solution.

For a true appreciation of the qualities of the proposed submarine a criticism from an outside source (such as Vickers) is desirable.

Although this appears to be a laborious tome, it is well worth a day's study by a keen Staff Officer.

I have my Admiral's permission to circulate these papers to service authorities.

(Signed) G Villar,
Engineer Captain,
Staff of RA(S)
7th Decr. 1934

The Admiralty reacted, within days, with a 'Secret and Personal' letter to RA(S), the head of the Submarine Service:

Sir,

I am commanded by My Lords Commissioners of the Admiralty to inform you that it has come to their notice that a paper criticising submarine construction extending over a long period has been written by Engineer-Captain G. Villar, RN, dated the 7th of December, 1934, and has been circulated to certain Service Authorities with a covering note, of which a copy is attached. In this you will observe that the statement is made that the author has your permission.

2. It is the intention of Their Lordships to make full enquiry into the issue of this paper at Portsmouth at an early date, and, as you will be required to give evidence, you will be formally appointed to HMS Victory to enable you to attend.

I am, Sir,
Your obedient Servant,

....
(Secretary to the Navy)

Rear Admiral (Submarines) ducked and got away with it; his staff officer did not. It did not pay to speak out. Villar was, according to his confidential reports, 'a most energetic and exceptionally efficient officer' and he had 'quite exceptional engineering knowledge'. Alas, he evidently knew little of politics and suffered accordingly. The board recommended that he never be employed again and he was put on half pay for several years before being re-employed on relatively mundane duties when war came. His outstanding abilities were thrown to waste by Admiralty pique.

Villar would have smiled wryly at a more recent instance of things not being 'nearly as well thought out as they should have been'. Despite American experience and advice, freely offered, mild steel was used for the primary loop in the first all-British submarine reactor at Dounreay. As US naval nuclear experts had predicted, it had to be exchanged for stainless steel with consequent long delays and at very considerable and unnecessary expense.

The lesson, which turns on not collaborating sensibly with one's friends, will recur in more sad tales about materials and inappropriate usages which emerge in the chapters that follow. But today there is a new factor to contend with, a successor to the old prejudice and propaganda but less substantial and harder to argue against – emotion. It is a poor substitute for reason when the stakes are so high and the costs are so great, but emotion plays a notable part in defence debates when submarines are brought into the argument – especially if the word nuclear is attached to them.

Submariners themselves can be emotional, make mistakes and cling to preconceived ideas; they would not deny that. Arguments in close confines on board are apt to be deliberately needling, prejudiced, enjoyably ill-considered and, at variance with the submarine's silent image, loud. Total ignorance of the subject in hand is no bar to debate:

in the wartime French boat *Rubis*, for example, the three most interesting topics discussed by the young officers were: how to furnish a bedside table for a honeymoon; whether the Papacy was valid; and whether His Majesty the King of England at the time (George VI) was Jewish. Today's discussions are equally up-market. But, when it comes to business, submariners know what they are talking about. They are more professional than any other specialists or surface 'skimmers'; they have to know what they are doing or else the sea itself would quickly win the battle.

Unfortunately, there are not many serving submariners who are permitted to express themselves publicly. They distrust the media (with reason) and this leads to something of a vicious circle. If submariners need public and political support, as they undoubtedly do, a major public relations exercise seems to be required. Credible PR, as an expression of capability, is an effective deterrent. Career PR men are not, in this case, necessarily the best people for the job: submariners must be allowed to seize their own PR opportunities if their message is to come across and be convincing.[6] It is not a time for modest silence if better protection is to be had by taxpayers for their investment in defence. Even though nuclear submarines are getting cheaper in real terms, a deep pocket is still needed to pay for them.

It is said that there are only six or seven men in Congress and a handful in Parliament who understand the requirements of underwater warfare. The estimate errs on the generous side. In the submarine field it can only be hoped that the political helmsman will listen with due attention to his or her naval advisers; but hot politics are too often preferred to cold logic.

There are no submariners in the Soviet Defence Council, but three quarters of the Politburo have engineering degrees – which ought to help considerably in making competent professional judgements.

Consisting of the general secretary, currently Mikhail Gorbachev, his deputy and three members representing the eternal equilateral triangle – the Party, the KGB and the army (meaning the armed forces) – the Defence Council runs the whole vast dictatorship. The headquarters (STAVKA) of the supreme military commander (who may be the general secretary himself, as Stalin was) is subordinate to the Defence Council, which has unrestricted powers and is where decisions are made. The Supreme Soviet, the nominal governing body with members elected because they are the sole and unopposed candidates (albeit selected by fellow workers in the first place), is no more than a front – the nearest thing in the Soviet Union to an internal public relations exercise: it meets only twice a year for four or five days and its deputies have absolutely no influence over political or military matters (which are not disparate in the USSR), so that it can in no way be compared with Parliament or Congress.

Thus Soviet citizens, who are not taxpayers in the accepted sense, have no say in how or why money is spent on the gigantic machine at sea, on land and in the air that calls itself generically the Red Army.

It could be pointed out that an American president can govern even when Congress is hostile (unlike a British prime minister who needs a majority in the Commons) but a president has no power remotely approaching that of the general secretary chairing the Defence Council. Total freedom from control affects the underwater scenario in several ways: notably it enables the Defence Council to make use of a weapon which can usefully be associated with the secrecy surrounding submarines – bluff. It is known that some of the gap-narrowing in the past between East and West has been more apparent than real. The Chief Directorate for Strategic Deception, formerly commanded by General N. V. Ogarkov, is expertly accomplished in the art of bluff. The first Soviet anti-ballistic missile (ABM) defences were sheer sham, but the trickery contributed significantly to the American president's signature on the Salt I agreement, with Ogarkov a smiling observer. If the real nature of rockets and installations, which can be observed by airborne surveillance systems, can deceive, how much easier it is for deception to be practised with submarines, which are rarely glimpsed. Looking from a distance at the Soviet Navy it may be as well to be cautious when considering its apparent strength. Nevertheless, in all too many respects its submarine force is now demonstrably well ahead of the West (see Chapter 6).

The battles between differing and ambitious factions in the Soviet defence organisation are fought even more bitterly than in the Pentagon or Whitehall – and the penalty for losers in Moscow can be draconian. But freedom from democratic debates allows development programmes to be consistent, cohesive and coherent. It has to be accepted that democracies, by their nature, are handicapped by requiring public agreement to their policies – public agreement being a principal purpose of this book. Admiral Mahan recognised the dilemma a century ago: 'Free governments have sometimes fallen short while, on the other hand, despotic power, wielded with judgement and consistency, has created at times a great sea commerce and a brilliant navy with greater directness than can be reached by the slower processes of a free people.'[7] The component parts of a naval organisation are so numerous and so costly that neither a single nation nor an alliance in the free world can possess them in entirety without unacceptable sacrifices. Only the Soviet Union, whose people have been disciplined to accept blindly that the Politburo knows what is best for them, can expect to acquire what might be called a total naval system – albeit at crippling cost to an economy whose health has been failing since the revolution and, indeed, before that. (The Warsaw Pact countries outside the USSR itself are not singled out because they form much more than an alliance: their forces are fully integrated into the Red Army and the most senior officers are all Russian.) It is not, however, sure that the Defence Council can continue to build up the navy at the present rate: the cracks in the economy are becoming a little too obvious and it is a reasonable guess that the Council will, for a while, seek to stabilise the situation and maintain the status quo while concentrating resources on the most cost-effective, flexible and open-option weapon system – submarines.

Although Mrs Thatcher was met with resounding applause, a detached listener might have accused the British prime minister of over-optimism when, addressing Congress on 20 February 1985, she said about the Russians: 'It is our strength, not their goodwill, that has brought them back to the negotiating table.' A better case could be made for saying that the Defence Council has sufficient confidence in the Soviet submarine force to accept that nuclear missiles based elsewhere could be numerically reduced without jeopardising Soviet defensive or offensive capabilities. That is doubtless what Mr Gorbachev had in mind when, in his 1986 New Year broadcast to the United States, he remarked (referring, of course, to the Strategic Defence Initiative) that it would be senseless to seek security through new types of weapons. Perhaps the answer on all sides would be to adopt the Chinese doctor principle – only paying politicians and admirals while peace lasts, and stopping their pay if war breaks out!

All things considered, it looks as if the Soviet Union regards the multitude of routes through inner space as freeways leading, perhaps with devious diversions, to the final objective. The West will need to establish more underwater toll-gates quickly.

2

The Realities of
Underwater Warfare

Despite revolutionary advances since the war, the basic principles of submarining continue to hold good. It will be easier to gauge the effectiveness of modern systems if the realities and practicalities of underwater warfare are broadly summarised, before evaluating the threat and examining present and future techniques in detail.

WEAPONS

It may be helpful to start with a brief reminder of the types of weapons available; however, it should be noted that weapons cannot sensibly be divorced from the whole package – the weapon system – which embodies search, location, identification and delivery. Indeed, the complete submarine should be considered as a coherent weapon system.

Submarines carry exceptionally heavy armament, which is out of all proportion to their size when compared with surface ships.

GUNS AND SHORT-RANGE MISSILES

Guns have been replaced by missiles in certain submarines because it is no longer possible to surface, without immediate retaliation, within gunnery range; but torpedoes remain the principal weapons in most boats.

Unsportsmanlike behaviour
American and German boats in the Second World War made comparatively little use of their guns. When they did, they usually stalked their prey on the surface, using weather and light conditions to best advantage. The British used gunnery much more and, with the stated aim of patrolling primarily submerged, perfected a technique of not surfacing until the the last moment. With a deliberate pressure inside the boat, the conning- and gun-tower hatches were flung open

while still just under the water and the gun's crew were practically jet-propelled to their stations, with air whistling out around them, before the boat had settled herself properly on the surface.

Apart from shore bombardment, only small, unescorted and preferably unarmed vessels were subjected to three- or four-inch gun attack. Captains who used guns might, forty years earlier in Edwardian England, have been the target of 'unsporting' epithets then aimed at submariners; but they had no option and ran great risks.

Whether or not submarining was, or is, a sporting affair, it has always been jealously competitive; so it came to be unkindly said, within the British submarine service, that the commanding officers who favoured gunnery most were those who did not have the knack of hitting with torpedoes. In a few cases there might have been some truth in this; but the main reason for using a gun was that the target was either not worth torpedoes or had too shallow a draught. Similar situations might arise today with small but nevertheless important vessels, including high-speed hovercraft and hydrofoils.

It is not impossible, therefore, that certain small navies will equip their submarines with simple, portable, deck-fitted missile packages for use in circumstances where guns were once employed. There are large sea areas – notably in the Far East and off South America – where the risk of surfacing for a few minutes would be negligible. It has been perfectly practicable since about 1907 to house a gun under the casing (decking) and raise it by air or hydraulics for firing. The same principle could easily be applied to a missile launcher, thus preserving the submarine's stream line.

TORPEDOES

There are still traditional torpedoes in service with some navies which are little changed since the Second World War – unexciting but reliable, straight running at forty-five knots for 5,000 yards. But the majority of 'fish', not proven in war, are now 'intelligent' – equipped with passive and/or active homing devices they can be wire-guided by the firing submarine to their surface or submarine targets out to very much longer ranges. Warheads can be conventional or nuclear.

Some torpedoes are partial air-flight weapons, which break surface and take wing after firing, to home in on a surface ship or to re-enter the water and explode against or near a submerged target.

TACTICAL MEDIUM- AND LONG-RANGE MISSILES

Tactical missiles may be fired at medium and long range, depending on
the type of system, and from the surface or submerged – the latter will be
the rule in future. Generically they have usually been known as
submarine-launched cruise missiles (SLCMs) – small, fast, unmanned
'kamikaze' jet aircraft – but some tactical weapons now have a ballistic
trajectory so the terms can be misleading. Warheads may be nuclear
(typically of 350 kilotons), conventional (HE), chemical (CW) or
biological/bacteriological (BW). Missiles have a better track record than
torpedoes in peacetime test firings, but they are generally more
susceptible to countermeasures than underwater weapons.

ANTI-AIR MISSILES

Anti-air (AA) guns have been abandoned, but a few Soviet boats are
armed with a defensive anti-air missile system about which little is known.
The equipment which has been glimpsed could possibly be a bluff; but if
such a system can be made to work – and there is no technical reason why
it should not – it would have a major tactical impact on operations by
anti-submarine aircraft and helicopters, neither of which carry any form
of defence. A self-initiated anti-aircraft missile (SIAM) is under
development in the US Navy.

Trouble in the air

Anti-submarine aircraft and helicopters have long been a menace. In
1957 the commanding officer of HMS *Springer* found an answer to one
of the latter by purposely ramming and wrecking the sonar ball which it
was dunking off Northern Ireland. It was an effective but costly tactic:
the helicopter itself was not pulled down but *Springer*'s captain only
narrowly avoided a court-martial. The incident provoked thought and
in 1964 – it took a long time for the idea to sink in – the possibility of
equipping boats with anti-helicopter, anti-small-ship missiles was
explored. In 1970, (six more years later) HMS *Aeneas* became the first
(and last to date) British guided-missile submarine (SSG) with a
battery of army man-portable blowpipe missiles on the periscopic radar
mast. They could be fired from periscope depth and worked quite well,
but submariners felt it was too much of a last-ditch defence. The
project was dropped when *Aeneas* was de-commissioned in 1972 – at
which time somebody painted SS *Gillette* on her stern, a cynical
forecast of the razor-blade fate that awaited her, together with the
grandly named SLAM (submarine-launched anti-aircraft system).

STRATEGIC MISSILES

Submarine-launched ballistic missiles (SLBMs) are fired when fully submerged (although a few old Soviet and Chinese boats have to surface), to ranges measured in thousands of miles – principally against territories, though it is not inconceivable that they could be targeted on groups of ships; and a megaton burst outside the atmosphere, at a height of a hundred miles, would disrupt communications and shore electrical power supplies, and wreck much unshielded shipboard (but not submarine) electronic equipment over an 850–mile radius. The warheads are always nuclear and usually multiple.

Long-range cruise missiles (SLCMs), formerly considered as purely anti-ship weapons, are now fully capable of shore bombardment: hence the distinction between attack submarines (normally nuclear-powered SSNs) which carry SLCMs, and strategic submarines (hitherto uniquely ballistic-missile-launching SSBNs) has become blurred.

MINES

Several types of mines can be embarked, conventional or nuclear, for laying in shallow or deep water.

Weapons that wait

Mines were a formidable submarine weapon during both world wars, but submariners disliked minelaying because it often took boats close inshore and necessitated, for tube-launched weapons, a reduced torpedo load. However, external vertical mine chutes, with little or no sacrifice of torpedo armament, proved entirely practicable in German, French and British boats. There were, for example, sixteen mines in the saddle tanks of First World War British E-boats at the marginal expense of two beam torpedo tubes; and HMS *Tetrarch* was similarly equipped, for a short trial period, at the beginning of the Second World War. The six French submarines of the 'Saphir' class carried thirty-two moored mines in external wells: FFS *Rubis* laid 683 of them in a record-breaking twenty-eight patrols between 1940 and 1944, claiming fourteen supply ships, seven anti-submarine vessels and minesweepers, and damage to one supply ship and a U-boat.

German U-boats laid 327 mines off the eastern American coastline resulting in eleven ships sunk or damaged. In addition, seven ports had to be closed for a total of forty days, equivalent in result to a great deal of tonnage being sunk – an intriguing aspect of submarine deterrence.

A total of 658 (tube-launched) mines were laid by Allied, mainly US, submarines in the Pacific resulting in twenty-seven Japanese ships being sunk or damaged beyond repair and another twenty-seven being damaged but repairable. Therefore, for each dozen mines laid, one was successful.

It was not obvious to an outside observer that a submarine was loaded with mines internally or externally – nor would it be any more obvious today.

Although it is not known for certain what caused the loss of some submarines between 1939 and 1945, mines probably accounted for about one third of the British boats which did not return from patrol.

LANDING AGENTS

Standard submarines frequently landed agents or reconnaissance parties in both world wars. Clandestine operations were remarkably successful, although the boats had to surface. Nowadays most boats have exit and re-entry facilities (stemming largely from escape arrangements) for frogmen while dived. Although details have not been revealed, it can be assumed that Special Boat Squadron (SBS) Royal Marines were landed by British submarines during the 1982 Falklands conflict.

DESIGN FOR WAR

The shape – circularity – and thickness of a hull, together with the material employed (usually but not necessarily metal), dictate both the diving depth and the resistance to underwater explosions. In turn, there are other considerations which can affect the strength of a hull. The German versus the British approach to submarine design before 1939 is especially interesting.

A question of priorities

German U-boats were not designed for comfort: they were designed for action and action alone. Everything was subordinated to fighting ability and one boat of a class was mechanically the twin of another, which greatly simplified training and maintenance. Nor were they built for a long life; but that was not because of a disregard for life itself – although Captain (soon Admiral) Doenitz, commanding the U-boat arm from 1935, had no illusions about forthcoming losses. The boats, like their crews, were intended only for war, and no war would last for twenty years – which was the designed life of British and Allied submarines.

This philosophy penetrated deep. It allowed the Type VIIC, the workhorse of the fleet, to be equipped with exceptionally high-capacity 'soft' thin-plate battery cells, which did not last long physically (a few patrols) but which gave twice the submerged endurance at top speed of the Allied batteries, which had a life-span of several years.

The hull of a Type VIIC was made of three-quarter-inch to seven-eighth-inch steel, instead of just over half an inch as in most comparable submarines. That was made possible by omitting features which submariners elsewhere would gladly have foregone if the advantages had been realised – and twice the diving depth was a notable advantage.

Incredibly, it was insistence on an accurate magnetic compass, to supplement the perfectly serviceable gyro, that was at least partly to blame for restricting the diving depth of British boats. The magnetic compass was placed outside the hull, in the position demanded by the Staff, vertically above the helmsman; and the Royal Navy would not accept steel within seven feet of the instrument, although the Germans were content with a distance of three feet and hence with a less predictable compass deviation. The accuracy was sufficient to get a U-boat out of trouble, but maybe not always have been good enough for confident navigation in pilotage waters. Presumably Doenitz asked 'So what?' The Royal Navy, insisting on one hundred per cent (and, still, by the way, not getting it), felt obliged to build conning and gun towers of non-magnetic bronze to satisfy this trifling requirement: bronze is heavy and its use prevented thicker steel being used for the main hull, besides adding cumbersome top weight.

U-boat hulls were also circular in cross-section from stem to stern: this was achieved by limiting the internal bow torpedo tubes to a group of four. Other navies demanded a salvo of six torpedoes forward (sometimes eight with external tubes as well), and that was arguably justifiable with fast, armoured targets in view. But six tubes could only be installed in an oval bow, which was not the best shape.

There were other factors which allowed German hulls to be tougher. U-boats were not provided with special escape hatches (which, anyway, in wartime were often shut and bolted externally in British boats to prevent them jumping during a depth-charge attack); there was no forward collision bulkhead; and the reserve of surface buoyancy was comparatively low – but still safe in the heaviest weather.

The starkly realistic German U-boat arm recognised that unnecessary and unwarlike features, which supposedly contributed to safety in peacetime, actually militated against success and survival in war. The point has relevance today.

SUBMERGED CONTROL AND PROPULSION

The natural condition for a submarine is submerged when, in neutral buoyancy, it exactly equals the weight of water it displaces and tends neither to sink nor rise. To maintain this bodily state, and to balance the trim longitudinally, the level of water in the internal trimming tanks has to be adjusted continually to compensate for differing seawater densities and changes in weight due to consumption of stores, fuel, weapons discharged, the movement of personnel fore and aft, and so on. Pumps are apt to be noisy and they are therefore run as little as possible. Some trimming officers master the art; others do not. Trimming is an obvious area for computerised automation, which is highly desirable for hovering and surfacing without damage in ice.

Water is not flooded in to go deep: on the contrary, compression of the hull makes a boat negatively buoyant and water has to be pumped out. However, many of the smaller submarines have an auxiliary tank ('Q tank' in British boats) which can be flooded very quickly, and subsequently blown, to give temporary negative buoyancy for rapid depth-charging.

When on the surface a submarine is supported on cushions of air in ballast tanks, which are usually outside the hull proper. On diving the air is released through main vents at the top of these tanks, allowing water to enter through free-flood holes at the bottom. In order to surface, the water is expelled again by blowing high-pressure air into the ballast tanks with the main vents shut.

External ballast tanks can play another significant role. If, as in modern Soviet submarines, the outer hull which they form is well displaced from the pressure hull, and if this is wrapped all around the submarine to make a complete double hull, it offers effective protection against conventional anti-submarine weapons. The force of an explosion underwater varies inversely with the cube root of the distance from impact. So if a weapon is detonated against the thin outer skin a few feet

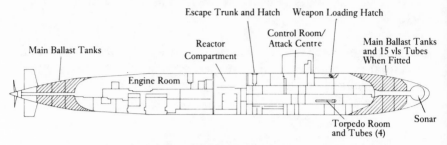

US NAVY LOS ANGELES CLASS SSN

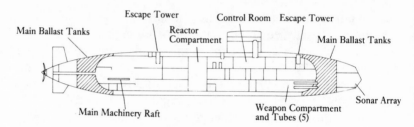

RN SWIFTSURE CLASS SSN

SINGLE HULL SSNs

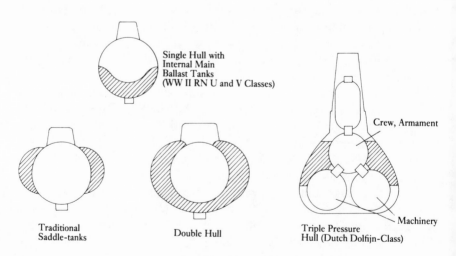

SUBMARINE HULL AND BALLAST TANK TYPES
(SCHEMATIC)

away from the pressure hull, relatively little harm will be done. A double hull can also accommodate fuel, torpedoes, missiles, mines, and equipment – sonar arrays, or perhaps batteries for secondary propulsion in a nuclear boat – for which there is insufficient space inside the submarine. The Soviets make full use of double-hull construction, which can also be used to shape a boat advantageously; most other navies have failed to adopt the principle, for reasons which are not apparent.

Hydroplanes and rudders control a submerged submarine just as they always have done, but now it is usual for one man watching over an autopilot with a single control column, not unlike that in an aircraft, to do what three men did before. A small movement of the after planes produces a violent angle at high speeds, so plane angles are limited above a few knots. Tabs may be fitted on trailing edges, as on the fastest Soviet boats, obviating the need to tilt the whole plane area. And, of course, there is at least one back-up system which can instantly be switched into operation if primary control fails. A submarine at twenty or thirty knots can change depth through hundreds of feet in seconds – an uncomfortably exhilarating sensation when not fully under control.

The safe diving depth is reckoned, as a rule, to be between a half and three quarters of the ultimate crushing depth – which can be calculated very precisely, as unmanned tests have proved. For submarines which can go well below 1,000 feet this safety factor seems unnecessarily high – the Soviets have probably cut it to a minimum, although there will still be a substantial margin for error, or for deliberate use if hard-pressed. U-boats during the war went to their absolute limits to evade counter-attacks, although well aware that if a depth-charge did explode nearby the effect would be greatly intensified by the pressure of water already exerted – 450 pounds on every square inch of the hull at 1,000 feet.

A porpoise or teardrop shape with a single propeller is the ideal for speed and control with a length-to-breadth ratio of about seven to one. Some modern boats come fairly close to this but, with all that has to be packed into the hull, something in the order of nine to one is more common for nuclear-powered attack boats (SSNs). An ideal shape is impossible to achieve for ballistic-missile submarines (SSBNs), which have a ratio of about thirteen to one and are therefore less manoeuvrable – although at full power they can make between twenty-five and thirty knots plus.

The first submarine
The first practical warlike submarine, USS *Holland* (SS–1), was designed by the Irish-American John Philip Holland before the turn

of the century. 'Holland' boats were subsequently adopted by nearly all the world's navies, including Russia, in the early 1900s.

They were short and fat – very well proportioned – but thereafter submarines became longer and thinner. It was not until 1954 that USS *Albacore* (AGSS–569) demonstrated the high speed and excellent control afforded by her fishlike shape, sometimes designated by her name but historically attributable to an Irish invention.

Holland was wrong about one thing. The depth for HM Submarine Torpedo Boat *No–1* (generally known as *Holland I* in the Royal Navy) was specified as 100 feet. Records suggest that she never went below fifty-eight feet – which was just as well because naval constructors, who examined the hull after the little boat was salvaged and put on display at the Royal Navy Submarine Museum in 1982, discovered that she would have started to collapse at sixty feet. Naval architecture was less exact in those days: the intrepid early submariners had two feet to spare between safety and disaster.

DIESEL-ELECTRIC PROPULSION

Diesel-electric drive needs little explanation: when on the surface or snorkelling, generators charge the battery or float the load to supply power to the propeller(s) and auxiliary circuits. A diesel-electric submarine (SSK) has no need to surface on passage or patrol; noisy periods when running the generator and exposing the snorkel mast to suck in air are cut to a minimum, at irregular intervals, and unless anti-submarine aircraft activity is intense in the area an alert watch should prevent the boat from being detected – or, if she is detected, from anti-submarine action being successfully prosecuted. However, if heard while running the generator by a nuclear-powered submarine (SSN) which subsequently uses active sonar to pin it down, the diesel boat is at a decided disadvantage and the chances of escape are not good. Against that, a diesel-electric submarine on electric motors alone – perhaps ninety per cent or more of the time on patrol – is virtually silent over the full band of sonic frequencies: it is therefore a near-perfect listening platform and safe from passive detection. SSKs usually prefer to be assigned inshore areas rather than patrolling in the open sea, where an exposed snorkel mast sticks out in calm water like the proverbial sore thumb.

The Isle of Wight cruise
In the summer of 1904 the Royal Navy's five 'Holland' boats, with four-cylinder gasoline engines, set out from Gosport to circum-

navigate the Isle of Wight – on the surface, of course. It was not an ambitious project, but three broke down before reaching Spit Sand Fort four miles from the start and only one got as far as Cowes a dozen miles away. The American Otto engines usually worked better than that, and the embarrassing failure to complete the course was evidently hushed up because later that year, on 17 November, the *Naval and Military Record* proudly reported that:

... a few Lieutenants and Sub-lieutenants have crossed from Spithead to Cowes and back in a submarine, doing the distance of about twelve knots [meaning nautical miles] each way in excellent time. To have navigated a vessel of this type safely across the Solent, with its currents and peculiar set of tides and its sandbanks, is regarded as extraordinary in modern naval practice, and that it should have been performed by these young officers makes the event additionally interesting. There is evinced on the part of officers and men of His Majesty's Navy a marked desire to serve on these vessels, and the volunteers for that purpose are far in excess of the requirements.

The conversion from petroleum to diesel engines, starting in about 1908 with HMS *D–1*, effected a revolution in underwater warfare that was almost as significant as the invention of nuclear power would be half a century later. The unreliable, dangerous and short-range gasoline 'submarine boats', with (in the RN) three white mice standing guard to give warning of carbon monoxide poisoning, were at best not much more than an extension of harbour defences. Diesel power enabled them to roam far afield, independent of support, in waters which had hitherto been considered as 'belonging' to one country or another. The consequences were profound.

Independence and long range, besides concealment and stealth, are a submarine's main attributes. An average diesel submarine has a range of 10,000 miles – at least twice that of a frigate which needs refuelling quite frequently at sea. The range of a nuclear-powered submarine is limitless for all practical purposes within crew limitations. US, British and Soviet nuclear-powered submarines have circumnavigated the world. The new Chief of the Soviet Navy, Admiral Chernavin,[1] organised a submerged round trip by a detachment of boats in 1966.

NUCLEAR PROPULSION

The fuel for a nuclear plant is U–235, an isotope – found in slightly less than one per cent of all uranium – which has three fewer neutrons in the nucleus of its atom. An atom of U–235 splits when hit by a neutron from another atom, giving off heat and radioactivity. Some of its neutrons shoot off and shatter other U–235 atoms, which in turn give off heat, radioactivity and more neutrons in a self-sustaining chain reaction. The reactor is then said to be critical.

The part of a nuclear reactor that produces heat, the core, is made up of fuel elements each of which is enclosed by a strong outer metallic case, or cladding. The elements are surrounded and separated by pure water – a moderator which slows down the emitted neutrons so that, instead of flying off into nowhere, they are more likely to hit and split a nucleus on their way. The fission process has been likened to throwing magnets at a steel wire mesh: if thrown too hard they sail through and do not stick.

The small core is enclosed in a large and very strong reactor pressure vessel (RPV), pressurised to prevent the water, which is a coolant as well as a moderator, from boiling – hence the name pressurised water reactor (PWR).

The hot coolant water in the RPV is radioactive and cannot be used for generating power directly: it is therefore circulated by primary coolant pumps through a heat exchanger, which generates steam for a non-radioactive secondary loop supplying the main turbine(s), turbo-generators and associated condensers – a conventional steam plant assembly. The reactor compartment containing the entire primary circuit is shielded by lead and polythene.

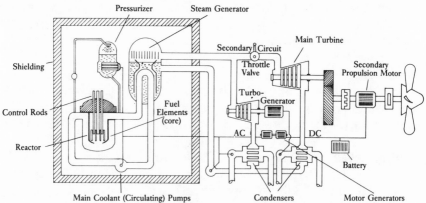

SCHEMATIC SUBMARINE PRESSURIZED WATER NUCLEAR POWER PLANT

The original two PW reactors (since replaced) in the Soviet 19,000-ton icebreaker *Lenin* (first commissioned 1959) were probably prototypes for submarine machinery and their published statistics are therefore interesting: they also indicate the small size of a reactor core.

RPV: Diameter 6.56 ft, Ht 16.4 ft, walls 4 ins thick.

Core: Diameter 3 ft, Ht 4.7 ft, No. of fuel elements 37 (enriched to 5% U235), No. of control rods 24.

Reactor inlet temp. 478°F, outlet 615°F

Steam generator pressure 430 lbs per sq. in, temp. 590°F

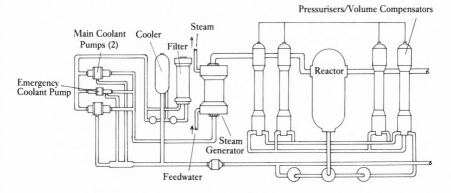

SOVIET LENIN ICEBREAKER – ORIGINAL PRESSURISED WATER REACTOR SYSTEM

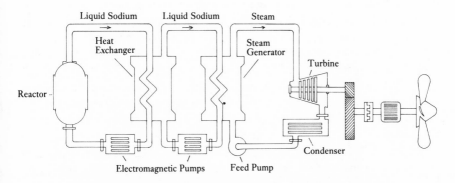

SCHEMATIC ARRANGEMENT OF ONE TYPE OF SODIUM-COOLED REACTOR WITH AN INTERMEDIATE HEAT EXCHANGER

When shutting the plant down Hafnium control rods, which act something like blotting paper and absorb sufficient neutrons to halt the chain reaction, are lowered into the core. In an emergency 'scram', due to a fault in the system, some or all of the rods are lowered automatically to bring the reactor to a sub-critical state. When the rods are withdrawn sufficiently to give a stable neutron population and fission rate, the reactor again becomes critical.

A nuclear plant responds immediately to an increase or decrease of power used without moving the control rods. If more energy (steam) is taken from the secondary circuit by opening a throttle-valve wider, the coolant (moderator) loses heat, becomes denser and slows down more neutrons, which collide with more atoms and instantaneously produce more heat until, very quickly, a balance is achieved at the new level of power required. If less power is demanded, the coolant (moderator) becomes hotter and less dense; fewer neutrons are slowed down to 'collision speed' and again the process stabilises. It is all elegantly simple.

REACTOR SAFETY

Risks, safety precautions and accident countermeasures have to be considered in any objective description of reactor operations; and any discussion of risk must cover the hazards of ionising radiation.[2]

At the simplest level, radiation hazards are of two types. Firstly, if given in high enough doses, radiation kills cells: the severe result of this action, sometimes referred to as radiation sickness, is death of the individual – although it must be emphasised that these effects do not occur if radiation doses are kept below a threshold level. Secondly, radiation may damage or alter cells, the most important result of this being the possible induction of cancer, which would manifest itself some years after the radiation is received. The probability of its occurrence increases, in the main, with the radiation dose, and there is no apparent threshold.

Radiation is not a new or modern hazard. Since its creation our planet has been bombarded by cosmic and solar radiation; naturally occurring radioactive isotopes are incorporated into our bodies so that we irradiate both ourselves and our companions; and the earth itself contains natural radioactive elements which irradiate us daily. These naturally occurring radioactive sources decay slowly with time. Thus, in bygone ages the natural radiation background must have been higher than today.

Since radiation is now used extensively in medicine and industry (the use of reactors to propel submarines is but a single example), national legislation must contain a system to control and limit the hazard. In principle the rules require that all radiation exposures should be kept as low as is reasonably achievable, but they go on to specify a definite limit beyond which radiation workers must not be exposed. The early effects of radiation, including sickness and death, are completely avoided by setting the limit below the threshold level at which they occur. However, in considering the risk of cancer and other long-term side effects for which the probability increases with radiation dose, comparison is made with the average risks of what are generally regarded as safe industries. A limit is also specified for members of the general public not exposed to radiation as part of their occupation: this limit is one tenth of the radiation worker's limit, and is made on the basis of comparison with the risks of riding on public transport.

In addition to those limits, which apply to planned uses of radiation, accident situations must also be considered. If, for example, radioactive gases are released, there are a number of countermeasures that can be taken, ranging from simple sheltering inside with windows closed to evacuation from the area. What is required in such situations is a clear indication as to the level of hazard at which such countermeasures should be instigated. It would obviously be very wrong to risk killing or maiming people in the panic of evacuation if the radiation hazard they were running away from would kill or maim nobody. In order to solve this problem there are now nationally promulgated 'Emergency Reference Levels' (ERLs), which advise the level of radiation at which the hazards exceed the risks of a given countermeasure, and hence when such a measure may be appropriate.

However, at the time of writing the effects of the extremely serious accident at Chernobyl in the Ukraine on 25 April 1986 are unknown. It seems that they will far exceed anything so far experienced from nuclear power plants, and point to the poor Soviet safety precautions.

When considering nuclear submarine containment and safety there are two very separate problems. Firstly, there is the day-to-day safety, during normal reactor operation, of the operators and the remainder of the submarine crew; and secondly, there is the identification of accident situations and the question of how these might affect both the crew and, possibly, the general public.

During normal operation, with the radioactive fuel and fission products contained within their cladding, the hazard to the crew derives from the possibility of radiation passing through the reactor pressure vessel. In order to protect personnel, shielding is provided both around the pressure vessel itself and the compartment in which it is contained. The design criteria for this shielding reduce this radiation to a level at which the doses received by nuclear submarine crews are within the nationally laid down limits. In fact, shielded as he is by the sea from cosmic radiation, free from the effects of the decay of natural radioactive elements present in the building material of most homes and, less fortunately, from the radiation emitted by a faithful and constant partner sharing a double bed, the position of the nuclear submariner could be advantageous.

Turning to the accident situation, it is obvious that a nuclear reactor is a complex piece of machinery containing many components and back-up systems. The effects of failures of individual and multiple components, together with some estimates of the probability of these events, is an area of vital study which must take place before operation is allowed. This process identifies many conceivable events of differing probability which form a spectrum between those which cause no hazard whatsoever to those which present the maximum credible danger. Within this spectrum of accidents the hazards can best be identified by looking at three conceivable situations.

It is impossible for a reactor accident to result in an atomic explosion; and the design, construction and operation of reactor plants are extremely carefully supervised and controlled to reduce the risk of any other form of accident to the absolute minimum. However, should the cladding fail and the primary coolant water become contaminated with fission products, the coolant system, which is itself a high-integrity system, would contain the release and prevent its further spread. Such an accident effectively moves part of the radioactive source around within the reactor compartment, and could therefore reduce the effectiveness of the shielding, with the result that the submarine crew might be exposed to somewhat higher radiation doses; but, with the fission products contained, there is no hazard to the general public.

Both of the other situations involve the melting of a reactor core as a result of loss of coolant. If the main coolant pumps fail simultaneously, due to disruption, for some reason, of electrical supplies, an emergency system takes over; nevertheless, there remains the remote possibility of a sudden and complete failure of the primary coolant water system. For this to happen, it would be necessary for a major component of the primary circuit to fracture completely, so that all the primary coolant water escaped into the reactor compartment. If the reactor core could no longer be cooled, the fuel elements would melt and some of the fission products would be released into the reactor compartment with an associated severe pressure rise. Such an accident could thereby result in two separate hazards.

The fission products which remained within the reactor compartment after an accident would be a source of intense gamma radiation transmitted through the hull in all directions. The intensity of gamma radiation is rapidly reduced by both distance and shielding, but excessive radiation doses could be acquired by personnel who did not immediately evacuate an area within close vicinity of the submarine. If, however, fission products were released from the reactor compartment, they would present a significant hazard – in the form of a radioactive cloud – to people further away and downwind of the accident.

In order to mitigate the effects of the release of fission products from the stricken submarine, the reactor compartment itself is constructed to provide primary containment, and to withstand the severe pressure rises associated with a melt. Although this containment is expected to remain intact, the presence of a small leak could result in a very slow release to the remainder of the boat, and thence to the outside atmosphere, of a fraction of the fission products discharged into the reactor compartment. In order to reduce still further the probability of fission products escaping to the outside atmosphere, the compartments adjacent to the reactor compartment are designed to form yet another barrier, known as 'secondary containment'.

The situation where primary containment functions as designed and, at worst, only a small proportion of the fission products are released to atmosphere over twenty-four hours, is often referred to as a 'contained accident'. The probability of this worst contained accident occurring is predicted at about once in 10,000 years of reactor operation.

An even less likely accident would be the sudden and complete failure of the primary coolant system occurring simultaneously with a breach of primary containment. There would then be a short-term release to the outside atmosphere of a much greater proportion of the fission products: this situation is usually referred to as an 'uncontained accident'. The probability of this accident occurring is predicted at about once in one million years of reactor operation.

The chances of a PWR accident of either type are clearly very small; but, of course, there is no way of predicting when one might occur. The remote possibility of an accident in harbour has to be taken into account, so well-prepared countermeasures can be implemented immediately, in the event of an accident, wherever a nuclear submarine berths – and the berth is always monitored. In addition to monitoring to detect if an accident has occurred, specialist teams, who are able to monitor at many sites, can be deployed. Experts are on call who are able to assess the monitoring information, quantify the radiation hazard and advise on the need for countermeasures. And finally, there are well-prepared and exercised plans produced in consultation with local authorities so that countermeasures, if required, can be speedily implemented.

Current plans involve the automatic implementation of countermeasures in a limited area 360 degrees around the submarine, with the extension of countermeasures to further downwind areas based on monitoring results.

There have been a number of reactor accidents in the Soviet Navy, and it is said that there is a hospital full of irradiated submariners at Murmansk. Some unconfirmed reports may be exaggerated, but there have certainly been incidents, some of them serious. The Soviet regime is often far too relaxed and careless about the safety of its people, and the catastrophe at Chernobyl is indicative of what could happen on a smaller scale in the nuclear plant of a Soviet submarine. Western nuclear boats are as safe as they can possibly be, and safety rules are rigidly applied. There is, undeniably, some very slight risk, but anybody who feels concerned about nuclear accidents would do well to consider the inestimably greater risk from the Soviet Union if nuclear submarines were not included in NATO defences.

Apart from accidents there are two other risks – one internal and one external.

An automatic scram is designed to protect the reactor, and it may be initiated by a fairly minor instrumentation or pipe-system failure at sea which is not necessarily catastrophic by itself. There has been much conjecture about what caused the loss of USS *Thresher* (SSN–593) and USS *Scorpion* (SSN–589), both in very deep water, in 1963 and 1968 respectively. Loss of power at a critical moment linked with a sudden, relatively small loss of watertight integrity would have been sufficient, despite more esoteric theories.

A nuclear submarine can keep depth on the hydroplanes at moderate speed even if negatively buoyant (heavy) by a large amount. Negative buoyancy can arise quite simply by inattention to the trim, and may not always be readily apparent to an inexperienced trimming officer while the planes are holding the boat up. More likely in these disasters, however, flooding through a fractured pipe or hull fitting would very rapidly add tons and more tons to the weight – again, the seriousness of the situation might not immediately be apparent so long as speed is maintained.

But if there is a scram, primary power is lost; the stand-by electric motor on the propeller shaft, supplied by a relatively small battery, only has sufficient power for about three to five knots – not fast enough for the planes to prevent the submarine sinking if by then it is very heavy. If the boat is already well below periscope depth and on the way down, the main ballast blows, against external sea pressure, might not be able to force out enough water to compensate quickly enough for the increasing weight inside the hull. Inevitably, in deep water, the submarine is then dragged down below crushing depth.

There are four ways of preventing all this happening. Firstly, *all* systems and hull connections subjected to seawater pressure must be thoroughly tested by ultrasonic and other methods in the building or overhaul yard. Secondly, the trim must be checked continually, even if this means slowing down from time to time. Thirdly, it must be possible to override an automatic scram if an operational emergency demands that power be maintained: a 'battle-short' which does this has been installed since the loss of *Thresher*. Fourthly, it is very desirable to be able to blow main ballast effectively, or otherwise get rid of weight quickly, at depth. It is believed that thought has been given to this, and British captains express confidence in their main-ballast blows down to full diving depth so long as the emergency arises from leaking rather than flooding. A degree of flooding can, however, probably be catered for in large Soviet boats with a double hull and an exceptionally high reserve of buoyancy.

Escape from submarines is something which submariners think very little about. It will not be discussed in this book, but it should be noted that escape from deep water is only possible by means of a 'mini-sub' deep sea rescue vehicle (DSRV) which is transportable by air and subsequently by submarine; but if internal bulkheads are to be strong enough to isolate escape compartments at great depths they add greatly to the overall weight in a boat which, crammed with heavy weapons and equipment, already encounters design problems related to the inflexible principle discovered by Archimedes twenty-two centuries ago.

The other – external – danger is that an enemy agent or crackpot could take a shot with, say, an anti-tank missile at the reactor compartment above water when a submarine is lying at its berth. This would probably *not* cause a catastrophic reactor accident. However, a limpet mine attached underwater by a frogman could be disastrous.

Although a pressurised water reactor is installed in all existing NATO nuclear boats, a liquid metal (sodium) coolant would be more efficient. The inlet and outlet coolant temperatures in a PWR are restricted, within quite a narrow band, to below the boiling point of water under high pressure. The temperature in a sodium coolant reactor, and thus in the heat exchanger, can be several hundred degrees higher over a wider range, making much more thermal energy available to the secondary circuit – in the form of superheated steam – from a comparatively small, quiet plant. USS *Seawolf* (SSN–575) used liquid sodium as a coolant – with graphite as a moderator – in 1957–58, but the metallurgical technology of the day was not, apparently, sufficiently advanced to cope with the thermal stresses imposed. There were problems of maintenance and safety, so the plant was exchanged in 1959–60 for a PWR that had been standing spare for *Nautilus*, the first nuclear-powered submarine.

It would be quite difficult to reduce the size of direct-drive steam turbines to take advantage of space saved by a sodium plant, but it should be possible to contrive a compact turbo-generator system for electric drive. A more esoteric method, employing magnetohydrodynamic (MHD) propulsion, will be discussed in the final chapter.

The Russians, in some nuclear-powered submarines, almost certainly took over liquid metal coolant designs where the US Navy left off. The Soviet Navy is more concerned with high power densities and less worried about safety. In the ten years between 1975 and 1985, Soviet submariners suffered a variety of accidents – more than 200 in all – some of them very serious (although not by any means all nuclear), resulting in the loss of several boats.[3]

CLOSED-CYCLE ENGINES

There have been a number of experiments with closed-cycle engines since the first German Walter design for the Type XVIIA *U–792* in 1943. In a typical system, an oxygen compound – usually concentrated high test peroxide (HTP) – is broken down by a catalyst to form oxygen and steam. The gases are then led to a combustion chamber where oil fuel is injected and ignited. Water is also sprayed in with the combustion products, increasing the volume of gas and reducing the temperature. The gas is passed to a turbine to provide the power and thence to a condenser which separates the water from the gases, mostly carbon dioxide which dissolves in seawater when discharged overboard.

There are now variants of the Walter system which seemed, at one time, to be a fairly cheap alternative to nuclear power. But HTP is inherently dangerous, unpleasant stuff to deal with and has proved expensive in practice. The two HTP boats, HMS *Explorer* and *Excalibur*, completed for the Royal Navy in 1956 and 1958, were both taken out of service by 1963. HMS *Explorer* made twenty-six and a half knots submerged on trials but top speed could only be maintained for less than three hours; at twelve knots the endurance was about fifteen hours. At full power the two 'exploders' (as they were known because fireballs and fires were not infrequent) cost, in old English money, one and eleven pence and three farthings a yard to run; and that – comparing like with like as far as possible – was twice the cost of running a nuclear plant.

Sprint speeds would undoubtedly have been useful if the Germans had been able to fling Walter boats, which came too late, into the Battle of the Atlantic; but it is doubtful if the delicate machinery and unstable fuel would have stood up to depth-charging.

Present-day versions of closed-cycle engines, notably the Stirling piston version, show more promise, but results in the past have largely been disappointing. Sweden and Germany are showing strong interest in developments; and other navies are expected to follow.

FUEL CELLS

Fuel cells for submarines have been seriously considered, discarded and reconsidered by turns since 1958. They are a practical proposition, proven in space and on land, and seem well worth pursuing for certain types of submarine. Germany now leads research in this field. Electricity is generated, and water is made, by continuously feeding into a cell chemicals in the form of gases, liquids or solids and combining them with a catalyst. In a common type, hydrogen and oxygen are fed to two terminals, or electrodes, where one of the gases gives up electrons and the other takes them up. The electrons flow in a circuit between the electrodes, constituting an electric current. The electrified atomic particles (ions) produced in the process combine to form water.

Fuel cells are compact power packs and efficiency figures of seventy or eighty per cent are quoted for them. However, they operate most efficiently at a constant current corresponding to a medium power rate: they are not good for high-rate discharges. A hybrid system, with a lead-acid battery for high power, recharged either by the fuel cell system or by a closed-cycle generator, would probably be best if fuel cells are adopted.

NOISE, QUIETING, SPEED AND DRAG

There are three main sources of noise radiated from a submarine: the propeller (or propulsor), the hull and the machinery.

Propeller cavitation, caused by air bubbles forming as a result of a boiling effect at the tips of the blades, was for long the bugbear of all submariners. The broad-band noise might start as low as five knots at periscope depth, and it can be heard and distinguished by quite primitive hydrophones. Cavitation is suppressed by increasing pressure as a submarine goes deeper, but it is less than convenient to keep changing depth for this reason alone. Multi-bladed, skewed propellers have eased the problem; and when a single efficient propeller is placed abaft control surfaces, where there is little flow interference, blade-rate narrow-band noise, which can be analysed and identified by suitable underwater listening apparatus (low-frequency sonar), can also be markedly reduced. Resonance – 'singing' – can also be a problem. Propulsors – basically pump-jets with a multi-blade rotor turning relatively slowly against stator vanes in a duct – can do much to reduce noise of this kind still further; a pump-jet is horrible for manoeuvring in harbour, but that has to be accepted. Propulsors, of one kind and another, are still evolving.

Hull noise is dependent on speed. The old superstructure and casing rattles have been eliminated (save in the oldest Soviet boats), but hydroplanes and stabilisers still vibrate; there may be some cavitation from external fittings; and turbulence where water flows fast over the hull also causes noise. All these problems are being reduced by various means that will be discussed in Chapter 12.

Machinery radiates noise, at discrete frequencies, through hull fittings to the hull and outwards. Nuclear-reactor main-coolant pumps are a particular noise source (not, of course, applicable to diesel-electric SSKs on main motors) which is why research continues into quieting the pumps, and into natural circulation systems, which are believed to be practicable up to higher power levels than was previously thought possible. Natural circulation is very desirable for ballistic-missile boats (SSBNs) on patrol at low speeds.

Machines are insulated from the hull by resilient mountings and, in a nuclear boat, the main machinery can be installed on a large raft which is itself flexibly supported on the hull. Flexible mountings bring their own problems when, for instance, the machinery which they carry has to be connected to a rigid propelling shaft – so they may have to be locked at high power.

Noise-reducing tiles can be affixed to the hull around machinery spaces to absorb noise; and an anechoic coating or tiling, made of decoupling materials, applied to the hull can significantly reduce the amount of energy reflected back to an active searching sonar – as can the submarine's aspect and the rounded external surfaces which the Soviets favour for superstructures.

There are four fundamental problems which a submarine designer has to face besides noise reduction, improving the efficiency of the reactor's conversion of heat to propulsion power and improving the efficiency of the propeller/propulsor itself:

a. The drag exerted by water on the hull increases enormously with increasing speed. Much has been done already to reduce drag; but, as a guiding rule, to double the speed from twenty to forty knots requires eight times as much power at the propeller/propulsor.

b. Since the power requirement has increased much more than the flow of cooling seawater past the steam condensers, it is becoming more difficult to reject waste heat to the ocean.

c. While propulsion and hull noises increase dramatically with speed, so does the temperature of the sea in the wake of the submarine – and this can be scanned by a sensitive air or space sensor.

d. The magnetic effects of a hull must be reduced, or preferably eliminated, to avoid triggering magnetic mines and detection by airborne magnetic anomaly detection equipment (MAD).

Ways in which some of these requirements are being met will be considered in the final chapter.

SHORE SUPPORT, DEPOT SHIPS AND REFUELLING

All kinds of submarines need support ships or overseas bases if operating for long periods away from home waters. The Soviet Navy is faced with this problem, which is the Achilles heel of its worldwide operations.

Nuclear and diesel-electric submarine endurance is limited only by the need of food and relaxation for the crews. A two- or three-month period submerged is perfectly tolerable and not unusual.

Nuclear-powered submarines (SSNs and SSBNs) only need to refuel every few years; in the past it has been the 'poisoning' effect on the core of accumulating fission products that has restricted its life rather than the consumption of uranium. No more than half of the U–235 has been used when a core has been replaced in some cases. It is assumed that 'poisoning' effects have been lessened in later reactor designs. A core-change is planned to coincide with a routine refit and overhaul of the whole submarine and can be accomplished well within the time allotted for the latter, so refuelling is not an inhibiting factor for a nuclear boat.

Shore support facilities back at home must be on a grand scale if operational time is to be maximised. The infrastructure – embracing control, communications, intelligence, weather reporting, stores and supplies, the provision of spares (reportedly unreliable in Soviet bases), maintenance, secure berthing, training, weapons system analysis, crew and family accommodation, and a host of other necessities – is very expensive, but it is often discounted when announcing the cost of a new submarine.

Refits and overhauls, which include the installation of updated equipment, are typically undertaken every five years and last about two years. They will be longer apart in future for new Western boats – possibly up to eleven years. Intermittent 'down time' for dockings and essential defects, depot ship or base repairs, working-up, training and leave periods necessarily take up a large proportion of a submarine's life – totalling something to the order of fifty per cent, and in some cases much more, especially in the Soviet fleet.

SSBNs (but not SSNs except in the French Navy) have two crews for each submarine to increase the time spent actually on deterrent patrol. The US Navy keeps about seventy per cent of its Trident force 'either in alert or mod-alert status at all times'.[4] In 1985, on the attack side, the US Navy 'surged' forty-four SSNs, each with a full load of Mark 48 torpedoes, Harpoon and other weapons, into the Atlantic – as an operational exercise – within twenty-four hours of the order. The Soviets are also good at 'surging', but spend less time, as a rule, at sea and the crews are said to be unhappy about not having enough sea-training.[5]

SONAR

Passive (listening) sonar is the most important submarine sensor today, but all boats have active (echo-ranging) sonar with a greater or lesser capability depending on the power and space available. The acronym

SONAR (SOund Navigation And Ranging) was first approved and published in the *US Fleet A/S Bulletin* in November 1943 and has since replaced ASDIC (from the initials of the Allied Submarine Devices Investigation Committee of 1914–18).

Underwater sound is attentuated by absorption and scattering, but suffers far less attenuation than underwater light or radio waves. Attenuation increases rapidly with an increase of audio frequency and is less at low frequencies. Hence a receiver/transmitter (basically a hydrophone or electro-acoustic transducer) has to be quite large to accept efficiently the long wavelengths (low frequencies) associated with long ranges and the especially interesting sound signatures at very low frequencies in narrow bandwidths. Higher frequency rotating transducers can be smaller: ranges are shorter but bearing (direction) can more easily be determined accurately with high-frequency equipment around ten kHz. A ten-kHz signal has a wavelength of 14.7 cms (5.8 inches); a 1 kHz signal 146 cms (4.8 feet); a 100 Hz signal 14.6 metres (48 feet); and a ten-Hz signal 146 metres (480 feet).

Sound travels

In 1960 sound waves from a small explosive charge detonated south of Australia were received off Bermuda, after travelling a distance of 21,000 kilometres (11,500 nautical miles), nearly four hours later. Acoustic information passing through water at 1,463 metres per second (varying with depth and pressure) is very slow compared with radio and radar propagation: however, sound underwater can be heard at extremely long ranges if conditions are right.

Mechanically rotating transducers generate their own noise and, anyway, at low frequencies the size needed would make physical rotation impractical. Furthermore 'searchlight' sets can miss a noise, particularly in the active mode, because they have to remain on the same bearing until the echo is received – 12.5 seconds at five nautical miles (9,144 metres). The solution was to construct a fixed circular or conformal array of transducers, whose beams could be formed and steered electronically. Equipment like the US Navy BQS–6 and the Royal Navy Type 2001 employ this principle and have a nearly all-round capability; but they are large and require a good deal of power, only available in a nuclear-powered submarine, when 'going active'. They are also subject, to some extent, to self-noise and most nuclear-powered submarines are now equipped with a long (passive) linear towed array which displaces the low-frequency hydrophones from the submarine itself and provides a long base-line.

Because the sea is not a homogeneous medium the propagation of sound in water is complex. The velocity varies with temperature, pressure and salinity; and consequently it also varies with depth, position and the season of the year. The result is a collection of waves which are generally refractive (bending) due to changes in sound velocity as a function of depth or horizontal distance, and waves which are reflective due to interaction with the surface, seabed or marked velocity boundaries. There are relatively few conditions when, at other than short ranges, the path does not bend in some way – sometimes horizontally as well as vertically – so refraction and reflection have to be exploited and allowed for.

There are four regions of differing sound behaviour in an idealised vertical deep ocean profile. The surface layer extends down to fifty or sixty metres and is susceptible to climatic vagaries, besides being cluttered with noise from the surface of the sea. In the next region, between sixty and 250 metres, there is a 'seasonal thermocline' or temperature gradient characterised by a negative velocity curve (temperature and velocity decreasing with depth) which moves up and down seasonally and in which sound is refracted downwards. Below that, between 250 and 1,000 metres, the 'main thermocline' is constantly negative. But in the fourth region, the 'deep sound channel', whose axis is defined as the depth where velocity reaches a minimum before the curve starts to become positive (temperature constant but pressure and hence velocity increasing), a wave generated remains trapped and travels by cylindrical spreading for long distances. This occurs at between 1,000 and 2,000 metres.

When a sound ray penetrates downwards by refraction to the deep isothermal layer (in the deep sound channel) it will eventually, if it does not strike the seabed first, be refracted upwards, to be reflected by the surface back down again; this process repeats itself in a series of 'convergence zones' at intervals of twenty-four to twenty-eight nautical miles near the surface.

If, on the other hand, a refracted ray strikes the seabed it is reflected upwards by 'bottom bounce' and can therefore be received, like convergent zone signals, at longer ranges than by the direct path.

Signal processing techniques enable these paths to be used at various optimal depths according to conditions, depth of water and the submarine's diving capability. A submarine that can go to 1,000 metres (3,280 feet) can clearly exploit all kinds of propagation to better advantage than a shallower boat; but, against that, its own radiated noise (if any) will be trapped in the deep sound channel which could carry it to very distant receivers at a similar depth.

It is not much help hearing a noise unless it can be accurately interpreted. Broad-band cavitation, if there is any, is very useful and will also suggest the speed of the ship or submarine detected. But, with submarines becoming quieter in all respects, other clues have to be looked for, primarily in the low-frequency range, where computer analysis can pick out specific frequencies related to a particular noise source.

Human sonar

In 1916, Sir Richard Paget, from the Board of Invention and Research in Cockspur Street, London, was acknowledged to have a very keen sense of pitch. To determine propeller frequencies, he was suspended by his legs over the side of a boat in the Solent while a submarine circled him. After a suitable period submerged, and before he actually drowned, this devoted scientist was hauled up humming the notes he had heard whereupon, safely back in the boat, he related them to the standard G-sharp which he obtained by tapping his cranium with a metal rod. He had the right idea but computers do the same thing rather more accurately and with less discomfort.

ELECTRONIC SUPPORT MEASURES

Most submarines have at least one periscopic mast devoted to electronic sensors which can detect radar and radio transmissions, either to help search for and identify targets or to give warning of anti-submarine activities, primarily from the air. The latter function is vital to diesel-electric SSKs when snorkelling. The level of a radar signal is measured and all exposed masts are (hopefully) retracted before the signal is strong enough to be reflected back to the searching aircraft. However, aircraft can 'cheat' by transmitting intermittently or only over certain sectors, so that a signal can be at danger level or above when first detected.

Electronic Support Measures (ESM) for Electronic Warfare (EW) cover a wide field of countermeasures and counter-countermeasures which are mostly applicable to surface and air units at the receiving end of missile attacks; but, of course, attacking submarines are keenly interested in all aspects of electronic detection. There is sometimes a narrow microwave duct, formed by water vapour just above the surface, which can be exploited to detect signals well beyond the horizon.

Jamming

Electronic warfare, in the embryonic radio stage, was first evidenced during the Russo–Japanese war which broke out in 1904. The Russians intercepted Japanese radio signals, noting a marked intensity when action was imminent – long before the enemy ships came within visual range. One wireless operator at the Port Arthur base – acting on instinct – jammed Japanese communicators by holding down the key of his spark transmitter. On the latter occasion the Japanese ships, intent on bombardment, were obliged to cut short their action and withdraw. Unfortunately, at the battle of Tsushima on 27 May 1905, Admiral Rozhdestvensky refused permission, for no discernible reason, to use tactical jamming which might have gone some way towards alleviating a disastrous defeat under the guns of Admiral Togo.

PERISCOPES

Many periscopes now have image-intensifiers or infra-red thermal imagers for use in darkness or low light conditions. Video signals can be taken to a remote monitor, primarily for the captain's use while another officer is at the periscope itself (although future systems may obviate the need for direct viewing altogether), and to a video recorder for subsequent analysis. Other optronics include laser ranging and anti-vibration optics, which enable a periscope to be used at unprecedented speeds of up to sixteen knots – but a dangerously visible wash (and wake) is created at speeds above about five knots. ESM radio antenna facilities may also be incorporated.

Periscopes today can therefore be more than an optical aid; they are sensors in their own right and are not redundant by reason of predominantly acoustic approaches. Even if sonar analysis is reliable, there is nothing to beat looking at a surface target, especially in a limited war where positive identification is crucial.

NAVIGATION

Nuclear submarines are equipped with SINS (Ship Inertial Navigation System) which senses movement by measuring and integrating accelerations relative to the earth. SINS is extremely accurate, but it is prudent to update or check the given position at intervals. SATellite NAVigation

(SATNAV) networks such as GPS Global Position System (NAVS-TAR), Bottom Contour (BC) navigation (now very reliable), celestial observations through the periscope and radio navigational aids like LORAN C and OMEGA are all available to supplement SINS or dead-reckoning. Unless something goes very wrong, there is no reason for the navigator of a modern submarine in the open ocean not to know his precise position at any time: in some boats the latitude and longitude are pounded out by an IBM typewriter every six minutes.

Lost at sea

Until a few years ago, and certainly during the war, submarines were quite frequently out of position by twenty, fifty, or occasionally more miles, thereby not only missing target intercepts but also laying themselves open to attack by friendly forces. The prize for being in the wrong place went to Kptlt Ernst Cordes in *U–763* who, after thirty hours of depth-charging off Selsey Bill on 6/7 July 1944, reckoned he had drifted to a position some twenty miles north of Cherbourg, probably between the Channel Islands. He therefore steered north towards supposedly deeper water. Early in the morning he ran aground. When he cautiously came to periscope depth he was faced, inescapably, with the fact that he was actually at Spithead, the most historically famous of all British anchorages. There was so much shipping in the area that he was able to work his way out and eventually return to Brest.

This incident is recalled to emphasise that a submarine inshore in the midst of a mêlée is very difficult to single out. To engage the enemy more closely, in Horatio Nelson's words, can still be the best thing to do in certain circumstances.

COMMUNICATIONS

Submarines seldom transmit on long-range high radio frequencies (HF) because the briefest transmission is liable to be detected, and a line of bearing established, by Direction Finding (D/F) shore or shipboard equipment. Super (SHF), Ultra (UHF) or Very High Frequency (VHF) two-way links with co-operating aircraft, surface ships or, via a satellite, with shore are fairly safe and have a high data rate; but they require a boat either to expose an antenna (and probably break off operations while doing so), or to send a buoy (which can be expendable) to the surface.

Very Low Frequency (VLF – around fifteen kHz) stations ashore transmit messages to submarines submerged; they can increase their receiving depth considerably by streaming a buoyant wire antenna, or by towing a communications buoy at set times – or continuously when a constant radio watch has to be maintained, as by nuclear-powered ballistic-missile submarines (SSBNs).

Extremely Low Frequency (ELF) transmitters (US Navy seventy-six Hz) have a much wider and deeper coverage than VLF stations because the attenuation of ELF signals in seawater is only a fraction of that suffered by VLF. ELF is also invulnerable to Electromagnetic Pulse Effect (EMP), nearly impossible in practical terms to jam, and is unaffected by abnormal propagation conditions. The snags are that the data rate is so low, because of the low bandwidth, that it can only carry short, simple messages – 'bell-ringers' – and the shore antenna must ideally be hundreds or even thousands of kilometres long.

Historically, submarine communications have been too often prone to fail of their own accord, but it is very probable that the Soviets will seek to sever NATO data links of all kinds at the onset of a serious crisis. On the other hand, no attempt was made to destroy radio communications between Doenitz and his U-boats during the last war because so much information was gleaned from them by the Allies. But with modern cryptography code-breaking is very much more difficult than it was forty and more years ago.

OPERATIONS UNDER ICE

Under-ice activities are, of course, unique to submarines: nothing else can penetrate the vast volume of sea beneath the polar icecaps, and submarine operations in this vital part of inner space embrace every aspect so far discussed.

Obviously, nuclear power, with total independence from the atmosphere, is needed to make full use of the Arctic seas but diesel boats are not barred from the whole area. For much of the year there are fissures, gaps and puddles (*polynyas*) in the pack which allow a boat to surface without having to break through thick ice. In any case, in the absence of *polynyas*, hardening the outer structure can enable practically any submarine to break through quite thick ice sufficiently either to gulp air (if it is a diesel-electric SSK), or to launch missiles (if it is an SSBN, SSGN or even a diesel SSB). Incidentally, a black submarine surfaced in white ice is surprisingly difficult to spot from the air; but the encapsulated US SIAM anti-aircraft missile would be very useful as a 'leave behind' defensive weapon for a submarine submerging in a *polynya* under pressure from the air.

A thinning of the ice overhead is usually detected by upward-looking echo-sounders or custom-built high-frequency active sonar, but submerged periscope visibility by day can be very good. The first serious diesel explorers in the 1960s (notably HMS *Grampus* and *Porpoise*) used the search periscope, from a depth of 150 feet, to look for the lightening that signified thin ice or a fissure a short way ahead. The difficulty comes in stopping, suddenly, under the chosen patch: going astern on the propeller(s) upsets the trim, but various methods of coming up in the right place have been extensively practised and it is no longer a real problem.

It is a strange environment under the ice, but no longer daunting. It would certainly become a battle zone in war and, for the Soviet Navy, it is a natural bastion in times of tension. Fighting under the ice will be discussed more thoroughly when reviewing anti-submarine and strategic-missile operations.

FIGHTING EFFICIENCY

Fighting efficiency is obviously a function of weapon-system effectiveness, but it is also dependent on morale and, self-evidently, training. During the last war there were clear indications that (given weapons which worked) men and morale counted for more than machinery and material. There is no proof that comfort, in European navies at least, came into the equation; but good habitability is important today for much longer patrols and in particular for efficient watch-keeping at the sensors. Living conditions in American boats are superb, in British boats not as good as they could be, while in Soviet submarines they are bad for the crew and moderately good for the officers. Compared with Western submarines, the majority of Soviet boats spend less time at sea.

Action and danger stimulate a crew and bring out the best in them. That is one great value of peacetime operations which bring about close encounters with the opposition. As the immortal Jorrocks said of fox hunting in Victorian England, intelligence-gathering on the high seas, uninvited participation in Soviet fleet exercises and surveillance operations are 'the image of war without its guilt and only five-and-twenty per cent of its danger'.[6]

It is the long days, weeks and even months of waiting, when nothing is happening, that are most testing because a submariner must be constantly alert: he who hears or sees the enemy first is likely to be the winner. During the last war initial detection was nearly always visual, either from the bridge or through a periscope, and the captain almost invariably sighted something before anybody else. That was not because he had superior eyesight – officers and lookouts were younger and probably had better vision – but he desperately wanted to find a target and concentrated his whole energy on so doing. Motivation is the modern word; and today it has to be inculcated into sonar operators, who can easily become bored, and thus liable to miss the first trace or sound and lose moments that are vital to subsequent manoeuvres. The danger is recognised, but avoiding it requires constant application in what can be a rather somnolent atmosphere, with monotonous background ventilation and machinery noises. The officers on watch, who can themselves be tired and stale, have to show continual enthusiastic interest in sonar performance; and the captain, in turn, has to keep his officers on their toes. Meanwhile, equipment and machinery has to be maintained at peak running efficiency by men working in small spaces where constant supervision is impossible.

Leadership is therefore as critical as ever it was: it underpins all else. Unfortunately, its importance has been partially obscured by the fascination of technology. It is no longer hammered home in Western navies after initial entry to the service and, although lip service is paid to it, the word leadership seems to be regarded in practice as old-school. Its decline as a stated first requirement for a submarine officer probably dates from the advent of nuclear power some thirty years ago: and, if blame there is, it might be laid at the door of the late Admiral Hyman G. Rickover of the US Navy.

Admiral Rickover's immense contribution to the nuclear submarine force was to insist on excellence as the norm and to force compliance with the highest standards. Only those with the most superior qualifications were considered after legendary interviews, said to involve harassment, verbal abuse and demeaning indignities which Rickover evidently believed would sift the grain from the chaff. The qualifications were technical and almost wholly concerned with the atomic power plant. The notorious interviews may, in some instances, have produced men who could stand up for themselves, but they were scarcely concerned with leadership. Nor were officers chosen with any regard for their likely tactical ability or for their skill in using the weapon systems – which are the only reason for building a submarine, however it may be propelled. The result, for many years, was that the weapons and their users at the sharp end were afforded less attention than the nuclear kettle and its minders aft. Moreover, as a distinguished United States officer has remarked, Rickover was the banyan tree under whose shade nothing else could grow. Under the Rickover personality cult, pressurised water-coolant systems for nuclear reactors became sacrosanct: innovation was not encouraged. It was arguably this conservatism in the United States Navy, which only began to break following the late admiral's retirement from the commanding scene, that allowed the Soviet Navy to leapfrog, in a disquieting number of areas, over Western submarines.

It was Rickover's personal drive (which is, by the way, not necessarily the same thing as leadership) which forced nuclear development ahead, but the side effects have been less than advantageous. Leadership takes many and varied forms: an odd quirk, an independent line or a touch of eccentricity can contribute remarkably to the qualities of a leader. But the art of leadership is in danger of being lost amidst the complexities of modern submarine systems overseen by officers with graduate engineering degrees or their equivalent.

The US Navy has line officers who are all qualified engineers while the Royal Navy has specialised technical and supply officers who are trained very thoroughly within their own departments. Seamen officers are thereby freed to concentrate their expertise on actual submarine warfare and tactics. Seamen officers must, of course, be leaders, although pushing – drive – is sometimes more practised than pulling or leading.

The disadvantage of the British system is that seamen officers find it hard to express their needs in engineering or mathematical terms when discussing them with weapon engineers or submarine designers. Hence, it is sometimes said that American submariners have better material, but that British submariners use what they have to better effect. The Soviets have, in the main, followed American practice in regard to engineering training.

Morale goes with good leadership, but it also depends, in war, on a conviction that weapons will perform as advertised. Such conviction would not, perhaps, always be apparent in Western submarines at present, for reasons that will be discussed in Chapter 4.

There is a different kind of personnel problem in the Soviet Navy which would alarm any Western commanding officer. Seventy-five per cent of the navy is made up of conscripts who serve for three years. They do five months' basic training and then go to a submarine training establishment, the largest of which is at Leningrad, before joining their boats where they form, on a cycle system, one third of the crew. Each conscript serves for two years in a submarine so, at any one time, less than half the crew has any meaningful experience. The rapid turnover presents formidable training difficulties, not the least of which is that one man is only trained for a single specific duty: he cannot usefully be employed on anything other than his particular piece of equipment which, it is claimed, he will be competent to operate one month after joining his boat.

Welding a Soviet crew into an efficient fighting team is therefore a continual, never-ending task – far greater than that implied by minimal cycle-replacement systems, involving men who are already fairly well trained, in the US and Royal navies. Soviet officers and petty officers have to spend a great deal of their time, which could otherwise be employed more constructively, making sure that individuals carry out their duties properly. This is not the way to run a submarine which ought to be ready for war at a moment's notice. Conscripts are poorly paid, but a carrot is held out to them: an outstanding man can become the equivalent of a chief petty officer in two years; and if he opts to serve for longer, he can be rated *michman* (senior chief with near-warrant rank) after a further year. Just one per cent of the conscripts avail themselves of this opportunity – which says something about conditions on board.

The Russian Revolution

A small squadron of British submarines operated from Revel against German shipping throughout the Russian Revolution. They were based on the depot ship *Dvina* – the first ship to haul down the Imperial Ensign and hoist the Red Flag on the Russian Easter Day 1917. At the same time the ship's name was changed back to the original *Pamyat Azova*, which had been renamed by the Tzar's order following her part in the naval mutiny of 1905.

There were other changes. Under the Tzar the crew had been accustomed to fall in by divisions each morning to be greeted by the captain, on his arrival, with a 'Good health, my brave sailors.' To which the ship's company would reply, in perfect unison, 'Good morning, Excellency. We are happy to serve under you.'

That impressive little ceremony disappeared. The conditions under which sailors would serve were laid down by the Central Committee:

a. No man to be removed from a ship without the approval of the ship's committee.

b. Undesirable officers to be removed at the demand of the committee. Any new officers to be approved by the same body.

c. Officers to be elected and promoted by the crew.

d. Work to start at 9 am and cease at 3 pm.

e. No saluting.

f. Officers and men have equal rights ashore.

g. All summary punishments to be awarded by a committee of three men and one officer.

h. All matters of routine and internal organisation of the ship to be run by the committee.

i. Food and pay to be improved.

Needless to say, the rules were rapidly revised when, with the Bolsheviks firmly in power, the country was run by the Central Committee of the Communist Party in Moscow. The great gulf between a submarine wardroom and the mess decks was very apparent in the Second World War; and officers and men are decidedly not equal today.

A further problem in the Soviet Navy is caused by the wide variety of languages spoken by different ethnic groups within the Soviet Union, which must make communication difficult in an environment where it is absolutely vital to safe and effective functioning. How is a Russian-speaking supervisor to know whether a blandly smiling Byelo-Russian, Ukrainian, Lithuanian, Moldavian, Georgian, Armenian, Uzbek, Tartar, Turkoman, Azerbaijanian, Mongol or Buryat conscript sailor – with at most a couple of years to go before he returns to his own people and language – has understood the message about the red light flashing on the warning console?

The performance of Soviet submarines in the Great Patriotic War of 1940–45 was abysmal. Stalin had shot most of the worthwhile submarine commanding officers in the massive purge of 1937. Good submarine captains are individualists, and individualists are bad communists: without wishing any more purges on the Soviet Navy, this fact of life in the USSR – leading to a lack of initiative – beams one of the few rays of light, seen from the West, on an otherwise dark and foreboding Eastern horizon.

Politics on board

In 1940 the state of Soviet submarine training did not merit the name. British advisers, so far as they were allowed, did their best to improve matters, but it was a struggle. There were no proper instruments or aids to attacking; director angles were estimated by rough and ready rules; there were no torpedo spacing and spreading tables; target identities were continually mistaken; the size and importance of targets was over-estimated, leading to hopelessly inaccurate periscope ranging; base and maintenance facilities were poor; torpedo performance was even more erratic than elsewhere and no vigorous efforts were made to improve it.

Worst of all, on the fateful day of 16 July 1941, a commissar was appointed to every submarine. The political officer knew little or nothing about submarines; nor was the squadron or division commander who invariably accompanied a boat on initial patrols (which indicates the small number of submarines at sea at any one time) well versed in their operation. The effect on a commanding officer of having two ignorant seniors on board, as well as one or more Party officials amongst the crew, does not have to be imagined: instances were artlessly recorded in the memoirs of Admiral Arseni Golovko,[7] the commander-in-chief of the Northern Fleet throughout the war.

For instance, the 'baby' 250-ton *M–172* (Captain-Lieutenant I. Fisanovich) was, on one occasion, directed to attack the roadstead of Liinakhamari Harbour through a narrow, heavily protected fjord. Captain Second Rank Kolyshkin, the flotilla commander, decided to tell the commanding officer, step by step, how to go about it.

'The steadiness and patience of Kolyshkin who knew,' wrote Golovko, 'as nobody else, how to choose the right moment for attack, had a most beneficial influence on Fisanovich ... First of all he suggested postponing the entry of *M–172* into the enemy harbour for twenty-four hours ... to study the position ... On the second day Kolyshkin again advised delaying the entry. This was simply a test of patience for the captain to school him for independent operations later on.'

Fisanovich was eventually permitted to con his boat through the fjord and fire a salvo at a merchant ship lying alongside a pier. It missed and the torpedoes exploded against the pier itself. (Had he known his job, incidentally, the flotilla commander might have warned the captain that a stationary target is the most difficult of all to hit.) *M–172* then retired to sea and had a shot at the hospital ship *Alexander van Humboldt*. To be charitable, he probably identified the target wrongly: but, in any case, he missed.

Perhaps genuinely unaware of these disappointing results (which were doubtless claimed as sinkings with the connivance of the political officer and the flotilla commander), Admiral Golovko was moved to comment that 'such was the outcome of the first combat sortie of Captain Fisanovich, achieved under the supervision of the flotilla commander'.

The sinister role of the political officer became clear in another, rather naive account of the happenings on board *Shch–421*. The captain, Malyshev, returned from patrol, on several occasions apparently, with unexpended torpedoes. That was not good enough. Senior Political Instructor Dubik reported that there had been ample opportunity to fire them and that the commanding officer 'bore the stamp of excessive, inexplicable caution'. A new, tougher commissar, Senior Political Instructor Tabenkin, was appointed to relieve Dubik and duly went on patrol to assess the cautious captain. He soon signalled the base at Polyarny (using his own code of course) asking for recall in view of the captain's palpable cowardice. The boat's gyro had become unserviceable and the captain, who happened to have been the division's navigating officer before, personally tried to repair it. He did not think that anybody else could do the job; but, unfortunately, his own efforts put the gyro completely out of action. At the subsequent court-martial, Malyshev, presumably after the usual softening-up procedure, stated that he had caused the damage deliberately, 'because he was afraid to carry on with his patrol'. Then, laconically, the account goes on to say that Malyshev was killed soon afterwards when the building in which he was being held was bombed during an enemy air raid . . .

No wonder that torpedoes were fired with abandon, small targets were reported as large and sinkings were claimed when there was not a shred of evidence for them. Some twenty years after the war, (by then) Admiral Kolyshkin remarked on the 'scrupulousness' of Soviet submarine captains in assessing their results, but did acknowledge that 'the subjective element would inevitably creep in' – which was a nice way of putting it.

Who's in charge?

As another example of the Party's power, there was the case of the battery explosion, caused by incorrect ventilating procedures to get rid of the hydrogen, on board *Shch–402* (Captain-Lieutenant N. Stolbov). The captain, political instructor and most of the officers were killed. The engineer officer, Captain-Lieutenant Bolshakov, a man of considerable seniority and equivalent to a lieutenant commander in the US Navy, was left, but it was not proper for him to assume command automatically. That was up to the secretary of the submarine's Party organisation, a senior chief petty officer whose first priority was to instate a new commissar. Naturally, he chose himself. Next he called a Party meeting, at which his suggestion that Bolshakov should move into the vacant post of captain went unopposed. There was neither doubt nor question about who should set up a new command structure; the hegemony was preserved and the all-powerful Party kept control.

The Soviet system of command and control was rigid in the extreme, and it still is. Western submariners could not possibly operate efficiently, offensively and successfully under such conditions. A commanding officer enjoys, and makes best use of, the freedom insisted upon by Doenitz for a U-boat captain: 'He is independent and master of his own decisions'.[8]

Freedom, in this respect, is a source of strength for Western submariners, and lack of it is a source of weakness, which we should seek to exploit, for the Soviets. The full effects of rigid control and conformity to ideological and tactical doctrines may not be fully apparent in peace, but must necessarily be inhibiting in war. No wartime submarine commanding officer has ever sunk ships by slavish adherence to a rule book or by consultation with a committee – which are prerequisites of the Soviet system. The constant presence of a political officer (*zampolit*) and Party officials in submarines, with the widest possible powers to praise or condemn, must make it difficult, sometimes perhaps impossible, for commanding officers to act quickly and resolutely in fast-changing situations, when every action may be argued on the spot and will certainly be criticised, for good or ill, later. Nor do captains know who may have been planted on board as a secret observer by the main political administration in Moscow. A commanding officer has to watch his step, and he knows that every step is being watched by others.

However, in a few of the latest boats, notably the 'Victor III' class of nuclear-powered attack submarines (SSNs), the reins seem to have been loosened a little. They are commanded by exceptionally senior officers who have presumably been vetted with extreme care in every regard[9] – unlike NATO officers and men, whose positive vetting must be a standing joke with the KGB. This extraordinary degree of freedom makes them a considerable nuisance in zones concerned with ballistic-missile submarine sailings and other sensitive operations, including areas where tests and evaluations are taking place. There are probably no more than a dozen submarines so privileged, and they are emphatically not typical of the Soviet fleet.

If anybody doubts the difficulties of a submarine captain encumbered by a division commander and a *zampolit* looking over his shoulder, the case of the luckless 'Whiskey' *137* illustrates them vividly. The old diesel submarine, claimed by the official Soviet statement to be 'on an ordinary training cruise in the Baltic', ran aground just outside Karlskrona in southern Sweden, one of the two most important Swedish naval base areas, at eight o'clock on the evening of 27 October 1981. The captain claimed variously that he believed his boat was some twenty miles north of the Polish coast when it rode up on the rocks, or north of Bornholm in the middle of the Baltic. Navigational uncertainties of that magnitude are inconceivable; and without a reliable compass, the submarine would have stranded on outlying skerries, islands and rocks long before it did. It did not reach a highly restricted area by accident. Why, then, did it ground?

Any submariner in the West dislikes having senior officers on board, although he is usually too circumspect to say so. They occupy the best bunks; they have a knack of hearing things they ought not to hear and seeing papers they ought not to see; conversation in the wardroom takes on an artificial, brittle air; and something inevitably goes wrong. Much more seriously, they get in the way during an attack or when the captain and the navigator are having a mild disagreement over the chart table. But in a 'Whiskey' there is even less room for four people to pore over the chart in the cramped navigational area abaft the control room. One can envisage the scene here, during a very difficult passage at periscope depth, with the captain trying to put a fix on the chart and lay off the next course while deferring to his political betters. The consequences became obvious to the world on that October evening.

Western submariners are, of course, bound by strict operational orders and positive 'Rules of Engagement' are brought into force in a crisis; but orders and rules allow them a great deal of tactical latitude because it is recognised that – with highly competent crews, dependable equipment, accurate navigation and reliable communications – a captain's freedom of action and initiative are the keys to success.

By comparison, the great majority of Soviet commanding officers are severely hampered by inexperienced crews and the dictates of the system: the conditions under which most Soviet submariners operate have to be taken into account when judging the nature of the threat. The realities of underwater warfare, especially where the Soviet Navy is concerned, are not readily apparent from the surface.

3

The Underwater Threat

What do we mean by the word 'threat'? The conventional definition that 'threat' equals 'intention plus capability' has a fair claim to being as accurate as need be, but as far as underwater operations are concerned it does have the disadvantage of implying hostile activity. This can be misleading, as one of the most important aspects of underwater operations is the fact that the very existence of a submarine capability can have a profound influence without the potential ever being exercised. The *Oxford English Dictionary* devotes over a page to the words 'threat' and 'threaten', and from this mass of words the section which reads 'to press, urge, try to force or induce, especially by means of menaces' is most apposite in this context. Nothing is more menacing than an unseen adversary whose very presence can inhibit all manner of activity.

So the word 'threat' has much the same connotation as a 'fleet in being', which may be able to keep its adversary in harbour without actually putting to sea. The actual blockade may not be necessary, but the ability and the determination to blockade if called for are the vital factors. The flexibility offered by submarines allows this principle to operate extensively at the many levels where intervention, interposition, presence or even long-range activity by a given fleet can be a device to 'press, urge, try to force or induce, especially by means of menaces'. In other words, a submarine can represent a threat without a shot being fired.

How does this work in practice when, say, a Soviet submarine is on patrol? A well-found submarine operating from Murmansk or Vladivostok can remain on patrol for anything up to three months. At the end of this time a short spell alongside one of the eighty or so Soviet depot and repair ships will render her fit for another lengthy spell at sea. Operations during these months could include clandestine minelaying which, if successful, will have an effect on international insurance rates; a sudden appearance amongst a neutral fishing fleet; participation in a focal point exercise which may well result in the vessels of local navies suffering unnecessary and additional wear and tear; or she may never appear at all. The very advertisement of her presence, whether true or false, will cause serious perturbation if her intentions are reported as 'menacing'. The knowledge that British nuclear submarines were at sea and that their instructions were to attack Argentinian naval vessels was a sufficiently potent threat in the Falklands Campaign of 1982 for the main units of that fleet to remain within their own coastal waters, once *General Belgrano* had been sunk.

But for a threat to be effective, it has to be believed that the submarine fleet is actually capable of hostile action. No matter how thorough the training, how many and successful the peacetime exercises, the abrupt transition to real hostilities is a testing experience for those directly involved in, or immediately contemplating, the fighting. The sudden realisation that other people are intent on killing you is, at first, liable to be unnerving, particularly for the young. The instinct of self-preservation promotes a heightened vigilance. But days stretching into weeks and months of this alert state cause weariness, and a tired and frightened man's efficiency can drop with alarming rapidity – those who have never suffered wartime conditions, and that embraces well over ninety per cent of serving submariners in all navies, are unable to judge how they would react in such circumstances. However, war has been described as lengthy periods of boredom interspersed with moments of intense fright. This was occasionally true in the past – some British submarines operating with the Far Eastern Fleet towards the end of the war against Japan in 1945 spent many weeks on patrol without sighting a single target. But today underwater war would be very different. Quieter, faster, far more effective submarines, improved means of detection, weapons with homing heads and wire guidance, the possibility of nuclear weapons – all these would combine to present continuing danger. Under these conditions boredom and its effects could have fatal consequences.

But, once the initial fear of the unknown passes and gratitude for continued survival takes a hand, other factors come into play. Amongst these, and most important of all, are motivation and morale, usually closely linked. Any member of a submarine's crew may be expected to be of a sufficiently high standard of intellect to ask himself and his friends: 'What are we doing here, risking our lives? Are those who control our political destinies justified in getting us into this situation?' The answers to these queries will depend very largely on past background. In any of the navies of the democracies there will be a variety of political opinions in even the smallest gathering – political indoctrination is not only abjured, but would be ridiculous when the complexion of the government may change every few years.

In the Soviet Navy and those of its satellites, the daily political plug is an essential part of life. From his earliest years the Soviet citizen is brought up to a single faith and creed, from the Lenin room at his kindergarten, through the various youth organisations, to the daily lectures by his political officer on the application of Marxist-Leninism to his present career. Added to this are the endless diatribes against the warmongering habits of the democracies, the continual harping on the dangers presented to the Motherland by the imperialists, and the lectures on the heroic deeds of their forefathers in the defence of their homes and institutions. If one is fed on a continual diet of boiled beef and screened from any knowledge of the delights of toad-in-the-hole or baked beans, one probably accepts the inevitable – boiled beef is the best. And, if the gastronomically inclined who question the fact that this is, in truth, the best diet are suddenly translated to psychiatric hospitals or labour camps, the compulsion to enjoy boiled beef is mightily enhanced. The motivation of the Soviet conscript is implanted at a very early age and is nurtured throughout his service, which takes place in that highly impressionable age bracket of eighteen to twenty-one.

But what of the gnarled veterans of twenty-two and more? These are the sailors who have volunteered to continue their naval careers, the chief petty officers and the *michmany* (warrant officers), and their future advancement depends on their acceptance of the doctrines and dogmas under which their country is governed. Probably no more than twenty to twenty-five per cent will be active members of the Soviet Communist Party, but they are all nationalists and patriots. The majority believes that their country is misunderstood, misrepresented and under threat.

The officers are somewhat different. Their training is highly specialised. After entry into the service there is a wholesale redistribution of talent – and the submarine schools receive a high quota of the most talented. Not all are expected to reach the pinnacle of command, but there is a common factor amongst them all: dissidence is disastrous and advancement depends upon acceptance, if not embracement, of Communist doctrine. After all, Admiral of the Fleet of the Soviet Union Sergei Gorshkov was a vice-admiral before he was nudged into becoming a Party member. Thus, amongst the officers there is a variation between the energetic Party member, who may thus achieve distinction, and the strictly professional officer, who achieves distinction as a result of his capabilities. This is not a new outcome of totalitarian rule – similar advancement for political reasons is apparent in the Greek order of battle more than 2,000 years ago. Whatever the reasons for advancement, the young officer can expect a long wait before he reaches the status of commanding a modern nuclear submarine of any type. A majority of such appointments are reserved for senior captains and, in one case, a rear admiral.

Forty years ago, when the Soviet Navy returned some British submarines loaned during the Second World War, the main point of discussion on the British side was the fact that, in a small 'U' class submarine, the meagre messes allocated to the senior rates and the sailors had been converted into cabins for the officers. This seemed to breach the principles of Soviet Communism, but no information was vouchsafed as to the resting place of those who were not officers. The rare sightings of officers' accommodation and that of junior ratings in modern Soviet ships suggests that this class differentiation continues today, a reflection of the gulf existing between the upper strata of Soviet society and the rest.

The Soviet Union expects . . .

In October 1904, as the Russian Second Pacific Squadron was about to set off from the Baltic prior to their annihilation in the Straits of Tsushima, Fleet Bulletin No 32 informed those interested that the Tsarina was to present a chalice to all ships with a chapel, knowing that 'in their inmost hearts all men of the fleet, both high and low, are but awaiting the time when they may effectually do their duty to God and to our country'. Not all the Russians at Tsushima covered themselves with glory – one battleship with a complement of 900 was surrendered with a total casualty list of twenty killed and forty wounded – but it is not the habit of the Soviet ideologues to recall such disasters.

Thirteen years later God was dropped from the reckoning but a powerful sense of duty to the *Rodina*, Motherland, is now reinforced by an urgent call to the banners of Marx and Lenin, and Western planners would do well to heed this powerful mixture.

The point of this excursion into the background of the so-called 'classless society' is to estimate whether the huge differences which exist between the volunteer officers and senior ratings on one side and the conscripts on the other would have any effect on the function of Soviet submarines in time of war. One cannot help feeling that the 'haves' would be hard pressed to carry out their professional duties and lead the 'have-nots' at the same time.

The efficiency of a fleet is the result of a complex amalgam of men and machines, in which the men take the lead. If a submarine fleet is to pose a credible threat it must have not only men capable of fighting effectively in time of war, but also a watertight chain of command. Command decisions may be greatly assisted by computer calculations, but there is an indefinable something, a feeling in the bones, which comes as a result of experience. This steady accretion lies behind the decisions of those whose task it is to direct the activities of the submarines at sea.

The amount of control exercised over any submarine operation should vary with the circumstances. Only on board is there an immediate appreciation of water and weather conditions, visibility and many other variables which affect the conduct of the patrol. If a regular flow of intelligence is passed to a fleet submarine the captain is the best, and often the only man who can decide how to make full use of this information. Any attempt by the staff to direct the course of events frequently results in failure or, at the best, frustration. Success in lone submarine operations depends on the ability of the commanding officer to grasp a fleeting opportunity and turn it to his advantage, as well as on his knowledge of the likely actions of his adversary.

In the Soviet Navy, however, rigid control by the shore staff, overriding that of the embarked political staff, is essential in some circumstances, and these occasions are multiplied as more submarines with varying capabilities become available. Co-ordinated attacks, which include not only submarines using torpedoes and cruise missiles of varying ranges but also surface ships and aircraft, are frequently exercised during Soviet naval manoeuvres. Such operations have been made possible by the ability of nuclear submarines to proceed at speeds equal to or greater than the ships on the surface. When Lord Fisher was British First Sea Lord in the early years of the century he wrote, 'The submarine is the weapon of the strong – that is if they are sufficiently developed and diversified and properly applied – but you must have quantity and multiplicity of species.' This extraordinarily prescient remark was made when submarines had little range, low speed and were armed with torpedoes of dubious capability. Today Fisher would find all that he believed necessary – in the Soviet submarine fleet. There one finds that development is continually taking place, there is a considerable diversity and multiplicity of species, and the total number of hulls is the largest in the world and the greatest achieved in peacetime by any navy.

What the First Sea Lord could not foresee was the impressive range of weapons available to submarines some eighty years in the future. At a time when the aeroplane was in its infancy the idea of airborne missiles would have strained people's imagination and credulity. But today they are a regular part of a submarine's armoury and it is worth considering the differences in their deployment by the two major navies, those of the USA and the USSR. The former has abandoned the construction of non-nuclear submarines and is concentrating all efforts on the production of a single class of attack submarines and one class of ballistic-missile submarines. This has an advantage in that continuity of construction at the only two yards available in the USA has resulted in a considerable reduction in real costs and dramatic cuts in building times.

But the fact that the US Navy had only one class of attack submarine under construction when the Tomahawk cruise missile became available has meant that this class, with only four torpedo tubes, now carries a mixed load of wire-guided torpedoes and three different types of missile – Subroc, Harpoon and Tomahawk. While this allows for versatility, it does also mean that at a critical moment it may be necessary to reload with different weapons, the ranges and capabilities of the three missiles being very different. From the end of 1985 this problem was partially resolved by incorporating a number of Tomahawk launching tubes external to the pressure hull.

The Soviet Navy has, ever since their first cruise missiles went to sea in 1956, adopted a different approach. Since then, separate classes of cruise-missile-firing submarines have been built in parallel with normal attack submarines. For instance, in 1967 the first boats of two new classes of nuclear submarines appeared, both with similar hulls and propulsion systems. One, though, was armed only with torpedoes, while the other had separate cruise-missile launch tubes external to the hull as well as a torpedo armament. This two-track method has continued until today: the huge 'Oscar' class carries twenty-four missile tubes, and three separate classes of nuclear attack submarines are under construction. These last are armed with torpedoes of two different sizes – the normal twenty-one-inch and the new 25.6-inch, as well as two types of comparatively short-range missiles, one of which carries a torpedo, the other a nuclear depth bomb. At the same time, non-nuclear submarines are regularly under construction, giving a further capability for operations in coastal waters where nuclear boats cannot use their full potential. It is the existence of this 'multiplicity of species' which calls for careful staff work in the allocation of areas and sectors to avoid mutual interference.

The Soviet submarine fleet has three main operational branches: the ballistic-missile, the cruise-missile and the torpedo-armed submarines. The first of these must be considered quite separately from the other two because its tasks are integrated with a separate Soviet arm – the Strategic Rocket Forces. At the same time it must be remembered that the ballistic missiles are not the only strategic weapons carried by submarines; cruise missiles also come into the picture. When the Soviet Navy converted a number of the 'Whiskey' class in the late 1950s and fitted them with SS–N–3C (Shaddock) missiles their purpose, in view of targeting problems against ships, was probably land bombardment. The maximum range of these missiles was 450 nautical miles – today the SS–N–21, carried by the later classes of nuclear attack submarines, has a range of about 1,600 nautical miles. This would effectively complement the use of long-range ballistic missiles, would penetrate below any form of space defence, and would present a deterrent in the event of 'wars of national liberation'. All these aspects will be considered in Chapters 6 and 11, but here it must be emphasised that the Soviet fleet of ballistic-missile submarines is by no means now, and will be increasingly less in the future, the only branch with a strategic capability.

No excuse is needed for occasional excursions into recent history – the neglect of history is often the downfall not only of arguments but also, frequently, of governments. In the education of the average naval officer it is often ignored and, in staff considerations, denied the vital place which is its right.

So let us give brief consideration to the history of Soviet submarines during the last forty years and then ponder on their current effectiveness as instruments of political intentions now and in the immediate future.

Despite the problems facing the diesel-electric submarine of forty years ago, a building programme of 1948 decreed the addition of 1,200 submarines to the Soviet fleet between 1950 and 1965. The initial rate was to be seventy-eight a year rising to 100. Of the total, 200 were to be long-range boats ('Zulu' and 'Foxtrot' classes), 900 medium range ('Whiskey' and, later, 'Romeo' classes) and 100 coastal submarines ('Quebec' class). As the interval from the announcement to the completion of the first of this series was barely two years, it was apparent that the plans had been made during the preceding three years, drawing heavily on German experience and designs. The task was formidable, not only for the shipbuilders but also for those who had to train the ships' companies. By the end of 1965 the number of men required for this huge fleet would have been some 65,000, plus at least half this figure as 'spare crew'. As all the junior ratings had to be replaced at the end of their conscript service, the total to be put through the training machine each year at the end of the programme could have been as high as 30,000, a figure to make the average Western submarine training officer feel a bit ragged at the edges.

This historical digression is necessary to make the point that the submarine is not a new device in the Soviet fleet. The Imperial Russian Navy had adopted various forms of underwater craft for some forty years before the Revolution and, when the first Soviet building programme was tabled in 1926, it contained a high proportion of submarines. By 1941 the total had risen to 280, the largest national fleet in the world.

The advent of nuclear power caused a rapid rundown of the 1948 plan. By 1955 the 'Zulu' programme was halted with only twenty-six out of forty built. By 1957 240 'Whiskeys' had been completed and between 1957 and 1961 only about twenty 'Romeos' were finished out of a planned total of 560. Only twenty-two of the little 'Quebecs' were commissioned, probably to the delight of their crews as the high test peroxide (HTP) used in the Walter turbines proved to be a somewhat inflammatory method of propulsion. Thus, by 1965, barely a quarter of the planned 1,200 boats were completed, although the 'Foxtrot' class, a much improved version of the 'Zulu', was commissioned at a much slower rate between 1958 and 1971. Only sixty-two of the planned 160 'Foxtrots' were eventually built, but once the requirement for non-nuclear submarines had been appreciated, the first of eighteen 'Tango' class submarines appeared in 1972. This programme finished twelve years later, although the first of the 'Kilo' class, a major departure from previous designs, was probably completed in 1979. Many more 'Kilos' can be expected as the later 'Whiskeys' and 'Romeos' finally run out of life.

The first nuclear-propelled submarine, USS *Nautilus*, was at sea in January 1955. At the same time the first of the Soviet 'November' class must have been on or very near the building slip – fourteen were completed between 1958 and 1963. No time was allowed for trials of a prototype and this faith in the designers and engineers has been amply proved, for twelve of the class remained active in 1985. When the class went into commission, there were two urgent requirements. The first was the need to utilise the potential of nuclear propulsion in the line-up against the carrier task forces. The second was to gather all available knowledge and experience to be incorporated in new designs.

It was, therefore, nine years after the original 'November' was commissioned that the first of these new classes appeared and these, with the 'Yankee' SSBN, were all commissioned in 1967. The hull form of the 'Victor' and 'Charlie' was quite different from the long, slender form of 'November', as was their propulsion, and this general pattern remained standard for the next seventeen years. In this period 'Victor I' was lengthened to become 'Victor II', which was probably the first Soviet class to carry the 25.6-inch torpedoes which had been developed since the mid-1960s. This class was completed in 1978 with the seventh boat, and was followed in the same year by the 'Victor III'.

There are five major attributes of a submarine which a designer must take into account – range, speed, armament, diving depth and silence. If the optimum figure is reached in all these elements one should have the ideal boat, based on the principle that the true submarine has no need to use the surface. But what is the optimum? Range is easy and could be defined as the maximum period during which a crew can remain sane and healthy – in fact with a true submarine using nuclear power the term 'endurance' is more applicable, and numerical assessment has little relevance.

High speed has two important effects. Firstly, it allows for rapid deployment. Secondly, it allows the submarine to engage or disengage at will if it has a speed advantage over the opposition and its weapons. This is a lesson learned long ago by the Phoenicians, and it has been thumped home over the intervening centuries. It is what Lord Fisher meant eighty years ago when he said, 'Speed is armour.' Thus the maximum attainable is the optimum – if it can be afforded and if other attributes are not prejudiced by cost.

Armament is primarily related to tasks – the specialised minelaying submarine was a perfect example of this fact. Today the ballistic- missile submarine is the modern edition of the type-cast boat. But with endurance limited only by the resilience of the men in the submarine (remembering the remark of a very wise intelligence officer, 'You will be making a great mistake if you judge Soviet rationing standards by our own'), flexibility is essential; the weapons must therefore be both as numerous as the size of the submarine allows, and as easily transferable. as effective and as accurate as the designers can produce.

The diving depth of a submarine depends on the several factors described in Chapter 2, to which can be added the efficiency of the builders and a certain amount of luck. When submarines were designed for a depth of 300 feet they frequently exceeded this figure in an emergency. Today 1,300 feet is a fairly standard figure, and tests of laminated hull structures down to 15,000 feet have been carried out. We can't all go down to profound depths in little round balls, nor would such an attainable condition be of much use in an operational boat. But, without going into the mathematics of the matter, depth capability is increasingly important as detection devices improve. The optimum is perhaps 3,000 to 4,000 feet.

Lastly, silence – this is really the nub of the problem, the vital element in survivability. Active sonar is a lighthouse towards which a submariner can steer or whose beams he can avoid. Passive sonar detection depends on the sounds, some tiny, some at very low frequencies, some at high, emitted by a submarine. Remove these sounds and the only alternative form of detection is active sonar. The task of silencing is the most difficult and the most demanding of any in the submarine world.

How do the Soviet submarines measure up to these criteria of excellence? Firstly, endurance: the average member of the Soviet armed forces is fit, well motivated and energetic. It is impossible to make an overall assessment of the character of these men, drawn from the fifteen republics and over a hundred races which form the USSR, but their leaders are determined and brave. The endurance of Soviet submariners will be the maximum possible, and this capacity has long existed.

Speed was, clearly, the second requirement placed on the Soviet designers. This is a very major element of survival and the Soviet submariner, like any other, is not only determined but encouraged to survive. Therefore the 'November' class was fast, but not fast enough. As the plans for the 1967 trio of classes was in hand, another design was on the drawing boards. This was to be the test-bed for the long-term solution and, when the first of the class appeared, the Western analysts, with what may have been extraordinary foresight, labelled it 'Alfa'. Her titanium hull, the shape of her fin, the smoothness of the upperworks and what may well be the use of super-conducting electrical machinery – these have resulted in an increase of a third in her speed, to forty-two knots, and a diving depth of 3,000 feet – twice that of previous classes. It matters not at all that the first boat was a failure and was dismantled. Very shortly number two was at sea, followed by five more. The Alfa has achieved the highest known speed underwater – and it may very soon be eclipsed. Today the optimum speed may be sixty to seventy knots: tomorrow, who knows? Other than the Soviet naval staff and their designers.

The next aim was to produce a weapon load which would provide the flexibility considered desirable. We have discussed the improved torpedoes in the 'Victor II' and other classes. Unlike men, torpedoes of greater girth can often go faster and further. In 1933 the Japanese introduced the twenty-four-inch Type 93 'Long Lance', which could carry with accuracy an 1,100-pound warhead to a range of 43,500 yards at thirty-six knots, a performance which stands comparison with most modern torpedoes. With two sizes of torpedoes, some fitted with nuclear heads and a proportion with a wake-homing capability, plus the SS–N–15 and 16 missiles and a minelaying capability, the Soviet Navy had a very firm grip on its armament by the late 1970s.

The ability to dive deeper into the ocean has many advantages for the submariner. How far have the Soviet designers advanced in this downward direction? It is clear that an increase in this plane was envisaged in the early 1960s, when the hull of 'Alfa' was being designed. The use of titanium alloys had been considered by Western scientists long before 'Alfa' appeared, but had been discarded as prohibitively expensive – fine for aircraft, but not so for submarines where solidity was required. What Western analysts failed to take into account was the Soviet doctrine that what's good for the military is affordable. The USSR has huge deposits of titanium – no doubt a great deal of experimentation went into its recovery, smelting and welding, at very great cost. But all this finance produced the first operational submarine to reach depths of around 3,000 feet In 1971 'Papa' went to sea – displacing 8,000 tons and with a titanium alloy hull – and is still with us. The point was sufficiently proved. Today 'Mike', the first of a class entering service in 1984, has benefited from these experiments and the first 'Akula', launched in mid-1984, may well be of the same construction. With the huge financial resources at his disposal, the Soviet submariner is going steadily deeper than his Western counterparts.

Western submarines had been much quieter than the Soviet boats for many years. If the earlier versions of Soviet submarines were to achieve their planned speeds a great deal of power had to be transmitted to the water, and this made a lot of noise. It seems that the designers, having achieved excellent range, speed, armament and diving depth, decided to tackle noise reduction. And so came 'Victor III'. When we consider variations in propulsion systems in Chapter 6, we shall find that these can contribute greatly to this end. An exceedingly quiet submarine is within reach.

One of the authors, with customary good fortune, was on his way to pay an account in London when he realised that he'd forgotten his cheque book. A few minutes later, his destination was demolished by one of the first V2 rockets launched by the Germans. The date was 1944. In less than a year, the Soviet authorities were in possession not only of the details of this missile, but also of the Lafferentz project to launch V2s from capsules towed by U-boats. The seed of an idea was planted; experiments, albeit unsuccessful, were carried forward with the Golem series of missiles and, finally, it was decided to enclose a launcher in a tube incorporated in the hull of a submarine. This took some time to fabricate, but in September 1955 the first submarine-launched ballistic missile was fired from a converted 'Zulu' class submarine. This was five years before the first ballistic-missile submarine of the US Navy, *George Washington*, was in commission. Admittedly the Zulu was not nuclear propelled (this being the same year as *Nautilus* first went to sea on nuclear power and three years before the Soviet 'November' class) and the missiles had a range of 300 nautical miles, compared with the 1,300-mile range of *George Washington*'s Polaris. The important facts are these: (a) the Soviets were first off the starting blocks; (b) only five months later Admiral Gorshkov took over as commander-in-chief of the Soviet Navy, a position he held until 1985. Thirty years of stability and continuity have provided the essential background for evolution and improvement. In 1958 a custom-built class of non-nuclear ballistic-missile submarines went into commission and a year later came the first nuclear-propelled version, the 'Hotels'. In 1962 both classes were converted to carry SS–N–5 missiles with a megaton head and a range of 750 nautical miles, while the construction of the Soviet 'Yankee' class began. Very similar in outline to *George Washington* (not surprisingly, as take-apart models of the latter were on sale in toy shops within a year of her commissioning) the 'Yankees' carried sixteen SS–N–6 missiles with a range of 1,300 nautical miles. The first was commissioned in 1967, and within two years at least two of this class were on regular patrol off the east coast of the USA. From that time onwards designs followed one another at an accelerating pace. In the late 1960s testing of the SS–N–8 missile for the 'Delta' class took place, the original version having a range of 4,200 nautical miles, and the second version one of 4,900 nautical miles. Thus when the first of the 'Delta I' class SSBNs was completed, to be followed in 1975 by the 'Delta II', the Soviet Navy had submarines whose missiles could cover slightly more than the entire northern hemisphere from the waters immediately adjacent to their fleet bases. SSBNs no longer had to run the risk of detection as they made the passage of the Greenland–UK gaps into the North Atlantic or sailed from Vladivostok or Petropavlovsk into the Pacific. The first 'Delta III', with three versions of the SS–N–18 missile – some with multiple heads and all with ranges of between 3,500 and 4,300 nautical miles, appeared in 1976, and ten years later came the 'Delta IV', carrying the more powerful and more accurate SS–N–23. In the midst of this series came 'Typhoon', a monster submarine configured for under-ice operations, carrying twenty SS–N–20 missiles with a range of 4,500 nautical miles, each carrying six to nine warheads. Three of this class entered service between 1983 and 1985.

A piece of string and a globe of the world will demonstrate a disturbing fact. If four modern Soviet SSBNs were deployed – one off Murmansk, one off the Kamchatka Peninsula, one off the Equator south of India, and one in the Antarctic area of the South Pacific, their missiles could be targeted on every major city in the world.

It is true that the US Navy's 'Ohio' class has the same capability, but the story of Soviet cruise-missile submarines shows a different pattern when compared with its US counterpart. The latter started trials with Loon missiles in two submarines in 1948–49 and, soon afterwards, converted a number of other boats, either with Regulus missile launchers or guidance systems. By 1965 the US Navy had abandoned the cruise-missile programme because ballistic missiles could now be deployed at sea. Not so the Soviet Navy. In 1958–60, after experiments with the only 'Whiskey Single Cylinder', the 'Twin Cylinder' variant became operational, carrying two missiles of dubious accuracy but undoubted lethality. In the next three years came the 'Whiskey Long Bin', with four missiles, overlapping the 'Echo I', the first nuclear-class submarine, which also carried the SS–N–3C missiles. From 1961 to 1969 the non-nuclear 'Juliett' class appeared, with only four launchers as opposed to six in 'Echo I', and simultaneously came the 'Echo II', another nuclear class with eight launchers. Twenty-nine 'Echo IIs' were launched in six years from building ways left vacant during the turn-over from the 'Hotel' to the 'Yankee' SSBNs.

Up to 1967 all cruise-missile submarines had to surface to launch their missiles. These had a range, in later classes, of some 300 nautical miles and a capability for attacking surface ships. This was a time of necessity – Western anti-submarine operations had considerably lessened the likelihood of a successful torpedo attack by any submarine which was not nuclear propelled. Only the dozen or so noisy 'November' class were available in the nuclear category, so the long-range cruise missile was essential. But, because it could be launched only on the surface, the range had to be sufficient to allow the firing submarine to operate beyond the range of the escorts of a task force, even if within the compass of embarked aircraft. Despite the advent of the Polaris missile, the carrier remained a considerable threat to the naval installations around Murmansk. However, the radius of her aircraft with nuclear weapons was only some 500 nautical miles at the most, and this meant that an 'Echo II' engaging a NATO task force might expect cover from her own shore-based aircraft while the carrier was still beyond range of the target.

This was less certain in the Mediterranean, where NATO airfields in Italy, Greece and Turkey could despatch strikes intended to disturb and destroy any submarine which chose to surface. The need for a cruise missile launched from dived was appreciated long before 1967, when the first 'Charlie' class was deployed. This was a nuclear boat of a totally new design which carried eight tubes for SS–N–7 missiles, each with a range of thirty-five nautical miles. These were constructed so that they could be launched from a fully submerged submarine – a third range-circle now had to be covered by the anti-submarine escorts of a task force.

In the succeeding years it was merely a matter of extending this range-circle by improving the performance of the missiles. In 1971 the single 'Papa' class was at sea with SS–N–9 missiles. This pushed the circle out to sixty miles and the same armament was fitted in the 'Charlie II' class, which was built from 1973 to 1980. The slow rate of construction of the 'Charlies' (only seventeen were built in thirteen years) portended another radical change. This came with the launch in the spring of 1980 of 'Oscar', a monster of 14,000 tons dived displacement. Her huge casing is sixty feet wide and contains six twin-launch tubes on either side. In these she carries twenty-four SS–N–19 missiles and the range-circle has taken a dramatic jump out to 295 nautical miles. With a speed of at least thirty-three knots and a powerful torpedo armament, 'Oscar' is well suited for independent or co-ordinated operations. Her speed is sufficient to maintain station on a carrier task force, be it NATO or Soviet commanded.

To what extent does this superb fleet pose a threat? Is it likely to offer menaces? And if so, what kind?

It is self-evident that a fleet of some eighty ballistic-missile submarines, about seventy cruise-missile submarines, and the best part of 215 attack submarines offers a grave threat in the event of hostilities. This is compounded by the fact that ninety-three per cent of the first, seventy-three per cent of the second, and thirty-two per cent of the last of these types are nuclear propelled. The primary aim of the Soviet Navy at the outbreak of war would be the protection of the ballistic-missile submarines on passage or station. This task would be shared amongst all branches of the fleet, including the naval air force, but the attack submarines would have an important function in attempting to track and destroy any NATO submarines seeking out the ballistic-missile boats. This would apply equally in the Pacific as in the Atlantic.

This is probably the only new task when compared with earlier submarine operations. Attacks on naval and merchant shipping, minelaying, the landing of agents and raiders, reconnaissance – all would have their place. The difference is that modern boats can carry out all these with greater efficiency and more quickly.

In the event of a 'war of national liberation' as defined by the USSR, a satisfactory result could be achieved in a limited area by the declaration of some form of 'exclusion zone' backed by an intimation of submarines being deployed to enforce it. In this case there would be a lot of huffing and puffing in the West, but very little action would be possible. The success of the Nyon Patrol, as described in Chapter 1, resulted from two of the world's largest navies combining, albeit late in the day. Today any Western fleet other than the US Navy is hard pressed if an additional couple of frigates is required abroad; the Japanese MSDF is restrained by politics and treaties, and the Chinese and Indians would probably prefer to avoid involvement. This would be a clear case of 'forcing by means of menaces' – less immediate than the American mining of Haiphong in the Vietnam War, but equally effective.

Some might call this 'international terrorism' or a dozen other names, but whatever the title such action becomes more likely as the aggrieved fail to react in a period of escalating violence.

The fact that the navies of the major democratic powers are stretched due to falling values, rising prices and continual cuts, either in the past or present, provides another possible activity for the Soviet submarines. Throughout the world, and particularly in the vicinity of the narrow maritime defiles, the USSR has obtained access to the ports of their sympathisers. In the Dahlak Islands off Ethiopia, Aden, Cam Ranh Bay in Vietnam, in Angola, West Africa, Mozambique and Cuba, anchorages are available for Soviet depot and repair ships; meanwhile the Kremlin continues to make advances to Tonga and other South Pacific states. The available havens are used from time to time, but a sudden deployment of a reasonable proportion of the eighty-one support ships which are available, followed by an equal proportion of the 300-odd cruise-missile and attack submarines would pose major problems of surveillance to Western navies. Satellites are all very well for keeping tabs on surface ships or submarines in harbour, but any accurate estimate of a submarine's intentions when at sea requires a more immediate scrutiny. Even that required for a watch on a two- or three-week exercise is very demanding on engine hours of both ships and aircraft. Extend that to a matter of months and the problems could mount rapidly.

It might be argued that all this is speculation. Of course it is – and every act of the forward planner is a matter of speculation – based on the best intelligence available allied with a sound knowledge of any historical background which may be relevant. In this case there is considerable intelligence of capability and a large body of case history. The latter includes both overt and covert acts which embrace such operations as the direct support of Ethiopia, surrogate support in a number of African states, subversion in areas like Baluchistan, activities in the Caribbean, illegal intrusion into the territorial waters of Norway and Sweden, the reinforcement of the Southern Kurils on Japan's northern coast – to mention some of many events. All have a maritime connection, all could be supported by submarine operations, and all are in areas vital to the survival of the democratic states. While the nibbling is ignored and the principle that the Soviet Union should be treated differently from other aggressive nations is adhered to, the threat will remain. It is a threat to all countries, great and small, and, to face it, there is a need, equally ignored in many places, for cohesion and determination. Europe and North America have maintained their co-operation in NATO, although this is circumscribed by tight rules and national susceptibilities. Further east the demise of regional pacts such as CENTO, SEATO and the possible dissolution of ANZUS can have no other effect than a loosening of control – at a time when this can only be to the advantage of the USSR.

4

Weapon System Development

'The only use of the *Holland* (SS–1), remarked Admiral O'Neil, US Navy, in 1900, 'is to discharge torpedoes and no weapon is more erratic.' There were plenty of submariners on all sides who came to agree, in time, with the Admiral's pessimistic verdict, delivered at the very beginning of practical underwater warfare development; but the point behind the words 'the only use' has time and again been missed: John Philip Holland, the father of all modern submarines, was in no doubt that attack (or the threat of attack, because Holland anticipated deterrence) was the boat's sole purpose, and he designed it around a weapon system comprising an eighteen-inch torpedo with two reloads and, initially, two nine-inch missile tubes.

Elsewhere, weapons tended to be an afterthought, something to be attached or added later if the hull proved sound. And from the turn of the century it is an extraordinary fact that, almost without exception, vehicles have taken precedence over weapon systems – with the honourable exception of strategic systems like Polaris. The first consideration has usually been speed linked with endurance – propulsion has been devised for that; and then a hull has been designed to accommodate machinery and fuel in a shape more or less suited to the speed and diving depth, with space for the crew; and, lastly, some weapons in vogue have been chosen to fit the hull.

It would have made better sense to decide what weapon system was needed for such and such a task and only then determine the most suitable platform to carry it. The snag in that line of thinking, from a submarine protagonist's point of view, is that the best platform may conceivably not be a submarine at all. Back-to-front thinking is quite evident today, especially where followers of a Rickoverian propulsion-first philosophy are concerned; as in the past, the consequences can be far-reaching and decidedly detrimental to weapon-system effectiveness – which is what, logically, submarine designers should aim for first and foremost. For one thing, Western weapon engineers have been, and still quite often are, constrained to a twenty-one-inch torpedo tube, which may or may not be in the best place for discharging a new kind of torpedo or missile; for another, far more money and effort is devoted to developing submarines than the tactical weapons which it is their ultimate purpose to fire.

In the words of a respected submariner, Vice Admiral Eli T. Reich of the US Navy, 'there is a tendency to forget that, in the end, it all comes down to placing an ordnance package alongside the other fellow . . . and making sure that it explodes!'

A submarine should be designed as a complete weapon system in itself, a package deal integrating weapons, fire-control and sensors with the most suitable hull and propulsion for the selected purpose or purposes. Although there have been proclamations of avowed intent to this end over the past thirty years, particularly in the US, British and French navies, the traditional priorities have generally asserted themselves at an early stage. The reasons for that will become apparent later; and some of them may prove inescapable when examined. But, without trying to reach a conclusion, which would need extensive wargaming/modelling, it will be useful to keep one basic question in mind: if a long-arm weapon system is reliable out to a certain range, what speed is required by the launching platform to deliver the weapon? The tactical speed ought to be quantifiable and not just 'as fast as possible'.

The question is important because high speed means high power and that is exceedingly expensive: an extra fifteen per cent at the top of the scale can add tens of millions to the price – a cost increase of around fifty per cent is quoted. And the fact is that a submarine is deaf, dumb and blind above a certain speed. For future boats, not yet on the stocks, twenty knots has been suggested as the maximum at which sensors can be expected to function with a reasonable degree of acquisition probability; and at present it is likely that the figure is a good deal lower.

Nuclear-powered attack submarines (SSNs) use full power more than in the past – when engaged in a 'dogfight' with another submarine, when closing or chasing a target, and when escaping torpedoes or other unwelcome attentions by the opposition. Diesel-electric submarines (SSKs) wind on full ahead less often because the battery is drained at an alarming rate. A ballistic-missile submarine (SSBN) would probably use every available knot after launching missiles because its position would, in theory, be known to the enemy within moments; the same applies in some circumstances to tactical missile launchers. But whether the costly increase from, say, thirty-two knots to thirty-five knots for an SSN or seventeen knots to twenty knots for an SSK would make much difference is difficult to say. Frankly, cost-effectiveness appears doubtful if there is a danger of speed-money robbing weapon-money.

At all events, submariners seem to agree that keeping very quiet is more desirable than going very fast if a question of priorities arises. The Royal Navy has now decided to design submarines 'to cost', at a price that can be paid, with Vickers (VSEL) the prime contractor, working closely with the Ministry of Defence from the preliminary sketch stage. 'If we don't pool our resources,' says the new Director General Submarines,[1] 'there is a danger within the Ministry of trying to create a submarine which may be more expensive than we can afford.' How right he is. The Royal Navy cannot possibly pay the price which the US Navy is willing to afford – one billion dollars or more for the planned SSN 21 (*Seawolf*) – and it has to be realistic.

Given a weapon system with adequate range – which is the key to the whole problem – it is suggested that *exceptionally* high speed is no longer crucial so far as tactics are concerned.

However, there are other factors which affect considerations of speed, not least the very real need for designers, engineers and shipbuilders to keep abreast of advancing technology. Above all, there is the requirement, more apparent in some navies than others, for rapid strategic deployment; and high speed is also needed if submarines are tasked to support a surface fleet. Nobody quarrels with a submariner's plea for speed: it is the level of that speed that needs to be determined.

Getting to the Falklands

Nuclear power made it possible for the UK Task Force Commander (Rear Admiral Woodward) to have three of his allocated attack submarines on station to enforce the 200-mile Maritime Exclusion Zone around the Falklands by 12 April 1982, ten days after the Argentinian invasion.

HMS *Spartan* was the first to leave Gibraltar, making the 6,500-mile passage to her operating area in less than ten days, implying a speed of advance of around twenty-seven or twenty-eight knots. Allowing for brief excursions to a shallow depth to receive messages and check on navigation, arithmetic suggests that, for this deployment, *Spartan* went flat out. The same was presumably true of *Conqueror, Splendid, Courageous* and *Valiant*, which followed closely. A long way astern came the diesel-driven *Onyx* – with a submerged speed of advance of eight knots she did not arrive for three weeks after the nuclear boats.

When on station there was one occasion when *Spartan* came slowly but inexorably – and inexplicably – to a complete halt. Eventually it became clear that the 4,900-ton 15,000 shp submarine had been arrested by a giant bank of kelp: the sea still has some surprises to spring and remains the submariner's most powerful enemy.

Onyx must have been missed in the early days of the campaign as a more suitable vehicle than the SSNs for launching and recovering Special Boat Squadron (SBS) raiders – a very important kind of weapon system associated with SSKs as well as with midget submersibles.

Another five knots for the SSNs would have saved thirty-six hours to the Falklands – a meaningful saving on that occasion, but it has to be asked what the likelihood is, in future, that British boats – in fact any nation's submarines other than those of America or the Soviet Union – will be required to deploy so urgently, so rapidly, and so far. Against that, one might reply that the Falklands conflict was wholly unexpected (which would not be entirely true) and that future surprises may be in store.

Either way, it is no use careering about in wartime at full power unless Admiral Reich's 'ordnance package' can ultimately be exploded alongside the enemy.

For Soviet submariners exceptionally high speed is fully justified for deployment, evasion and attack with the systems it has selected. Paradoxically, an extremely long-range weapon – a tactical missile capable of two or three hundred miles or more and intended primarily for defending the homeland against an advancing fleet – does require the carrier submarine to have high speed to 'end around' if necessary and intercept the enemy before he can launch strike aircraft.

It is a case of horses for courses: what one navy needs is not necessarily the same as another. The same is true of the continuing argument for and against diesel as opposed to nuclear power. The two types have different jobs to do in, usually, differing environments. Unfortunately, the price difference between the two, in Britain anyway, is not turning out to be nearly as wide as it should be. The Royal Navy can certainly not buy five diesel SSKs for the price of one nuclear SSN, as once hoped. The figure is more like one and a half or two to one.

TORPEDO ATTACK AGAINST SURFACE TARGETS

History is only another word for experience, so it is worth recollecting some of the lessons learned during the last full-scale underwater war from 1939–45. Only two submarines have made successful torpedo attacks since then. The first was the Pakistani *Hangor* (a French 'Daphné' class SSK) which sank, with simple acoustic-homing unguided torpedoes, the Indian 'Blackwood' class frigate *Khukri* from about five hundred metres and severely damaged the *Kirpan* at the entrance to the Gulf of Khambhat north of Bombay on 9 December 1971. The second was HMS *Conqueror* (SSN) which sank the Argentinian cruiser *General Belgrano* from a range of about 1,200 yards with two 'fish' from a salvo of three Mark VIII** straight-running, non-homing forty-five-knot torpedoes (whose design dated back to 1928) on a near right-angle track on 2 May 1982.

There are two important points to note from these incidents: elderly weapons, bordering on the antique in the latter case, did the job required of them in strictly limited war situations – indeed it was whispered, rightly or not, that *Conqueror*'s more sophisticated Tigerfish torpedoes either failed or were not considered as suitable because the Mark VIIIs packed a far more powerful punch and were sure to work. Secondly, *Conqueror*'s nuclear power enabled her to track, trail and choose the moment for attack when authorised to do so.

In neither of these two confrontations was the USSR directly involved. The Anglo-Argentinian conflict might have taken a very different turn if the Soviet Defence Council had chosen to interpose just a few attack-type nuclear submarines – perhaps if only to lay mines, as they might have been expected to do in what the Politburo chose to classify (for the Falklands) as a 'war of national liberation'. Presumably it was more interesting for the Soviets to watch the two sides slogging it out: there were tests of resolve and ability to be observed and, doubtless a fascinating prospect, there was a possibility of tactical nuclear and chemical weapons being used. It can hardly be thought that Moscow did not intervene because of the British nuclear deterrent.

In the light of these relatively recent 'old-fashioned' attacks, and bearing in mind that minor threats will continue to involve more or less pre-1945 tactics for some years to come, it is worth recollecting how a classical wartime torpedo attack used to be conducted.

Delivering fish

A submerged attack started with a periscope sighting of masts on the horizon five to ten miles distant. The simple Second World War directional hydrophones (best in the US Navy) might hear asdic/sonar 'pinging' or faint screw noises (cavitation) further away, but the search periscope, raised about three feet above the surface, was usually the principal means of detection. If a submarine was on the surface at night, sightings through binoculars were apt to be uncomfortably close; but radar in American fleet boats could pick up targets out to horizon range.

Night attacks were often made entirely on the surface, but since they are very unlikely to be attempted today it is only dived attacks that deserve description.

The problem was to determine the target's range, course and speed and then close the projected track to an ideal firing position – about half a mile on the enemy's beam – without being detected. The maximum submerged speed in all submarines was around eight knots and, generally, that could only be maintained for one hour before the battery was flattened – a highly undesirable state of affairs when enemy vessels were milling around overhead.

The captain closed the track with bursts of speed deep (to avoid surface disturbance and detectable cavitation) for a few minutes at a time, returning to periscope depth after each burst for another periscope observation and a check on escorts. If one of the latter was close it was best to present an end-on target – bow or stern – to minimise the chances of being 'pinged' and discovered; but that, of course, interfered with the all-important business of closing the target.

Without continuous angling gear for the torpedoes, the captain had to point his boat, like a shotgun, a calculated number of degrees ahead of the target and fire a salvo, one torpedo after another, on the same line of bearing exactly the right number of seconds apart, so that the enemy's own movement would effect the required spacing and spread. Submarines turned slowly at slow speeds – twenty or thirty degrees a minute – so that rapid mental arithmetic and nice timing were needed if the submarine was to achieve a firing position and score hits with a 'hosepipe' salvo on a zig-zagging target. The chances of hitting an anti-submarine vessel coming in fast on an unpredictable course were practically nil.

The difficulties are obvious, but British and European Allied 'hosepipes' scored 1,363 hits out of 3,220 attacks (42.3 per cent) and 1,040 ships were sunk for 5,121 torpedoes (20.3 per cent). Considering that the majority of targets were zig-zagging at quite high speeds and were often heavily escorted, the statistics are impressive. They were due to relentless training during the 'Perisher' Command Course (attended by most European Allies), meticulous periscope observations, a captain's personal skill, a determination to get at the enemy, and, very importantly, the ruthless analysis of both peacetime and wartime attacks by a small, tough, dispassionate, unimpressionable team of experts back at base.

All this suited the British temperament very well (less so the French), and the very fact that fire-control was rudimentary in the extreme forced commanding officers to make their attacks with great care and accuracy.

By comparison, American fire-control systems were greatly superior. A TDC (Torpedo Data Computer) continuously generated a firing angle and applied it electrically to the gyros of torpedoes waiting in the tubes. When the 'fish' were fired they automatically turned to the calculated hitting track with an appropriate angular spacing between them. This meant that the boat itself did not have to turn on to a firing track and there was thus no danger of altering course too late and losing an opportunity ('missing the DA' in British terms). Tactics were thereby simplified and it was possible to torpedo menacing destroyers. But the results were not so good: US submarines fired 14,748 torpedoes using angled fire, mostly against quite simple targets (because the Japanese never really understood anti-submarine tactics or submarine countermeasures such as zig-zagging) and sank 1,314 enemy ships – 8.9 per cent, or less than half the British and Allied sinking rate per torpedo fired. The comparison is not entirely meaningful because American captains were profligate with torpedoes (when, eventually, they ran true), but it is nevertheless a fact that the more sophisticated equipment did not achieve better results.

There were a number of reasons for this. It must have been tempting to fire from the hip without accurately determining the target's course, speed and range: periscopes had only a graticule lens graduated in minutes of arc, requiring a Stadimeter slide-rule to translate a rather rough angular reading into yards, and readings were not nearly so exact as those obtained by the miniature gunnery-type range-finder incorporated into British periscopes; sonar and radar bearings were also significant sources of error because they were inherently inaccurate (sometimes wildly so), but were apt to be trusted implicitly and were not checked frequently; and blind sonar attacks from deep – an advanced concept for the day – simply did not work in action.

The comparative roominess of American fleet boats in the last war had an inbuilt disadvantage compared with the smaller European submarines. It was difficult for a captain to maintain intimate contact with all that was happening throughout the boat. He depended a great deal on instrumentation and there was sometimes a natural tendency to rely upon dials rather than on his own skill and judgement.

There are vastly more dials and digits in the attack centre of a submarine today and it is not unknown for them to hypnotise a commanding officer, misleading judgement and common sense.

Wishful thinking

The US Navy Submarine Service was further hampered at the beginning of the war by a total lack of realism in peacetime exercises. Nobody, except the Germans, was very realistic, but American boats compounded unrealism by having to be successful (on paper) in the light of the creed that only excellence merited promotion. Exaggerated claims of success in peace – seldom, if ever, investigated by the kind of analysis which British commanding officers were subjected to – and unwillingness to risk reputations led, after Pearl Harbor, to a few commanding officers being over-cautious for a while and to admirals being over-confident. These serious qualitative failings (which, it must be said, have been disputed by some ex-wartime captains)[2] were to be overcome – magnificently – but they could have been avoided in the first place by objective, implacable auditing.

The habit of inflating successes in the US Navy was a source of embarrassment when post-war investigation revealed a spectacular drop in several scores, the greatest disparity being Commander Roy M. Davenport's credits while commanding USS *Haddock* and *Trepang*. These were reduced from 151,900 to 29,662 tons, with eight ships instead of seventeen sunk.

Wishful thinking was a temptation anywhere, but the Germans recorded only one glaring example ('We are an honest firm,' said Doenitz) while the British had none of significance.

Torpedoes were spaced and spread in a salvo to cover errors in estimating target movement while giving a high probability of one or more hits. A spread also made it difficult for a target which saw the clearly visible tracks of the usual oil/air or oil/air/steam forty-five-knot 'fish' to avoid all of them by making an emergency turn – provided that the salvo was not fired from too far away.

Electric torpedoes, which were wakeless, were used throughout the war by the German Navy, but they were slower at thirty knots and, during the U-boat heyday, they were generally fired singly at extremely close range from the surface against merchant ships in convoy. They very seldom missed, but they would not have met Allied requirements against primarily naval targets.

U-boats scored their greatest successes on the surface: they were really conceived as submersible torpedo boats and, despite the comparative excellence of their submerged performance, they started to lose the Battle of the Atlantic from the time that Allied anti-submarine measures forced them to keep their heads down in 1943.

Ironically, at almost exactly the same time as the battle turned, a rocket from Peenemunde, heralding the ballistic missiles that have changed the whole concept of war, rose gracefully from its launching pad under the direction of a certain Wernher von Braun. The rest, as they say, is history.

MODERN ANTI-SURFACE TORPEDOES

A fair number of SSKs today have nothing better than the old wartime torpedoes for attacking surface ships, and for these anti-surface-vessel approaches are little changed. But full submerged speed is now at least double what it was during the war, the boats are much quieter, and fire-control is greatly improved with all-round angling, so that there is now a chance of hitting fast, zig-zagging escorts, as well as more sedate targets, with non-homing torpedoes.

Needless to say, better weapons are needed and even in the Royal Navy, which has lagged sadly, they are beginning to appear in submarines of all types. However, 'intelligent' torpedoes are, or will be, susceptible to countermeasures (jamming) and decoys which straight-running fish, like the British Mark VIII** (similar to the old US Navy Mark XIV), and Soviet equivalents, are not. It may be a little premature to ditch such trusted and proven weapons altogether; and in any case it is doubtful whether every navy can afford full loads of modern replacements at up to four hundred times the price per unit. There are longer range 'unintelligent' torpedoes in Soviet service, developed from German wartime FAT pattern-runners which cross and recross a convoy's track, but the hit probability is, surprisingly, not greatly increased. However, a fifteen-kiloton warhead (the estimated yield of Soviet nuclear heads) on any torpedo would do immense damage to a group of ships.

The objections to an oil/air torpedo are manifold: it leaves a clearly visible wake; its range is short (hit probability for a salvo declines sharply outside about 3,000 yards); and it is noisy. But for attacks against merchant vessels from short range, as well as for the sort of use which the

(ABOVE) A Soviet sixteen-SLBM (SS–N–6 1300/1600-nautical-mile) 'Yankee' class SSBN. The sail-planes would have to be rotated vertically when surfacing through ice and they look sufficiently robust for that. The rail running around the casing is for crewmen safety harnesses – a very necessary precaution when working on the upper deck, especially after breaking upwards through the ice and shifting blocks off missile-tube caps. The slots in the outer hull imply noise: in this respect, unless carefully designed to avoid turbulence, a double hull can have disadvantages at speed, as well as marked advantages. (BELOW) USS *Michigan* at Electric Boat in 1979, due for launching on 26 April 1980. The existing (1986) eight 16,600/18,700-ton 'Ohio' class SSBNs, based at Bangor, Washington, are 560 feet long and carry twenty-four Trident I 4,350-nautical-mile SLBMs; but SSBN 734 (due to commission in January 1988) and on will be equipped for Trident II D5 6,000-nautical-mile (approx.) missiles. Costs have escalated since *Ohio*, the lead boat, was laid down in 1976: not counting missile development, research into countermeasures and support facilities, it looks as though boats building now (1986) are passing $1,500 million and heading higher. However, with vastly expensive peripherals (training, shore support and communications notable amongst them) it is difficult to calculate the real cost of an individual boat.

(ABOVE) A missile technician first class (immensely responsible, but none too well paid) sits at a control room console in USS *Ohio* (SSBN–726) during a simulated missile firing for pre-commissioning training: the first actual patrol was carried out from October to December 1982, a year after commissioning. Two crews, Blue and Gold (British equivalent – Port and Starboard), each of 133 (sixteen officers, 117 enlisted men) enable an 'Ohio' class SSBN to maintain a continuous cycle of seventy days on deterrent patrol and twenty-five days in harbour. Hopefully, overhauls will be at nine-year intervals (conforming to the nuclear core life) and – again optimistically – they will occupy no more than twelve months. (BELOW) The control room of USS *Ohio* (SSBN–726) during simulated submerged operations before commissioning. The chief of the watch is on the left, planesman/helmsman at centre, and diving officer on the right. (*US Navy*).

(ABOVE) The dining hall on board USS *Ohio* (SSBN–726). There is little difference in the facilities compared with a surface ship, the food is excellent, and there is no seasickness to contend with. (*US Navy*) (Below) USS *Woodrow Wilson* (SSBN–624), seventh of the 'Lafayette' class and built at Mare Island naval shipyard, commissioning on 27 December 1963. Displacing 8,250 tons dived, the SSBNs of this class have a top speed submerged of about thirty knots (twenty knots on the surface). The pressurised water S5W reactor supplies two geared turbines (15,000 shp) driving a single shaft and the nuclear core provides energy for approximately 400,000 miles without refuelling. Like most SSBNs and SSNs (other, possibly, than some of the Soviet boats which have two reactors and two shafts) there is a diesel-electric snorkel system as a stand-by (very seldom needed, but prudently kept in good shape) and a small auxiliary propeller which can be lowered if required. The maximum diving depth is close to 1,000 feet.

(ABOVE) USS *Henry M. Jackson* (SSBN–730), the fifth of the 'Ohio' class, commissioned on 6 October 1984. One pressurized water S8G reactor supplies the single shaft through geared turbines (of 60,000 shp). Two and a quarter times the displacement of preceding SSBNs, the 'Ohios' have four times the shaft horse power (shp). The maximum diving depth is 985 feet, according to *Jane's*.

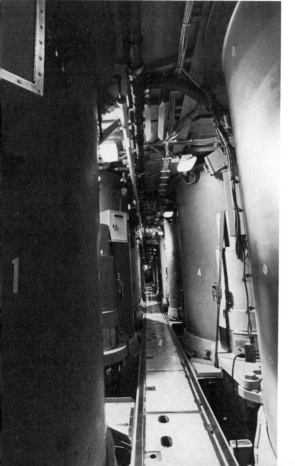

(LEFT) The ballistic missile compartment in USS *Ohio* (SSBN–726) designed for Trident C4 (UGM–96) SLBMs. (*US Navy*)

A monstrous Soviet *Typhoon*, 557 feet long with a seventy-five-foot beam, now reckoned to displace at least 25,000 tons submerged. It seems very likely that there are twin hulls for deep diving. However, there is some doubt about whether the light, outer double-hull concept has also been followed sufficiently to afford the anti-submarine protection evidently favoured by the Soviet navy: it could be expected, but it is difficult to make the supposed measurements fit. There is almost certainly a third, upper pressure hull housing the control room and attack centre (seen in the photograph), and there could be yet another for the torpedo space forward. Top speed is probably less than twenty-five knots (with one 40,000 shp plant in each hull). This is the only class anywhere where the missiles (twenty SS–N–20 with a 4,500-mile range and six to nine re-entry vehicles) are forward of the sail. The anechoic tiles on the outer hull are clearly visible in this photograph.

(OPPOSITE PAGE TOP) SLAM (submarine-launched anti-air missile), the simple system consisting of four Blowpipe missiles mounted on HMS *Aeneas*' redundant raisable mast (left) in 1970. This, basically, is the kind of method which Soviet submarines may have adopted for an anti-air missile system for use from periscope depth against helicopters and fixed wing anti-submarine aircraft. (Centre) A Soviet 'Juliett' class 3,500/4,300-ton SSG with four SS–N–3A 250-nautical-mile anti-ship missiles and six bow torpedo tubes (eighteen torpedoes carried) – an unsophisticated but quite powerful development of the Whiskey Long Bin with radar for missile mid-course guidance. It may have silver-zinc batteries for greater submerged endurance. (BELOW) A Soviet 'Echo II' SSGN, 6,200 tons dived, armed with eight missile tubes. Of the twenty-nine built in 1961–67, some ten of the class are now equipped with SS–N–12 295-nautical-mile anti-ship missiles, and the remainder with SS–N–3A 250-nautical-mile anti-ship missiles, all with radar for mid-course guidance. It is likely that, for SS–N–3As anyway, an 'Echo II' requires at least twenty-five minutes on the surface to prepare missiles for launch, and must then use guidance radar – probably also while on the surface or very shallow. Six twenty-one-inch bow torpedo tubes and two sixteen-inch stern tubes are also fitted (twenty torpedoes). The boats are divided between the Northern and Pacific fleets and are quite often deployed to the Mediterranean and the Indian Ocean. (ABOVE) A Soviet 'Charlie II' SSGN, 335 feet long and displacing 5,500 tons dived. It has eight tubes for submerged launch of SS–N–9 sixty-nautical-mile anti-ship missiles as well as six twenty-one-inch torpedo tubes (fourteen torpedoes). A 15,000 shp reactor plant drives a single shaft for a maximum speed submerged of twenty-four knots. Well equipped with LF passive/active, MF active and (torpedo) fire-control sonar, it represents a powerful threat to surface forces, and is probably also effective in the anti-submarine role. There seems, from the photograph, to be a complete double (outer) hull.

(ABOVE) A Soviet 'Oscar', the newest known type of Soviet SSGN, first at sea for trials in late 1980. This huge boat, 492 feet long and displacing 14,000 tons dived, has an outer hull which embodies twenty-four SS–N–19 295-nautical-mile supersonic anti-ship missiles. Two reactors and two steam turbines delivering 60,000 shp can probably drive the Oscar at up to thirty knots submerged, making her well capable of taking station on the bow of a task group. Twenty-one-inch and 25.6-inch torpedo tubes are also fitted and a substantial number of mines can be embarked. (BELOW) USS *Halibut* (SSGN–587), commissioned in 1960, the US Navy's only SSGN, carrying five Regulus I (shown launching one here) or two (larger) Regulus II land-attack missiles. Re-classified as an SSN on 25 July 1965 after the US Navy had discarded the submarine Regulus force (i.e. rejected guided missiles for land attack in favour of SLBMs), *Halibut* became involved with DSRV trials before going out of service in 1976.

British put it to against the *General Belgrano*, it remains a viable weapon with one third of a ton of high explosive in the head. With a number of spread torpedoes in the water for no more than a minute, the average merchantman will find it difficult to avoid being hit – and sunk – even if its captain detects the salvo immediately and takes drastic evasive action.

So far as noise and wake are concerned, more modern torpedoes destined for more sophisticated targets are certainly quiet and wakeless with thermo-chemical or electric propulsion. But, unfortunately, the ejection system – compressed air or water ram discharge – may give the game away at the moment of firing if the target is equipped with sonar of the kind that some Soviet submarines are credited with. There are ways of dealing with the problem – notably 'swim-out' systems which are nothing new, but have snags – and they will be discussed in Chapter 12. Meanwhile, submarines may be hampered by potentially detectable discharge systems which could probably have been avoidable if hulls had been designed around weapons rather than weapons being matched to hulls.

It has proved difficult to produce an effective, heavyweight torpedo with both anti-ship and anti-submarine characteristics, although the American Honeywell wire-guided NT 37E performed well during trials from 1981–1984. It is a further development from the original nineteen-inch electric swim-out Mark 37 Mod O free-runner anti-submarine weapon which first underwent evaluation in 1958 and has since grown into a family of mainly wire-guided types in service with at least sixteen navies. The two-speed NT 37E – powered, like most modern fish, by OTTO fuel, with a rotary piston cam engine – has a number of optional modes, with anti-ship passive snake and circle homing, or it can be fired straight and in salvoes. Its deficiency is the rather small 330-pound warhead – little more than one third of the honourable old British Mark VIII** – but this should cope adequately with lightly protected, fast, surface targets. Not very much has been heard of the torpedo since the dual-version Mark 48, which the Australian Navy is particularly enthusiastic about, came into service; but it is compatible with British, West German and Dutch fire-control systems as well as with US Navy boats equipped to fire Mark 37 torpedoes of other types.

The Royal Navy's wire-guided electric Tigerfish Mark 24 has encountered problems in the anti-surface-vessel role. These are said to have been overcome, but British submariners are looking forward to the new Spearfish, due to arrive by 1990, with some eagerness.

Torpedoes on trial

The American and German navies were both bedevilled by torpedo failures at the outset of the last war. For a long time a combination of torpedoes running too deep and the unreliability of magnetic-influence warhead pistols (to maximise effect by exploding beneath a target) denied submariners, on both sides, the successes they deserved.

The underlying reason for these compounding faults was undoubtedly a lack of realistic trials. It was, admittedly, costly to carry out extensive test firings; but savings made in peace were to prove exceedingly expensive in war. Besides false economy there were other factors which militated against exhaustive proving trials: these included scientific self-assurance backed by unjustified, self-interested commercial claims; secrecy (although this was poorly preserved and a cynic could think that security was used as a smokescreen); and, for Doenitz, political and practical restraints on conducting exercises in the Atlantic, where the battle would be fought.

Another trouble in Nazi Germany was that the Torpedo Experimental Establishment, in charge of torpedo development, built a torpedo, tested it, and then itself decided if it was fit for operational use. Doenitz rightly believed that the whole process 'should never be left in the hands of one single authority'.[3] The situation was not much different in the United States, where the 'Gun Club' (Bureau of Ordnance) with its Newport Torpedo Station were self-accounting.

Time and again torpedoes ran too far below their targets or failed to explode on contact. As Lieutenant Commander 'Red' Ramage (USS *Trout*) sourly remarked to Ralph Christie, then his squadron commander but previously involved in torpedo research, 'If I get twenty-five per cent reliable performance on your torpedoes I'll be lucky . . .' Lieutenant Commander 'Moke' Millican (USS *Thresher*) complained that during an attack on a Japanese boat his weapons had 'merely clinked 'em with a clunk'. Christie was not prepared for any 'wrangling in print' and said flatly that the torpedoes 'were fine'. Millican was ordered back to the States for a rest and involvement with submarines then under construction. The Gun Club closed its ranks and its members' insistence that torpedoes ran true was, in fact, supported by a fair number of hits.[4]

There were many reasons for torpedo failures, and no doubt personnel errors on board accounted for a proportion of them: but there were two particular faults which underlined the essential requirement for thorough trials under wartime conditions.

The US Navy eventually discovered (amongst other things during urgent post-failure examinations) that on a ninety-degree track – the ideal shot – either the exploder mechanism was crushed or the firing pin was bent out of line before it struck the detonator caps. When, on the other hand, a warhead hit on a poor track (forty-five degrees or less) the mechanism worked in about half the number of cases – hardly a creditable performance but an improvement on a long series of duds. It appears that the Gun Club had concentrated pre-war trials on fine-angle shots, believing them to present the most difficult situation for a warhead.

In the German Navy there was an even more subtle cause of malfunction – in this case resulting in 'eels' running too deep below their targets. (In fact, it almost certainly contributed to bad depth-keeping elsewhere, although it was apparently not discovered.) During a prolonged dive – never experienced during trials – air pressure built up in a boat, as all submariners knew, due to inevitable small leaks from high-pressure air lines. But the balance chamber of a torpedo was not designed to resist an insidious increase in ambient pressure over a long period, and when the torpedo was fired the hydrostatic valve, working against a set spring, was therefore already biased. Consequently the torpedo 'thought' it was shallower than it really was; so it headed downwards until the reinforced spring counter-action against the hydrostatic valve was overcome and balanced by sea pressure at a depth greater than intended. In all other respects the training and operational evaluations that Doenitz insisted upon were as realistic as they could possibly be. But practice firings were not conducted, in this last vital respect, under wartime conditions.

The lessons from wartime failures are plain enough. Absolute realism, in every smallest detail, is mandatory for peacetime technical and tactical evaluations, whatever effort and expense are involved. A three-dimensional facility like AUTEC (Atlantic Undersea Tests and Evaluation Center) in the Bahamas is invaluable: it should produce much more trustworthy results than in the past – just so long as everybody realises how dangerous it is to 'cook the books' and is prepared to accept objective, and sometimes painfully embarrassing, analysis. The further that wartime experience fades into the past, the more important it is to underline the lessons learned.

ANTI-SHIP MISSILES

Those SSNs which are equipped with Sub-Harpoon are happy with the system. No wholly underwater weapon can compare with a missile, launched from submerged, for speed and range; and a missile does not have to struggle with the vagaries of underwater sound. Its qualities are more and more important for a submarine attacking a surface ship, especially for an SSN helping to defend a task force or convoy against surface attack, when speed of delivery is a vital factor. The enemy warships, themselves armed with long-range missiles, cannot be allowed to come within striking range, and there may well be no time to make the relatively long, stealthy approach required for a torpedo attack. The Harpoon system can take out one target after another with rapid and simple fire-control inputs; and it demonstrably works.

Harpoon, as a sea-skimming missile maintained at the desired height by a radar altimeter and propelled at high subsonic speed by a turbojet engine with a range of fifty miles plus, was remarkably successful from its start in May 1971, when McDonnell Douglas Astronautics were awarded a sixty-six-million-dollar contract for development. The main contract followed in July 1973; and by 1975 some thirty prototype weapons had been launched, three of them from submarines. Later developments are highly classified, but the original homing system was an active radar-seeker which searched, locked on, and finally commanded an abrupt pull-up and swoop-down on the target from above.

Sub-Harpoon is contained in a capsule which is ejected from a submarine's tube like a torpedo. When the missile clears the tube its control fins deploy and the capsule glides to the surface. On sensing the broach, the nosecap and tail of the capsule are blown off and the missile slides out using a booster motor. The missile's main engine then starts and the 'bird' ascends to its pre-programmed flight level, at which height the mid-course guidance system steers it towards its target until the terminal guidance system takes over.

Sub-Harpoon can be launched in practically any sea conditions from tactically convenient depths. Trials have been far more encouraging than ordinary torpedo trials are prone to be. Operating out of San Diego, HMS *Courageous* (SSN) fired fifteen Sub-Harpoon missiles from July 1981 to February 1982 and all functioned correctly. In addition, eighty-one verification rounds – inert missiles – were launched as part of the Royal Navy's assessment of the system. By any standards the results were astonishingly good: at long last Harpoon gives submarines an anti-surface weapon that is compatible with their long-range sonar and classification ability, while not being too long range for the submarine itself to supply the necessary fire-control data.

Although the Royal Navy initiated its own Staff Target in 1964, the British clearly did well to buy Harpoon from America at a cost in the order of £750,000 per unit – a fairly modest figure for a potent weapon (the price in the USA had dropped from $1 million to $625,000 by early 1986), but it does not, unfortunately, include the millions required to install the fire-control system. It would have been considerably more expensive, especially on a smaller production run, to proceed with the original plans, jettisoned in 1975, for a unilateral weapon based on the French Martel missile – even assuming that the expertise would have been available for development in a reasonable time-scale.

The Soviet SS–N–7 and SS–N–9 Siren missiles in 'Charlie' and 'Papa' class SSNs are broadly similar to Sub-Harpoon, but are launched vertically from custom-built tubes. SS–N–7 has a slightly shorter range, but the weapon was in service several years before Harpoon. Soviet warheads are probably a good deal larger, at about 1,100 pounds of high explosive or 200 kilotons of nuclear explosive.

Tomahawk is the latest US submarine-launched cruise missile (SLCM), with alternative (but not interchangeable) variants for use against surface or shore targets. Fitted in the 'Los Angeles' class, SSNs 688–720 carry, or will carry, twelve encapsulated weapons as part of the torpedo load, but SSN 721 and her successors will have fifteen vertical launch tubes in the bow between the inner and outer hulls – the first serious indication that double-hull advantages are recognised. In the anti-ship role Tomahawk flies at close to 500 knots out to a maximum of 250 miles – a little less than the faster (mach two) Soviet SS–N–19, launched from 'Oscar' class SSGNs.

Either missile is liable to be quite a long time in the air before reaching the target area at a distance of, say, 200 miles – twenty-four minutes for a Tomahawk and fifteen minutes for an SS–N–19. A submarine cannot, with its own sensors, identify or pinpoint, let alone produce a tracking solution for, a target beyond fifty miles away – and that is probably an optimistic figure. A ship is liable to shift position by five or ten miles during missile-flight time at the longest ranges, and there may be a non-target vessel, between the attacker and its objective, which would attract the missile. Limiting range brackets can be applied and wide-scan terminal homing is feasible; but flying around in a search pattern will destroy the element of surprise and make a missile comparatively easy to shoot down or be rendered harmless by decoys and electronic countermeasures – to which the answer is electronic counter-countermeasures, and presumably counter-counter-counter-measures, because that is the way that electronic warfare is going on – at no small expense.

SSGNs must, therefore, depend on external control and upon data from satellites and other tactical intelligence sources with, perhaps, missile-guidance from aircraft or helicopters like the Ka–25B embarked on 'Kirov' class cruisers. It is conceivable that an SSGN could dispense with mid-course guidance partners if it launched missiles 'down the throat' of an oncoming task group; but submarine co-operation with air and surface units has been established Soviet philosophy for more than forty years.

Soviet SSGNs have advanced along the logical weapon development guidelines that the West has almost studiously ignored over the years: targets have first been determined, missile-systems have been devised to take them out, and submarines have been designed around them – all at a very brisk pace.

There are grounds for suspecting that the US Navy, while developing Tomahawk, did not address itself wholeheartedly to the total system which, for long-range missiles, must include command, co-ordination, control, intelligence and targeting – probably best managed from shore (e.g. by COMSUBLANT) in the light of political and strategic considerations, as well as for most efficient use of the weapons available in a given area. There might, physically, be nothing to stop a submarine captain from launching missiles independently if he is able, by some means, to gather sufficient intelligence and positional data for fire-control; but there is some risk of him going for the wrong target at the wrong (political) time, and this may not be acceptable in the scenario of a 'limited' war at sea.

If nuclear warheads are to be employed there is also the question, both for American and Soviet SSGNs, of their being authorised. Soviet naval commanders will press for permission to use nuclear heads because a very large number of conventional missiles would be needed to put important, distant targets out of action: it is to be hoped that they are refused.

ANTI-SUBMARINE WEAPONS

The British Tigerfish Mark 24 ASW Torpedo (already described in its surface role) has had to be redeveloped from the original weapon. It took more than twenty years to appear on the scene in anything approaching a reliable or effective form. The history of this particular torpedo is indicative of the kind of delays that can occur – delays that magnify costs and outdate a system before it is in service.

The Staff Target (a broad sketch) for the Mark 24 was drafted in 1961, at which time Soviet submarine capabilities were nothing like they are now, although intelligence assessors, largely unheeded, were predicting what would come. After the customary elephantine processing in Admiralty departments, culminating in a feasibility study, the Staff Requirement (a more detailed paper) was signed by the Controller in 1964.

The Admiralty Underwater Weapons Establishment (AUWE) then undertook all research and development, but handed over responsibility for the active/passive homing head to Marconi Underwater Systems Limited, as sub-contractor, in the late 1960s. The Mod O weapon was, to put it mildly, disappointing. In 1977 Marconi were given the whole problem to sort out – which they duly did with a 'get well' programme that resulted in the Mod 1 finally being accepted by submariners, with a fair degree of confidence, in 1983.

It would have been more sensible to have given the whole project, feasibility study and all, to a commercial company in the first place. An established firm has to be businesslike and work quickly to be commercially viable: a service department does not. Alternatively the research could have been undertaken by a naval establishment and development responsibility given to a commercial firm. As Admiral Sir Lindsay Bryson remarked in 1985, 'It is essential to separate research from development . . .' and '. . . it is vital that defence research establishments not be allowed to do the development.'

The actual performance of Tigerfish is secret, but unclassified publications suggest a dual-speed capability with an estimated maximum of fifty knots out to ten miles, the range presumably depending on the primary battery endurance at top speed.

It might be advisable to pause for a moment and see why long range, wire-guidance and changeable high and low speeds are needed for anti-submarine attacks. At ranges beyond three to five miles a single free-running homing torpedo has a low hit probability. Even a modern gyro cannot steer closer than half a degree from the set course and a small error of that order may displace it enough – fifty feet per mile – to prevent target acquisition: but, more importantly, alterations of course or speed by the target – or errors in calculating course, speed and range by the attacker – are almost certain to result in a torpedo passing outside acquisition range. A target may also suddenly go quiet – too quiet for passive homing – while the torpedo is on its way so it must be possible to switch it to the active homing mode. It is also clearly desirable for the fish to travel as far as possible at high speed (geometry suggests seventy-five knots would be needed to intercept forty-knot submarines) before slowing down to listen.

The solution is to retain control of a weapon in the water. Tigerfish, like other wire-guided torpedoes, is therefore steered, by commands through a wire, towards the target, which is held by the attacking submarine's sonar, and commanded to do whatever is necessary to intercept until contact (active or passive as selected) is gained by the torpedo's own small but very efficient three-dimensional sonar set. At that point (signalled back down the wire) the weapon is allowed to home in for the kill under appropriate commands from its own computer; but the operator retains over-riding control even after a torpedo has entered its terminal homing phase – a valuable capability in a confused situation where the fire-control team, assisted by the submarine's systems, can modify the pre-programmed responses of the torpedo. Two weapons (at least) can be controlled simultaneously by the latest fire-control equipment, either to take on more than one target at a time or to increase the chances of hitting an evasive enemy submarine. The hit probability demanded by the original Staff Requirement for a single shot was 0.8 (eighty per cent): no figures have been published to show whether this has been achieved, but it seems reasonable.

The attacking submarine (like the Tigerfish itself) must be free to manoeuvre after firing without cutting or tangling the fine guidance-wire; so the latter, neutrally buoyant, is dispensed both from the submarine and the torpedo in such a way that it remains stationary.

All in all, Tigerfish – late but welcome – is a good weapon and is capable of sinking a wide range of submerged targets or, more likely perhaps against a double-hulled Soviet boat, causing serious damage that will put it effectively out of action and achieve a 'mission kill', which is quite enough for the purpose.

The US Navy Mark 48 torpedo, also in service with the Australian and Netherlands navies, is beyond question the best existing anti-submarine torpedo anywhere – also the most expensive. The basic weapon, which is wire-guided in much the same way as Tigerfish, has undergone a reliability improvement process and all production torpedoes were upgraded by mid-1985. Since the improved torpedoes have been returned to the fleet there has been a 100 per cent success rate in twenty test firings. It is to be hoped that the tests were carried out under simulated wartime conditions. The required hit probability under standard conditions is not known.

The Mark 48 programme, under RETORC II (REsearch TORpedo Configuration), was initiated in November 1956; required and obtainable characteristics were determined in December 1960; and by May 1962 the development of the torpedo, then known as EX–10, was put out to tender. Pilot copies were authorised in 1970 for two competing versions, and a production contract was awarded to Gould Ocean Systems Division in July 1971. Production began in 1972 – sixteen years from conception to multiple birth. The Royal Navy bid for some weapons in 1971–72 to bridge the gap caused by delays with Tigerfish, but was refused because all available torpedoes were urgently needed for the US Navy, not surprisingly after such a long wait.

Some 3,250 Mark 48s will have been completed by the end of 1986, 157 of them further modified to ADCAP (ADvanced CAPability) status for which the Operational Requirement was issued by the chief of naval operations in 1975, in the light of the enormous strides being made by Soviet submarine technology. The ADCAP programme was accelerated in September 1979 when the depth and speed capabilities of the Soviet 'Alfa' class had been confirmed.

The torpedo is propelled by an axial flow pump-jet propulsor driven by an OTTO mono-propellant gas piston engine designed by the contractor. Gould, and the Hughes Aircraft Company contracted for ADCAP digital guidance and control electronics, appear to have done a good job. However, certain shortcomings of the original torpedo have been openly criticised – notably the tactical constraints on the firing submarine when positioning for a shot, questionable under-ice characteristics, and a warhead which may not penetrate Soviet double-hulled boats.

ADCAP improvements have not been made public in detail, but they aim to maximise acquisition range, minimise adverse environmental and countermeasure effects (including Soviet double hulls and anechoic 'Clusterguard' coating), minimise limitations on the attacker's manoeuvring, and enhance the anti-surface capability. The published characteristics for the Mark 48 without ADCAP give it a maximum range of nearly twenty-one nautical miles and a maximum depth of 3,000 feet.

ADCAP's performance 'in the most stressing environments' has been described as 'superb'[5] (presumably meaning a kill probability close to unity – 100 per cent), but the modification kit was in 1986 reckoned at nearly three million dollars for each torpedo, while the unmodified weapon cost $1 million. However, the price seems to have been cut because defence authorisation for fiscal year 1986 was $417 million for 123 Mark 48 torpedoes – $3.4 million a shot – still very expensive, but it is the price that has to be paid for meeting the Soviet threat.

Fish lore

'No man has ever cost the world so much by an invention as did the late Mr Whitehead of Fiume.'

Commander E. Hamilton Currey, 1910

'In the old days many of the torpedoes were distinguished and known by pet names. Those that were inclined to get out of hand were not allowed to run often, and then only when the omens were good. They still have their lucky and unlucky days.'

Rear Admiral D. Arnold-Forster, 1931

Very little information is freely available about Soviet torpedoes, but it is presumed that American, British and French technology has been employed and some cautious deductions can be made from that assumption. Twenty-one-inch (533-millimetre) tubes are standard bow armament, but several of the older classes (including 'November' and 'Echo' SSNs) have two or more sixteen-inch (406-millimetre) tubes at the stern. The new Soviet boats have 25.6-inch (650-millimetre) tubes for missiles and torpedoes, as well as twenty-one-inch torpedo tubes; and it is thought consideration is being given to forthcoming US and British boats having larger tubes.

Stern tubes, where still fitted, probably carry decoys now, but they were originally conceived for specialised work in countering anti-submarine vessels, carrying weapons like the wartime German 'Gnat' and anti-submarine torpedoes of a fairly basic kind like the Mark 20s, which used to be fired from the stern countermeasure tubes of British 'P' and 'O' class SSKs. It would be logical for Soviet submarines nowadays to be equipped with external launchers loaded with instantly deployable decoys.

ANTI-SUBMARINE MISSILES

There are significant gains to be had by employing missiles for anti-submarine as well as anti-surface warfare. A submerged target may be moving very fast – within a few knots of most of the fastest torpedoes currently in service – implying a large lead angle and a long chase; it may change its speed and course suddenly and unpredictably – perhaps resulting in fire-control problems too great for torpedoes to overcome; sonar contact may be too brief or spasmodic for confident torpedo fire; or the enemy may pose such an immediate threat to a force that it has to be attacked immediately. Speed of reaction, in many circumstances, is the essence when a submarine target is positively identified.

If aircraft or helicopters are available to co-operate with the SSN or SSK they can be vectored to the target directly or via a surface ship; but absolutely reliable and secure communications are mandatory. Each unit must know very precisely where friendly faces are in order to avoid mutual interference (a euphemistic term for friendly kills); and, in practice, vectoring procedures can be unacceptably time-consuming. Hence, a self-contained, self-initiated air-flight weapon system is much to be preferred.

The urgent need for a submarine rocket (Subroc) became clear in 1955 following (mainly unsuccessful) attempts at sub-air co-ordinated attacks and equally disappointing trials at the time with anti-submarine torpedoes. A rapid development programme for a torpedo-tube-launched weapon was put in hand by the prime contractor, Goodyear Aerospace, and by 1958 a prototype system was ready. It then took, understandably, some eight years to solve the problems associated with submerged launch, rocket motor ignition, precise airborne trajectory to the target's future position, and underwater detonation. Unlike ballistic missiles, fired vertically, Subroc required an exit angle of about thirty degrees. Shock, vibrations and accompanying trajectory disturbances took a long while to overcome. And then a charge had to be exploded in the water at the end of flight.

Clearly, only a nuclear warhead (lethal at three to five miles, in general, but probably less so against modern Soviet boats) would compensate for the inaccuracies expected at long range. Subroc necessarily became a nuclear weapon with no conventional alternative, and with all the associated political and tactical inhibitions. In that respect, a nuclear explosion at sea is apt to be conjectured as just a very big bang. It is unimaginably more than that – unimaginably because there is no published information about the effects. But they are bound to be cataclysmic for the underwater environment, sound propagation and underwater communications over a wide area.

The key question, even harder to answer than when missiles are used against surface vessels, is whether a distant submerged target can be identified with enough surety to justify a nuclear attack. The reply to that is implicit in the development of the new anti-submarine stand-off weapon Sea Lance, which can carry a lightweight torpedo as an alternative to a nuclear depth bomb.

Subroc began to be deployed operationally in 1965; improvements to the system were initiated in 1977–8 to face the increasing threat; and by 1982 some sixty-four US submarines were equipped with the system, four to six weapons being embarked in each boat. It is now considered obsolete and is being withdrawn from service.

Meanwhile, the shorter range (twenty-five miles) Soviet SS–N–15 equivalent (probably in most SSNs and 'Tango' and 'Kilo' SSKs) and the SS–N–16 carrying a lightweight torpedo payload ('Victor III', 'Akula', 'Mike' and 'Sierra' SSNs) are fully operational – the SS–N–16 having come into service some years ahead of the planned new US anti-submarine stand-off weapon. It is interesting to note the Soviet adoption of a homing torpedo for the SS–N–16. As usual, the Soviet Navy is keeping its options open, and is not tied to nuclear weapons only.

Gone are the days when the Russians were struggling to catch up with the West; but it would be unreasonably pessimistic to think that Soviet weapons work, in each and every case, as intended. That has never happened in the history of modern warfare and, as we have remarked before, there is ample scope for bluff – internal and external. However, it must be repeated that, in general, missiles are more reliable than torpedoes – and missiles are, predominantly, what the Soviet Navy has gone for.

FIRE-CONTROL AND TACTICS

Passive, bearings-only sonar attacks used to present a nice mathematical problem for those interested in such things. The range, course and speed of a target took a long time to estimate – and estimate was the right word. Today, computers quickly generate a solution, derived from passive sonar alone, which is sufficiently accurate for fire-control – provided that human common sense is applied to a computer's calculations.

A passive solution may be backed up at the judicious moment by one or more active transmissions – or a captain may decide to 'go active' intermittently throughout an approach and sacrifice stealth altogether, using noisy speed in bursts as well, if necessary, to get to grips with the enemy. Stealth is a tricky subject constantly being argued amongst tacticians. Uniquely available to a submarine (and, to a lesser degree, to a helicopter) it is something not to be given up lightly; on the other hand, if active transmissions and/or speed are necessary to achieve the aim and make a kill, caution cannot be allowed to stand in the way. All that can be said is that the decision rests with the individual commanding officer at the time, and he will have to take into account the possibility that a third-party undetected submarine may be in the vicinity while he is approaching the selected target.

Lengthy periods of transmission on active sonar are presumably avoided by all sides, and there could be dangers in the future arising from homing-on-active anti-submarine torpedoes. Transmissions can, theoretically, be disguised to sound like fish noise, or whatever, but this is a way forward that does not appear to have progressed very far. There are formidable difficulties in pushing out high power at tens of kilowatts while imitating a burping whale. However, at comparatively low power there are said to be ways, in theory, of emitting something like random noise which would conform to and imitate ambient conditions. The computer software would be complex, but not, apparently, impossible to produce.

In other words, powerful active SSN sonar – which can cover huge areas of inner space by exploiting the optimum depth for the area and time of year – is not employed in the same way as surface sonar.

The Soviets have obviously appreciated that many of their submarines are noisier than NATO counterparts, and it can be assumed that they have devised defensive tactics and weapon systems to cater for the case where a Western boat has stealthily closed the range and is suddenly detected in a dangerous, potential firing position. A submariner under the threat of imminent attack in this situation would either take violent, high-speed evasive action, or – very likely before doing so – he would release one or more decoys, 'go active' to obtain an instant fire-control solution himself, and fire a couple of active/passive homing torpedoes at his would-be attacker. He might well, at the same time, endeavour to jam any homing weapons already in the water and heading for him, if he knew the frequency of their search and acquisition sonar and could tune to it – hence the need for tight security with regard to weapons like the Mark 48 and Tigerfish.

It is also not impossible that the principle of electronic countermeasures and counter-countermeasures could be extended to sonar to produce noise jammers and spurious contacts.

The Soviet tactics suggested above are no more than conjectural, but they would be natural for a nuclear submarine captain who knows he is at a disadvantage because of his own boat's noise, and who has to reckon, all the time, on being 'jumped'. Assuming that the Soviet submariners see the problem in this light, it would be rational to expect two of the bow tubes to be loaded with relatively unsophisticated but fast active/passive homing torpedoes capable of being fired, on active sonar data, within seconds – just as soon as the bow caps can be opened. The fish would not have to be quiet or particularly clever; but fire-control equipment, linked with fire-control sonar, would best be computerised because of the need for an instant response. It is known that modern Soviet submariners depend heavily on computers. Their design philosophy is that anything simple is done by men and anything complex by automation – which is good thinking so long as total, blind reliance is not placed on machines. In the US and Royal Navies manual data processing is still the mainstay; and until – in the not too distant future – computer systems become fully integrated and until the software and displays start to match the capabilities of the human mind, a degree of conservative manual processing and evaluation may not be altogether bad.

Western SSNs and SSKs cannot afford to be complacent just because they are quiet. If Soviet submariners are tactically minded, as surely they are, they will be ready to shoot very quickly indeed if an anti-submarine submarine gives the game away by any means at any stage during its approach – by a noisy weapon-discharge, for example, or by careless acoustic housekeeping, such as allowing stores and spared gear to be stowed behind machinery where they 'short-circuit' resilient mountings. It is all too easy, amidst a welter of sophistication, to neglect a vital facet of the noise game either in system development or in tactical usage; and, as experience has shown in the past, the greater the complexity the easier it is to lose sight of simple essentials.

INTEGRATED AND SUPPORTING SYSTEMS

At present a submarine's weapon system usually comprises a number of more or less independent sub-systems for sonar, fire-control, weapons and weapon-discharge, decoys, electronic warfare, communications, periscope observations, and navigation. Often enough these sub-systems are at differing levels of development, some analog and some digital, which makes integration difficult if not impossible. The US SUBACS (SUBmarine Advanced Combat System) has been designed as a total, computerised package from the start: central processing will, if it comes to full fruition, bring about very marked and worthwhile tactical advantages – and maybe some economies. But SUBACS, the successor to AN/BQQ 5 sonar and Mark 117 fire-control, had grossly overrun its budget by May 1985 and its full development was jeopardised.

Problems had arisen with the IBM SUBACS, notably with the fibre optics for the computers designed to digest and produce information on several enemy targets at once: this key part of the system has apparently been eliminated. Hopefully it has been substituted by something more practicable. Costs were cut from the original $205 to $190 million, and the revised proposal was renamed the 'SSN–21 combat system'.[6] It is devoutly to be hoped that the change in name does not imply a reduction in capability and that the step forward is large enough to last for a long time, allowing operators to become thoroughly proficient before yet another improvement or modification is presented to them. Training for a fire-control team is not just a matter of becoming accustomed to a different kind of console. Attack teachers ashore, as well as continuation training on board, are another area where cost-cutting economies cannot be afforded.

The need for taking on a number of targets simultaneously is not always apparent in peacetime exercises, where NATO safety rules preclude a flock of 'enemy' submarines operating and attacking in close proximity to one another. We can be sure that the Soviets will not bother about safety spacing between boats in war. We can expect them to fling large numbers into battle wherever important targets present themselves; they will not attack one by one in successive geographical areas as the enemy sails majestically past – which is what anti-submarine exercises have led media observers to believe over the years. True, NATO exercises are much more realistic than they were; but quite apart from safety rules, there are not enough submarines in the 'loyal opposition' to begin to simulate the wave after wave of Soviet SSNs, SSGNs, and SSKs which, by every indication and sheer logic, are intended to break with shattering effect on convoys, strike fleets, task groups, amphibious forces – or whatever else is deemed to be threatening the Soviet Union.

If Western submarines are to have any real effect on the numbers game – for that is how Russian military philosophy has always regarded war – they must have the means to engage as many opponents as they have weapons at the ready. To deny SSNs an expensive system like SUBACS, which will cater for a numerically superior enemy, is to deny the potential of very expensive submarines and very expensive weapons – and it is the way to lose the battle.

Besides SSBNs and SSNs, British SSKs are entering the computer age – not before time – and the ageing O class should be able, soon, to make better use of newer weapons and improved equipment, including the excellent towed-array sonar which is now being fitted. There is no way of processing the mass of information which sensors of all kinds nowadays provide without powerful computers; but it cannot be said too often that the human element, with override, is as important as ever. No computer can ever replace a captain's determination to engage the enemy come what may. Even with defensive automated sensors there are dangers. For instance, ESM equipment which is precisely set to give automatic warning of discrete incoming frequencies could be fooled by an enemy transmitter which is, by accident or design, detuned.

Well-trained, thinking operators, who are in short supply for the Soviet Navy, are still needed for sophisticated and computerised systems. Above all, although computerised presentations for the captain and his team are essential, very rapid command decisions must still be based upon long experience and a willingness to take calculated risks. There is no way that a computer can be taught to make tactical decisions covering all the eventualities, especially when things break down or go wrong – as, inevitably, they do under counter-attack. Even in peace a submarine captain can suddenly find himself rubbing shoulders with the opposition. Every situation is different, and by no means all the possible tactics in three dimensions can be pre-programmed. Nor can a captain afford rigidity in his own thinking – inflexibility is probably the principal shortcoming of all but a handful of Soviet commanding officers.

Training a submarine commanding officer is expensive – more than a million pounds for a British 'Perisher' – but it would be madness to seek savings.

OFFENSIVE MINES

From Tzarist days the Soviet Navy has been the keenest proponent of minelaying for defence – the traditional concept everywhere – but mine warfare has now entered an offensive era. Mines constitute a significant (and perhaps insufficiently appreciated) part of the Soviet Navy's armoury. All Soviet submarines, possibly including SSBNs, are capable of carrying a quantity of mines instead of – or in addition to – a torpedo/ missile load; and it has already been suggested that they may be stowed in chutes externally as well as in the torpedo compartments.

Soviet submarine-laid 1,000-kilo (AMD–1000) ground mines, laid on the seabed, are magnetic, acoustic (high and low frequency passive), pressure or combination-influence types; and they are thought to be effective against submarines down to 600 feet. All except the most secret pressure and combination variants have been widely exported to client states and Warsaw Pact countries.

Additionally, there are two kinds of Soviet submarine-laid offensive moored mines. Rising mines are tethered until they detect (passively) a pre-programmed target noise-source, when they are released and driven upwards to their targets by underwater rocket propulsion under guidance from an active location device; the older version is designed for the continental shelf and the newer is for deep water. A still more sophisticated weapon senses the underwater electrical potential of its victim and is thereby known as the 'UEP' mine. The 'risers', of whatever variety, are singularly unpleasant. They would be laid around NATO submarine bases and across transit lanes. Although primarily intended for anti-submarine purposes, rising mines, depending on where they are laid, would presumably threaten surface units as well. It is assumed that SSKs would be used to deposit mines around European bases and at related choke points while SSNs (and perhaps SSGNs) would be deployed to lay their eggs further afield, off the American coastline and in deep water. The Soviets also have a stockpile of nuclear mines with yields between five and twenty kilotons.

Mines were not popular in the wartime American and British submarine services for reasons explained in Chapter 2 and, latterly, because mines like the Royal Navy's (now obsolete) S Mark 6 were liable to damage a torpedo tube on discharge. Nor, in peacetime, until the last decade, was the anti-submarine mining threat taken very seriously; 'wiping' (demagnetising the hull) and similar precautions were duly observed, but perfunctorily. It is believed that prudence now prevails. The modern mine could turn out to be more dangerous than any other anti-submarine weapon: one wonders whether NATO sees it in that light and is prepared.

The US Navy Captor (encapsulated torpedo) is the most advanced in-service Western offensive mine and can be accommodated in a twenty-one-inch torpedo tube, although it can be laid by aircraft and surface ships as well as by submarines. Laid in deep water (and under the icecap if required) Captor embodies a Mark 46 Mod 4 lightweight homing torpedo. The latter is released by a detection and control unit when an enemy sound signature has been recognised for a certain length of time (at a range out to about half a mile) and when, following recognition, an active ranging/homing device has been triggered. The sensor mechanism is programmed to disregard surface traffic.

There were doubts about Captor's effectiveness in 1980, but modifications have evidently corrected its deficiencies because the procurement programme was resumed in 1983 at a cost of around $450,000 per unit (1985 price). The Mark 46 by itself is a well tested, very reasonably priced torpedo at about $200,000 a unit (1986 cost of the latest upgraded version), and is in service with the aircraft, helicopters and anti-submarine vessels of two dozen navies – which suggests that its capabilities are known in entirety by the Soviet fleet. Perhaps the latest type (presumably incorporated in Captor) is something special for the US alone; it is known that one object of the upgrading programme was to restore the homing capability against Soviet submarines which had been given an anechoic (Clusterguard) hull coating; but the 43.5-kilo (ninety-six-pound) PBXN 103 explosive warhead is on the small side for dealing with Soviet double hulls – unless a Mark 46/Captor has a directional charge or unless the weapon is propeller-seeking (that is, disabling), which might be thought sufficient, particularly under the ice.

If Soviet submarine-laid offensive mines have a capability approaching Western estimates they have the edge on Captor and a large margin over anything else available in NATO fleets. The fact that mines are relatively inexpensive (compared with the Mark 48 torpedo for example) is no reason for treating them as poor relations. If mines on both sides function as advertised (and maybe priority should be given to ensuring that NATO mines do) minefields could negate a fair proportion of the effort put into submarine hulls, weaponry and tactics – much, in fact, of what is discussed in this book – unless adequate wide-ranging mine countermeasures are introduced. One method for NATO of dealing with the mining threat will be suggested in Chapter 10.

However, there are two recurrent themes running through any review of underwater warfare – bluff and kill (or mission kill) probability. Both are apposite to mine warfare and the mining threat. As an aside, it is suspected that mines are probably tested even less, in realistically simulated 'wartime' conditions, than torpedoes and missiles. It also has to be remembered that offensive mines (as opposed to classical defensive mines) have a limited life – more likely to be measured in months rather than years. Moreover, selective mine sensors have to be updated to match enemy advances (such as sound and other signatures changes), which underlines the need, as for all systems, of continual underwater intelligence-gathering – another quite costly business, in terms of time and effort, that cannot be skimped.

ASSAULT SWIMMERS

Most boats can launch and recover agents or assault swimmers (frogmen), basically using systems intended for escape from a sunken submarine –

although these can be markedly improved, or custom-built, if that seems worthwhile. Agents were frequently landed and recovered during the last war but, invariably, the parent submarine was on the surface. Surfacing offshore is not impossible today, but the risk is considerable on all but the most remote and unguarded coastlines. It hardly seems practicable to plan on being able to mount assault operations from the surface; and it is not exactly comfortable, either, for a large submarine to engage in such operations submerged when close inshore.

A raiding party is, in its way, a submarine weapon system – and an effective one at that – but it would best be sent ashore nowadays, from the parent boat, in one or more midget submersibles of the kind discussed in Chapter 10.

PROCUREMENT

The procurement of weapon systems is a very lengthy business – some would say needlessly so. Proposals for cutting time and cost while improving effectiveness (the three considerations are closely related) are included in Chapter 12; but a few preliminary notes and comments will help to set the scene.

The United States has vastly greater resources for defence, including a wealth of talent and expertise, than any other country and, in many respects, still enjoys a technological lead (albeit diminishing) over the Soviet Union. One third of the national budget and ten per cent of the gross national income (compared with eighteen per cent in the USSR and six per cent in the UK) is geared to defence; one in four American scientists and engineers are involved in it. If arms production, and all that is related to it, were halted the economy would collapse inwards like a house of cards when the bottom deck is removed.

America, therefore, can and must continue, under the present economic system, with research, development and procurement for new weaponry. The question is whether money is being wasted; and there are clear signs that it is – which is sad when the budget deficit arising from defence is so large (pushing up interest rates around the world), and when money could be so well spent on benefits at home and on aid overseas.

Waste is only readily quantifiable (without access to voluminous records) in one notorious respect – overcharging, generally on overheads, by defence contractors. For the rest, the evidence tends to be qualitative, but there are indications of exceedingly large sums being involved, ranging from $200 million a month[7] to Senator Edward Kennedy's claim that one third of the total defence budget (around $300 billion in 1985) is being lost due to fraud or mismanagement. Defence figures are so enormous that they are difficult to grasp in real terms. For interest, a dozen responsible people, chosen at random, were recently asked how many noughts there were in a billion: not one of them was quite sure! Accusations and estimates may be wildly inaccurate, but it seems undeniable that dollars have been going down the drain on a large scale.

The temptation for corruption becomes almost impossible to resist when astronomical amounts are poured into a military-industrial complex which was the recipient of $1,800 billion up to 1985 from Defence Secretary Caspar Weinberger and a (then) compliant Congress. Of the top 100 defence contractors, forty-seven have been under active investigation for creative accounting, but apparently not all the account books were opened to the auditors. An investigative staff of 7,000 was recruited, headed by Joseph H. Sherick, Pentagon Inspector General (a post created by Congress in April 1983), and a further 18,000 were contemplated for 1986: it will not be cheap to put matters right and keep them so.

On the submarine side General Dynamics were awarded some spectacular headlines concentrating, unfairly, on gifts valued at $67,628 to Admiral Rickover and his wife over a sixteen-year period. General Dynamics was also heavily fined for defrauding the government, and was obliged to repay a large sum to the Department of Defense. Mr Sherick means business.

Shady dealings

Shenanigans are nothing new in submarine procurement. The Holland submarine boat contracts awarded to the Electric Boat Company came under scrutiny in 1908 by a Select Committee from the House of Representatives[8] following allegations by Representative George L. Lilley (Bridgeport, Connecticut) on behalf of competitor Simon Lake. Forged letters (said to have been traced by a typewriting expert to Lilley's own office), bribery, sabotage and excessive costs (1,476,296.60 dollars) during the period 1902–5 were bandied about, but the Electric Boat Company (founded on the Holland Torpedo Boat Company) came out of the hearings pretty well – Lake and Lilley less so, the latter appearing to have been, putting it mildly, badly briefed.

Items that came under scrutiny in 1985 included $7,600 coffee machines (capable of withstanding a twenty G shock), $91 sheet metal screws, $435 claw-hammers (priced in shops at $7 but, by some quirk, actually justified by auditors at $436), and $650 ashtrays (subsequently reduced to $50). Such inflatory prices may have been exceptional, but it is quite usual to charge 100 per cent for overheads: contractors have only to prove costs, not values.

Navy Secretary John Lehman has voiced his determination to effect a cure and will not accept the 'we will pay up if you catch us' attitude; but at the same time he pointed out that the Pentagon does not want to cut off its nose to spite its face. Major defence contractors like Electric Boat are good, and it would be unthinkable to dispense with their services. The difficulty lies in not having sufficient open competition: thirty-five per cent of defence contracts go to suppliers who face no competitors, and competitive energies tend to be directed in the Pentagon itself between the armed services. It has been estimated that between $4.5 and $5.5 billion a year could be saved by going to open contract.

Weinberger clearly appreciates that public support for defence spending is essential, especially now when Congress is urgently seeking economies. The Department of Defence will have to put its house in order before that support is forthcoming; and meanwhile, with Congress alarmed by deficits and outraged by abuse, the Pentagon is hostage to domestic politics and subject to the 'feasts and famines' of the 1960s and 1970s, when defence expenditure bore little relationship to real security interests. That is one reason why it is so very important for submariners to make their requirements properly understood by Congress and the public alike.

The British procurement system has been reformed in recent years, and with Peter Levene, a noted industrialist and entrepreneur, at its head since March 1985 it will hopefully be more efficient than it has been.

Besides having very limited resources compared with the Pentagon, the Ministry of Defence is traditionally hampered by appallingly slow paperwork. A non-operational docket can take nine months to circulate through the Ministry and return to its originator; courier mail between the headquarters at Northwood and an out-station seventy-five miles away can take a week or ten days to arrive; and, lower down the scale at local level, straightforward letters may not be answered for a couple of weeks. Hold-ups are habit forming: they would not be tolerated for a moment in industry, where time means money.

There are several reasons for delays in advanced procurement for the Royal Navy, but one root cause until now (and there are no obvious signs that it has been eradicated) is that the operators, represented by

MoD staff now headed by the Director Operational Requirements
(Sea), have tended to concentrate on, and overbid for, the evolutionary
near future to the detriment of big jumps into the more distant future
which is when new systems will, anyway arrive. This has led to shorter
term capabilities sometimes being set too high for current budgets –
leading to protracted bargaining with the Treasury – while inhibiting
longer term projects: there is seldom enough money and effort
remaining to embark, with a clean sheet of paper, on the radical changes
demonstrably needed in light of predicted or known Soviet advances.

There are all kinds of financial figures quoted for the difference
between 'good enough for most cases' – say a 0.7 or 0.8 (seventy or
eighty per cent) probability of success against the majority of targets –
and 'caters for every situation – all singing, all dancing' (near certainty).
The differences vary, naturally, with the equipment concerned, but they
are all large. At the lower end of the scale (moderate performance,
simple technology), a twenty or thirty per cent improvement costs eighty
per cent more; in the middle bracket, a ten per cent improvement costs
100 per cent more; and at the top end (high performance, high
technology) the difference between ninety per cent and something close
to 100 per cent capability can cost ten times more, although a probability
approaching unity is in practice hardly ever achieved.

As an example of these general rules, looked at in another way, a
recent ninety-one per cent increase in spending on (American) land-
based missiles resulted in only six and a half per cent more weapons
being built.

Of course, if an extra ten per cent means winning, and going without
means losing, a weapon system is worth every penny of whatever it costs,
but that is very seldom the case. It is almost always better value in war to
go for quantity – and that can be done without sacrificing quality to an
unacceptable extent.

Unfortunately, Parkinson's Law[9] bears heavily on waste in procurement: 'Work expands so as to fill the time for its completion.' Parkinson,
choosing the Admiralty as a specific example in his later arguments, goes
on to say that:

> The number of officials and the quantity of work are not related to each
> other at all. The rise in the total of those employed is governed by
> Parkinson's Law and would be much the same whether the volume of the
> work were to increase, diminish or even disappear.

He also presents two axioms underlining the tendency defined by the
law:

1. An official wants to multiply subordinates, not rivals.
2. Officials make work for each other.

Statistics cited in this perceptive work revealed, *inter alia*, that in 1914 there were sixty-two capital ships in commission in the Royal Navy and 2,000 officials in the Admiralty; in 1928 there were twenty capital ships in commission and 3,569 Admiralty officials – a decrease of 67.7 per cent at the sharp end and an increase of 78.5 per cent at the blunt end.

Although it is difficult to establish Ministry of Defence numbers meaningfully now, because of amalgamated staffs (and civil servants have recently, it is claimed, been cut by a small percentage), the trend has continued and it now extends to headquarters and squadron levels, where staffs have swollen disproportionately in comparison with the number of submarines in the flotilla. A case has doubtless been made for expansion, but it does not appear to have been accompanied by an increase in speed and efficiency. Parkinson's Law remains valid.

The Pentagon is plagued by no less than 10–12,000 'staffers' (aides) now employed on Capitol Hill, each of whom is entitled to call for an immediate answer on this or that subject. Thankfully, the British Ministry of Defence has not yet reached that level of political communication. One would hesitate to say that time spent on serving political masters is wasted, but it is scarcely productive.

Under the British procurement system it has been necessary to reckon, in general, on a good idea taking up to ten, a dozen or fifteen years to be translated into serviceable hardware; and then a further two or three years have passed before the particular item has been fitted throughout the fleet, and operators have been trained to use it. American methods, involving commercial contractors to a much greater extent, have been notably quicker, and if the Royal Navy follows suit (as now seems likely) more rapid results should be possible.

A submarine itself takes a long time to get from paper to sea. HMS *Swiftsure* (SSN) started life in the Admiralty dockets at the beginning of the 1960s, as SSN OX (no number being assigned because it was impossible to say where the new design would come chronologically). The hull, which in fact became the Royal Navy's seventh SSN, was laid down on 15 April 1969. The boat was launched on 7 September 1971, and commissioned into the Third Submarine Squadron on 17 April 1973 – a dozen years after the Staff Target was written. 'First-of-class' trials and training to peak efficiency probably took a year or two longer – less with follow-on boats in the class.

A submarine has a normal life of at least twenty years: it follows that, if the pattern continues, planners must contemplate their initial design still being in service some thirty-five years ahead, and maybe more. In practice one should reckon, unless preliminaries can be shortened, on a forty-year period when putting forward a new proposal for procurement, whether major or minor, bearing in mind that modifications during the life-span are exceedingly expensive and that a submarine should be a complete weapon system from start to finish. When periods between refits are, very desirably, lengthened – to perhaps ten years or so – it will be even more important to install advanced, long-lasting equipment on building: financiers will have to be convinced of this very real necessity.

Delays (leading to unduly early obsolescence) make it more difficult for the planners concerned with looking ahead to formulate the answer to a future threat; they also add considerably to ultimate costs (because of needful modifications) and cast doubt upon future effectiveness. In all this it does not help, in the Pentagon and Ministry of Defence, to relieve the officers concerned with planning every two or three years: it takes several months to learn a complex job and Treasury officials, always happy to watch time pass without expenditure, can make mincemeat of a 'new boy'. Savings at the outset (assuming that the project is viable) can also be very costly in the long run: a refusal to order a full set of spares for the 'Swiftsure' class, when the decision was finally made to go ahead, was a major factor (made worse by dockyard strikes) in prolonging the refit of HMS *Swiftsure* herself to a record-breaking five years. 'Down time' of this order is downright waste.

It goes without saying that success depends upon the user – the command team – as much as on the weapon system when it has finally been procured; and here there can be waste of a different kind.

During the last war, in rough figures, twenty-five per cent of US Navy submarine captains sank seventy-five per cent of the Japanese merchant shipping that went down to American torpedoes.[10] On the German side four per cent of the U-boat commanders from 1914–18 sank thirty per cent of the shipping; and from 1939–45 2.2 per cent sank thirty-one per cent. The latter statistic is not entirely fair because U-boats early in the last war had a heyday which was certainly not enjoyed by latecomers; but there is no doubt that a few achieved the most. Amongst the Royal Navy's submarine captains during the Second World War, 8.6 per cent sank thirty per cent. Soviet figures for the Great Patriotic War are extremely hard to determine because they are concealed by gross exaggeration and propaganda, but *very* few boats were at all successful: the relationship was in the order of two per cent sinking ninety per cent.[11] A statistician could drive a coach and horses through these raw figures, which ought to be qualified by sundry factors: nonetheless, they are highly indicative.

The wartime implication is obvious. Weapon systems will not be used to full advantage unless the performance level is raised for the majority of command teams. Set-piece exercises have not achieved that in the past; but there is a better chance today of improved performance in war by a fair proportion of British and American boats – those which are given the opportunity, in peacetime, of operating at close quarters with the Soviet fleet. As suggested earlier, surveillance, tracking, trailing and intelligence-gathering on the high seas all involve, without provocation, tactical training which is arguably as valuable as the information which they are presumed to bring back. The Soviets are plainly aware of this, but they probably send only their small proportion of trusted aces on such expeditions.

The probability is that the percentage of Soviet captains who will use their weapon systems to best effect in battle will be low, but sheer numbers could well result in shattering sinkings and mission-kills. American and British commanding officers, on the other hand, could be expected to produce correspondingly better results in war if they were all afforded opportunities for tangling with the opposition in peace. Such opportunities are fun, extremely good for morale and valuable beyond price. They sort out the men from the boys and, for the first time in submarine history, they should make it possible, within bounds, to gauge a peacetime commanding officer's potential for war. Hitherto the qualities required for peace and war, with the usual low percentage of exceptions, have not been found in the same man – and waste is implicit in that.

In summary, procurement is bedevilled by various factors, not least inefficiency and short-sightedness; avoidable waste, in terms of related time and money, seems widespread; but it would be wasteful in every sense to spend huge sums on weapon systems while denying what it costs to match – and prove – men and material before they are put to the ultimate test in war.

5

The Western Order of Battle

There are only two large navies in the world and these are the only fleets which can afford nuclear-propelled submarines in sufficient numbers to make a significant impact in any foreseeable major hostilities. The Soviet submarine force is reviewed in Chapters 3 and 6; here the Western order of battle must be headed by the other large navy, that of the USA.

The submarine fleet of the US Navy must be considered in two groups, both consisting of nuclear-propelled submarines – the attack submarines and the ballistic-missile submarines.

When USS *Nautilus* was 'underway on nuclear power'[1] on 17 January 1955 the end was in sight for the American programme of diesel-electric submarine construction. The last of these, the three boats of the 'Barbel' class, were completed in 1959, by which time a further six nuclear submarines were in commission. The significance of this fact is the trust placed in the development of nuclear propulsion at a time when nothing of the kind had been tested at sea: in the programmes for fiscal years 1953–6 the allocation for diesel-electric boats was minimal – one in 1953, one in 1954, one in 1955, and the 'Barbels' in 1956. Prior to these commitments the six boats of the 'Tang' class had been ordered by 1949, all other submarine development being limited to the various 'Guppy' programmes applied to submarines of the various wartime designs.

This trust in the future of untried nuclear power plants is all the more remarkable when it is remembered that it was not until January 1948 that the Department of Defence asked the Atomic Energy Commission to design and build a propulsion plant suitable for submarines. The period from first request to first operation of what was known as STR Mark 2 (later renamed S2W) was seven years, yet within two weeks of first operation the plant was run at full power and, a further two weeks later, *Nautilus* was under way. This remarkable combination of foresight, confidence and technical ability gave the US Navy a head start in the race for underwater supremacy. It was over three years before the first

Soviet submarine of the 'November' class was at sea. In these three years a great deal happened in the US submarine world.

Hull form is an essential element in the search for speed and silence. Both are inhibited by a shape which causes turbulence and eddies, and this was the situation with most of the pre-1945 submarine designs. These were basically little more than surface ships with an ability to dive for comparatively short periods. In December 1953 the US Navy commissioned USS *Albacore*, a 'hydro-dynamic test vehicle' which was a further illustration of the foresight of those then concerned with submarine planning. Whereas normal designs had a length to beam (L/B) ratio of something like 11.5 to one and were propelled by twin screws, *Albacore* had an L/B ratio of 9.3 to one and was driven by a single screw. With a smooth, uncluttered outer skin she achieved what were then unprecedented speeds, and submariners all over the world spoke reverently of her performance.

While her early trials were in progress *Nautilus* was under construction, but her hull was of a conventional 11.6 to one L/B ratio. Her immediate successor, *Seawolf*, was even stringier, while the first class of nuclear boats, the 'Skate' class, was closer to *Albacore* with an L/B ratio of 10.7 to one. The giant *Triton* was of a shape not dissimilar to *Seawolf*, and the other two 'specials', *Halibut* and *Tullibee*, were 12 and 11.7 to one respectively. Thus the submarines in which novel ideas were being tested were of conventional shape, but they were soon overtaken by the acceptance of the *Albacore* school of thought.

The last diesel-electric class, the 'Barbels', registered 7.6 to one, while the next class of nuclears, the 'Skipjacks', were very slightly different at eight to one. Its increased horsepower gave this last class a notable improvement in dived speed which has been maintained in all later classes, although the L/B ratio has varied around the figure of 9.3 to one set in *Albacore*.

Speed and silence must be complemented by effective sensors and weapons. In the earlier classes, up to and including the 'Skipjacks', the sonar used was the BQS 4, an adaptation of the earlier BQR 28 with an active component added. This allowed for the mounting of six torpedo tubes in the bow, but in 1960 USS *Tullibee* was commissioned, the first submarine to carry the BQQ 2 sonar system. This is a combination of the BQS 6 active sonar, which has its transducers mounted in a metal sphere fifteen feet in diameter, and the BQR 7 passive sonar. This has a conformal array of hydrophones along the forward section of the hull. The size of the BQS 6 sphere, almost half the maximum beam of the average nuclear submarine, required it to be housed in the bow, an arrangement which effectively prevented the siting of any torpedo tubes up forward. As a result, the total was reduced to four and these are mounted at an angle amidships. This reduced number of torpedo tubes may cause a shudder amongst those who recall the original boats of the British 'T' class, which had six internal tubes and four external tubes, all pointing forward, and one stern tube. It must be remembered, however, that in the Second World War the success of an attack depended on the captain's visual observations – from which the enemy's course, speed and range were calculated. Radar scarcely existed, though sonar of a primeval type was available in some boats. The attack was conducted so that a spread of torpedoes would be fired over a linear spacing, which it was hoped would allow for errors of estimation as well as inaccuracies in the performance of the torpedoes. Under these conditions, one commanding officer in the course of twenty-three war patrols in 1943–4 managed to hit with forty-three per cent of the torpedoes he fired.[2]

Now the situation is totally different. In the latest US Navy submarines of the 'Los Angeles (SSN 688)' class an advanced sonar arrangement incorporates a long-range acquisition set, a short-range set, and a towed array containing multiple hydrophones. Signal processing equipment and an UYK–7 computer provide an up-to-the-minute analysis of all information available, which is fed to the torpedo fire-control system. The captain has a choice of weapons and this is where the small number of torpedo tubes is a disadvantage. Dependent on the type of target and its range, the submarine can launch a Mark 48 torpedo with a range of some twenty miles, wire guided with its own sonar homing head, or an obsolescent Subroc with a twenty-five to thirty-mile range and carrying a nuclear head, or an RGM 84 Harpoon missile with a sixty-mile range. One of the probably forgotten lessons of the Second World War is that, despite a careful analysis of available intelligence, the target which is expected is frequently replaced by a totally different member of the opposition. One may be on an anti-submarine patrol when a surface ship, previously hidden from surveillance by bad weather, is detected. This can require a rapid change of weapons if the fleeting chance is to be taken, and four tubes could be insufficient for this reversal of tasks. But until new types of sonar are introduced, the US submarines will suffer from this disadvantage.

With advances and changes in the form of weapons it has become difficult to assign specific designations to various classes of submarines. In the days when the torpedo-armed diesel-electric submarine was the only major underwater vessel, the type letters SS were allocated. These had various letters appended to describe specific tasks but, when *Nautilus* appeared as the first of the nuclear boats, she was described as SSN. The B was added for those submarines equipped with ballistic missiles launched from special tubes – thus we had SSBs or SSBNs. A G was found necessary for the submarines whose primary task was the discharge of guided missiles from tubes external to the pressure hull – these are the SSGs or SSGNs. But technical progress has invalidated this careful compartmenting. Very soon a majority of American SSNs will be able to discharge not only torpedoes, Subroc and Harpoon, which would qualify them for an SSGN tally, but also the 1,350-mile Tomahawk land attack missile. Now this is not a ballistic missile, but it is one with 'strategic' value, to use the modern jargon. So the rigid systems of nomenclature are useless in defining a modern nuclear submarine's capability. She can engage a ship or submarine with torpedoes, fire a nuclear-tipped Subroc, a long-range Harpoon, or a very long-range Tomahawk. This overall ability presents not only the captain but also the planning staff with a crisis of options.

Rules and regulations

Forty or so years ago the choices available for a submarine's patrol orders were relatively simple, and could be put in an order of priorities. She could be told to sink enemy ships and submarines, she could tow 'X-craft' (midget submarines), carry out beach reconnaissance with enemy attacks as a secondary task, lay mines, land agents, bombard shore targets – within limits it was all pretty cut and dried. In certain cases the captain was given some discretion, but in others – the delivery of X-craft or agents for instance – there was no way that the orders could be circumvented. With luck an agent landing could be put aside if an enemy battleship or cruiser crossed one's path, but this was a rare event. Yet, despite all these provisos, the submarine captain of the last war had considerable freedom of action. Unwelcome instructions could be ignored with the excuse of poor radio reception. Today, in the same way that football jerseys have given way to collars and ties, the activities of submariners are far more regulated. Part of this change is due to improved communications, part to the enormous cost of a modern nuclear submarine, and part to the weapon load embarked.

Today the only line of demarcation between the two basic types of nuclear submarines is whether they are capable of launching missiles which fly on a ballistic trajectory, high in the earth's atmosphere, or are not. Of those that are not, the US Navy now plans to have 100 in the front line, an increase from the ninety planned during the Carter administration. This is probably the most that can be achieved without a very considerable change of emphasis. With only two submarine building yards (General Dynamics Electric Boat Company at Groton and the Newport News Shipbuilding and DD Company) remaining, the average order is no more than four hulls per year. This could possibly be increased if funds were made available, but the most included in any fiscal year programme was six in 1973 and this merely resulted in cost and time over-runs. If a hull-life of twenty years is assumed a rate of five hulls per year will be required to maintain the 100 level once it has been achieved. By April 1986 the struggle to maintain numbers had become a close-run thing – with thirty-five 'Los Angeles' class, two submarines of single classes, and thirty-seven 'Sturgeon' class, the total of hulls within the twenty-year bracket was only seventy-four. A further thirteen 'Thresher' class came within the twenty-five-year bracket – with a further eleven from classes over twenty-five years old, the total can be jacked up to ninety-eight. This would be more than enough were it not for one thing – the likely opposition. Every year the Soviet Union commissions about ten submarines of various kinds – in 1985 the US Navy commissioned five SSNs and one SSBN, to which could be added the single SSN commissioned in the Royal Navy. Seven compared with ten – not bad, some might say. Those who play with figures to boost their morale could also say that the Soviet rate represents about three per cent of their total submarine fleet, while that of the US Navy totals six per cent. This juggling with numbers is a favourite preoccupation of US Congressmen – rarely of their female counterparts. It usually confuses the issue and obscures the truth. In this case the issue is that the Soviet Navy already has three and a half times the strength of the US submarine fleet, and this includes almost twice as many nuclear-propelled boats. The truth, even more disturbing, is that the USSR has additional yards and slips available should there be a need to accelerate the building rate, while, as we have already seen, the US Navy relies on only two, the yards at Mare Island, Portsmouth, New York, and Pascagoula having ceased submarine construction.

Another area of comparison is the introduction of new classes. In the five years from 1981 two new classes of SSBN and four other nuclear-propelled classes entered service in the Soviet Union. In the same period the US Navy continued with the 'Ohio' class SSBNs and the 'Los Angeles' SSNs. The effect of political decisions may be seen from a short examination of authorisations over twenty years.

FY	SSNs	FY	SSNs	FY	SSNs	FY	SSNs
1970	3	1975	3	1980	3	1985	4
71	4	76	2	81	2	86	4
72	5	77	3	82	2	87	4
73	6	78	1	83	3	88	4
74	5	79	1	84	3	89	2

As keel laying normally occurs about two years after the fiscal year figure (for example, SSN 750 of the 1982 programme was laid down on 3 March 1984) and the building time averages two and a quarter to three and a quarter years, the effect of a decision to cut the building rate has no immediate effect for about five years. With an administration's term of office set at four years this leaves the successors to clean up the mess, normally at far greater cost than if a steady, rolling programme had been achieved. The obvious answer, a bi-partisan procurement programme, is unfortunately impossible in a country where huge sums of money are involved, where huge Congressional staffs assume an all-knowing stance, where there is a continual awareness of the effect of a powerful statement on retrenchment on the electorate, and where not only both parties but a large proportion of Congress have their own views on how to cope with a colossal Federal deficit.

In the table above the drop to two hulls planned for 1989 is due to the expected introduction of the next class of attack submarines (if that title really means anything), the 'SSN 21'. This somewhat delayed design is the product of a special organisation within the Sea Systems Command, which is charged with knitting together the plans for the later submarines of the 'Los Angeles' class, those already prepared for the 'SSN 21', the SUBACS, or its derivative, and the latest developments in electronics and submarine development. The 'SSN 21' design will be larger than its 6,900–ton predecessors – its L/B ratio will be significantly different and its dived displacement may well be in the 9,000-ton range. A new type of pressurised water nuclear reactor is expected to provide sufficient power for an increase in underwater speed. These improvements will be much needed – if the five-year lead time already mentioned is achieved (perhaps a little ambitious for the first of class) the 'SSN 21' could enter service by 1995. By this time the Soviet Navy will probably have made a selection from their new designs for series construction, and could have added a further forty SSNs of advanced type to their fleet. Whether these will match the American submarines will be discussed later.

The first launch of a ballistic missile from a tube carried by a submarine took place in September 1955. This was achieved by a Soviet 'Zulu' class. Within four years two new classes, 'Golf' and 'Hotel', were entering the Soviet service – the former diesel and the latter nuclear propelled. Both classes were fitted with three launching tubes and, in all, twenty-eight of this design were built by 1962.

However, an astonishing programme in the USA nullified this early Soviet advantage. On 11 February 1958 a supplement to the Fiscal Year 1958 building plan was approved, providing for the construction of the US Navy's first three SSBNs. The hull for *Scorpion* (SSN 589) was lengthened by almost 130 feet and fitted with sixteen tubes for Polaris missiles. On 9 June 1959, USS *George Washington* was launched, to be commissioned less than seven months later. Within fifteen months four more of the class were in service; thus, before the Soviets completed the 'Golf' and 'Hotel' series a far more potent and efficient class was at sea. The Polaris A–1 missiles had a range of 1,200 nautical miles and were launched whilst dived. The Soviet boats carried 300-mile missiles which were launched on the surface. Three years after *George Washington* appeared, the majority of the 'Golf' and 'Hotel' series were converted to carry 750-mile missiles which could be launched from dived. But it was not until 1967 that the Soviet 'Yankee' class appeared, bearing an extraordinary resemblance to the early American SSBNs. They, too, carried sixteen tubes for 1,300-nautical-mile missiles, but by this time the US Navy had completed forty-one SSBNs in six and a half years. Their missile ranges varied from 1,500 nautical miles (Polaris A–2) to 2,500 nautical miles (Polaris A–3).

This remarkable activity in four US shipyards placed the Soviet Navy at a grave disadvantage, and this lasted until 1972. But it instantly faced the Pentagon planners with a very major problem. The production of forty-one submarines in six and a half years meant that those same submarines would require replacement over approximately the same period in twenty to twenty-five years. Fortunately for these planners, advances in technology and design overcame the need for a one-for-one replacement schedule. Larger submarines could carry more launching tubes, while larger and more modern missiles would have greater range and carry more heads with a MIRV (Manoeuvring Independent Re-entry Vehicle) capability. Thus fewer hulls would be required – a comforting thought at a time when the number of building yards was being drastically reduced.

The missile design outstripped the submarine design, and between September 1978 and December 1982 twelve of the later boats already in commission were converted to carry the Trident I (C–4). This was larger and heavier than the Poseidon (C–3) 2,500-mile missile, which was the successor to Polaris, and C–4 has a range of 4,350 nautical miles. The conversion included re-ballasting of the submarines as well as the fitting of extensive modifications to the fire-control and missile systems. The first conversion, including extensive post-refit trials, took thirteen months.

This very commendable period compared sharply with what was afoot at Groton, Connecticut, where the first of the new class, *Ohio* (SSBN 726), was in hand. She was the largest submarine ever to be laid down in a Western shipyard, as well as the most expensive. The construction contract was signed on 25 July 1974 and the keel was laid on 10 April 1976. A series of problems in Washington and Groton delayed her building and, shortly before her launch in April 1979, it was found that the General Electric turbines were faulty. These had to be replaced at considerable cost. On 11 November 1981 the submarine was eventually commissioned, five years and seven months after keel laying. By the time the fifth of class was in service this period had been cut by two years.

Allowing for deletions of the earlier submarines, the American SSBN force by mid-1986 consisted of seven 'Ohio' class with twenty-four Trident I missiles apiece, twelve 'Lafayette' and 'Benjamin Franklin' classes with sixteen Trident I missiles, and nineteen of the latter two classes with Poseidon on board. Those who choose to quote figures will find that already, with thirty-eight instead of forty-one submarines, the number of missiles available has increased by eight. In addition the far greater range and capability of Trident I allows for greater choice of deployment areas and much-improved hitting power. Both will be further enhanced when Trident II (D–5) is fitted in the ninth and subsequent members of the 'Ohio' class from late-1987 onwards. The range will be extended to over 6,000 nautical miles and, if current progress is maintained, a higher-yield re-entry body, Mark V, will further enhance the weapons' performance. Operating from the two Trident bases at Bangor, Washington and King's Bay, Georgia these squadrons will have tremendous flexibility in deployment and, with a nine-year core life, exceptional availability.

The eventual total of the 'Ohio' class is planned as twenty-three, but this is a programme stretching into the 1990s and thus susceptible to political interference at any time. For instance, when the Fiscal Year 1979 programme building funds were requested for the eighth 'Ohio', the request was rejected by Congress, which substituted about a fifth of the desired sum – and this smaller budget was to be spent on long-lead items for the eighth and ninth of the class.

The most sinister aspect in the future may be Congressional attitudes to service pay. The dire conditions which existed only a few years ago, when chief petty officers had to apply for food stamps to supplement their income and the US Navy was, as a result, seriously undermanned in many vital categories, has been overcome. But all this can change at the flick of a voting counter. Any form of ship is merely an exceedingly expensive luxury unless there are sufficient people adequately trained to provide the ship's company. With two crews for each SSBN – the only way to ensure full usage of the submarines – something like 11,000 officers and enlisted men are needed; and this total takes no account of that vital element ashore required to control and maintain the fleet. If a significant proportion of these men are allowed to drift away to civilian employment, where their nuclear skills are much sought after and in which they may expect not only higher remuneration but also the chance to be with families on a regular basis, the whole of defence planning will be frustrated. An all-volunteer navy has many advantages, but it also imposes great responsibilities on those whose duty it is to care for the welfare of the volunteers. It may take four years to build a submarine, but it takes a great deal longer than that to train men to the pitch of excellence which is needed to operate her.

It is now just over thirty years since the world's first nuclear-propelled submarine was commissioned into the US Navy. Since then experiments have taken place with various forms of propulsion – liquid sodium cooled reactor (*Seawolf*), turbo-electric drive (*Tullibee* and *Glenard P. Lipscomb*) and a natural convector circulation reactor (*Narwhal*). None has been repeated, and the 'SSN 21' will retain the pressurised water reactor and geared steam turbine which have been the normal fit in all the main classes. Even so, with standard classes of considerable numbers of submarines, the total fleet for the first line is still well behind the desired strength. If Congress tinkers with the funds required the optimum force may never be attained. If, in addition, there is a failure to consider the well-being of the personnel, it may be impossible to man what is available.

CANADA

In 1914 the Royal Canadian Navy bought its first two submarines, a bold move for a four-year-old navy. The pair had been built for Chile, but were sold to Canada by their US builders. During the First World War a submarine building programme of 'H' class boats was started by Vickers in Montreal for the Royal Navy, and in 1919 two of this class were presented to the Royal Canadian Navy. By 1922 all four submarines had been deleted and it was exactly forty years later when the Ministry of National Defence announced that Canada was, once again, to enter the submarine business. Three of the British-built 'Oberon' class were commissioned between 1965–8, all having had improvements made to their inadequate air-conditioning system. Rectification of this fundamental defect would have been welcomed by many British submariners. From 1982–6 a major up-date was carried out in all three boats to incorporate new American fire-control and Sperry Micropuff passive ranging.

Does Canada need submarines? Why can't reliance be put in aircraft, which now have a high surveillance ability and good anti-submarine properties? Such queries from intelligent Canadians suggest that they have paid as little attention to their country's geography and meteorology as did a succession of governments to their country's defence. Canada's coastline is over four times more extensive than that of the USA and its defence in both the Pacific and Atlantic oceans is the duty of the government in Ottawa. Only two countries in NATO spend a smaller proportion of their gross national product on defence, and Canada's expenditure per head is only a little more than a quarter of that of the USA. It is, therefore, not surprising that such questions are raised in a country whose geographical separation from European NATO and lack of worldwide obligations have allowed the government to shelve its basic responsibilities. Nor do the experiences of other peaceable countries seem to have had any effect on governmental thinking. Both Norway and Sweden have played host to intruding Soviet submarines surveying their coastline for possible landing areas and safe havens for both ballistic-missile and attack submarines. On Canada's west coast, over 200 miles of deeply indented coastline lie between Queen Charlotte Sound and the Alaskan border and, to the east, some 650 miles of the sparsely inhabited coast of Labrador offer many safe havens of equal value to the Soviet Navy. With the 250-mile-wide Davis Strait covering the southern exit for one of the Soviet routes from Murmansk to the Atlantic there are, therefore, huge areas to be covered if the combined duties of the Canadian Armed Forces are to be discharged to the benefit of their own country and NATO. The weather conditions in these areas, which extend from 50 degrees north to beyond the Arctic Circle in the east, can vary from flat calm to hurricane force winds with blizzards. The latter puts a clamp on air reconnaissance, but is most advantageous for a submarine transit of Baffin Bay and Davis Strait. In this case the only possible detection could come from another submarine.

But with only three boats, one of which is always in refit or maintenance and a second probably on passage, the chances of making such a detection are minimal. The west coast has no cover at all. If Canada is to operate submarines for any other purpose than anti-submarine training a minimum of nine boats is required, with a sensible total of twelve. Such a programme would certainly cost money, possibly a 2.5 per cent increase in overall defence spending, or something like seven dollars per head per year – maybe a bottle of rye or a few Cokes.

GREAT BRITAIN

Any visitor to HMS *Dolphin* at Portsmouth, the home of British submarines, will see ample evidence of a commitment to this form of warship stretching back to the turn of the century. At the conclusion of the Second World War the survivors looked back on a busy and successful conflict, but wondered a great deal about the future. Twice in six years there were sharp cuts in manpower, much in line with events in the surface fleet. Improvements in radar and sonar were affecting out-dated ideas of tactics, and the search for greater underwater speed attracted much attention. Two boats incorporating the German Walter high test peroxide turbine were built, but these turned out to be a sideline when USS *Nautilus* commissioned in 1955. The choice had, very clearly, to be made in favour of nuclear propulsion, and in June 1959 the first British SSN, HMS *Dreadnought*, was laid down. But the design had outstripped the efforts of the engineers, whose nuclear plant was some years in the future. To avoid delay an American S5W pressurised water reactor was obtained, one might say charmed, from the US Navy, and *Dreadnought* commissioned in April 1963. The main task of those in charge of her was to evaluate the capabilities of such a submarine so that, when the next class appeared between 1966 and 1971, there would be adequate data on which to base their operations and deployment. The year following the arrival of the first of this 'Valiant' class saw the completion of the last of the 'Oberon' class, delayed by two years as her predecessor had been transferred to Canada. The rapidity of this programme had ensured another problem of block obsolescence for the 1980s – from 1958–64 twenty 'Porpoise' and 'Oberon' class were commissioned, with the last arriving in 1967. Half-way through this programme an unfortunate decision was taken which shaped the future for the British submarine fleet. The First Sea Lord, with the second SSN approved, sought agreement from the Chiefs of Staff for a continuation of this construction programme. This was given on one condition – that no further diesel-electric submarines should be built. This was a caveat of extraordinary idiocy, the equivalent of saying to the army 'no mortars if you have guns' or to the air force 'no helicopters if you have fighters'. But the navy lost the battle, despite arguments based on Britain's geographical position on the continental shelf and the short passage time to suitable patrol areas. These were both the reverse of the conditions affecting American choices and were of great importance – not only to Britain but also to NATO. The result was very simple – the Royal Navy ran out of sufficient submarines. In the late 1970s the urgent need for a new class was acknowledged – a design was prepared and the first of class was ordered in November 1983, five years after the first of the 'Porpoise' class had reached her twentieth birthday. As an interim measure modernisation of the 'Oberons', a design of the early 1950s which owed not a little to the American 'Tang' class and the German Type XXI, has been undertaken. The need for numbers at a time when finance is constricting all the Royal Navy's new construction programmes has forced the Ministry of Defence into this necessary if unsatisfactory compromise. Twenty years ago, at the time of the 1966 Defence Review, recommendations that the Chiefs of Staff decision should be reversed and thought given to the construction of non-nuclear submarines to a West German design were intended to fill the forecast gap while relieving the burden on the design staffs, which were then involved in the construction of SSBNs and plans for the next class of SSNs. In retrospect it is hardly surprising that this scheme was rejected with acerbity. The navy was about to lose the last of its aircraft carriers and, in the prevailing political mood, any suggestion that the nuclears needed a back-up might have been fatal to the future. The good Lord may have comprehended what was in the minds of ministers and civil servants, but it was most unclear to the fleet.

The design of British submarines in the last forty years has been marked by periods of uncertainty and inefficiency. The Second World War was fought using designs conceived in the early 1930s, the 'S', 'T' and 'U' classes, as well as the larger submarines of previous classes which were a hangover from the somewhat confused thinking of a previous generation. The trio, which ranged from the small to the medium-sized, were popular and successful within the limits of their time. But the increased use of aircraft was soon forcing submarines, particularly the German U-boats, below the surface. Long periods dived meant that three things were essential – a higher battery-charging rate, higher surface speeds, and improved air-conditioning. The 'A' class was designed for the war in the Pacific and achieved the first two requirements. The air-conditioning was almost useless in tropical waters, and the first of class tended to dive unexpectedly in heavy weather, necessitating the addition of a bow buoyancy tank. As a 'design-for-task' the 'A' boats were less than successful.

The arrival of the 'Porpoise' class was awaited with interest – after the first eight a revised version, the 'Oberons', was laid down. They were better streamlined, quieter, and basically somewhat more habitable than the 'As', though the air-conditioning was still inadequate. The stress laid on this last aspect, one which causes no problems in nuclear submarines with their great power availability, is intentional. A non-nuclear submarine with inadequate air-conditioning can easily become an operational liability. In the tropics the efficiency of the ship's company falls alarmingly if a poor internal atmosphere is allowed to persist. Heat stroke, rashes, and prickly heat are physical manifestations – more dangerous is the drop in mental acuity. In the Arctic sheets of ice are liable to form on the interior of the hull – drips can cause havoc to electrical machinery, and cold is as numbing to the faculties as heat.

By 1986 the Royal Navy flotilla of SSNs included four 'Trafalgar' class, with a further three under construction or ordered, six 'Swiftsure' class, and five 'Valiant/Churchill' class. In addition thirteen 'Oberons' and the last two 'Porpoises' represent the non-nuclear boats, with orders placed for the first four 'Upholder' class.

Until 1962 there had been many discussions, staff meetings, papers and dockets under way in the various service ministries on the subject of Britain's independent nuclear deterrent. With the cancellation of the air force version the task was handed to the navy. After an unbelievably hasty gathering of the facts Cabinet agreement was sent to the Prime Minister, who was visiting the president of the USA. The Nassau Agreement of December 1962 was the result. At this meeting it was decided that five SSBNs were to be built by Britain, and that they should each carry sixteen Polaris A–3 missiles. The weapons systems, except for the Polaris warhead, would be provided by the USA, while all the remainder of the hardware would be of British manufacture. In February 1963 the decision to build the submarines was announced and, with astonishing faith, the operational date for the first of class was given – 1968. A staff operation of dazzling efficiency was set up – the Polaris Executive – and in May 1963 four submarines were ordered.

The fate of the fifth was only decided in February 1965, when the new Labour government embarked on a policy of defence retrenchment. The design was based on the current 'Valiant' plans, the hull being lengthened by 140 feet, but the propulsion system remaining unchanged. The first of class, *Resolution*, was laid down on 26 February 1964 and started sea trials three years and four months later. This remarkable effort had one major effect on the SSN programme. The completion of *Valiant*, building at the same yard, was delayed by ten months, a consideration to which we shall return later. But the extremely high standard of construction of the SSBNs has, so far, ensured that only four submarines is an adequate force to keep one constantly on patrol. The fifth was originally requested to provide a reserve in case of accidents or damage and her cancellation has proved acceptable, although it is doubtful whether governmental faith in British craftsmanship was the reason.

As has been seen in the discussion of the US Navy the Polaris A–3 missile was rapidly overtaken by Poseidon and, subsequently, by Trident I. But, whatever the missile, there was a need for a missile-servicing depot close at hand to the submarines' base and, with Faslane on the Gareloch chosen for the task of servicing the submarines, Coulport, over the hill on Loch Long, received the vote. For twenty years the Armament Depot has maintained what are now elderly missiles and dealt with their up-grading with the very expensive Chevaline warhead. With *Resolution* reaching her twentieth birthday in 1987, followed by her three sisters over the following two years, the British government was faced with a number of decisions. Was Britain to maintain a nuclear deterrent? If so was it to be seaborne? If so was it to be a British or American missile? If the latter was it to be Trident I or II? This may sound like the old story of the 'two alternatives' which, in fact, is a fair description of the advertised government stance. However, the vigour with which the programme has been defended since a decision was reached by a small Cabinet group in July 1980 suggests that 'Morton's Fork'[3] might be a more accurate title for what has become both a dramatic and traumatic affair. The Conservative government had been in office for a little over a year when, on 15 July 1980, they announced their decision to procure from the USA the Trident weapon system with Trident I (C–4) missiles. That this was a hasty decision is apparent when one considers that the Trident II (D5) was already in development and that the date for commissioning the new submarines could not be much earlier than the 1990s. On 11 March 1982 the government changed horses – the Trident II (D–5) was the chosen missile, to be deployed in four submarines each with sixteen launch tubes. Of some 15,000 tons displacement, they are due to enter service in the mid-1990s.

The questions raised by this decision are very numerous – ranging from the emotional to the more practical. The various political parties have what appear to be entrenched positions, but these can vary substantially after a party political conference or an election. The basic queries for the average voter are: 'What will it cost?' and 'Can we afford it?' The answer to the first question differs from source to source. The Ministry appears to be stuck at somewhere around £9–10 billion (thousand million), while independent analysts range up to £12–14 billion. The answer to the second question, in view of the extraordinary cuts in public expenditure that have been in progress in Britain since 1979, is apparently 'No'. But, say Trident's proponents, a huge proportion of that sum will be ploughed back into the economy. So what? Aren't there other naval projects which could have an equally beneficial effect?

Perhaps it is time to investigate a more practical question. If British Trident submarines are in service by the mid-1990s will they be effective in the circumstances for which they are designed – threatening nuclear retaliation? Very recent studies make the answer to this query somewhat dubious. The target would clearly be the Soviet Union, where the government has been investigating anti-satellite and anti-missile defence for many years. The situation in the mid-1980s is not encouraging for the West. The Strategic Defence Initiative of the USA has been met by an intensive propaganda campaign conducted worldwide by agents of the Kremlin, a move hailed by many in the West as an earnest of the peaceful intentions of the USSR.

But the facts tell a different story. The programmes needed to provide strategic defences for the Soviet Union were under way in the late 1960s. The largest laser development programme in the world now employs 10,000 scientists and engineers working on at least seven various types, a number of which have weapon potential. Their power sources for ground-based lasers already include a fifteen-megawatt rocket-driven magnetohydrodynamic generator, while the construction of large mirrors suitable for space-based lasers is under way. Thus the laser situation is:

a. Ground-based lasers are in existence which could interfere with satellites.
b. Testing for ground-based anti-ballistic missile lasers could be undertaken in the late 1980s, with full-scale deployment soon after 2000.

About this time, or soon after, a space-based particle beam weapon aimed at warheads could be reaching the operational stage. By then kinetic energy weapons firing streams of heavy metal particles designed to wreck weapons in space or the outer atmosphere could be operational, based on an experimental model developed in the 1960s.

The Soviet campaign is clearly designed to prevent the West challenging what is currently a monopoly in space weapons. This has been achieved by the investment of huge sums of money, the employment of great numbers of highly trained scientists and technicians, and the use of a great deal of Western technology obtained openly or by normally nefarious means.

Thus by 1995 Western ballistic missiles, if launched in small numbers, could have some five years of life before their efficiency is threatened by the Soviet equivalent of the Strategic Defence Initiative, now in its third decade of research and development. It may never come to that, but it is a point rarely mentioned in the debate.

FRANCE

An earlier book on submarines had this to say about the history of France's underwater capability: 'The inception of the French Submarine Service was so marked by examples of fascinating ingenuity, flair and enthusiasm that it is extremely difficult to choose a starting point.' With that advice it is probably best briefly to consider the French submarines of forty to forty-five years ago and then move rapidly to the most interesting developments in the current French fleet.

In 1940 the submarine force was composed of small submarines, medium-sized submarines, minelaying submarines (including the incomparable *Rubis* and her dog), large submarines, and the monster *Surcouf* of 4,304 tons dived. This last boat demonstrated the extraordinary flights of fancy of the between-wars designers. Her twin eight-inch gun turret took longer to set up and fire than the submarine did to dive, and her lamentable end (she was rammed by a friendly merchant ship) was in keeping with her general uselessness.

Once the Second World War was over the period of French rehabilitation did not encourage expensive naval programmes, and it was not until the 1950s that the 'Narval' class was laid down. Then came the 'Arethuse' class, small boats of 667 tons, the 'Daphnes' of 1,043 tons, a successful export model and, finally, in the non-nuclear range, the 'Agostas'. While these were still on the building slips it was announced in 1973 that their successors would be a class of nuclear-propelled submarines.

This was not such a leap into the unknown as it might seem. In March 1964 the first of a class of nuclear-propelled ballistic-missile submarines was laid down at Cherbourg, to be followed by four more of the same design over the next ten years. Thus the French had followed the British into the nuclear propulsion business; but they had developed their reactors in a very different direction: those for the SSBNs were cooled by natural convection flow and this design was continued in the SSNs.

But when the details of the SSNs were released in part, there was considerable surprise that this forty-eight-megawatt reactor was fitted in such a small submarine. With a length of 72.1 metres and a dived displacement of only 2,670 tons, this was the smallest operational nuclear design in the world. The puzzling fact, not yet resolved, is the comparatively slow speed of twenty-five knots credited to this class. If the published figures, other than the speed, are correct, and despite the very upright fin structure carrying the fore-planes, this class should, theoretically, be capable of at least thirty-eight knots. Perhaps they are, and the French authorities simply preferred not to risk their reputations with apparently over-inflated claims. The first two of this 'Rubis' class were operational by 1986, with a further three under construction. A sixth boat of an improved 'Rubis' design was ordered in October 1984, and the next pair are to be included in the 1986–8 programmes.

The French Navy has taken the same course as was forced on the British Admiralty in 1962. With only four modern non-nuclear boats and only two more under twenty years old, they have embarked on an all-nuclear programme. The results of this policy are plain. All construction will be centred on the single yard at Cherbourg; the not inconsiderable area of continental shelf water under 200 metres will be an area where their submarines will be unable to employ their full potential; and a high proportion of the requirements of basic training will have to be fulfilled by very expensive submarines. The second of these problems may be aided by the small size of the 'Rubis' class, but the need for long passages at high speeds is nowhere near so pressing as it is for the Americans. A non-operational point is that the French are putting their lucrative foreign market at risk. This is based entirely on non-nuclear designs and, although the French advertise new diesel-electric varieties, purchasers are more likely to clinch deals with yards which are already building the classes on offer.

The French SSBNs have already been mentioned. These were part of de Gaulle's *'Force de Frappe'*, and were started at the time when France chose to opt out of the NATO military command. Although their particulars, including the sixteen missile tubes, are very similar to the British SSBNs, their design and that of their missiles was entirely French. The latter have undergone similar improvements to the American weapons, starting with the M1 and M2, the latter being installed from 1976. The M2 had a range of 1,300 miles with a 500-kiloton head; it was soon overtaken by the M20, which has an improved range of 1,500 miles and a megaton (1,000 kiloton) head. Shortly afterwards the M4 missiles were available, providing a range up to 3,000 miles and a head (possibly MRV rather than MIRV) carrying six 150-kiloton re-entry vehicles. By 1987 the first submarine carrying the M4/TN71, a version with a range of 3,125 miles, will be at sea.

In 1985 the single submarine *L'Inflexible* was commissioned. An improved version of the previous class of five, she was built to carry the M4 missile, her construction having been delayed for three years to enable this to be carried. From good sense and management, the French government accepted the operational penalties, saved the cost of a very expensive refit, and now has six of these submarines – of which two are continuously on patrol and one in refit. A new class is planned for the 1990s, to succeed the first quintet which are due for deletion from 1997 to 2008. Whether the facts concerning Soviet advances in anti-ballistic-missile defences, which were discussed earlier in this chapter, will affect this programme remains to be seen.

FEDERAL REPUBLIC OF GERMANY

The Imperial German Navy was the last of the major fleets to embark on a submarine building programme. Although three 'Karp' class were begun at Kiel in 1904 for Russia, the German *U1* was not completed until December 1906. In the less than eight years before the start of the First World War the German designs had advanced rapidly, and by 1914 a building programme – of boats whose dimensions and displacement were very similar to those of their successors of the 'Type VII' thirty years later – was in full swing. During the four years of that war over 350 submarines were built. Their effect on Allied shipping needs no emphasis here.

In 1939 the new German submarine programme had been under way for only about five years and, once again, a huge acceleration took place. The results were even more disastrous for the Allies than in the previous

U-boat war – a result of greater numbers of very effective submarines operating from bases from northern Norway to the Spanish border. Continual research and development showed the remarkable capabilities of German designers. These came to their peak in the astonishing 1,819-ton 'Type XXI' which, had the war lasted longer and the planned run of over 120 operational boats been achieved, could well have affected the outcome. The underwater speed of sixteen knots was unique, as was the battery capacity which allowed a dived endurance of six knots for two days. The submarines which were produced had six bow tubes with power reloading and carried twenty-three torpedoes – plans were in hand for the 'Type XXI B', with twelve tubes, and the 'XXI C', with eighteen. Neither of these got further than the drawing board. A class of much smaller submarines, the 'Type XVII', benefited from experiments with the Walter turbine, fuelled with high test peroxide. This had been under development for some time and had its first sea trials in V80 in 1940. The designed speed of 'Type XVII' A was twenty-six knots, with a dived displacement of 259 tons.

By 1945 a great fund of knowledge of all aspects of submarine design was available. The schnorchel had been generally fitted from mid-1943, while power reloading in the 'Type XXI' allowed all six torpedo tubes to be reloaded in twelve minutes, half the time it sometimes took to load one tube in earlier boats. Battery capacity was greatly improved; non-electric propulsion systems independent of the atmosphere, the Walter HTP turbine, and the Ingolin closed-cycle diesel were developed; air-conditioning and food freezers were introduced in the 'Type XXI'; in the 'Type XXIII' of 256 tons, the torpedoes were loaded through the bow caps, a system utilised again twenty years later. The launching of V2 rockets from an encapsulated tube was planned, and designs without conning towers were on the drawing boards. Meanwhile, the *Kleinkampf-verband*, a separate department from the main U-boat headquarters, was set up in 1944 to develop small underwater craft. At least a dozen designs were considered – some reached mass production, some only the prototype stage, while others got no further than the design office.

This long catalogue has a purpose – to establish not only the advantages which the navy of the Federal Republic held when they once more began to build submarines in the early 1960s, but also to indicate those designs which the Soviet authorities collected during their advance to Berlin.

In March 1962 the first U-boat built since 1945 was commissioned and named *U-1*. She and her sister, *U2*, were unsatisfactory and were scrapped. The second *U-1* was commissioned in June 1967 and, in fact, followed *U9–12*, which were of the same design as the first *U1*, but were built of steel with non-magnetic properties – an idea dating back some years. The size of German submarines was, at this time, restricted, but the Baltic requirements were little affected by these strictures. Comparatively shallow water is usual throughout most of that sea, distances are short, and the German Navy had much experience of the area up till 1945. In January 1969 the twelfth boat of the 'Type 205' design was commissioned, to be followed in April 1973 by the first of eighteen submarines of the 'Type 206'. This class was larger than the '205' by five metres in length and fifty tons in dived displacement; it was built to a most effective and capable design, mounting eight torpedo tubes and with a dived speed of seventeen knots. The knowledge gained during the Second World War was put to good use, with additional refinements and improvements: the schnorchel system was better, the batteries improved, the introduction of new electronic equipment allowed a reduction of the complement to twenty-two, the torpedoes were loaded externally – the designers at Kiel had produced an excellent interim submarine to carry out a specific task in enclosed waters. But these men were looking well beyond such circumscribed horizons – they were looking for means of extending their building runs and improving the underwater performance of their boats.

The first was achieved by an energetic programme of sales and marketing – throughout the world there was a need for fairly small, effective submarines which were comparatively cheap in both capital and running costs. In 1964 *U3* was loaned to Norway for three years, and in 1965 the first of fifteen submarines of 'Type 207' were commissioned for that country. This class was an improvement on the 'Type 205', with an increased diving depth. In 1970 two of the original 'Type 205' were completed in Copenhagen for the Royal Danish Navy. In 1977 the British yard of Vickers completed three 'Type 540' boats under licence to a West German (IKL) design. This consortium of Ingenieurkontor in Lubeck, Howaldtswerke in Kiel and Ferrostaal in Essen were in a powerful position to meet the worldwide desire for submarines. A new basic design, the 'Type 209', which was to appear in a number of variations, hit the front in September 1971, when the first of what was to be a run of eight submarines for Greece was commissioned. Since then the tally has mounted. With the USA, Great Britain and France opting out of the non-nuclear field at that time, there was little competition. Argentina, Brazil, Chile, Colombia, Ecuador, India, Indonesia, Peru and Turkey have all signed up with IKL since 1968 – making a total of thirty-three submarines to be added to previous programmes for an overall ninety-seven.

With this background, while rivals were scratching about for single orders and the Iranians, Malaysians, Saudis, Taiwanese and Thais were entering the bidding, it is not surprising that it is a West German yard which is leading the way in a new application of a long-known technology.

The fuel cell, in an embryonic form, was first produced in 1839 by an Englishman, Grove. His cell, a device for converting the chemical energy of a fuel into electrical energy, was not fully developed until Francis Bacon took the matter in hand in the years immediately following the Second World War. Today there are many land-based applications of this energy source and it is a vital element in American spacecraft. But it has been left to the West German designers to apply the fuel cell to submarine propulsion.

The first design produced was labelled the '1800H' class. Once again the 'Type 209' is the basis for this, and the '1800H' is a derivative of the '1500' class with a quarter of the main battery replaced by a hydrogen/oxygen fuel cell. The advantages of this system are the very few moving parts involved – with a resultant improvement in silent running – and the fact that the only exhaust is fresh water. The probable endurance of a small fuel-cell submarine would be a fully air-independent patrol of twenty-eight days at a speed of 4.7 knots. In larger submarines this could be increased to sixty days at four knots. Endurance would obviously be reduced by prolonged use of the maximum speed of twenty-two knots. Once the inevitable teething problems of a new and revolutionary system have been cleared, the plans for an all fuel-cell submarine will be completed, and this could be at sea in the early 1990s. Some underwater experience with fuel cells has been obtained in the two American deep submergence recovery vehicles, producing much valuable information, but a period of intensive trials in a full submarine will be necessary before the system becomes fully operational.

Meanwhile the German Navy is continuing its programme of conventional diesel-electric submarines. With a current fleet of six 'Type 205' and eighteen 'Type 206', future plans provide for the modernisation of twelve of the latter and the early construction of a further twelve of the new 'Type 211' to enter service from 1991–6. This design is very similar to the 'Type 210', of 1,450 tons dived displacement, for which the Norwegian government signed an agreement on 6 September 1983.

THE NETHERLANDS

As one of the first navies to include submarines in their fleet, the Royal Netherlands Navy has maintained a regular building programme since

01 was completed by K. M. de Schelde at Flushing in 1905. Over the next forty years Dutch submarines with K numbers became a familiar sight in the East Indies, while 0 numbers remained in the Netherlands area. This system was abandoned and the named submarines, which operated with great gallantry and effectiveness in the Second World War, were transferred from the Royal Navy. Some of these formed the nucleus of the post-war force, until Dutch designs were available from the yards at Schiedam and Rotterdam. The first pair of four submarines of unique design, *Dolfijn* and *Zeehond*, were laid down at Rotterdam in 1954, five years after the original budget vote in 1949. These were of a triple-hull form, the upper cylinder containing the living and operational areas, as well as four torpedo tubes at each end. Below this on either side were two similar cylinders, each containing propulsion machinery, batteries and storerooms. With a dived displacement of 1,826 tons, their twin screws propelled them underwater at seventeen knots, and they could dive to a depth of 300 metres. This was a remarkable achievement for a country recovering from five years of occupation.

The immediate successors to these four submarines, the 'Zwaardvis' class, reverted to a normal hull configuration, though the Dutch length-to-beam ratio (L/B) of 7.8 to one is notably better even than the American *Albacore* at 9.3 to one. The current building programme comprises two 'Walrus' class, slightly larger than the 'Zwaardvis', but in which the L/B ratio has increased to 8.1 to one, to be followed by a further two and, possibly, more. Thus by 1988–9, if all goes according to plan, the flotilla will consist of two 'Potvis' class (a later 'Dolfijn'), which will be replaced by the second pair of the 'Walrus' class, the first two 'Walrus', and two 'Zwaardvis'. This is an inadequate number for a navy with not only a fine submarine tradition, but also a major part to play in NATO's Atlantic operations. However, as with so many of their European neighbours, cost remains an inhibiting factor.

SCANDINAVIA

The three navies in this area, though geographically close, have very varied requirements. Norway has a 1,500-mile coastline, extending from the Arctic border only fifty miles from the Soviet Northern Fleet bases in the Murmansk area to the border with Sweden at the inner end of the Skaggerak. An archipelago of islands fringing a coast indented by numerous fjords, with deep water only a few miles offshore, provides a series of havens for opposition submarines. The Danes have a totally different problem. With the exception of a small patch in the Skaggerak, their patrol areas in the Baltic approaches and within that sea are all in water of fifty metres or less, with varying densities to the north and south of the main islands. Similar problems face the Swedish submariners, although their main area of interest lies within the Baltic. Here densities vary with disturbing frequency. The spring melt brings in huge quantities of low-density fresh water and, in what is virtually a land-locked sea, Western submarines require re-ballasting to enable them to dive. Once down, extraordinary things can happen. Layers of water make handling difficult and sonar conditions unpredictable. Some 400 miles from Stockholm is the Soviet base at Kronshtadt; half that distance away are the submarine base at Tallinn and the naval base at Riga. In peacetime the main task of the Swedish Navy is to monitor Soviet incursions into their coastal waters; in wartime they need to protect their shores from amphibious assault. The major factor in the latter situation is the very brief warning time which results from the short distances involved. Dived speed could be of prime importance, and all the submarines now available or under construction have a minimum of twenty knots.

The 'Draken' class is now well into its third decade and will soon have been paid off. This will leave the five boats of the 'Sjöormen' class, dating from 1968–9, the three 'Näcken' class of 1980–1, and the four 'Västergotland' class due to be completed in 1987–9. The Swedes have the advantage of two submarine building yards, at Malmö and Karlskrona, and this underlines their interest in building for export.

Denmark entered the submarine business at a somewhat later date than some of her neighbours, but by 1914 she had nine submarines operational, three of which were built by Whitehead at Fiume and the remainder in the Royal Dockyard at Copenhagen. A further six, slightly enlarged at 369 tons dived, were completed at the latter yard during the First World War; they were equipped with Burmeister and Wain Danish. diesels. By the beginning of the Second World War the Danes had given up their submarine service, but this was rejuvenated in the post-war years. Now, forty years later, the Royal Danish Navy is caught in financial straits, which have resulted in many problems for a number of years. The country's politics and the powerful peace lobby are making a mockery of the aim of collective NATO defence. Denmark is the cork in the Baltic bottle, but internal wranglings obscure her vital importance to the Alliance. Her present force of four submarines is now outmoded, and it is planned to hire replacements to maintain even this vestigial force. But the importance of a competent submarine squadron in the

Royal Danish Navy would become evident were there to be a Soviet advance through southern Sweden. This would outflank the Baltic Approaches command of NATO and, if the main bulk of Norwegian submarines were deployed in the north, only those of Denmark would be available to disrupt Soviet sea-borne advances from the Malmö/Oslo area.

Finance is a major problem for the Norwegians too. With a tiny population, equivalent in total to that of a major city, the provision of adequate funds for the nation's defence is a considerable burden. One has to ignore the protection of the very considerable Norwegian Merchant Navy – this is a task far beyond the country's resources. But the defence of the Norwegian coastline is a task which must be addressed, and in this the Norwegian submarines play a major part.

On 28 November 1909 the first Norwegian submarine, *Kobben*, was commissioned – built to a German Krupp-Germania design. From then on the strength of the squadron stemmed mainly from the building yard at Horten, with both diesel and electric motors built in Norway. By the end of the Second World War five Horten-built boats of an Electric Boat design, and two British 'V' class were operational. In July 1959 a programme jointly funded by Norway and the USA was announced, and in 1963 the first of fourteen boats of the Type 207 was laid down at Emden. By mid-1967 the whole programme had been completed – a sterling effort, but one which posed the problem of block obsolescence in the mid-1980s.

The Type 207s are small submarines of 435 tons dived displacement, based on the Federal German Type 205 design. On 6 September 1983 the Norwegian government signed a contract for the construction of six Type 210 submarines, which, at 1,300 tons dived, were much larger. The design, known as Project 6071, was a joint effort between the Norwegian and the Federal German designers. The hull is very similar to the latter's.Type 211, and the equipment for both types is shared between the two countries – weapons-control systems by Kongsberg of Norway, sonar, periscopes and torpedoes from West Germany. The first of the Type 210 is due for delivery by Thyssen Nordseewerke in 1989, two years ahead of the first of the Type 211. With a reported diving depth of 250 metres and an underwater speed of twenty-three knots, these six Type 210 submarines will be a valuable addition to the fleet, although the overall drop in numbers must be a source of concern to NATO staffs.

THE MEDITERRANEAN

There is a long history of underwater activity, if not of governmental enthusiasm, in many countries bordering this sea. The French effort has already been discussed. South of the Pyrenees, there has also been a burgeoning of designs. Monturiol and Garcia constructed their first submersible in 1862, and were followed by Isaac Peral with his pioneering work on battery-driven submarines. Although his work reached fruition in 1887, he failed to penetrate the imagination of officialdom, and it was not until 1914 that the Spanish Navy ordered its first three submarines – to be named, ironically, after the three great pioneers. The 1915 programme provided for the construction of twenty-eight boats, and in July 1916 the first Spanish-built submarine for thirty years was laid down at Cartagena. Although the considerable effect of submarines on maritime operations was demonstrated during the Spanish Civil War, by 1945 there were only eleven submarines available. Of these, five were becoming aged, one was an interned German U-boat, and two were Italian submarines purchased in 1938. By the late 1950s a number of changes had taken place – the five oldest boats and the two Italians had been paid off. Three (*D1* to *D3*) which had been ordered in 1926–7, but whose construction had been delayed by the Civil War, were completed in 1947 to 1954 and then modernised; a programme of four boats ordered from Cartagena in 1945 had been cancelled in expectation of the transfer of US submarines; and four midget submarines had been completed. These last, two of thirty and two of sixteen tons, were eventually classified as 'assault submarines', a very rare appellation. In 1959 the first US submarine arrived, to be followed by four Guppy modernisations in 1971–4. But by this time the Spanish yard at Cartagena was in full swing. In 1973–5 four submarines to the French 'Daphne' design were commissioned, with a further four to the 'Agosta' design entering service in 1983–6 – all the US boats being paid off in 1982–4. A new Spanish design is on the drawing boards, and three of these are included in the programme up to 1990.

Further to the east greater enthusiasm was shown for submarines. In 1895 the Italian Navy completed *Delfino*, of 107 tons dived displacement, but it was thirteen years before the first of the five boats of the 'Glauco' class appeared. By late 1914 five yards were building submarines, and at the end of the following five years a total of fifty-one operational Italian-built submarines were in commission. These included two of the earlier minelaying submarines, *X2* and *3*, built by Ansaldo of La Spezia to a Bernardis design.

By 1940, when Mussolini booted Italy into the Second World War, the submarine fleet totalled 103, with a further sixteen boats under construction. The most noteworthy contribution by Italian submariners during the next three years was the exceptionally brave and skilful manner in which they operated the 'SLC' (Maiale), similar to the British Chariot. These achieved considerable success off Gibraltar and in Alexandria harbour.

But one of the results of this unsuccessful foray into a war for which Italy was ill-equipped was the ban on new warship construction. This expired on 1 January 1950, and the five-year programme then announced included several submarines. However, by 1955 the navy possessed only five boats – two of the US Guppy type, and three reconditioned survivors from the war. In fact one, *Bario*, had been sunk in harbour and salvaged. Ten years later the total was unchanged, though a third American boat had replaced one of the Italians', but in 1965 a pair of Italian-designed submarines was laid down, the first such programme since 1943. These were small boats of only 582 tons dived displacement, a reflection of past Italian conviction that it needed two types of submarine – the coastal and the ocean-going. Such a distinction may have advantages on a purely national basis, but it does present restrictions for NATO planners. It can be argued that the British operated successfully from Malta and La Maddalena with 'U' class submarines from 1940–5. These were small boats of only about 730 tons dived, but the distances to their patrol areas were correspondingly brief – 250 to 400 miles. The 'U' class design philosophy, though primarily based on training, also envisaged the use of this class only in the North Sea against German targets. It was fortuitous that their main area of operations turned out to be the Mediterranean, where the retention of Malta and the occupation of Sardinia provided bases close to their main operating areas. It may also be argued that the British 'U' and 'V' classes operated successfully in the Indian Ocean, but this was never a comfortable task and was performed far better by the larger submarines of the 'S' and 'T' classes.

In the Mediterranean there could well be NATO requirements for Italian submarines to operate 1,000 miles from base and, for this task, the four new boats of the 1,630-ton 'Sauro' class, and their larger successors now on order, are far better fitted. The Italian fire-control systems are the product of a great deal of co-operation between the various providers of naval equipment, and are of a very high standard. Innovation is frequently a product of the Italian system of design and construction, and is well illustrated in these new classes.

Some building yards persist throughout submarine history, and one of these is Monfalcone, currently the only Italian submarine construction yard. In the days of the Austro–Hungarian Empire, before the border adjustments handed this area to Italy, this same yard shared the load for the Imperial Navy with Pola (now Pula) and Fiume (Rijeka). The first of these is now one of the two submarine yards used by the Yugoslav Navy, the second being at Split. Only nine years elapsed between the acceptance of the first Austro–Hungarian submarine, built to a Simon Lake design at Pola in 1908–10, and the eclipse of the navy itself. Twenty years later at the start of the Second World War, Yugoslavia, which incorporated, since the Peace Treaties, the Adriatic coast from Istria to Albania, had a small navy which included four submarines. Of these, two were built in Britain to an 'L'-boat design, and two in France. One of the former, *Nebojsa*, was operated by the British from 1941, the remainder being lost – two after capture by Italy. As an illustration of the sturdy construction methods of that period, *Nebojsa*, on her first test dive in British hands, exceeded her designed diving depth by a factor of 3.28. This occurred because the depth gauges were marked in metres, instead of the feet to which her new crew were accustomed.

It was not until 1957 that the first Yugoslavian designed and built submarines, *Sutjeska* and *Neretva*, were laid down at Pula. In 1968–70 three more were commissioned, two at Pula and one at Split, and in 1978 and 1981 two more of an improved 964-ton design were completed at Split. Plans exist for a further reinforcement of this squadron, which could have important effects on any operations in the Adriatic.

The Royal Hellenic Navy, possibly as a result of its justifiably tentative attitude to *Nordenfelt I* in 1886, may have been late in the race to obtain submarines, but its first acquisition moved straight into the history books. Two boats of 460 tons dived displacement, *Delphin* and *Xiphias*, were launched in 1911 and 1912 by Schneider's of Creusot. Their armament was five eighteen-inch torpedoes and, with the Balkan War against Turkey in full swing, *Delphin* carried out the first recorded dived torpedo attack in December 1912. The target was the escorted cruiser *Medjidieh*, and *Delphin*'s captain was the first in a long line of submarine commanding officers of several nationalities to have his attack fail due to torpedo malfunction.

These two boats survived the First World War and it was not until 1926 that two new submarines were launched in France, to be followed by four more in 1927–8. This was the total strength when the German invasion of Greece caused their withdrawal to ports under British control. Four of these were sunk in 1941–3, to be replaced by the Italian

Peria, renamed *Matrozos*, and six British 'U' and 'V' class, transferred in 1943.

There was a pause in the post-war period until, with the last of the British boats being paid off in 1957–8, two US 'Gato' class were transferred in 1957, and a 'Balao' class in 1965. Two of these were relieved by two of the 'Guppy' type in 1972–3, but by then the first four of a new class of Type 209 had been completed for Greece by Howaldtswerke of Kiel. Four more followed in 1979–80, and these eight are now a most valuable allied reinforcement in the Aegean. Although the Greek elections of 1985 returned a government whose attitude to other NATO countries can, at best, be described as ambivalent, a Warsaw Pact advance through Bulgaria into Thrace would most likely be fiercely resisted by the majority of Greek patriots. In this event, reinforcement through Thessaloniki, Kavalla and Alexandroupolis would be essential and protection of the ports and beachheads on this coast would be a joint sea/air operation in which submarines would play an essential part.

The Turkish Navy has a more difficult wartime task. With some 800 miles of coastline facing the southern boundary of the USSR and the Soviet Black Sea Fleet – the Bosphorus offering the only exit from that sea – and a Mediterranean coastline of the same length as that in the north, the major question for the naval staff in Ankara is how to deploy available resources. For a warlike Turk the apparent answer is to attack the enemy at the earliest opportunity – in the Black Sea. But this would not provide support for the armies about Erzurum and Thrace, which would be opposed by land armies with internal lines of communication. The centre must fall, like the traditional ripe plum, if the wings are defeated. So the strategy must be to provide maximum support for the armies on either flank; and here the problem is the same as that facing the Greeks in Thrace. Reinforcement must come through the main ports of Iskenderum and Izmir, both vulnerable to enemy forces in the Mediterranean – which would in turn be vulnerable to submarine attack from Turkish forces.

Different problems in the late nineteenth century had prompted the Turks to follow the Greek example – the Imperial Russian Navy was reported to be experimenting with a large number of small submarines. What extraordinary idea prompted people to assume, in an era when there was neither a means of detection nor an effective form of attack, that submarines should be set against submarines remains a mystery. One disastrous dive by the first of the two unsuccessful Nordenfelt boats dissuaded any potential volunteers, and the Turkish government, from further participation in the project.

There was, apparently, an attempt to resurrect the two Nordenfelt boats during the First World War. According to *Jane's Fighting Ships* of 1919, 'the reconstruction of these curiosities proved an absolute failure'.

By 1939 the Turkish Navy had overcome this trauma and had commissioned a variety of submarines – two from Rotterdam, two from Monfalcone, one from Cadiz, and two from Kiel, with two which are listed as 'built at Istanbul'. This last pair may well have been assembled on the Golden Horn from parts provided by Germany – a small part of a carrot designed to persuade Turkey to provide much-needed support for Hitler. As a further diversification, four boats were completed by Vickers of the UK, although all were held by the Royal Navy – as P611, 612 and 614 – from 1941–2 to 1945 (P615, *Uluçali Reis*, being lost on patrol). By the end of the war the Turkish Navy had ten submarines, but in 1950 the first of a series of American submarines was transferred. By 1976 the total of these boats had risen to ten, but a new element was arriving. In July 1975 the first of a growing number of Type 209 submarines was completed at Kiel. These have a dived displacement of 1,185 tons, and an underwater speed of twenty-two knots. A total of twelve of these boats is planned, all but the first three to be built at Gölcuk on the Gulf of Izmit. These are the first submarines built from the keel up in a Turkish yard, and the trimming of the building time after the first of class is notable. But would twelve be sufficient in a crisis? Even at a very high availability rate based on adequate warning time, eight or nine might be operational. The task would be a testing one – reinforcements would be essential if the supplies to NATO's eastern hinge were to be fully protected.

6

Soviet Developments

Innovation has frequently been part of the Russian approach to submarine matters. Some twenty years after the German Wilhelm Bauer had carried out well over a hundred trials of his various submersibles off Kronshtadt, he was succeeded by Drzewiecki, whose first boat was completed in 1877. Two years later a number of pedal-operated submersibles were ordered to the latter's designs. None showed any more promise than the underwater craft commissioned by Peter the Great in 1729.

Despite the setbacks some of the nobility on the naval staff continued their quest for an efficient submersible. Submarines tended to be thought of at this time as purely defensive devices. Designs were pursued in a somewhat amateurish way, which is reflected in the high failure rate of some of the schemes and the disastrous conclusions to others. Training was either non-existent or inefficient and the superior attitudes of the officers to their men was hardly conducive to the competence and teamwork essential to the proper conduct of life in a submarine. The insignificant contribution of Russian submariners to the naval operations of the First World War need not detain us.

In the post-revolutionary navy there was little cash available and new construction was rare. However, in 1926 a programme was begun which steadily gained momentum until, at the time of the German invasion of the USSR in June 1941, the Soviet Navy had the largest fleet of submarines ever assembled in peacetime. But in this war three problems did much to negate the courage and commitment of a number of their commanding officers: they lacked modern equipment; technical training was poor; and Stalin's purges in the 1930s had destroyed a high proportion of the leadership.

But with the war over, Stalin ordered a massive submarine building programme – 1,200 boats were to be built between 1950 and 1965. The starting date was dictated by the need to develop new designs and by the period needed for the rejuvenation of the building yards. In 1953 two matters caused a change of plan – Stalin died and the first design for a nuclear-propelled submarine was completed. Of the planned 1,200 submarines only 388 were eventually completed, but where quantity was sacrificed quality took over. When Admiral Gorshkov became commander-in-chief in 1956 a great deal was afoot. The first of the nuclear-propelled 'November' class attack submarines was well advanced, the conversion of the early 'Whiskey' class cruise-missile-firing boats was under way, the first ballistic missile had been launched from a submarine in September 1955, and the designs of the 'Golf' and 'Hotel' classes, the first of the custom-built ballistic-missile submarines, were far advanced. The speed with which all this activity was conducted was comparable only to the US Navy's programmes, and by the early 1960s a formidable force was well in the making.

By 1967 the order-of-battle was;

SSBNs ('Hotel' class)	13
SSBs ('Golf' and 'Zulu' conversions)	35
SSGNs ('Echo I' and 'Echo II' classes)	25
SSGs ('Juliet' and 'Whiskey' conversions)	22
SSNs ('November' class)	12
SS ('Foxtrot', 'Zulu', 'Romeo', 'Whiskey' and 'Quebec' classes)	300

All the diesel boats (SS) resulted from the original post-war programme, while the ballistic- and cruise-missile submarines were the result of advances in missile development. Nuclear propulsion was beginning to take its place in both the missile and attack submarines, but 1967 was a year of profound significance in the story of Soviet submarines. In that year the early submarines of the 'Yankee' class of SSBNs, the 'Charlie' class of SSGNs and the 'Victor' class of SSNs made their appearance. The building yards for these new classes – Severodvinsk ('Yankee'), Gorky ('Charlie') and Admiralty Yard, Leningrad ('Victor') – were widely dispersed, but the total impact was immense.

The 'Yankees' carried sixteen SS–N–6 missiles with a range of 1,300 miles and had a dived speed of at least ten knots more than the 'Hotels', which by this time had been refitted to carry three SS–N–5 missiles with a range of 750 miles. The search area for SSBNs on patrol was thus vastly increased, and the eastern cities of the USA from Detroit to New Orleans were now within the target area.

Although the 'Charlies' showed a minimal speed advantage over their predecessors, they had one aspect of superiority which was of fundamental importance – they could launch their SS–N–7 cruise missiles from dived. The 250-mile SS–N–3 missiles then carried by preceding classes far out-ranged the SS–N–7, but this was because the former required the launching submarines to surface before firing. This had many disadvantages: apart from the risk of detection there was a third party involved – an aircraft or vessel was needed to provide mid-course guidance for the missiles. This was a clumsy method of attack, allowing the defence forces to engage the launcher, the 1.2 mach missile, or the guidance ship or aircraft. Yet the 'Charlies' were also saddled with problems. Their missiles had, and have, a range of thirty-five miles. If the submarine is attacking a thirty-knot carrier battle group and is using 1,100-pound high-explosive heads on its missiles, the accuracy needed can be achieved only when the submarine is approaching the target. If pursuing, the speed required allows for only intermittent and, possibly, inaccurate sonar or radar information. The alternative is to use a 200-kiloton nuclear head, an action which might be contrary to current rules of engagement. However, these difficulties aside, the 'Charlies' added a troubling element to Western anti-submarine defence planning which is still around today.

In 1967–8 Western defence had to allow for cruise missiles launched from 250 miles and thirty-five miles, as well as torpedoes fired well within the latter bracket. The deep diving (400 metres) and fast (twenty-nine knots) 'Victor' class SSNs provided an additional threat in the close-in engagement. Their hull form and propulsion, like those of the 'Charlie' class, were of a new design, more streamlined and less noisy.

Soviet designers achieved a fast, deep-diving submarine with the 'Novembers'. The 'Charlies' and 'Victors' incorporated some elements of sound quietening, and had a hull form very different from their predecessors. Their nuclear plants were an improvement on those of the 'Novembers', but the real and startling developments still lay in the shipyards and drawing offices in 1967.

First amongst these was the lead boat of the 'Alfa' class, which was completed in 1971. Comparatively small at seventy-nine metres in length and 3,700 tons dived displacement, this was a design which must have been worked on since the early 1960s. The hull was of titanium alloy, a material of very notable advantages, but considered impractical by Western designers due to its high cost and the many problems in shaping and welding it. But the Soviet Union has large deposits of titanium ore and had purchased specialised welding equipment in the USA in the 1960s. Furthermore, cost was a relative term in a military-orientated society; what the armed forces could convince their masters they needed, they got.

The first 'Alfa' was a disaster. This was more likely to have been the result of the liquid metal cooled reactors giving trouble rather than the titanium alloy hull being found inadequate. In the USA *Seawolf* had been fitted with a liquid sodium cooled reactor and, when this proved a danger, the whole idea was scrapped. Soviet ideas on nuclear safety are very different from those in America. Personal reputations are at stake, as well as lives, in the USA. In the USSR eventual success takes little account of dead men, and reputations depend on ultimate achievement. The first 'Alfa' was scrapped in 1974, but within a year the first of six more was under way. The programme was finished by 1983, but these six submarines, which appear to be differing versions of the same trials design, had set the pattern for future construction. Their dived speed of forty-two knots and their diving depth of over 900 metres set new standards of submarine performance, but these were questioned by a number of experts. However, if facts are unassailable, as is this quoted speed, and counter-arguments on the basis of current technologies are valid, as they appear to be, there must be some unexpected explanation – unexpected, that is, on the basis of Western developments, but not so if the background of Western research and published information on Soviet work is taken into account.

The fact that resistance in electric motors decreases under conditions of super-cooling (super-conductivity) has been known for the last seventy-five years, but the necessary technology for the incorporation of this knowledge into an operational unit had been lacking. Over the last twenty years this has become increasingly available, and the use of super-conducting motors is now more generally available. They have been manufactured in the USA and discussed as possible propulsors in Great Britain. The advantages are tremendous reductions in weight for the same power output; the disadvantages are the very considerable costs.

In 1971 the prototype for future cruise-missile submarines entered service in the form of the one example of the 'Papa' class. Once again it seems that titanium alloy was used for the pressure hull and that two pressurised water reactors are housed in the 109 metres of hull. 'Papa' is a fairly large submarine of 8,000 tons dived displacement, but despite her size she can achieve a speed of at least thirty-seven knots dived. The cruise-missile armament was increased to ten launchers from the eight in 'Charlie', and the type of missile improved. In 'Papa' the SS–N–9 missile, with a range of sixty miles, replaced the SS–N–7, but her activities suggest that she remained more of a test vehicle than an operational submarine.

At about the time that 'Papa' appeared from the Severodvinsk yard in north-west Russia there was even greater activity on a nearby building slip. From this came the first of eighteen 'Delta I' class SSBNs, somewhat larger than 'Yankee', but carrying only twelve missile tubes.

The reason for this was that the SS–N–8 missiles she carries are considerably bigger than the SS–N–6, and as a result they carry their single warhead to a range of 4,200 miles – the later version (Mod II) carrying for 4,900 miles. The Soviet Navy had achieved a very important goal – from now on their SSBNs could launch their missiles to any part of the Northern Hemisphere without leaving home waters and, therefore, without risking detection in the island gaps in the Atlantic and Pacific, or from the US SOSUS bottom surveillance chains. To provide for the needs of both oceans, the eventual construction run was, like that of the 'Yankees', split between Severodvinsk and Komsomolsk, north of Vladivostok. In 1976 a short run of four 'Delta II' class followed, enlarged versions of 'Delta I' carrying sixteen missile tubes, to be supplanted in the building yards by 'Delta IIIs'. The first of these was commissioned in 1978, and production of about two a year continued until at least 1985. Although of much the same size as the 'Delta II', this class has a taller missile compartment, made necessary by the greater length of the SS–N–18 missiles which have replaced the SS–N–8s. This missile is a considerable improvement on its forerunners and comes in three varieties. It can have either three or seven MIRVs with a range of 3,500 miles, or a single warhead with a 4,300-mile range. With a missile CEP (circle error probable, the miss distance) of 1,500 yards, the potential of these submarines needs no emphasis.

In February 1984 there was a further addition to the 'Delta' group. Five metres longer than 'Delta III', the first 'Delta IV' was launched at Severodvinsk, and it is one of the ugliest of modern submarines. The huge housing abaft the fin covers the launching tubes for sixteen SS–N–23 missiles, another type of liquid-fuelled rocket incorporating seven MIRV heads of greater power and accuracy than those of the SS–N–18.

But in 1983 the first of a totally different class of SSBN had been commissioned. The 'Delta' series were no more than enlarged editions of the original 'Yankee' design, which dated back to the early 1960s. Their equipment, in the shape of navigational aids, sensors and communications, was continually improved, but the cumbersome missile section allowed only a comparatively modest maximum speed of around twenty-four knots. The new recruit turned out to be a revolutionary vessel which had been under construction since 1977. Compared with this, the building rate of the evolutionary 'Deltas' was almost mass production. 'Typhoon' is about the same length as the American 'Ohio' class, but there any resemblance finishes. 'Typhoon's' beam, at twenty-three metres, is 1.8 times that of 'Ohio', and gives a length-to-beam ratio of 7.4 to one, a vastly different situation from the 13.3 to one of the 'Delta IVs'. She sits high in the water when surfaced, an indication of a very adequate reserve buoyancy. The hull is remarkable in many ways. It is smooth and uncluttered, lacking the mass of limber holes which are such a prominent feature in the 'Deltas'. A considerable part of this saving results from the incorporation of the twenty missile tubes within the main casing, thus dispensing with the missile housing. The next revolutionary move was to place the missile tubes in the forward area rather than abaft the fin, as in all other SSBNs, irrespective of nationality. One can only speculate as to why this arrangement was chosen, but one pointer came to light on 12 October 1982 when the first of class carried out a test launch which involved a simultaneous discharge of *four* missiles. The answer might be, therefore, that it is easier to cope with such violent and massive variations of trim if they occur up front. The forward hydroplanes, of a retracting design, are set less than twenty-five metres from the stem, and would be available for instant correction should control become difficult.

As to whether the missile tubes are housed in a separate compartment or lodged in the main hull, the standard Western view is that 'Typhoon' is a twin-hulled design and, if this is correct, the missile compartment may be located between the two pressure hulls. If the reported length of the SS–N–20 missile which a 'Typhoon' carries is correct at 14.9 metres, then the depth of the submarine from casing top to keel must be about two metres more than this – 16.9 metres (55.4 feet). This would allow for two pressure hulls of about 7.5 metres (24.6 feet) in diameter, with a central circular section between them into which the bases of the missile tubes could be fitted. If this is the chosen design and the twin hulls are 7.5 metres in diameter, their outer sides will be at the edge of the casing. This alignment would be very different from another new class, 'Oscar', which will be referred to shortly. In this design of SSGN the placing of the cruise-missile tubes external to a single pressure hull has resulted in well over three metres of space between the outer casing and the pressure hull, a most valuable form of protection against torpedo hits, particularly those using shaped charges in their warheads. This technique is well known to Soviet designers yet, if the above assumptions and calculations are anywhere near correct, they have preferred to exclude the very useful protection in the 'Oscars' from the 'Typhoon' design.

There is no reason why 'Typhoons' hulls should not be expanded in wake of the missile compartment. In this case the diameter might be increased to ten metres, each containing one set of propulsion machinery. Other requirements concern the areas allocated to the control room and attack centre, the sonar equipment, and the torpedo armament. The siting of a separate, small pressure hull in the base of the fin would suffice for the first of these. The positioning of the sonar arrays should have presented few problems, but the torpedo area could have required another separate pressure-tight compartment set at the forward end of the missile tubes. Only by the latter device would it have been possible to site the six tubes of both 533 and 650 millimetres on the centre-line.

The configuration suggested here presents a major problem. If the outer casing continues in the same form underwater as it does above there will be a very large cubic capacity unfilled by the various pressure hulls. Working only on published data and photographs it appears that this void (in other words free-flood) area is approximately half of the whole, the latter being very approximately 40,000 to 50,000 tons. The idea of having this amount of free-flood water is somewhat surprising, and could suggest either a different hull configuration or a requirement for an external water jacket. Without any further evidence, this enigma must here remain unresolved.

Other problems result from two photographs in particular. Both were taken within a very short period of each other and shortly after the submarine surfaced. The shot from the starboard quarter shows a series of patches of broken water up the side. These could result from blowing out the ballast tanks. But in the second shot these patches have disappeared; instead there is a haze over the fore-casing, which might suggest that the submarine, her captain having spotted the interloping aircraft, is diving. But there is no such haze on the after casing, and the water at the stern and along the side shows little sign of forward movement.

Many other queries arise from an inspection of the 'Typhoon' pictures – here there is no space for any further conjectures, but one point must be emphasised. The fin structure appears to be some forty-five metres long, over two and a half times the length of that in the 'Delta III' class. This suggests that there may well be an upper 'hull' within the structure, which could be forty metres (131.2 feet) long, more than enough to contain all the controls and firing systems, as well as the radar, sonar and communications offices, and cabins for the senior officers. This, in turn, suggests a number of other things which cannot be substantiated, although one appears to be certain. The fin is very powerful, the sides well rounded, and the whole is well suited for surfacing in pack ice. The after end is fitted with horizontal limber holes while, rather surprisingly, the forward end is surrounded by a more than ample walkway.

The 'Typhoon' is clearly a very large, tough submarine with a reserve of buoyancy greater than in normal Western practice. Emphasis on the survivability of submarines is frequently stressed in Soviet writings, and this class is probably a prime example of this approach. But the cost of such a monster, with the many innovations and variations in her structure, is obviously very high, an adequate reason for the simultaneous construction of both this class and 'Delta IV'. At the same time this diversification of SSBNs with twenty and sixteen missiles apiece provides an increased number of hulls available if the USSR intends to abide by SALT restrictions.

The Soviet Navy has been alone in having a continuous and considerable building programme of specialised cruise-missile submarines. The single boat of the 'Papa' class has already been discussed. In 1978, only seven years after 'Papa' entered service, the first of a new class of SSGNs was laid down at Severodvinsk. When she was launched in April 1980 it was evident that, once more, the designers had made a very major increase in size. 'Oscar', with an overall length of 145 metres (475.6 feet) and a beam of eighteen metres (fifty-nine feet), has a dived displacement of 14,000 tons, nearly three times that of the 'Charlie I' class of 1967. The emergence of 'Oscar' is an indication of the intensity of Soviet submarine design effort. Four years after 'Charlie I' came 'Papa'; two years later, in 1973, the first 'Charlie II' was commissioned; five years later 'Oscar' was on the slips. It is not surprising that this continual quest for improvement has produced new and innovative designs. How many land up in the waste-paper basket one cannot tell, but at least the Soviet designers probably would have little reason to say, as a British surface ship designer once remarked, 'That's the thirteenth I've done in fifteen years and not one has got beyond my drawing board.'

'Oscar's' outer hull, when viewed from above, appears gigantic. The length-to-beam ratio of eight to one results from the twenty-four missile tubes being fitted in six pairs on either side of the pressure hull, stretching from some eight metres forward of the twenty-seven-metre-long fin to a similar distance abaft it. Within the casing the pressure hull is probably twelve metres in diameter, with some three metres separating it from the outer shell. Survivability of this class should be high – once again the reserve of buoyancy is considerable and the range of the SS–N–19 missiles (295 miles) allows for a much longer distance from the target than the 'Charlies' – even 'Charlie II' with its SS–N–9 armament. Such long-range engagements require high-grade sensors and ECM/ESM equipment and communications. The great length of the fin suggests that these can all be comfortably accommodated.

By 1986 the Soviet Navy was operating a variety of classes of cruise-missile submarines. The 'Juliett' and 'Echo II' classes have to surface to launch their missiles; but with some ten of the latter class now equipped with the 270-mile SS–N–12 (a considerable improvement on the 250-mile SS–N–3A), this group of forty-five submarines provides a useful capability, particularly where there is an absence of enemy Airborne Early Warning. The seventeen boats of the two 'Charlie' classes are available in the thirty-five/sixty-mile zone, while 'Oscar', with a speed of at least thirty-five knots, can operate at will.

There is, however, one aspect of cruise-missile operations which is not covered by this group, and that is land attack. The earliest applications of cruise-missile technology were directed to this use – in 1947–9 the US Navy had carried out trials with Loon missiles, and then built submarines to carry Regulus as a strategic bombardment weapon. This programme was overtaken by Polaris, but in 1958–60 the Soviet 'Whiskey Twin Cylinder' followed the single prototype and were equipped with two SS–N–3C missiles – suitable only for shore attack. As with Regulus and Polaris, this function was taken over by the 'Golf', 'Hotel' and 'Zulu' classes equipped with SS–N–4 and 5. Now, however, trials with a new weapon, SS–N–24, have been under way for two to three years, and 1987 may well see the appearance of an even larger SSGN than 'Oscar', designed to carry out shore attack with large cruise missiles from a range of 2,000 miles or more. This would add an unknown element to the Strategic Defense Initiative equation, in the same way as the long-range Tomahawk caused some consternation in the USSR.

The third category of submarines has a title which is both misleading and irrelevant – 'attack submarines'. In the days when submarine operations were far less complex than they are now, the practice was very simple. One sank one's target with torpedoes, if it justified such an expenditure, or surfaced and sank it by gunfire. Today the torpedo remains a primary weapon, but the gun has been superseded by the missile. Whereas enemy submarines were attacked with torpedoes, today a far more effective method is to launch a missile, which can easily be fitted with a nuclear head.

The 'Los Angeles' and other classes of American submarines are now equipped, as we have seen earlier, with torpedoes, 'Harpoon' missiles, and 'Tomahawk' missiles. All are discharged from the same tube, but each has a different purpose. Therefore an admiral facing these submarines in time of war must expect some form of attack from 1,350 miles inwards. This adequately explains why the US Navy does not operate cruise-missile submarines as a separate type. But now the Soviet Navy has the same capability, and it is becoming increasingly difficult to differentiate between the so-called SSGNs and SSNs – the two have become complementary.

The 'Alfa' class, to which we have already referred, was essentially a trials submarine, with a new hull form, material and propulsion. But this may have been the forerunner of a hybrid type, able to fire both torpedoes and tube-launched missiles. This latter capability was expanded in the 'Victor II' and later classes, which carry both the SS–N–15 and 16. These are in many ways similar to the American Subroc, which can carry either a torpedo or a nuclear warhead to a range of about fifty miles. These are described as anti-submarine weapons, but a nuclear explosion, even if intended for a submarine target, would seriously endanger any surface ship in the vicinity. The truth is that, with the introduction of the variety of weapons designed to be launched from standard torpedo tubes, the differentiation between attack and cruise-missile submarines is no longer valid.

Let us, therefore, review the Soviet building programmes for submarines which are not equipped with cruise-missile-launching tubes. As the construction of the astonishing 'Alfas' continued, so did that of the 'Victor' class. The first of seven 'Victor IIs' appeared in 1972. This boat was nine metres longer than 'Victor I', an increase which may have been due to the introduction of the 650-millimetre torpedoes and the tube-launched missiles. In 1978 came the first of twenty 'Victor III' class, a further enlargement of the basic 'Victor' design. It was probably this class which was chosen for the test launching of the SS–N–21, a winged cruise missile with a range of some 1,600 miles. It seems likely that these missiles, closely akin to the American Tomahawk, are now part of the standard outfit in modern Soviet SSNs.

These are almost bewildering in their variety. In 'Victor III' there was a considerable improvement in sound-quieting, but with a hull form which was merely an extension of a design of the early 1960s there were, inevitably, deficiencies in this area. The length-to-beam ratio had crept back to 10.2 to one as opposed to the 8.9 to one of 'Victor I', and with any form of stretched hull there must be some problems with flow noise – the whole is very different from that which originated from earlier calculations.

But 'Victor III' is a good submarine. She has a remarkable reserve of buoyancy, her single propeller is split into tandem screws, and she carries a large pod, about eight to nine metres long, slung on the top of her after fin. The function of this pod will be discussed later (p. 152).

The apparent successor to 'Victor III' was 'Sierra', launched at Gorky in July 1983. In this class the hull configuration appears to be not unlike that of 'Victor III', with a single screw and a considerable number of large limber holes along the casing; but the beam has been increased to give a length-to-beam ratio of 8.8 to one, compared with 'Victor III' at 10.2 to one – thus the 'Sierra' ratio has crept back to that of the original 'Victor I'. With a dived displacement of about 8,000 tons, a high reserve of buoyancy, a speed possibly in the high thirties, six tubes forward capable of handling both 533-millimetre and 650-millimetre torpedoes as well as SS–N–15, 16 and 21 missiles, this class could well be the steel-hulled, multi-purpose submarine of the immediate future.

One of 'Sierra's' main identification points is the large pod on her after fin, very similar to that on 'Victor III'. This is absent in the second new design, 'Mike', launched at Severodvinsk in May 1983. This design is somewhat larger than 'Sierra', 120 metres (393.6 feet) long with a dived displacement a little under 10,000 tons, and may have a direct relation to the 'Alfa' design. The hull is probably of titanium alloy which, in view of previous experience, may have greater strength than anything previously used. This is by all standards a big submarine – and size always confers dual advantage: it can contain a more powerful propulsion plant, and more weapons.

There appears every probability that 'Mike' has twin liquid-metal-cooled reactors, and there is no apparent reason why she should not have superconducting motors for her single shaft. If this is the case the single screw would be hard-pushed to transmit the available horsepower to the water, even if the tandem screw pattern of 'Victor III' has been adopted. Until adequate photographs are available, speculation is of no value.

But there are some points which can be made. With a titanium alloy hull of improved design, a diving depth of 1,000 metres could be achieved. When running very deep the efficiency of the propulsion would be increased, and a speed at least in the high thirties might be achieved. The absence of a pod suggests that, if it is a towed array in other classes, it is not needed, or if it is an auxiliary propulsor, this is not necessary. 'Mike' might therefore be a high-speed platform for SS–N–21 operations, with additional tubes in an ample hull, be they horizontal or vertical.

With the first of the next class, 'Akula', launched in mid-1984 there is very little data on which to build. Perhaps a little smaller than 'Mike', this design has some very notable features. The fin is far more streamlined than any new design since 'Alfa', and the after fin is again crowned with a large pod. Perhaps this is the true successor to 'Alfa', built with silence and speed in mind, possibly of titanium alloy, possibly with an advanced super conducting propulsion system and, if these surmises are correct, designed for anti-submarine operations.

If any of these conjectures are anywhere near the mark, the Soviet Navy could be planning more than a run-off between three SSN contenders. Each one might have its separate task, and the building rate over the period to 1995 could give evidence of intent. One 'Mike' to two 'Akulas' to three 'Sierras' – but no bookmaker would take the bet.

In the less exotic field of non-nuclear submarines there has been far less variation. The evolution of this type has been steady. The navy has continued to provide considerable numbers of these boats to operate worldwide. Their particular value is probably in the shallower waters around the Soviet coastline, but many have been deployed to the Mediterranean and Indian Ocean. After the first great post-war building programme slowed down with the advent of nuclear propulsion, the fleet contained 240 'Whiskey' class, twenty 'Romeos', and twenty-six 'Zulus'. Between 1958 and 1971 sixty-two 'Foxtrots' were commissioned, and in July 1973 the new 'Tango' class appeared for the first time.

This was an improvement on 'Foxtrot' with a slight variation in its length-to-beam ratio from 11.4 to one in the early class to 10.2 to one in 'Tango'. By the time the latter was in series production tube-launched missiles were embarked as well as torpedoes, and the building rate rose to two a year at Gorky. By the time this came to an end in 1982 nineteen had been built, and the first of the new class, 'Kilo', was in the water.

This is a radical departure from previous designs. She has a length-to-beam ratio of 7.8 to one, is probably the first true diesel-electric submarine the Soviets have built, is, like 'Tango', coated with anechoic anti-sonar tiles, and may have an improved underwater speed with her single screw. The first boats of the class were built at Komsomolsk, but other yards in the west of the USSR have joined in the programme. The dived tonnage is 3,100, large enough to provide for worldwide operations and, at a time when the first export version of this class has been transferred to India, others may be planned for use in foreign navies as well as the Soviet fleet.

Small programmes of specialised submarines have been completed over the last twenty years. Most, like the four 'Bravo' padded targets, have been diesel boats – the two 'Indias' for rescue duties, and the

'Lima' research submarine – but two small nuclear boats, 'Uniform' and 'X-Ray', have been built for unidentified research work. As well as these custom-built submarines, many conversions have taken place over the years – some for trials and experimental purposes, others with an operational function, such as the communications submarine of the 'Hotel' and 'Golf' classes.

For many years it was the custom in the West to speak of the Soviet Navy as having a ten-year technology gap compared with the more modern ships and submarines of NATO. Nobody was very specific about the areas in which this gap existed, but developments over the last ten years have shown that, if it really did exist, it has been very firmly and effectively bridged. The sceptics will very likely claim that any advances made are the result of a massive campaign of espionage on Western developments, but this is by no means the whole truth. No doubt there have been many aspects of electronic and computer technology, signal processors and the like which have been 'transferred', to the considerable advantage of the Soviet Navy. These trawlings from an ill-protected society have saved a great deal of research funds and, particularly, time.

But there are certain fundamental areas where native genius has been entirely responsible for very major advances. The extraordinary progression of missiles has already been mentioned. This has probably been accelerated by the use of information and hardware from the West, but the speed of introduction has been quite exceptional. Today the modern Soviet submarine carries a mixed load of tube-launched weapons, one being the 650-millimetre (25.6-inch) torpedo. This, the largest torpedo since the Japanese Long Lance, carries a wake-homing head to a reported range of fifty kilometres (thirty-one miles) at fifty knots, or 100 kilometres at thirty knots. Being larger and longer (thirty feet) than standard torpedoes, it can carry not only more fuel but also a bigger warhead. This development must have been built in response to a need stated by the Naval Staff for a weapon whose range would assist in the survival of the attacking submarine.

Survivability has a high priority in Soviet submarine thinking. As a result their designs incorporate greater reserves of buoyancy than in Western submarines, strong double hulls with a significant separation between the inner and outer, increased diving depths, achieved in some areas by the use of titanium alloys, significant advances in sound-quieting, and notably higher speeds.

It is the last two of these factors which are particularly relevant in dispelling the misapprehension of Soviet designers riding on Western backs. As has been stated, there are three basic sources of noise from a dived submarine: the hull passing through the water; the main and auxiliary machinery; and the propellers. A smooth, well-shaped hull goes a long way to reducing the effects of the first of these. The aims must be to reduce the friction between the water and the hull, to avoid any roughness or protrusions which will cause turbulence, and to provide a hull shaped to cause minimum resistance to the water molecules.

The new 'Victor' and 'Charlie' classes of 1967 showed a trend towards the streamlined hull with curved fins which is so notable in the 'Alfa' and, later, 'Akula' classes. Limber holes in the free-flood casings are shut off when not needed, and the whole hull is coated with anechoic covering, which serves both as a smooth surface and as an absorbent for active sonar transmissions. The fitting of these tiles was first mooted in the West at a time when, judging by the amount of Soviet literature on the subject, there was intense research on such coverings in progress in the USSR. In fact, from the late 1950s a stream of learned papers appeared from the Moscow presses, running in parallel with similar productions in the West.

The two other sources of noise, machinery and propellers, have also received a great deal of attention. In the early 1960s both American and Soviet designers published descriptions of research into electromagnetic propulsors – a principle of very long standing which, like the fuel cell, could not be fully developed until the advent of modern technology such as superconductivity. The main contender in this field is MHD (MagnetoHydroDynamic) propulsion, and the most likely current application may be the pod which is perched on the tail fin of 'Victor III', 'Sierra' and 'Akula'. This is approximately nine metres long, and if the details of Soviet patents, now more than ten years old, are applied it could provide a means of auxiliary propulsion up to a speed of six to seven knots. In 1974 Captain-Lieutenant A. Popov wrote a description in *Krasnaya Zvezda* of a device in which water was drawn in at the forward end of a tube lined with a flexible membrane. This is made to pulse by inducing an electric current in a highly conductive liquid metal packed against the flexible membrane. The end result is the expulsion of a jet of water at the rear of the tube. In the most general terms this is a description of what could be turned into an effective and silent method of propulsion. The improvements in ferromagnetic fluids recently reported would provide great efficiency. The use of liquid helium for cooling to the point of superconductivity would certainly be required.

So are we seeing a new form of submarine propulsion in its embryonic stage? Are the small research submarines, which have been completed recently, test-beds for what could turn out to be a very powerful and silent system? At the moment we can do no more than speculate. But the plain fact now is that, far from Soviet submarines being at a disadvantage compared with those of Western navies, they possess a number of superior qualities. There is no reason, in view of the immense strides taken over the last twenty years, why this superiority should not be extended, unless NATO designers take the challenge seriously.

7

Fences and Defences

This chapter is mainly concerned with submarines in anti-submarine warfare, and they certainly embody some – arguably most – of the best systems for the task; but they are only a part of the gigantic anti-submarine effort required to meet the Soviet threat. In turn, NATO submarines have to face the powerful Soviet anti-submarine organisation in and on the sea and seabed, in the air, and in space. Although we are looking at anti-submarine warfare (ASW) from a submariner's viewpoint, submarines cannot, as we said in the beginning, be treated in isolation; and to run down a surface fleet in favour of submarines and aircraft – as John Nott, former British Secretary of State for Defence, intended before the 1982 Falklands confrontation demonstrated the dangers – would be to imbalance and topple the ASW guard. If one thing has been learned, the hard way, about anti-submarine warfare it is that every possible system must be deployed continuously and vigorously: even then a proportion of submarines will get through the defences.

Submariners like to display a periscope photograph of a frigate captioned: 'There are only two kinds of ships – submarines and targets.' It is a pleasantly chauvinistic poster, reminiscent of other traditional sub-surface jibes down the years, but it is very far from the truth. Submarines do have a margin of advantage over surface vessels, just as, with a few ups and downs of the submarine/ASW see-saw, they always have done; but submariners do not have it all their own way today in the face of surface and air opposition – and, of course, opposing submarines. The new developments are not all in their favour.

The latest and most worrying anti-ship submarine weapons – tactical missiles – can be used at long range, and this tends (but only tends) to work against the element of surprise which was formerly the key to submarine successes, because air-flight weapons, of whatever kind, take a comparatively long time to reach their objectives and are detectable *en route*. Moreover, anti-missile defences are improving steadily. Experience during the Falklands conflict was invaluable in revealing shortcomings and requirements; but what percentage of submarine-launched missiles will in the future be shot down, decoyed, or jammed electronically before reaching their targets is very hard to judge; it could be quite high.

On the other hand, torpedoes, once they are in the water, are difficult to defend against: although they can be seduced by towed noisemakers or, conceivably, jammed, such devices are a considerable hindrance to sonar operators who are trying to find and counter-attack the firing submarine(s). Wake-homing weapons could be a particular problem.

In all cases it is best, of course, for ASW forces to find and destroy a submarine before it shoots – or, by manoeuvring and harassment, try to prevent it from firing. A 'flaming datum' – the result of a submarine penetrating the ASW screen and firing before it is detected – is no longer so likely to be the first indication of a marauder's presence. However, if a number of boats make a more or less co-ordinated attack – and concentration of force is central to Soviet doctrine – the defences could be swamped; and it is not at all easy to introduce mass attacks into peacetime exercises in order to see what might happen.

Soviet homing and pattern-running torpedoes can be fired at long range – out to many miles – with a reasonable chance of hitting something in a force or convoy; and it is improbable that the fish themselves will be heard by sonar before it is too late. Missiles can be launched from twenty miles out to around 300 miles. Thus the radius of ASW concern has now been pushed out to about 300 miles – from the few miles that it was when torpedoes were always fired from only a few thousand yards; but there are still second- and third-line submarines equipped with short-range, noisy, 'unintelligent' torpedoes which will seek to deliver their salvoes from very close range if they can slip through a screen which, stationed on a larger perimeter, is less dense physically than it used to be, even if sonar cover is much more capable.

If a boat does get past the escorts and hits with torpedoes before it is discovered, a comparatively small sector (out to about ten miles) can immediately be established for ASW search; and if an attacker uses high speed to clear the area there is a good chance of quickly gaining passive and then active sonar contact, albeit really too late. The same principle applies to short- or medium-range missiles like the Soviet SS–N–7 (or US/UK Sub-Harpoon) launched on fire-control data (including target classification/identification) provided by a submarine's own sensors, implying that the sector is still quite small in area: it can be searched quickly and to good effect – so long as VDS (Variable Depth Sonar) is available if the attacker tries to shelter beneath a density/temperature layer. In fact, there is said to be some debate in the Royal Navy about whether SSKs, with their limited mobility compared with highly mobile SSNs, should be equipped with Sub-Harpoon, which is detectable by enemy radar when within horizon range and is liable to reveal the approximate position of the launcher at the time of firing.

It is singularly un-Nelsonian to worry about what might happen after one has manoeuvred to 'engage the enemy more closely', but post-attack evasion is evidently now a more serious tactical consideration, on both sides, than formerly. Nevertheless, it is a fair bet that the ace captains – perhaps a quarter (less in the Soviet Navy) of any particular group – will press on regardless of the consequences; and it is equally fair to wager that, in a mêlée with the fog of war all round, a substantial proportion of them will get away with it. Indeed, a submarine at large in the middle of an escorted surface group is in a paradoxically safe position. It poses a nasty problem for the defenders because there is not only a huge amount of ship noise to confuse and degrade the performance of surface sonars, but conditions will also be greatly disturbed by underwater explosions (not a feature of peacetime exercises) resulting from submarine weapons and ASW counterattacks; and there will be decoys, false 'non-sub' noises and echoes (some of them deliberately created), and the inevitable 'ichthyological gefuffle'[1] to contend with as well. Then, almost certainly, there will be more than one actual submarine around which will shoot at escorts as well as prime targets whenever (or before) a hunt takes place. A frigate does not come to a spluttering stop with a hole in its side during an exercise and, human nature being what it is, signalled submarine attacks are apt to be ignored until the subsequent wash-up.

If an SSGN launches anti-ship missiles at long range (employing external data for fire-control) it will be much more difficult to reckon where it is: taking to its heels it could have moved seven miles by the time the first salvo of incoming missiles is detected by the defence, and, say, fifty miles by the time shore-based or carrier aircraft reach the estimated firing position. The sector for search is then very large indeed, and the prospects for prosecution do not appear bright unless intelligence and/or second guessing (a 'gut feeling' is not to be despised), together with an adequate number of aircraft, enables the force commander accurately to saturate the danger zone.

Heavy air coverage in support of a Carrier Battle Group (CVBG) is quite feasible, so long as the shore-based Long Range Maritime Patrol (LRMP) aircraft still have airfields to operate from in support of carrier-borne fixed-wing ASW aircraft and do not come under attack. Those provisos are considerable.

(ABOVE) One of the fourteen original Soviet SSNs of the noisy 'November' class commissioned between 1958 and 1963. One sank south-west of the UK in April 1970 and another was probably scrapped a few years later. Twin reactors and steam turbines provide 30,000 shp for the two shafts, giving a maximum submerged speed of thirty knots. Displacing 5,000 tons dived and 360 feet long with a twelve to one length-to-beam ratio (only a trifle better than the disastrously unmanageable British 'K'-boats of 1917), the 'November' has eight twenty-one-inch bow tubes and two sixteen-inch stern tubes. The complement is ninety-two and the diving depth is about 1,000 feet. It is the only Soviet SSN not covered with anechoic Cluster Guard tiles. (BELOW) The technologically advanced and agile Soviet 'Alfa' SSN, the fastest submarine in the world – capable of forty-two knots plus and powered, probably, by two liquid-metal cooled reactor plants developing about 47,000 shp to drive a single shaft via an electric motor. The titanium alloy hull would allow a safe diving depth of about 3,000 feet. Very well shaped, with a length-to-beam ratio of 7.9 to one, this 3,700-ton (dived) class of six, armed with six twenty-one-inch torpedo tubes, may be at least partly experimental – a very big step forward on the way to new designs which include the heavily armed missile-torpedo 9,700-ton 'Mike' and the 8,000-ton 'Akula' types. The 'Alfa' is thought to be computerized in all respects and is crewed (forty total) almost entirely by officers and *michmany*, with perhaps only a small handful of junior ratings for menial tasks. A difficult submarine to catch – still more difficult to sink with existing weaponry when at high speed and capable of a very quick reaction to a threat, the 'Alfa' has not, of course, demonstrated her abilities in the anti-submarine or anti-ship roles in time of war. Forty mines can be carried instead of torpedoes.

(ABOVE TOP) A Soviet 'Sierra' 8,000-ton SSN equipped with twenty-one-inch torpedo tubes and 25.6-inch tubes for land-attack missiles (1,600-nautical-mile SS-NX-21s). Two pressurized water reactors and one steam turbine provide 40,000 shp for the single shaft, which should give a top speed of about thirty-two knots. Diving depth approaches 2,000 feet and there are about eighty-five men in the crew. The nacelle at the stern has variously been assessed as an advanced auxiliary propulsion unit or a housing for towed array sonary (and/or a decoy system). (ABOVE BOTTOM) The French SSN *Rubis*, commissioned on 28 February 1983. At 2,670 tons dived this is (apart from the US Navy's 400-ton NR-1 engineering and research vehicle) the smallest class of SSNs (five laid down) ever designed, and the good sense of this in several respects is evident – particularly in the face of active sonar by anti-submarine surface and air units and submarines. An unusual cooling system has enabled the forty-eight megawatt reactor to be smaller. The top speed of twenty-five knots is perfectly adequate for the tasks assigned and, with eighteen torpedoes (four twenty-one-inch tubes) or mines and the tube-launched 'fire-and-forget' SM-39 thirty-nautical-mile anti-ship missile (a variation of Exocet), this type is formidably armed. The diving depth is 980 feet. To maximize sea-time, *Rubis* and her sisters will – uniquely for SSNs so far – be manned by two alternating crews, each consisting of nine officers, thirty-five petty officers and twenty-two junior ratings.

(ABOVE) USS *Albuquerque* (SSN-706) at launch on 13 March 1982. Nineteenth in a long line of 'Los Angeles' (SSN-688) submarines, she is 360 feet long with a length-to-breadth ratio of 10.9 to one. The diving depth is 1,475 feet. A pressurized water S6G (GE) reactor plant with two geared turbines (35,000 shp) powers one shaft for a top speed of more than thirty knots. With four twenty-one-inch torpedo tubes, set well back and angled out, Mark 48 torpedoes are the principle weapons for the class; but most can now carry twelve Tomahawk missiles (torpedo-tube launched), and SSN 721 onwards will be equipped with fifteen vertical launch tubes for Tomahawk in the outer hull (foward). Mines (such as CAPTOR) can be embarked instead of torpedoes. The complement is twelve officers and 115 enlisted men. It is equipped with BQQ-5 long-range sonar, which has been well proven, together with the towed array, BQS-15 for closer range and the Mark 117 fire-control system. Hopefully the latter will soon be replaced by fully integrated and comprehensive computerized SUBACS or something very like it.

(ABOVE) HMS *Turbulent*, the second of seven 5,208-ton (dived) 'Trafalgar' class SSNs commissioned on 28 April 1984. 280 feet long with a length-to-breadth ratio of 8.7 to one, the class has a single propulsor powered by a 15,000-shp pressurized water reactor plant giving a published (*Jane's*) top speed of thirty-two knots. Passive and active sonar systems, with a passive towed array, are excellent, as is the intercept set (seen forward of the fin). Sub Harpoon (RNSH) and Tigerfish weapons (twenty-five in all) are fired through the five twenty-one-inch tubes: mines can be substituted. These boats are exceptionally quiet and, built by Vickers, they are good value at around £200 million apiece (1985). But the crew of 130 is large – more automation/computerization would seem highly desirable – and is an expensive part of the real total cost. The pressure hull (single with ballast tanks forward and aft) is covered with anechoic tiles. (BELOW) A Soviet 'Victor I' class 5,300-ton SSN. The 'Victor' types I, II and III (the latter two types, at 335/341 feet, are longer) operate out of area actively and widely and are often commanded by very senior and trusted officers. Two pressurized water nuclear reactor systems provide 30,000 shp for a single shaft at speeds of up to twenty-nine knots. They can dive to 1,300 feet with a large safety factor (the crushing depth is in the order of 2,000 feet) and are ideally shaped with a double hull. Two small auxiliary propellers can be lowered, presumably in case of damage to the main propulsor when operating in the ice-field. The long-range LF and shorter-range MF fire-control sonars are good and Types II and III have 25.6-inch tubes for SS-N-16 Subroc type thirty-nautical-mile anti-submarine weapons, and SS-N-15 and torpedoes which can also be launched from the 21-inch tubes.

(LEFT) A Soviet 'Victor II' SSN, a powerful and versatile twenty-nine-knot 6,000-ton boat armed with SSN 15/16 Subroc type anti-submarine weapons and torpedoes, or with up to thirty-six mines. (*US Navy*)

(RIGHT) HMS *Torbay* (SSN) launched at Vickers on 8 March 1985 by the wife of the renowned and greatly respected captain of the wartime boat of that name, the late Rear Admiral Sir Anthony Miers VC, KBE. (*FOSM*)

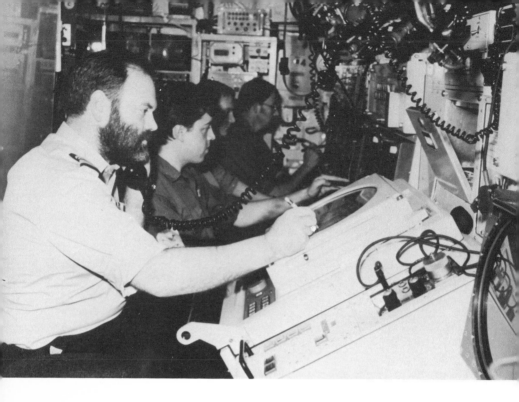

(Above) HMS *Trafalgar* (SSN), with the Ops Officer at the computerized Action Information (AIO) and fire control system. The type 2020 sonar slave display is in front of him. (*FOSM*) (Below) At the controls of USS *Los Angeles* (SSN–688). (*US Navy*)

(ABOVE) HMS *Sovereign* (SSN) at the North Pole. (BELOW) HMS *Conqueror* (SSN) returning to the Faslane base and flying the Jolly Roger to signify her exploits during the 1982 Anglo-Argentinian confrontation during which, on 3 May, she sank the cruiser *General Belgrano* – an absolute military necessity, as seen at the time, which caused an immediate and continuing outcry in Parliament and elsewhere. However, to flaunt the flag of piracy – albeit an honourable tradition originated by Max Horton (HMS *E-9*) in 1914 and perpetuated throughout the Second World War – was perhaps a little tactless in the circumstances.

(ABOVE) USS *Williams H. Bates* (ex-*Redfish* SSN-680) with DSRV I *Avalon* embarked. The two deep submergence rescue vessels in service are road, sea, submarine (modified SSN or SSBN) and air (C141 and C5) transportable. Operable down to 5,000 feet and precisely manoeuverable with a tilting control shroud aft and four ducted thrusters, a DSRV can be launched and recovered by the mother submarine submerged – and under the ice-cap if necessary. Connecting directly through a transfer skirt with a disabled boat, this is the only practicable means of escape from great depths. At shallower depths the usual method of escape in most navies is through a special escape tower with escapers wearing protective suits, but *not* supplied, as formerly, with neat oxygen which is lethal under pressure. (BELOW) One of the two Soviet 'India' class rescue submarines carrying two DSRVs. There would be little difficulty in substituting military midgets on an 'India', or on several other types of submarine.

Fixed-wing ASW aircraft search and attack primarily with passive, followed by active, sonobuoys, but they might well be alerted by ESM equipment if a submarine briefly uses its radar or transmits on radio; and they may glimpse cautiously exposed masts or snorkels on their radars with subsequent classification by eye, low-light television or infra-red scanners. The outstandingly good British Searchwater radar can also detect sea-skimming missiles out to forty-five miles. Localisation (that is, pin-pointing a hitherto approximate position) immediately before dropping weapons can be achieved by magnetic anomaly detection, but MAD sweeps a very narrow path and requires a low pass over the submarine: this could give warning that an attack is imminent, allowing precious moments to take evasive action.

Active sonobuoys provide an attack solution for lightweight air-dropped homing torpedoes – led by the new British Stingray, claimed to have a notably high single-shot kill probability, and the American ALWT (replacing the Mark 46) with a directed-energy warhead to improve effectiveness against double-hulled targets. Nuclear depth bombs (type 57 is the US Navy version) are in the kiloton range and can be carried by aircraft or large helicopters: one of them could spoil any submariner's day, even in a toughened boat.

Sonobuoys, passing sound signals by radio, come in three types, and are preceded by a bathythermograph buoy which tells the operators the best depth for the sonobuoy transducers in the existing water conditions. The USA, UK, Canada, France and Italy have all produced their own models, although this is an uncomplicated area for achieving efficiency and economy by co-operation and standardisation.

Passive omni-directional sonobuoys, like the twelve-inch US Sparton Dwarf Omni equivalent of the standard AN/SSQ–41B thirty-six-inch cylinder, are the simplest kind. The UK relation is Jezebel, which is now also miniaturised (Type SSQ 904), enabling three times as many units to be carried. A buoy is parachuted into the water and the hydrophone descends to the required depth to listen through a sonic range typically from five or ten Hz to five or ten kHz. Data is transmitted on thirty-one or ninety-nine preset VHF channels, depending on the type, and transformed into spectral lines in the aircraft's processing equipment.

When responses have been identified from one or more omni-directional buoys, directional buoys (DIFAR) can be laid to track the contacts, although tracking is possible by omni-buoys alone. Current types include the Sparton Dwarf DIFAR, and the AN/SSQ–77 VLAD (Vertical Line Array DIFAR) for use in a noisy high-density traffic environment, which supplies a long-felt need.

Finally, active sonobuoys may be laid to generate the best air-dropped torpedo-attack solutions. Two of the latest types are AN/SSQ–62B DICASS, which is directional and command-activated (a considerable tactical bonus), and the UK command-activated CAMBS.

The principal US and British LRMP aircraft are the 410-knot Orion P–3C (operated by ten navies) and the 500-knot Nimrod Mark II: both have a central processor and an accurate navigational system. The Russians mainly employ the Tu–95, broadly similar to the Nimrod, and the Il–38, which is more like the Orion but slower. Maximum ranges are typically in the order of 1,500–2,500 nautical miles with two hours on patrol.

Besides their great search ability, the advantage of LRMP aircraft, although the crew do not see the results, is that they oblige submariners to keep their heads down: the greatest effect is, of course, on diesel boats (SSKs). Some SSN and, to a greater extent, SSGN activities are also inhibited by aircraft being in the area, and no submariner likes having one overhead: there is no means of knowing what it is up to or whether it has put sonobuoys in the water.

Friend or foe?

Until at least the 1960s it was common for aircraft-generated datums to be ten miles or more in error. Submariners and aircrews alike would prefer to forget the number of times during the war that submariners were attacked by 'friendly' aircraft, usually due to navigational errors which were, often enough, mutual. As Vice Admiral Charles Lockwood US Navy remarked, 'Frequent bombings of our submarines by "friendly" planes had not impressed one with the earnest desire of the Army Air Force to co-operate with other forces.'[2]

In general tactical usage, fixed-wing aircraft patrol the fringes 200–300 miles around a force; submarines and surface vessels employ passive sonar (towed arrays) – TACTAS – in the midfield, with carrier-based fixed-wing aircraft and light airborne multi-purpose system LAMPS helicopters to search for and prosecute submarine contacts; and the inner zone, fifteen to twenty miles from high-value targets, is guarded by frigates and helicopters using active sonar.

Fixed strategic defences – SOSUS listening arrays on the seabed and minefields (such as CAPTOR) – are backed up by LRMP aircraft and submarines at choke points. The archetypal choke passages are those between Greenland, Iceland, the Faeroes and the United Kingdom;

they are, in total, about 600 miles wide. Their importance is obvious: the bulk of the Soviet Northern fleet has to pass through them to gain access to the Atlantic, across which American support to Europe must flow. A Soviet view (which compares pretty well with what has been said openly in the West) is that four LRMP aircraft will be constantly on station over the gap (requiring about twenty-five aircraft to be operationally available for this task alone), co-operating with seven patrolling submarines (eleven operational boats needed for an extended period), and that one thousand CAPTOR mines will be laid between Greenland and Iceland, where an attrition rate of thirty per cent has been quoted against noisy submarines. Presumably operations of this magnitude would be mounted if tension threatened to escalate a crisis. It has already been implied that things may become very difficult for patrolling aircraft when the shooting starts.

The Soviet Navy is very conscious of omnipresent fixed SOSUS warning chains, the rapidly deployable air-laid systems (RDSS), and the towed surveillance arrays (SURTASS). Warning installations, which are not confined to the Eastern Atlantic, do, without question, give US and NATO commands a constant and remarkably clear idea of Soviet movements: the processed information, integrated with airborne, space-borne, surface and sub-surface systems, provides a critical 'war indicator' of the kind that used to be derived less reliably from more nebulous intelligence.

The protection of shipping – whether or not to organise traditional convoys – is, as in the past, a matter of argument and divided opinions. Distilling the requirements for military transports (immediate and continued reinforcement) and for the economic requirements of Europe in crisis and war, it looks as though some forty ships a day, on average, would be needed from across the Atlantic. If there is no apparent nuclear threat, sufficient air, surface and submarine escorts could conceivably be afforded, as in the last war, 'to ensure the safe and timely arrival' of quite large convoys, although they would constitute a very heavy drain on resources urgently required for more offensive operations in the Eastern Atlantic and Norwegian Sea. But if one-mile anti-nuclear spacing between ships is necessary, a super-convoy of the size sometimes envisaged, comprising 300 tankers, cargo vessels and transports, would be at least twenty miles wide and about sixty miles long – an almost impossible area to defend. SSN wolves, approaching from any angle, would surely get amongst the sheep and make every weapon tell, while SSKs would not find their task too difficult with such a vast procession taking three or four hours to pass a given spot.

An alternative way of safeguarding ships is to protect a lane along which all traffic will pass, but this too would be difficult, and sooner rather than later the enemy would determine the route, discover the inevitable weak points and concentrate against them.

It has been suggested[3] that a combination of the convoy and lane concepts might be the best way of using scarce resources. Fairly compact convoys of forty to sixty ships would be given three or four escorts, which could include an 'Arapaho' container merchant ship with prefabricated facilities for operating a small squadron of helicopters – not as cheap an idea as it sounds but a very good way of providing more helicopters for ASW work where most needed. These convoys would not all follow exactly the same track, but their routes would differ only enough to confuse the enemy's picture. It would then be possible to form the remaining available ASW escorts (including SSNs and LRMP aircraft) into at least three route-in-use support groups which, operating well clear of noisy merchant vessels, should have numerous detection opportunities.

Merchant vessels can also contribute significantly to their own defence. Acoustic deception equipment is feasible for fast, independently routed ships, while speed itself is still an excellent defence against torpedo attack as any submariner will grudgingly acknowledge; and anti-submarine weapons, notably IKARA – a rocket torpedo carrier with a ten-mile range – can be installed in boxed or simple form inexpensively on many merchant decks for use in conjunction with an adjacent escort's fire-control data. The concept of self-protection, to some degree, for merchant ships could be taken a good deal further without prohibitive cost. The more ASW systems and devices there are at sea, the more difficult it is for a submarine commanding officer to take them into account; and anything that confuses or deceives him – from course and speed variations (zig-zags) through camouflage and ESM to any way of exploding charges in his vicinity – is a worthwhile addition to the ASW bag of tricks.

It is a great pity that old-fashioned depth-charges have largely been discarded: even dropped at random they can be very off-putting to a submariner. One simple alternative would be to convert a number of gunnery shells to explode at depth.[4]

Looked at from a Soviet submariner's point of view, the ASW systems arrayed against him must appear formidable although not impregnable, especially to a mass assault. The best way of gauging their effectiveness might be to follow the fortunes of the Northern Fleet boats in an *imaginary* scenario where tension rises to the point of crisis and open warfare at sea.

The difficulty is that imagination has to play such a very large part in predicting the turn of events; and practically no prediction in the past has proved correct. The more closely one examines various possible situations, in fact, the less conceivable they seem to be!

Commentators usually propound their theories at the stage when battle is joined. But when and where will that occur? Who will fire the first shot? Will so-called tactical nuclear weapons be employed at sea? At what point, if ever, will strategic nuclear weapons be launched? Will bases and communications remain intact if the conflict is non-nuclear? Will there be a formal declaration of war? If not, will it be obvious that NATO units, specifically submarines, have been attacked by Soviet forces? At what point can fully operational barriers be established and minefields activated without triggering open conflict if shots have not already been exchanged? Do politicians, anywhere, have a clear, unambiguous policy that lays down limits – political or military boundaries – which, if transgressed, will oblige them to initiate actual fighting? If they do (which is doubtful), will they seek to limit the area of fighting and the weapons used, or will they fling all available forces into the entire arena?

These questions, and too many others like them, are impossible to answer with any degree of conviction, but they are particularly relevant to underwater warfare because of its covert nature: we are no longer faced with a clearly visible, cut-and-dried, don't-do-it-or-else military situation, as Britain was in 1939. Submarines can pose an immediate threat without necessarily raising the political temperature. When and how should NATO respond?

Some kind of answers have to be found even if they can be no more than guesses – and highly imaginative guesses at that – because otherwise our anti-submarine fences and defences cannot be erected in time to prevent submarines from the Soviet Fleet gathering in the Norwegian Sea and pouring into the Eastern Atlantic, which is generally agreed to be the most crucial area in any major warfare scenario.

So, with a multitude of provisos and reservations at the back of our minds, let us imagine a 'Red Alert' in the Soviet Northern Fleet arising from heightened tension between the superpowers due, like as not, to affairs in the Middle East.

The three prime NATO war-management intentions – maintaining the initiative, defence in depth, and containment – are well known in Severomorsk, Kola HQ. Now, two carrier battle groups comprising the

NATO (mainly US Navy) Striking Fleet in dispersed formation are in the Eastern Atlantic, edging towards the Norwegian Sea; although contact was not maintained with them during their Atlantic crossing, they are now being tracked continuously by satellites, aircraft and two SSNs. Operational NATO SSBNs are assumed to be on patrol, but their positions are not known; two Soviet SSNs off the American east coast and one off Faslane, Scotland, are waiting to try to trail any further SSBNs which may be sailed. All available NATO SSNs and SSKs have been fully stored for war and are at sea. It is presumed that choke points are being patrolled. British and American LRMP aircraft are certainly covering the southern Greenland–Norway area, while a Norwegian P–3 is on surveillance patrol off the northern Norwegian coast, covering the exit from the Barents Sea, and a US P–3 is reporting movements in the centre of the Norwegian Sea.

NATO forces in Norway have been strengthened and an amphibious force – clearly destined for further reinforcement – supported by a battleship surface action group (BBSAG), centred on the USS *Iowa*, is moving towards Iceland.

Transports and supply ships are assembling into ten fifty-ship convoys on the US Atlantic seabord for sailing at four-day intervals from the declared day plus six; and two or three small, fast ten-ship convoys are somewhere in mid-Atlantic, as well as some fast, independently routed container ships. The British Naval Control of Shipping organisation has been brought into effect. Fifty-ship convoys will each have ten dedicated surface escorts; the fast ten-ship convoys already at sea have three escorts each; and two or three support groups are expected to guard the flanks of sea-lanes, but the routes that will be followed are not known. (In fact, Soviet intelligence has probably overestimated the number of escorts available and their speed of advance.)

The Soviet Union has been warned politely, at the United Nations, that any submarines passing submerged between Greenland and Iceland run the risk of mines. Intelligence suggests that this is bluff at present, but will soon become an established fact.

The KGB and GRU have not advised Moscow of French (non-NATO) intentions, which probably means that the French do not know themselves. Three French SSBNs and half a dozen SSNs/SSKs are at sea, but are not expected to take an active part, initially at least, if hostilities commence.

As a convenience for our purpose in this hypothetical scenario, we will say that the commander-in-chief Northern Fleet at Severomorsk has too much on his hands to concern himself with what the Black Sea and Pacific

Fleets may be doing (in fact he would probably not be told) or what is happening on land, but he knows that the Baltic Fleet is preparing to sail four SSGNs and twelve SSKs against naval forces and shipping around Northern Europe, and that some of these boats will lay mines. He also knows that, at an appropriate time, Spetsnaz units not under his direct control, KGB hit squads and established agents in Europe, Scandinavia, Greenland and Iceland will be signalled to destroy communications and early warning installations, wreck bases and undertake numerous *mokroe dela* (wet jobs) – the assassination of important political and military personages. American cruise-missile bases in Europe will also come under covert attack, notably at Greenham Common, where female Spetsnaz operators are said to have infiltrated women's anti-nuclear protest groups.[5]

The Politburo has announced its intention of 'taking all appropriate measures' to prevent Western aggressors from threatening Soviet territory by landing more troops in Norway. An Amphibious Force, waiting in the Kola Inlet and itself destined for Norway, is one of those measures.

The commander-in-chief's orders, emanating from the Defence Council, are straightforward and he has translated them into Operation Orders for the submarine forces under his command which are immediately available, some units being out of area:

a. Non-operational SSBNs in harbour to prepare as many missiles as possible for firing.
b. Submarine, air and surface protection to be augmented for the twenty fully operational SSBNs in the Barents Sea and under-ice bastions – four SSNs committed to this task, *Group Okhrana*.
c. *Group Aktiv*. Three SSNs to support own amphibious force.
d. *Group Bitva*. Ten SSGNs and seven SSNs to oppose the Striking Fleet.
e. *Group Vilka*. Five SSGNs, two SSGs, two SSNs and ten SSKs to oppose the NATO amphibious force and blockade the North Norwegian Sea against advancing NATO submarines.
f. *Group Glava*. Three SSGNs, two SSGs and fifteen SSKs to straddle Atlantic supply routes. A second wave – mainly SSKs forming Group *Doroga* – prepare to follow (bringing the total number of anti-shipping SSKs in the Atlantic to forty).
g. *War outfits*: twenty-five per cent nuclear warheads, seventy-five per cent conventional.
h. *Nuclear weapons*: NOT to be fired without explicit authority.

The Defence Council's appreciation of the situation is that NATO will pursue its forward defence strategy and not only endeavour to contain

Soviet forces in the Norwegian Sea but, while strengthening its Norwegian flank, seek to drive them back towards the Soviet Union. Control will be vested in NATO's Northwood HQ, where the new Upcon command and control system has been installed. This system is a target for two Spetsnaz units already in the vicinity.

The various Northern Fleet and Baltic submarine groups are duly deployed. There has been no declaration of war but, in response to the Kremlin's threat of taking 'all appropriate measures', NATO, led by the United States, has announced that any Soviet forces, including submarines, which put themselves in such a position as to threaten the safety of NATO military forces or shipping will be considered as a threat and will be attacked.

NATO makes no mention of a specific exclusion zone, presumably because of anti-British criticism during the 1982 Falklands campaign resulting from the *General Belgrano* being sunk outside the declared zone. There is a clear implication that NATO Rules of Engagement are not inhibiting, and that individual commanders have been given wide powers of discretion. Intelligence suggests that Soviet SSBNs will be trailed if possible, but not attacked until ordered.

On the Soviet side, no unit of any kind is permitted to use weapons of any kind against surface or air forces without the authority of the Defence Council, transmitted via the commander-in-chief Northern Fleet – unless it comes under attack itself, when it is to counterattack and report. Submerged submarines, however, are to be attacked immediately without prior authorisation whenever opportunity arises. SSBNs are the priority targets and territorial limits are to be ignored.

It is now *Kraisiz* day – 'K-Day' – in Soviet HQs. On K minus two primary NATO communications were seriously disrupted and vital electrical supplies were severed; remaining radio circuits are now being jammed as far as possible. Widespread strikes in Europe, particularly in the UK, are restricting movements; dockers are refusing to load cargoes at major American ports, and large sections of the media are blaming the United States for warmongering. Hysteria is rampant and the British Cabinet is thankfully congratulating itself on mobilising the bulk of UK forces in good time and relaxing the Rules of Engagement to the extent that commanders at sea can, largely, act on their own initiative if communications from Northwood Upcon fail completely for a time. Communication channels to US and British SSBNs are expected to remain intact, with back-up systems available if necessary.

We will now stretch our imagination still further to see what happens, through Soviet eyes, when the opposite forces meet.

On K plus one an SSK, Foxtrot 351 (Captain-Lieutenant Arvanov), which has been operating out of area, finds itself in the grain of a vast NATO armada south of Iceland. The crew go to action stations and the captain, *zampolit* and Party officials hold a conference in the wardroom. No permission to engage has been received and the only safe thing to do is to surface – but that is unthinkable. Instead, the consortium decides to snorkel at top speed (ten knots) out of the way and transmit an enemy report. It is the last that is ever heard of Foxtrot 351.

The signal is intercepted by several ships in the Striking Fleet and D/F bearings are plotted. Almost simultaneously, F–351's ESM equipment picks up aircraft radar signals which rapidly rise to danger level (indicating that the aircraft is receiving return echoes). F–351 stops snorkelling and goes deep: Arvanov knows he has been nailed but does not admit that to the *zampolit*. At 100 metres (there is no layer and sonar conditions are good) he sets course north-east at eight knots, which he can maintain for about twelve hours. He can hear the thundering herd astern, but there are no indications of his being tracked. (In fact, passive sonobuoys have been dropped and the Nimrod which discovered him is plotting distinct signals.) The screws are not cavitating, but F–351 has been at sea for several weeks and the casing is rattling badly.

The American ASW commander, in conformity with instructions, orders one of the two Sikorsky helicopters despatched to the scene to drop small grenades by way of 'firing a shot across the bow'. Arvanov realises that he is being ordered to surface and is inclined to do so now that the enemy knows where he is; but the *zampolit* forbids it and embarks on a stirring Marxist lecture to the crew on the intercom. None of the American tactical signals on UHF has been heard by Soviet listening stations.

The Nimrod, circling overhead, watches while the helicopters dunk their active sonars. Arvanov hears transmissions in the ten kHz band and knows well enough what they signify. But which way to turn? There is no means of calculating where a helicopter will dunk next: it cannot be tracked or evaded like a surface ship. Wriggle though he does, loud transmissions come now from this direction, now from that. He has sat himself in the proverbial Russian puddle.

After thirty minutes of this the American ASW commander reckons he has been patient enough. The main body is only a few miles now from the datum: the PROBSUB will have to be attacked.

Arvanov and his people listen impassively as sonar transmissions sound through the hull. It comes as no great surprise when they are joined by the distinctive high-pitched pinging of ASW torpedoes: the

choppers have dropped two Mark 46 active homers. One is a dud and
goes dead almost immediately; the other circles and homes relentlessly.
The explosion, when it comes just abaft the engine room, is followed
by a massive inrush of water, which bulkheads and watertight doors
cannot resist. Arvanov and his crew in the control room are engulfed.
A few survive for long minutes in very highly pressurised pockets of air
forward, but the remainder are mercifully knocked unconscious before
they drown.

The commander-in-chief Northern Fleet is not, of course, apprised
of Foxtrot 351's loss, although he realises from his Ops Room Chart
that the boat is likely to have been overtaken by the Striking Fleet and
he is well aware of enemy air activity. First blood to NATO and still no
authority to shoot from the Kremlin – but the Defence Council is
ready to give the word and is more or less permanently in session in
the nuclear-proof deep underground Supreme Command Post
beneath the huge natural granite monolith at Zhiguli, 400 miles south-
east of Moscow.

On K plus three the NATO amphibious force is in the southern
part of the Norwegian Sea and a landing is assessed as imminent. The
Soviet amphibious force, with three guardian SSNs, is off Narvik to
the north. The Striking Fleet is manoeuvring south of the gap between
Greenland and Iceland, which is now assumed to be CAPTOR-mined.
It is, nevertheless, of such importance to engage the Striking Fleet
when ordered that two SSGNs and two SSNs from Group *Bitva* are
routed through this dangerous passage in line ahead. Three boats get
through.

Minefield tactics

In the spring of 1942 submarines of the Red Banner Fleet breaking
out into the Baltic were directed to keep to shallow water in order to
avoid minefields, but where this was not possible they were directed
to try to pass beneath the mines: when the noise of a mooring wire
was heard scraping past the hull, they were to 'stop motors until the
sound has ceased'. Soviet submariners left no record of their reaction to this bland instruction.

On the same day the remainder of Group *Bitva* pass through the
Iceland–Norway gap: their passage is detected by submarines and aircraft. For a long while numerous contacts are tracked, but the NATO
boats can only pass enemy reports because the transitters are not
posing a definite threat. SOSUS chains are flooded with information.

When Group *Glava* – five nuclear-powered submarines preceding fifteen diesel boats – also surges through the gap the NATO commander loses track of the situation: all he can be sure of is that an awful lot of submarines are loose in the Atlantic.

Meanwhile, emboldened perhaps by the thought that he is close to home and its defences, Captain Second Rank Anatoly Bogdanov in the 'Charlie II' SSGN *Murmanskiy Komsomolets* (Group *Vilka*) comes very shallow to observe the hovering NATO amphibious force with ESM and, if possible, visually. The Charlie's electronic equipment is sophisticated and Bogdanov keeps a careful ESM anti-aircraft watch while having the electronic-visual look that few submariners can resist; but the masts are sighted by a Sea King helicopter which is keeping electronic silence (like the rest of the force at that time) and which Bogdanov fails to see through the periscope, so confident is he in his ESM. The Sea King makes a flash sighting report and the amphibious force commander orders two Type-42 destroyers, each with its Lynx Mark 2 helicopter, to search and attack. The chatter is intercepted, relayed to Bogdanov and to the commander-in-chief's headquarters in the Kola, where it is accurately interpreted. Within minutes the Defence Council authorises 'all defence measures to be implemented forthwith'. The very short (three-letter) coded signal is transmitted to all Northern and Baltic fleet submarines on ELF, VLF and HF simultaneously, and repeated at fifteen-minute intervals for the next six hours. The situation is correctly appreciated at Northwood, with agreement in Washington, and the NATO commander lifts the few remaining restrictions on conventional systems.

Bogdanov recognises that he has started the Third World War, but after all both his division commander (who is on board) and his political officer approved his original action in positively identifying the NATO force. Unfortunately he is closer to the enemy than he would wish: his six SS-N-9 missiles (out of the total of eight) which have conventional heads are not intended for firing at virtually point-blank range, so he decides (after due consultation with his naval and political superiors) to open the range by retiring in a north-westerly direction at high speed. His movements are limited – as are all submarines in their respective groups – by the size of his group's operating area; if the *Murmanskiy Komsomolets*, or any other boat, goes outside its assigned group patrol zone (which can be advancing with time in a moving haven when required, as it is for Groups *Bitva* and *Glava* for example) it risks attack by its own forces – particularly when so near to the Soviet coastline. Looking at his chart Bogdanov sees that he can only retire for twenty miles or so, which means launching missiles from about thirty miles where, in fact, his own updated fire-control data will suffice.

The destroyers, with a best speed of thirty knots, will take a long time to catch the SSGN at twenty-four knots, but Bogdanov is living in a fool's paradise: the Lynx helicopters speed on ahead, dunking their sonars from time to time, controlled by the destroyers, while a Norwegian Orion lays sonobuoys in his path. The Orion will be shot down by Soviet fighters in an hour or so, but while it still flies it guides the ASW forces unerringly towards their noisy target.

When Bogdanov slows down and comes quietly to periscope depth his sonar operators report destroyers approaching at high speed and occasional helicopter sonar transmissions. He has a paradoxical feeling of being cornered in the open sea. He wonders what the rest of Group *Vilka* is doing: none of the boats, in these circumstances, can talk to each other without giving away their positions. It is, suddenly, rather lonely. All he can do is to fight it out; but the British destroyers remain outside the danger range of his torpedoes while refining their plots and directing their helicopters. Happily for Bogdanov the immediate ASW attack is unsuccessful, and while the ships are standing off, fully occupied with what they classify as a PROBSUB, an undetected 'Victor' SSN classifies itself as a CERTSUB by sneaking up and putting two fish into the water – one of which hits and stops the leading destroyer, temporarily wrecking the ASW picture.

This gives Bogdanov the opportunity he is looking for: his computer-ised system instantly updates fire-control data on the main force. Guessing that the *gelikoptery* are now lacking effective control and are, for the moment, not a direct menace (there ought to have been a loud bang by now if they were), Bogdanov starts to launch missiles, from submerged, at the amphibious force, aiming 'into the brown'.

Meanwhile, the other SSGNs, SSGs and SSKs are not being idle. Torpedoes and missiles are showering the force, and USS *Iowa* receives no fewer than five torpedo and six missile hits which put her out of action. Other ships are also hit: two transports and a tanker are sunk and a carrier is severely damaged. However, both SSGs, one of the SSGNs, and two SSKs are destroyed by NATO SSNs before firing their weapons.

The NATO Striking Fleet is also under attack and a number of ships are disabled in the first encounter. (It will appear, from subsequent analysis, that five or six missile hits are required to put a carrier out of action and that the hit probability against a large defended target is quite low. In addition, about one in three missiles malfunction.) The smaller ships have received very few hits because the missiles automatically went for the larger targets and numerous decoys.

On the Soviet side submarine casualties are heavy. The ASW opposition is unexpectedly tough – much tougher than the commanding officers were led to believe from last year's summer exercise, when they were opposed by their own submarines and surface units. American and British SSNs account for three SSGNs and as many SSNs in the outfield almost before battle has been joined: the ADCAP Mark 48 torpedoes are not audible until too late (intelligence was wrong about that), and the British Tigerfish, rather surprisingly after such a chequered career (the GRU has provided a comprehensive briefing), actually performs as the makers claim – or, at least, enough of them have functioned correctly during this particular battle. Two giant 'Oscars' (SSGNs) are among the victims of fixed-wing and surface teams: their vast bulk (14,000 tons) has proved all too detectable by active sonobuoys and surface sonar at extreme range.

While all this has been going on, a US '688' class SSN encounters a monster 'Typhoon' SSBN under the ice. The 'Typhoon' is quiet, but not quiet enough. Admittedly the '688' virtually stumbled across the leviathan, but passive detection (at quite close range) in the low-frequency, narrow band quickly led to positive classification and the development of a fire-control solution. One ADCAP Mark 48 found its mark before the 'Typhoon's' captain (a man of immense seniority and dignity but not blessed with much awareness of tactical problems) was aware that a US boat was anywhere around. Although badly shaken, the huge submarine had no difficulty in surfacing through seven feet of ice, where it became invulnerable to further attack, and the crew immediately set about repairs that would get it back to base.

Another of the 'Los Angeles' class, one of the early SSNs of the '688' class, was on surveillance patrol off the North Cape when the signal to engage all Soviet forces was received on VLF. The skipper, Commander Blackjack Barnacle III, is gung-ho and raring to go. He has heard a seemingly endless stream of Soviet submarines go by without being able to do a thing about them. Now he can shoot whatever turns up.

BB III is an action man. The dull details of acoustic housekeeping are not for him. Although there have been incidents in recent days which should have cautioned him that, from time to time, the opposition has had a sniff of him, he reckons he can outfight any Russkie: the immortal words of Admiral David F. Farragut, uttered as US ships entered a minefield during the Battle of Mobile on 5 August 1864, are framed above the desk in his stateroom: 'Damn the torpedoes! Captain Drayton, go ahead! Jouett, full speed!' Caution, says BB III, is cowardice.

His crew think BB III is the greatest; and he cares for them above all else. He pays little attention to voluminous regulations: rules are meant to be broken – and many great men would agree with him. Unfortunately, some of the wise rules have been jettisoned with the 'bull'. Neither he nor his officers probe and peer into odd corners because they believe that would be interfering with the crew's privacy. Consequently kit, spare parts and stores are crammed into spaces where they should not be; and in several places they are short-circuiting the sound insulation of machinery so that noise is transmitted directly to the hull – and out.

BB III does not have to wait long. Sonar detects and classifies a 'Delta IV' SSBN and an 'Alfa' SSN, presumably escorting the 'Boomer', on a course that will take them to the ice-edge. BB III starts his approach at twelve knots, noting that the 'Alfa' is between him and the 'Boomer', which is his priority target.

The Soviet boats continue on course until the '688' is 4,000 yards from the Alfa, with the 'Boomer' beyond and coming into firing range for a couple of Mark 48s.

Suddenly the 'Alfa' whips round, like a terrier, straight towards the American boat and makes a succession of very loud transmissions on medium-frequency fire-control sonar. Almost at once two torpedoes are heard approaching and transmitting. BB III has been heard and nailed. He just manages to get two Mark 48s into the water, aimed at the 'Alfa', before the Soviet torpedoes arrive; but the 'Alfa' has loosed its decoys and gone deep and quiet. BB III's housekeeping is to blame: he and his crew are dead.

At about the same time, and not far off, a British SSN is sunk by a mine. In other areas, too, there have been losses due to mines: the indications are that a British SSBN has been damaged in Scottish waters and that four NATO SSKs have been sunk in the North Sea and Baltic (no German U-boats are amongst the latter because they have taken exceptionally prudent precautions in their designs for anti-mine protection).

On K plus five the first fast convoy (ten ships and their escorts), steaming at twenty knots, comes under attack from a sub-group of five SSKs from Group *Glava*. Only one commanding officer is, on this occasion, Nelsonian: he closes at seventeen knots (flattening his battery) and fires a full salvo at a rear container ship from 3,000 yards, achieving one hit and stopping the ship. He has been heard by one escort for about ten minutes, but it has been impossible to put any ASW unit between the attacker and its quarry in time to prevent the determined approach, and there are no depth charges available to drop and scare him off. With a 'flaming datum' and a flat box, he has no chance of escape: he becomes a posthumous medal winner. The other SSKs are very cautious and fire from long range – nearly 10,000 yards – discovering in the process that it is very hard to hit fast targets. All the torpedoes miss, but the attackers are not counterattacked.

The other sub-groups of SSGNs, SSGs and SSKs endeavour to place themselves on the most probable convoy routes, but they have no real idea of what these are, and the commander-in-chief of the Northern Fleet does not know either. In fact, he has a major problem sorting out the situation. Friendly and enemy forces are inextricably mixed in the Norwegian and Barents seas (Soviet aircraft have already attacked two Red Fleet submarines by mistake), and the flocks of boats now out of area, engaged with the Striking Fleet and convoys, are more or less out of positive control. Northern Fleet communication systems are now partially jammed, and the overall plot at Murmansk is exceedingly confused. The whole affair, on both sides, has by now become a 'roller-bearing, self-adjusting shambles' – an expression that was once used in describing to a senior officer the flight deck and hangar operations of an aircraft carrier.[6]

The Norwegian Sea and its approaches and exits comprise quite a limited area, further restricted by US and Soviet mining. A very large number of ships, submarines, fixed-wing aircraft and helicopters are liable to be milling about in a confined space at the outbreak of practically any kind of imaginable conflict.

Let us say – because an ending has to be devised – that a certain state at the eastern end of the Mediterranean (the one which caused all the trouble at the beginning) detonates a nuclear device as the final solution to its own territorial confrontation. The superpowers instantly perceive – and agree over a revived and red-hot hotline – that this is the beginning of the end unless they extinguish the atomic spark together forthwith. All the forces in the Atlantic and Norwegian Sea withdraw licking their wounds.

We have brought communications sketchily into the play and, for simplicity, we have assumed that strategic and tactical circuits are operable, albeit that secondary links may have replaced primary systems which have been put out of action. But the Soviets are keenly aware that everything depends upon command, control and communications: if the latter are almost totally disrupted on either side – perhaps only temporarily – our make-believe story might have been very different.

Suppose that on K-Day the Defence Council orders an SSBN, equipped with at least one suitable weapon, to launch a megaton warhead set to detonate one hundred miles above the earth's atmosphere in a carefully calculated position – say south of Iceland at the latitude of Glasgow – such that the Eastern Atlantic, UK and Western Europe, North Sea and Norwegian Sea approaches are subjected to electro-magnetic pulse effect.

Would this by itself trigger a nuclear exchange? The probability is that it would not. But it would immediately have a devastating effect on communications, as well as on unshielded shipboard, airborne and shore devices which use integrated or printed circuits, semi-conductors and micro-electronic chips, including digital computers and electronic sensors. It would, on the other hand, be much less likely to damage equipment which uses old-fashioned vacuum tubes or low-current switches and relays. Critics sneered at the MIG–25 Foxbat whose pilot defected to Japan with his aircraft in 1976 because relatively antiquated vacuum tubes rather than solid state electronics were included in many of its unprotected avionic systems; but in the light of EMP effects, the Foxbat was sensibly designed. High-power, high-current systems like radar are not affected by EMP, although there will be a lengthy radar, as well as a communications, blackout.

An enormous amount of effort is going into 'hardening' ships, aircraft and systems against EMP; and fibre optics, which do not conduct electricity, can be employed instead of conducive wiring. The cost is very high. Submarine equipment, however, is not susceptible and there is no need for expensive hardening.

Presumably it is intended that all ships and aircraft will be protected from the effects of EMP in due course. If they are not the results of a single nuclear explosion in space could be catastrophic.

EMP problems aside, a conflict at sea, in what the Soviets term the 'Atlantic Oceanic Theatre of Military Operations', has the seeds of chaos. It is to be hoped that, if fighting starts, our SSNs are on station, ready to stem the tidal wave, and that the situation will allow them to shoot before containment is breached. Whatever happens, common sense suggests that mining – with some involvement by our submarines – will be an essential adjunct to Western operations; and mines will certainly be employed by the Soviets in large numbers. Soviet SSGNs and SSGs could undertake preliminary minelays without detracting too much from their main objectives.

Reverting to the commander-in-chief Northern Fleet's viewpoint, let us see what he might reasonably expect his submarines to achieve against the USA–Europe Sea Line of Communication (SLOC). If they are deployed as we have pictured he will have twenty boats available for the first wave of attacks on the first convoy (fifty ships) which sails on K plus six and will be passing through the eastern Atlantic from about K plus eleven (twenty knots) or K plus fifteen (fifteen knots). It has been assessed[7] that the Soviet net will be widely spread and that only twenty per cent of submarines deployed will be able to engage a particular convoy. This means that four boats will engage the initial and most urgently needed convoy of all (after the two or three initial ten-ship military convoys that we have, rather optimistically, said were sailed early in anticipation of trouble). It has been reckoned[8] that, given the ASW protection proposed earlier (ten dedicated surface escorts), two of the four submarines will be lost, disabled or otherwise eliminated (for instance, by weapon exhaustion) from the immediate scene, in exchange for two merchant ships per attempted submarine attack – that is, eight merchant ships go down. Thus forty-two merchant ships get through – eighty-four per cent.

If, however, deployments are made in time for forty submarines (first *and* second waves) to threaten the convoy routes before the gaps are blocked and submarines start being lost in transit, eight boats could engage the first convoy with four losses in exchange for six merchants, allowing thirty-four to get through – sixty-eight per cent.

On the whole, given that only a small proportion of Soviet submarine captains are 'aces' and that a fair number of conventional weapons malfunction, the estimate of merchant ship losses in the open eastern Atlantic might be thought a little on the high side – so long as the 'aces' do not maroon the escorts in mid-ocean by clobbering the tankers intended to replenish them.

So far, the figures, as we have conjectured them, do not look too discouraging; but, unfortunately, we are still far from the end of the tale. When the convoys cross the continental shelf and come into relatively shallow water the ASW problems increase exponentially. Towed sonar arrays are of little use; non-subs (false contacts) abound; old wrecks have not, apparently, been marked with distinctive sonar responders; tides and currents complicate matters; ships are constrained geographically so that it is difficult to take evasive action, let alone adopt evasive routing; and in bottlenecks (inshore choke points) a submarine, with ship-noise all around, should find it difficult to miss, and fairly easy to escape the consequences. The unglamorous inshore ASW battle is not, regrettably, a simple extension of majestic ASW in the open Atlantic Ocean and Norwegian Sea. It is relatively easy to spot a rabbit in the middle of a field, but catching it running through the hedgerows is very much more difficult. However, NATO SSKs should be invaluable in winkling out the opposition inshore – if enough are available in the task.

One can play with figures endlessly, but there appear to be some fairly credible constants:

a. The first convoys, which will be almost wholly military in content, are bound to be the most critical: without them Europe would be easy meat if the Soviets advance on land through the central front – and such an advance must clearly be guarded against even if our limited scenario did not imagine it.

b. Hence, the first convoys need the most protection; so it might be thought prudent to divert a carrier battle group (CVGB) from the Striking Fleet, together with SSNs, for convoy support – although this might go against what has become a traditional aggressive posture for the US Navy. The Soviets might take the possibility into consideration and deploy more submarines against convoys and less against the Striking Fleet. However, it is difficult to envisage forty submarines, the number often quoted, being thrown into the anti-shipping battle at the outset; the later waves are liable to suffer heavy losses, principally from SSN attacks, while breaking out of the Norwegian Sea – if NATO boats are allowed to engage early enough.

c. Missiles have to be launched in very large quantities if they are to disable high-value units (HVUs) and abort their missions ('mission kills'). Extrapolating such information as there is,[9] five or six conventional hits would be needed to disable a large carrier and seven or eight missiles would be required to saturate the defences: in other words, the price of admission, as it has been called,[10] is twelve to fourteen missiles. Assuming that some missiles malfunction (which, from all experience, is inevitable) the figure is actually more like fifteen to twenty for a minimum disabling salvo against a single HVU.

d. The numbers above apply to a self-defended single-ship target. If there are numerous ships in a CVBG, as there will be, and the missile-launcher wants to be, say, eighty per cent sure of neutralising an HVU he must fire many more missiles: the number depends on the number of other ships around as well as on missile discrimination capability, but it could be in excess of fifty.

e. 'Echo II' and 'Charlie I' and 'II' SSGNs have eight missile tubes; a 'Papa' has ten and an 'Oscar' twenty-four. We have suggested that about a quarter of the weapons embarked might be nuclear.

Taken together, the various (somewhat simplistic) factors which we have assembled lead to the conclusion, which we devoutly hope is justified, that the commander-in-chief Northern Fleet is not going to have the easy ride that Western media would have us believe; his cronies elsewhere will have their problems too. But there is one vital proviso: NATO cannot possibly afford to decrease its current level of ASW forces under the sea, on the sea and in the air. The balance is scarcely in our favour and further Soviet submarine advances will demand numerically more, not less, ASW platforms, however high their individual quality may be.

It goes without saying, however, that if nuclear-missile warheads are employed the whole picture changes dramatically. In that case practically all that we have suggested is meaningless, and the only ASW platforms which will be able to operate effectively and continuously will be SSNs. The prudent priority for the provision of ASW units in the light of this very real possibility is obvious – SSNs; but, unfortunately, it is equally obvious that ASW surface and airborne forces may not be reduced to make up submarine numbers. ASW is an unavoidably expensive game.

There are limitless variables in anti-submarine warfare and our scenario has simply illustrated a few possible situations: the assumptions and consequences may be justified or unjustified – and, for sure, the plot is too set-piece. It is anybody's guess what will really happen if war breaks out, and if a predicted pattern of events turns out to be correct it will be purely coincidental.

Full-length, multi-act ASW dramas have been acted out very much more thoroughly in high-level war games with stage settings à la carte, numerous changes of scenery and a full supporting cast. The dramas must be difficult to judge for realism, but they can certainly allow for certain interactions and re-runs which exercises at sea cannot. Further upstream, computerised modelling is an invaluable (and still underemployed) method of refining tactical data and determining operational requirements a good deal more precisely than picking them off the deckhead.

Presumably, realistic assessments about ASW possibilities and probabilities in war have been made and agreed, although we have been unable, as yet, to find any published reference or abstract which quotes them. If they exist and are too highly classified for publication that is understandable: but we suggest that open, informed debate about ASW need not prejudice security and that, along the lines discussed in this chapter, it could be profitable. Security of truly secret material is vital, but if our broad ASW capabilities are made public, assuming that they are good enough to boast about, they will bear importantly on deterrence. If, on the other hand, our ASW effort is not good enough it will be essential to gain political and public support to improve it. Either way, it will be no bad thing to talk about it.

8

The Smaller Navies

With modern techniques and weapons a smaller navy with several high-performance ships and craft could well turn out the victor if engaged by a much larger fleet of elderly vessels. In the later years of the twentieth century the habit of counting numbers of ships, even of adding up the total tonnage of a fleet is, and will become even more so, an exercise both futile and misleading. In some cases, when manipulated by unscrupulous or ignorant politicians, it is even mischievous.

Here the overall title is used to indicate those navies not covered by previous chapters, but which vary in the strength of their submarine force – from the growing power of the extremely efficient Japanese Maritime Self-Defence Force to the pair of boats operated by Colombia. For convenience it is divided into three sections: Soviet provided, South American, and a general list. Submarine forces are very widely dispersed geographically and may be encountered practically anywhere.

Before launching into the first of these sections a few points on submarine efficiency must be considered. The most important single factor is, as in every maritime context, the men who operate the submarines. In a surface ship, if errors short of the catastrophic are made the vessel will continue to float. In a submarine small errors of commission or omission can, in both peace and war, result in the loss of the boat. In June 1939 HMS *Thetis* sank in Liverpool Bay because the test cock of a torpedo tube had not been adequately cleared of paint.

Given a well-trained crew remarkable things can be done with a submarine, even when the designers have produced something which the operators consider inadequate for the task. Nevertheless, submarine design requires continual attention to every sort of detail and is greatly assisted by the continuity resulting from a steady building stream. The remarkable success of the West German submarine yards stems from the application of innovation to a steady flow of designs conceived by a permanent group of naval architects.

But no submarine of any type, no matter what its design or means of propulsion, will function satisfactorily without regular and meticulous attention to maintenance and refit schedules. If these are in any way skimped or delayed the result can be fatal – the effect of continuing and total immersion in seawater has an insidious effect on many areas of the submarine. Whereas the surface ship's hull is subject to reversals of stress caused by wave motion, that of a submarine is constantly affected by variations in water pressure as it changes depth. Periodical docking and examination are essential.

Having provided a well-designed submarine with a well-trained crew and made arrangements for regular maintenance, the next responsibility of the operating authorities rests in their own offices. The patrol cycle of a squadron in wartime, and the requirements of exercises, trials, weapon training, foreign visits and leave in peacetime require very complex calculations of availability before the final plan is laid. In wartime and in peacetime exercises the command must have a clear appreciation of what are feasible tasks, what might be rewarding and successful tasks, and when to refuse the more outlandish demands of their superiors. The old adage, 'The possible we can do now, the impossible will take a little longer,' is an idiot's creed if applied to submarine operations. Because of extraordinary circumstances inordinate and improper demands can be made on a submarine command. When the invested Japanese garrisons on the Pacific Islands in the Second World War were in trouble they were supported by stores landed from submarines diverted from proper operational tasks. Because of inadequate numbers there have been occasions when submarines have been despatched on patrol with inadequate maintenance and tired crews. The almost inevitable result of 'missing, presumed lost' resulted from a failure to observe the old but still valid rule of thumb when operating non-nuclear submarines that, to retain one on patrol, a total of three is needed – one on station, one on passage, and one in harbour. The only variation to this rule is when the distance to the patrol area is short, such as in coastal surveillance operations in home waters.

In a number of the navies to be considered here this task is probably at the head of the list and accounts for the small size of the submarine force. Conversely, the small size of the naval budget may dictate the size of that force and, therefore, the tasks which it can undertake. But the infrastructure required to support two submarines needs very little expansion to accommodate double that number – the peak in overheads flattens into a gently rising plateau until the number is notably increased. Docks and workshops may have to be worked harder, but they will remain adequate.

None of the navies in this chapter possesses nuclear-powered submarines, although some have pretensions in that direction. These will be mentioned in passing, but the enormous increase in capital, training and support costs must rule out this option for the great majority.

SOVIET PROVIDED

Once the Soviet post-war submarine building programme was under way and the new 'Whiskey' class boats were becoming available in abundance, the USSR was in a position to offload some of its more elderly craft on its friends. The first of these, as discussed in the following chapter, was China. The new navy of the PLA was barely three years old when, in July 1953, the first 'M' class boat – a mobile training craft – arrived. Nine months later in 1954, a surprisingly short gestation period for a submarine force, two 'S' class arrived, to be followed in October by two 'M5' class. The first steps had been taken in the formation of a Sino–Soviet Pacific fleet, in which it seems likely that submarines were planned to play an important part.

In the Black Sea Romania had taken over her first submarine, an Italian-built boat, in 1936. In 1938 she began her own construction programme at Galatz, using German designs for the only two submarines completed. In 1957 these three were joined by four Soviet 'M5' class, soon to be followed by eight larger submarines of the 'Shch' class, but by 1962 all the submarine group had been deleted – either scrapped or returned to the USSR. This remarkable volte-face, presumably agreed with the Soviet Navy, cannot be explained here; the Romanian Navy remains bereft of submarines.

The sturdy Bulgarian ally received a complete navy in the post-war period, ranging from a destroyer to a tug and including three 'M' class and two 'Whiskey' class submarines. For an organisation which had numbered only eleven small patrol and torpedo craft in 1945, this was an expansion which must have strained the available training organisation. The 'M' class were rapidly disposed of, two being replaced by the 'Whiskeys', which remained in service until 1972–3. Their replacements, two 'Romeo' class, were then over ten years old and were certainly due for replacement by the mid-1980s.

A somewhat operatic performance had, meanwhile, taken place in the Mediterranean. As the Soviet incursion into Greece failed, so they sought other areas where they could establish their influence. Albania offered an inviting haven – staunchly Communist, and occupying an important strategic position roughly half-way along the Mediterranean and commanding the mouth of the Adriatic. In 1960 the transfer of two 'Whiskey' class and a depot ship was designed to strengthen these ties, but in less than two years the political differences between the minute state and the vast USSR had reached breaking point. The Soviet forces were shown the door, but the Albanians very sensibly seized two more 'Whiskey' class as their guests prepared to depart. But that was in 1961, and without spares from the building yards and with the depot ship converted into a merchant freighter, the efficiency of the surviving submarines must be in doubt.

A rather larger spares problem arose at a later date on the southern shore of the Mediterranean. In June 1957 the USSR transferred four 'Whiskey' class and one 'M' class to Egypt, a new venture for a navy whose surface forces were, until 1956, almost entirely of British and American origin. Following General Neguib's coup of 1952, Nasser's move to the front in 1954 and to the Presidency in 1956, and the Anglo-French invasion of Suez, the way was opened for the establishment of a Soviet naval presence in Alexandria. As well as the arrival of ships and submarines of the Soviet Mediterranean squadron, three further 'Whiskey' class were transferred in January 1958, and another eight arrived four years later. By then the solitary 'M' had mouldered into obscurity, and there was a long training period still ahead before the Egyptians were fully capable of operating their boats effectively. The discovery that their allies were using the wrong lubricants and had left a number of submarine batteries on the dockside uncovered to the sand and sun may have influenced the Soviet advisers to return two 'Whiskeys' to the USSR in 1966, to be replaced by two 'Romeos', and to send a further pair back to Leningrad in 1971. By this time the 'Romeo' numbers had increased to six, with three more joining in 1966 and one in 1969. Thus by 1971 Egypt's total submarine squadron consisted of four 'Whiskeys' and six 'Romeos', a handy force if properly handled. The Egyptians clearly had a grip on the situation; they also had the advantage of the infrastructure which the Soviets had installed at Alexandria – docks, workshops, the lot. When President Sadat closed Egypt to the Soviet Union and expelled their advisers in 1972, there was little which the departing Russians could remove from their main Mediterranean base. As in other cases, such as the Soviet departure from Berbera and the American expulsion from Cam Ranh Bay, the unwilling host became the heir to considerable naval riches. But these did not include sufficient spare parts, nor any new submarines to replace ageing boats. Egypt was faced by the growing power of Libya on her western border and needed reinforcement. The first move was to buy new submarines from Spain, which has now also provided her with two frigates. But that seems to have been the limit of the Treasury's resources – the submarine programme came to nothing and an order for six missile craft was cancelled. Then came help from the East. In March 1982 China transferred two 'Romeos', and these were followed by a further pair in early 1984 and two more in 1985. The balance had been temporarily redressed. These transfers were backed by the arrival of Chinese frigates, missile craft and patrol craft. The motives underlying this considerable activity are not hard to determine. The Suez Canal is a vital waterway for the growing Chinese overseas trade; Libya's increasing armament is a threat to this area and is backed by the USSR, whose African ambitions China has long sought to thwart or outmanoeuvre.

It is now thirty-five years since the United Nations declared Libya an independent kingdom. Ten years later, in 1961, the Libyan government asked the British Admiralty to advise them on the formation of a coast defence navy, and in November 1962 a British Naval Mission started training the first recruits at HMS *St Angelo* in Malta, while officer cadets were taken in at the Royal Naval College, Dartmouth, and technical ratings were accepted at British naval electrical and engineering training establishments. This piece of history is included to preserve it at a time when the government of Colonel Gaddafi has been seeking to obscure the origins of their fleet, now largely provided from Soviet sources. In his early days in power Colonel Gaddafi sought to borrow an Egyptian submarine in order to sink the British liner *Queen Elizabeth II*, which was on passage to Haifa with many hundreds of Jewish tourists. This request failed, but was soon answered from a different quarter. Since 1976 a steady stream of Soviet vessels, missile craft, mine countermeasures vessels, amphibious ships and submarines have been transferred to this navy, which will celebrate its twenty-fifth birthday in 1987. In a little over ten years this fleet has achieved a material capability which makes it a dangerous weapon in the hands of one of the least predictable and most violent of the present world leaders.

Arriving between December 1976 and February 1983 the force of Soviet 'Foxtrot' class submarines has grown to a total of six. This may not seem a major force, but with at least two submarines available on patrol at one time the danger is surely evident. Capable of carrying twenty-two torpedoes or forty-four mines, all supplied courtesy of the USSR, these two submarines, if engaged in the sort of undeclared war favoured by the Libyan leader, could wreak very considerable damage on unsuspecting targets. Gaddafi's extraordinary capacity for indiscriminate mayhem was clearly shown in 1984, when the converted Libyan ro-ro ship *Ghat* sprayed 190 mines, of a Soviet type designed for submarines, across two focal points in the Red Sea. The fifteen countries of registry of the eighteen ships damaged varied from the USSR to the Bahamas – a fair cross-section which showed the total disregard for the property of friends or the normal standards of international morality which characterises the current Libyan regime. Six submarines under the charge of such a man could be a sudden and unexpected threat if the crews were up to anything like normal standards. However, this is by no means proved – incompetence has been evident in the Libyan surface fleet and may be mirrored in their submarines. But this is no excuse for a failure in vigilance by other users of the Mediterranean – a few zealous officers and senior rates can transform a submarine's performance.

Only very recently has Algeria become a focus for Soviet submarine interest. Although there have been visits by the Soviet Mediterranean squadron and its ships have anchored off Algeria, it was not until January 1982 that the first Soviet 'Romeo' class submarine made her permanent home in Algerian waters. In February 1983 came the second, and these two now operate regularly in this area. It is interesting to ask why this particular transfer took place. It has already been pointed out that a total of two boats is inefficient except for very limited patrols, and the addition of a couple of elderly submarines (approaching their thirtieth birthdays) offers very little operational advantage to the Algerians. They could be there as anti-submarine targets for the Algerian and Soviet fleets; they might be there as training boats before the transfer of more modern submarines; or their presence might be an insurance that maintenance facilities would be continually available for Soviet submarines operating in the western Mediterranean. It could be a combination of all these reasons.

The only other country within European waters which has benefited from Soviet transfers is Poland. The somewhat pitiful group of three elderly 'Whiskey' class which now wear the Polish ensign compares poorly with the five modern submarines and their crews that were in commission in 1939. Those of their company who successfully brought their submarines to British waters made considerable names for themselves, and those of their hosts who survived the baptism of gin or vodka laced with red pepper conceived a great affection and respect for these somewhat unconventional yet highy effective submariners.

Declaration of war

It was a Polish submarine captain[1] who, when told after he had gained a firing position on an Italian freighter in the Second World War that Poland was not officially at war with Italy, replied: 'I, Boris, declare war on Italy. Fire One.' The target sank. No doubt the same spirit lurks within Boris's modern counterparts – it might be a reason for the niggardly contribution of the USSR to the Polish submarine branch.

The only recipient of Soviet submarines in the Indian Ocean has no similar submarine tradition to that of the Poles, yet occupies a vital position in world strategic planning. Until 1947 the Royal Indian Navy wore the White Ensign and an Indian jack. The ships of the RIN were mostly sloops and sweepers. In ten years the new fleet consisted of a carrier, two cruisers, three destroyers, fourteen frigates and a number of smaller ships and craft. All the major ships came from British yards, and this was only marginally changed in 1967 when the Mazagon Yard in Bombay began building frigates to the British 'Leander' design. But matters were on the turn. In 1965 very senior Soviet officials began to pay court in Delhi, and on 16 July 1968 the first submarine of the Indian Navy, *Kalvari*, of the Soviet 'Foxtrot' class, was delivered to her new owners. As the make-up of the Indian Navy changed dramatically over the next fifteen years and what was, for one of the smaller navies, massive Soviet reinforcement took place, so the submarine force grew. With the personnel trained in the USSR, a further seven 'Foxtrots' had been transferred by December 1975. Although the construction of this class had ceased for the Soviet Navy in 1971, a separate building stream was retained for export to Cuba, India and Libya. Thus this class of eight will remain operational until the 1990s.

In 1982 a Soviet delegation visited Delhi and discussed future transfers. As well as the procurement of cruisers and destroyers, an additional four 'Foxtrots' were included in the package then agreed. India was clearly a favoured customer, and in 1984 another Soviet group headed by Marshal Ustinov, the defence minister, descended on Delhi. In the ensuing discussions further transfers were discussed and these included six 'Kilo' class. This shows an unusual largesse, as the first 'Kilo' for the Soviet Navy was not launched until 1980. But by 1986 two other yards, apart from Komsomolsk on the Amur River, had taken up the building of this class. The new yards at Gorky and Leningrad will have a capacity far greater than that needed for the Soviet Navy, and additional foreign transfers are expected.

While these contacts with Moscow were maintained the Indians continued the same 'belt and braces' policy which they have adopted ever since 1968. This is to continue the use of Western designs, which are being built at an increasing rate in expanded Indian yards, while accepting Soviet reinforcements. From the submarine point of view the application of this policy dates from 11 December 1981. On that day an agreement was signed with Howaldtswerke of Kiel which had four basic parts:

a. Two '209' class (Type 1500) submarines were to be built in Kiel for India.
b. 'Packages' for two more were to be supplied to Mazagon Yard, Bombay.
c. Howaldtswerke were to train groups of specialists to supervise the construction of the submarines in (b) above.
d. Howaldtswerke were to supply logistic services during the trials and early periods of all the submarines' commissions and provide consultative services at Bombay.

The first boat was laid down at Kiel in 1982 and started trials in September 1985. The first Mazagon boat was laid down on 5 June 1984. It was in this year that the Indians announced that a further two submarines would be built in Bombay for a total of six. The Type 1500 is unique to the Indian Navy. With a dived displacement of 1,850 tons it is the largest of the '209' class, has eight torpedo tubes, and (a new departure) a central bulkhead with an integrated IKL rescue system. At twenty-two knots their dived speed is five to six knots faster than either 'Kilo' or 'Foxtrot', and they require only forty men as opposed to the seventy-five in a 'Foxtrot'.

Thus by 1991 the Indian submarine fleet could be composed of eight 'Foxtrot' (four being twenty or more years old), six new 'Type 1500', and four to six 'Kilo' class – a formidable group. When a submarine fleet of this consequence is being formed it is natural to wonder why, but no form of answer to this query can be attempted if the underwater group is considered in isolation. As has already been mentioned, a considerable number of surface ships is reportedly on order from the USSR. These could all have been delivered by 1991 and the maximum strength of the navy by then could be two aircraft carriers, two cruisers, twelve destroyers, twenty frigates, at least twenty-two missile craft of various sizes, eighteen amphibious ships and craft, eighteen MCM vessels, a goodly turn-out of support and service forces, as well as the twenty or twenty-two submarines already listed. With a growing naval air arm and main bases at Bombay, Vishakapatnam and Cochin, smaller bases at

Calcutta, Port Blair and Goa, and naval air stations at Dabohin and Arakkonam, this is already the largest regional navy in the Indian Ocean. By 1991 it will have a preponderance over all the rest of the littoral navies combined. Most importantly, this will be a strong and balanced fleet capable of deep water or amphibious operations, blockade or shore strike. When she was prime minister, Mrs Gandhi made little secret of her feelings concerning Pakistan, but the more conciliatory approach by Rajiv Gandhi may succeed in cooling the atmosphere. Is this, then, to be a defensive fleet in case of a miscalculation by the major powers which might result in conflict in the area? Is it intended as an adjunct to Soviet squadrons in the Indian Ocean? Or is it merely the result of Mrs Gandhi's open-handedness to the armed forces as a recompense for their remaining aloof from the busy grind of politics? In a country where a very large proportion of the huge population lives in poverty, the great expense of such a navy must have been justified by some compelling argument. India's neighbours must be constantly aware of this enigma.

THE CARIBBEAN AND SOUTH AMERICA

Although several of the South American navies were well provided with battleships and armoured cruisers in the early years of this century, little attention was paid to submarines until well after the major naval powers had embarked on considerable building programmes.

Argentina was the last of the more effective South American fleets to include submarines in their strength. Three Italian-built boats were completed in 1931–2, and these remained the only boats in Argentinian waters until they were paid off in 1957–60, being relieved by a pair of American 'Balao' class, which in turn were relieved of their names and duties by a pair of 'Guppy' boats in January 1971. At about this time Argentina was looking for new construction on a partial do-it-yourself basis. In 1968 two '209' class, Type 1200, were ordered from Howaldtswerke, Kiel, to be delivered in sections for assembly at Tandanor, Buenos Aires. Both were in commission by mid-1974.

In 1977 a contract was signed with Thyssen Nordseewerke of Emden – originally for two classes of varying size. This was soon altered to provide a class of six TR 1700 Type submarines of 2,300 tons and twenty-five knots when dived. Of these, one was commissioned in November 1985. Back in Buenos Aires (Tandanor) there was considerable activity as construction of the remaining four boats was put in hand. By mid-1986 the third was fitting out, sections were being fabricated for the fourth, steel had been cut for a fifth, and a start on a sixth was awaited. At a time of retrenchment in the Argentinian armed forces it is not clear if all six will be completed. If they are the navy could have eight modern, high-performance submarines by 1990.

Brazil was faster off the mark than her southern neighbour. In 1912 she acquired three submarines from Fiat, San Giorgio, and when these had disappeared from the scene another Italian boat was delivered in 1929. In September 1937 three more of the smaller (853 tons dived) 'Perla' class were taken over at La Spezia; this quartet was eventually superseded in January 1957 by the first two of four American submarines transferred on loan. The first pair were eventually returned in 1967–8, leaving the two 'Guppies' alone until they in turn were replaced by four 'Guppy II' and 'III' type in 1973. That year saw the commissioning of the first of three British 'Oberon' class, and the arrival of the last of these in 1977 brought the total to seven, the highest figure so far in the Brazilian fleet. More were planned – in October 1984 agreement was reached for the construction of three of the Howald-tswerke '209' class, 'Type 1400', the first to be built in Kiel, the next pair in Rio de Janeiro. The first two of this order were laid down in 1985, so by 1990 Brazil plans to have six boats in service. At present there is considerable discussion abroad about the acquisition of nuclear submarines for the Brazilian Navy. There is certainly a programme of nuclear research in hand in the country, but the conversion of this into a nuclear propulsion plant and the construction of a submarine which would require the very highest standards of welding and quality control seems unlikely – and this is quite apart from any consideration of the enormous costs involved for a country which has one of the highest foreign loan debts in the world, and one of the lowest standards of living among its predominantly poor population. It may be an exciting prospect for senior naval officers, but it will almost certainly remain no more than that for many years to come.

Of the three neighbouring countries to the west of Brazil, Venezuela, Colombia and Ecuador, only Venezuela benefited from the hand-out of American submarines in the post-war period. She acquired a single 'Balao' class in 1960 and in 1972–3 took over two 'Guppies'. By this time all were aged, and it was a prudent move when two '209' class 'Type 1300' were ordered from Howaldtswerke, both being laid down in 1973 and commissioned in 1976–7.

Colombia, with no previous experience of submarines, jumped in at the deep end in the early 1970s. In 1972 the first of four 'SX–506' seventy-ton submarines was delivered in sections by the Italian firm

Cosmos, to be followed by three more. These small submersibles are designed to carry eight attack swimmers and two tons of explosive, but the tasks likely to be assigned to the two that remain are somewhat obscure. Not so the tasks which the pair of '209' class 'Type 1200' are expected to fulfil. Commissioned in 1975 they can operate from either the Caribbean HQ at Cartagena or the Pacific HQ at Buenaventura, although to change areas they must use the Panama Canal.

It was again the busy men from Howaldtswerke who led Ecuador into the acquisition of submarines, this time a pair of the '209' class 'Type 1300'. These two, commissioned in 1977–8, operate from Guayaquil, fifty miles across the Gulf from the northern border of Peru. This country's navy has had a comparatively long association with submarines, its first purchases being in 1912–13, when two Laubeuf-designed boats were delivered by Schneider-Creusot of France. As these passed out of service four 755-ton submarines were ordered from the Electric Boat Company, Groton, Connecticut, the first pair making an unescorted and successful delivery passage to Callao in 1926. This business connection was continued in 1952, when Electric Boat began building four of the US 'Mackerel' class for Peru. When these had been in commission for a few years in 1960, their predecessors were paid off. In 1974 reinforcements arrived in the shape of two American 'Guppy 1A' boats, and the first of what was to become a group of six '209' class 'Type 1200'. By this time the staff of Howaldtswerke must have been fairly evenly split between Kiel and South America.

At first, however, this moving band of West Germans made little impression in Chile. Both Peru and Chile have maintained a form of balance between their fleets for the best part of a century, and it was not surprising that Chile entered the submarine business at about the same time as Peru. In 1911 she acquired two Holland boats, and in 1917 received six US-built 'H' class, originally destined for the Royal Navy but transferred to Chile as part payment for those of her warships which were taken over by Great Britain while building in 1914. These excellent submarines of the 'H11–H20' group remained in service until the 1950s, having received reinforcement from three of the British 'O' class, built for Chile by Vickers–Armstrong in 1927–9. These survived until 1958–9, the then denuded submarine force being resuscitated in 1961 by the transfer of two American 'Balao' class, which remained in service until 1973–5. Before this time Chile had again decided to buy British – in 1969 two 'Oberon' class were ordered, to be delivered in 1976. But the men from Kiel were not to be denied – in 1980 Chile ordered two '209' class 'Type 1300'. Both commissioned in 1984 with an interesting alteration to suit the customer: their fins and masts have been extended by fifty centimetres to cope with the heavy sea and swell experienced off the Chilean coast. A small thing, but what a difference such details can make.

Last in this list, out of place in one way but kept for this section because of her possible impact on South American affairs, is Cuba. When Castro seized power in 1956 he inherited a naval force of six frigates of varying types and a bunch of patrol craft. Six years later, as the KGB were arriving to spread the Soviet gospel, there was little change, but much was about to happen. From 1962 onwards the USSR entered the rent-a-fleet business; missile craft, corvettes and fast attack craft began to appear in droves. Before long the Cuban Navy had more punch than all the rest of the Caribbean navies put together. In February 1979, hard on the heels of reports of Cubans training in Soviet submarines, came their own 'Foxtrot' class – followed in May by a single 'Whiskey'. The latter was not intended for operational use and is employed for training and charging. In January 1980 came the second 'Foxtrot', with a third following in February 1984. In twenty-two years the Soviet Union had presented Cuba with an instant navy which has a base barely a hundred miles from the Florida Keys. If Castro is prepared to do as Moscow bids the presence of this fleet, particularly its submarines, could have a very unsettling effect on American plans in a crisis.

THE REST OF THE WORLD

Of the nine countries discussed in this section, two have had long association with submarines, one has a considerable naval tradition which does not include submarines, and the remaining six are states created in the last forty years.

Japan's claim to preeminence in this company is justified by a long history of involvement in submarine affairs and a notable ingenuity in design. It was the war with Russia in 1904–5 which focussed Japanese minds on the potential of underwater operations and in 1905 they ordered their first five Holland type boats from Fore River Yard in the USA – these were shipped to Japan in sections for reassembly. In the following year Japan built her first pair of experimental submarines. By the outbreak of the First World War the navy had seventeen boats available, although not all were operational. Various designs were favoured – British from Vickers, French from Schneider-Lanbeuf,

Italian from Fiat-Laurenti, as well as Japanese adaptations of these. The first truly indigenous design, the 'K3' class, was ordered under the 1918 programme, to be followed next year by the 'K4' class armed with twenty-one-inch torpedoes. From then on programme after programme produced variations in design, with dived tonnage ranging from 1,000 to over 4,000. The Japanese were afflicted with the same unfortunate addiction to large submarines for spurious purposes which had infected Western navies. In the giant 'AM' class, of which only two were completed, the dived tonnage had reached 4,762 on a length of 372.2 feet; two seaplanes were carried and an unsuccessful attempt was made to incorporate a snort mast. But they were underpowered and had a speed of only 16.7 knots on the surface and 5.5 knots dived. Both speeds were noticeably less than the majority of the contemporary patrol submarines, for which 'AM' and their predecessors of the 'J3', 'A1' and 'A2' classes were designed to act as command submarines. This was an additional task demanded by the Staff, as were the first designs for very large submarines, 'J1' and 'J2', were conceived prior to 1924 to provide long-range marauders equipped with reconnaissance seaplanes, 5.5-inch guns and a normal torpedo outfit.

The reasons for this search for big submarines are not difficult to find. In the inter-war years the battleship and the big gun were still looked on as the arbiters of naval conflict. Despite the success of the U-boats in the First World War, the submarine was still considered an adjunct of the surface fleet while the advantages conferred by the use of aircraft were still hotly debated. While the Japanese moved swiftly into the air supremacy league – a branch of naval operations requiring large and impressive surface ships – it is far from clear whether the naval staff appreciated the proper role of the submarine. The evidence of the types of submarines demanded from the designers and the yards suggests that they did not. In this failing they were by no means alone.

The big league

In 1918 Germany's *U142* was a large submarine armed with two 5.9-inch guns – probably a legitimate design in an era when anti-submarine detection was in its infancy and aircraft were of small concern at sea. In 1915 the British had set up the Admiralty Committee on Submarine Development, and from the subsequent recommendations stemmed the designs of the 'M' class with a single twelve-inch gun, and the *XI* of 3,585 tons dived with four 5.2-inch guns. These were all in commission by 1925, but apart from the three 'River' class of the mid-1930s, which at 2,680 tons dived with a

surface speed of 22.5 knots were a throwback to the old idea of a
fleet-support submarine, the British concentrated on smaller boats.
In the USA USS *Argonaut* appeared in 1928 – of 4,080 tons dived she
carried two six-inch guns and was designed for minelaying. She was
followed in 1930 by the two 'Narwhals' of 3,960 tons, but from then
on the Americans concentrated on designs of 2,000 to 2,400 tons.
These showed the adequacy of their size and performance in the
extraordinarily successful submarine campaign during the Pacific
phase of the Second World War.

Lastly comes *Surcouf*, the lone French monster, designed in 1926
to carry two eight-inch guns and a seaplane on a dived tonnage of
4,304. This was the only foray into the world of large submarines by
the French, whose subsequent designs were all of 2,000 tons or less.

In four major submarine fleets the concept of the big boat was
discarded, while in Japan it was continued right up to 1945. Yet there
was a capacity in the design field which was not accepted until too late
for it to have any effect on the outcome of the war. In 1937 the Japanese
laid down Submarine *No 71*, an experimental boat of 240 tons dived
which achieved twenty-two knots underwater. She was scrapped in
1940, but in the exhilaration of the preparation for and the conduct of a
series of all-conquering campaigns nothing further was done. With the
tide of victory on the ebb and following consultation with the German
designers of the 'Type XXI', a totally new class, 'ST', was laid down. Of
1,450 tons dived with two main motors of 5,000 shp (the same as the
'Type XXI'), the underwater performance of nineteen knots was
superior to that of her German counterpart, although the armament was
substantially less. But only three were completed by September 1945
and over a hundred were scrapped or cancelled. Had the lessons of No
71 been applied as soon as available and had the full capacity of the
excellent Japanese submarine building yards been utilised for such a
design, the problems of the US Navy in the western Pacific would have
been greatly multiplied. A surface range of 6,000 miles at fourteen knots
and a dived endurance, as a result of increased battery capacity, of
forty-five hours at three knots, coupled with a snorting capability, would
have provided a large shoal of elusive submarines.

Where the results of the experience gained in No 71 and the 'ST'
class went in the post-war period is unknown, but they appear to have
been preserved. The first of the Japanese submarines laid down after
building restrictions were lifted was *Oyashio*. Built under the 1956
programme, she was commissioned on 30 June 1960. The similarity

with 'ST' was considerable. Of 1,420 tons dived *Oyashio* achieved nineteen knots dived with twin shafts and main motors of 5,960 shp. Her armament of four tubes with a total of ten torpedoes was the same as that in 'ST'.

Two classes followed in the next five years. The four 'Hayashios' were completed in 1962–4, while the first of five 'Oshio' class was commissioned in March 1965. While 'Oshio' had a conventional length-to-beam ratio of 11.3 to one, the smaller 'Hayashio' class came nearer to the *Albacore* shape, with a ratio of 9.3 to one. The 'Oshios' were much larger – 2,450 tons dived with a ratio creeping back to the conventional form at 10.7 to one. The larger hull allowed eight tubes to be mounted instead of the three in the 'Hayashios', and the dived speed was now eighteen knots.

In 1971 the first of seven 'Uzushio' class was commissioned, a design with a true *Albacore* hull whose ratio was 7.3 to one. Her dived tonnage was very little different from that of 'Oshio', her dived speed was twenty knots, and the six torpedo tubes were mounted amidships to make way for a large bow sonar. The last of this class was completed in 1978; less than two years later the first 'Yuushio' class was in commission. A little larger and a little faster than their immediate predecessors, their completion rate of one every March is impressive, particularly when it is realised that the period from 'laid down' to 'commissioned' has been, since No 2, two years and eleven months. The eighth is due in service in March 1987, and the tenth boat and onwards are planned to be of an improved class.

A flotilla of fifteen submarines strategically placed at the various exits of the Sea of Japan would be a major deterrent to surface ship or submarine transits of these narrow straits, all within a very short distance from Japan's various bases. This is one of the occasions when the equation of three boats for one on patrol comes unstuck because passage time is reduced to a minimum.

Far to the south, Australia has to cope with the very reverse of this situation. Vast distances lie between her bases and probable patrol areas, and without a specialised depot ship to support them the few submarines in the Royal Australian Navy would be hard pushed to operate from Darwin or Exmouth Gulf for any but the briefest period.

Australian involvement with submarines has been spasmodic. Two of the earliest British 'E' class were transferred as *AE1* and *AE2* – one was lost off the Great Barrier Reef and one in the Dardanelles. In 1919 the surviving six submarines of the British 'J' class were transferred to the RAN, but this was a short-lived experiment. In the post-war period a division of three British 'T' class boats was based in Sydney, and these were relieved by the first of the 'Oberon' class, of which four were commissioned in 1967–9 and two more in 1977–8. The Australians have shown great originality in the re-equipment of their 'Oberons'. From 1977 to 1985 all six have been transformed by the replacement of their original systems by West German sonar and American passive ranging arrays, American fire-control systems, Mark 48 torpedoes and Harpoon missiles. Although this has resulted in a much-enhanced performance, the hull life of the first boats of the class will reach twenty years before 1990, and replacements are planned. Of the seven original contenders for this contract, only two remain – in Sweden and West Germany. The need for submarines is only one of several major requirements of the RAN: MCM vessels, helicopters, airborne early warning – the list is extensive and daunting for a huge country with a small population. But one thing is sure – submarines are a vital part of any naval plan for the defence of Australia.

In 1959, fourteen years after Indonesia proclaimed her independence and ten years after the Netherlands acknowledged it, the first ships of a considerable fleet of Soviet vessels was transferred to the republic. By 1962 fourteen 'Whiskey' class submarines had been handed over and the Indonesian Navy took the unusual step of placing six of these in reserve and using two for spare parts. In the following year, 1963, the confrontation with Malaysia began, and it lasted until Sukarno was removed as prime minister in 1966. During this period the Indonesian submarines were not noticeably active, contenting themselves with exercises in the coastal waters of Java.

The recovery period after Sukarno was finally deposed from his post as president in 1967 was long and difficult. The many islands forming the republic were in a state of poverty, but in 1980 the government under Suharto decided that the ramshackle remains of the ex-Soviet fleet should be paid off, and over the next twenty years a navy suitable for keeping some form of order along the huge coastline should be acquired. The composition of this new fleet was to include six submarines. In 1983 the last of the 'Whiskeys' were deleted, two years after two '209' class 1300 Type had been delivered by Howaldtswerke. It is presumed that the remaining four in the plan will be ordered from the same yard.

There was nothing as dramatic in the acquisition of submarines by Pakistan. In 1970 three French 'Daphne' class were delivered, with a fourth purchased from Portugal in December 1975. In 1978 two 'Agosta' class were acquired when the Republic of South Africa, for whom the two had been built, came under an arms ban imposed by the

United Nations. These 'Agostas' were valuable reinforcements – a total of six submarines allows at least two, maybe three, on patrol at one time. With one port, Karachi, as the country's vital link through which all its imports are channelled, and some 480 miles of generally sparsely inhabited coastline, early warning in a crisis would be essential. Submarines would provide a most valuable element in this task.

The South Africa Navy has well over 3,000 miles of coastline, including that of Namibia, to care for and precious few ships with which to carry out this task. Her three French 'Daphne' class acquired in 1970–1 are, as a result of the United Nations interdict, her only submarines – too few for the area to be covered. But, with the same energy and ingenuity with which South Africa has overcome many other problems of armament, this gap may be filled to some extent by home production. With pressure hulls built in sections in Johannesburg and transported for assembly and fitting out at Simonstown much might be achieved. It might be possible to deploy the resources of the Rand's expert welders to the Cape, providing a much easier solution, but if South Africa decides new submarines are essential there seems every likelihood that she will build them.

Israel has advanced her defence industries in much the same way as South Africa. In October 1958 she acquired two British 'S' class submarines at a time when no trained crews were available. By the time these boats were delivered after refit in December 1959 and May 1960 an astonishing feat of preparation had taken place. Working at an extraordinary pace men who would have felt more at home landing by parachute were converted into keen and knowledgeable submariners. By 1968 the first 'S' boat was paid-off as 'worn out', a hardly surprising condition. Three 'T' class were transferred at Gosport in 1967–8, but sadly one was lost on passage to Israel. In 1972 a contract was signed with Vickers for the construction of three 'Type 540' submarines of 600 tons dived, to be built to a West German IKL design. These were all commissioned in 1977, by which time the remaining 'S' and 'T' boats had been paid off.

In 1985 Israel began negotiations for the construction of 1,000-ton submarines which will probably be built at Haifa with assistance from both the USA and West Germany. There is no doubt that, with the current naval situation in the Mediterranean, submarines have an important place in Israel's maritime plans.

North and South Korea share a peninsula which from 1910 to 1945 had been governed by the Japanese. With the Second World War over, Soviet troops occupied the country down to the 38th parallel of latitude

North; below that line the American army provided the occupation forces. It was roughly along this parallel that the boundary between the Communist and the non-Communist Koreas was drawn after the war of 1950–3.

The North Korean Navy consists almost entirely of vessels built in the USSR or North Korea, with the exception of some of its submarines. In 1960 the Soviet Navy handed over four 'Whiskey' class and in 1973–5 China transferred seven 'Romeo' class. Presumably the building drawings were part of this deal, since in 1975 local construction of 'Romeos' began, and this had yielded a further eight boats by 1982. In addition a number of small submarines have been completed, but details of this programme are very uncertain.

With nineteen submarines operational in the navy of her irascible and uncertain northern neighbour, South Korea has made plans, yet to be fulfilled, for submarines to be built in her own very efficient and productive shipyards. The modernisation of this navy is long overdue and an underwater squadron would be an excellent start.

Taiwan's two 'Guppy II' class are now over forty years old, and are to be replaced by a pair of Netherlands-built submarines ordered in September 1981. These are similar to the 'Zwaardvis' design but with Taiwanese variations, and their construction has been plagued with problems. Obtaining the approval of the Netherlands government was not easy, and when the customers asked for a further pair, with an option on another two, the safety curtain came down. Financial problems bedevilled the building yard, but by 1984 construction was again under way. So Taiwan will have two submarines operating close to home ports – once again a useful reconnaissance capability.

In the remaining years of this century there will be other navies undertaking submarine programmes. The most likely candidates are Iran, now seeking to re-establish contracts cancelled when the Shah was overthrown, Malaysia, Saudi Arabia and Thailand. In each of these cases a good argument can be advanced for such a step, and it will be interesting to see who proposes the successful contracts.

9

The Chinese Enigma

Any research into the recent background of the Chinese Navy is fraught with problems. An inspection of *Jane's Fighting Ships* over the years will make this point clear. In 1914 the navy consisted of seven cruisers and a number of smaller craft. In 1919 the Chinese section opened with a correction: 'Following warships are at Canton, under the local government, which has declared its independence of the central government at Peking.' In 1939 we were treated to a 'Special Note', which read: 'Pending the termination of hostilities between China and Japan it has proved impossible to obtain a reliable list of the ships of the Chinese Navy that remain in service. But it is believed that the following have been destroyed or otherwise lost . . .' and there follows a list of forty-one surface ships of various sizes. By 1945 matters were still in a state of confusion. Fourteen ships (with others possibly in existence) were listed in the Chinese Navy, but a further six appeared under the somewhat quaint heading 'Nanking Quisling Government'. One's heart bleeds for the wretched editor, but by 1955 the new man was back in his stride. Now there was a clear differentiation between China (Communist) and China (Nationalist), and a brief note appeared under the former heading: 'Reported to have 4 'M' type and 4 'S' type Russian submarines.' The Nationalist pages, however, though filled with American and Japanese ships and craft, showed no sign of submarines.

So, following the success of Mao in 1949, in July 1953 to October 1954 the USSR provided the first submarines known in any of these varied and fragmented Chinese navies. One of the 'M5' class and two of the 'S1' class survived into the 1970s. Between 1956 and 1964 the first five of twenty-one Soviet 'Whiskey' class were assembled in Chinese yards, but in 1962 a production programme of the Soviet 'Romeo' design was set in hand in those same yards. At the same time the remaining sixteen 'Whiskeys' were being built, although this programme may have started earlier, in 1960. The first boats of the latter class were probably 'Whiskey IVs', the remainder being 'Whiskey Vs', but the important point is that although the Chinese Navy was in the submarine business maybe sixty years later than many, it was clearly determined to remedy the backlog. Three yards were soon in operation – at Canton, Shanghai and Wuzhang. By 1963 China was on her own so far as the Soviet Union was concerned, the growing split having widened into a gulf, and from then on it was a question of combining Soviet designs with Chinese manufacturing ability.

There are some who insist that politics have no place in naval discussions – the absurdity of this approach is apparent when one considers the state of the Chinese Navy in the late 1960s. It was in mid-1966 that the Red Guards were loosed by Mao and China started on the way to becoming a cultural desert. The universities were as much a target as any other manifestations of civilisation. With their near total suppression went the education of those who might have been qualified to design new naval types and classes as well as modern equipment. The result of this intellectual blight, which lay on the country for ten years and was described as the 'Cultural Revolution', can be seen in the current order of battle of the submarine fleet.

The 'Whiskey' class is an even older design than the 'Romeo', the latter dating from the mid-1950s. Nevertheless the 'Romeos' remained in production until the mid-1980s, and with a total of ninety-one constructed it is the second largest series run of one class in the post-war years, exceeded only by the Soviet 'Whiskey' programme. It is clear that the Chinese recognised the need for replacement designs in the mid-1960s, probably just before the Cultural Revolution was in its first and most violent period. This was a staff decision as far-sighted as those being taken in Moscow at the same time, and it contained the seed of a modernism which has grown into a somewhat under-nourished plant.

Between October 1964 and December 1968 the Chinese exploded eight nuclear devices. Preparatory work for this successful outcome must have started some time about the period of the Korean War (1950–3), a time when the USSR was providing the new People's Republic with all manner of equipment for her armed forces. Some of the many emissaries visiting Moscow from Peking may well have been Chinese scientists who, at a time of amity and support, could have profited from the great amount of work on nuclear physics and engineering then in progress in the USSR. Amongst the many Soviet programmes currently in hand were the construction of the early nuclear-tipped ballistic and cruise missiles, as well as the nuclear reactors for the icebreaker *Lenin* and the first of the 'November' class SSNs.

The gestation period of the first American nuclear reactor for USS *Nautilus* was seven years, but in the background was a wealth of experience from the participants in the work at Los Alamos and the Manhattan Project. The Soviet designers, profiting from the results of espionage, may have achieved a reduced time scale, allowing them to start the design of their seaborne reactors in about 1950. The Chinese, with the new government having been formed in September 1949, were in no condition to make an orderly approach to research and development; a great deal of simmering down and reorganisation was needed and this took place simultaneously with the squabble with the USSR. But the Chinese nuclear programme was clearly in full swing. The production of missiles was the first priority, but by the early 1960s nuclear propulsion had become a matter of great importance, and in 1971-2 the first Chinese nuclear-propelled submarine was laid down – now known as the 'Han' class. Alongside this came the first-ever native design for a non-nuclear submarine, the 'Ming' class. The first 'Han' is believed to have run her early trials in 1974 after an understandably long building period. Apparently there were problems with the power plant and with political funding, but the second boat was reported to have been launched in 1977, and the third in the 1980s. This is an excruciatingly slow programme which may have resulted from a combination of these two problems. But there is another possibility: over the next few years Great Britain will find that the guts are taken out of her SSN programme by the construction of the four 'Trident' submarines. It is reported that the first Chinese SSBN of the 'Xia' class was laid down in 1978 and, as in Great Britain, such a programme is liable to monopolise those with important abilities in a country with a small submarine-building capacity. The 'Xia' class will be dealt with later, but its probable impact on the 'Han' programme must be recognised here.

But this argument cannot be applied to the 'Ming' class. This is reported as a diesel submarine with a dived displacement of 1,900 tons, a length of seventy-nine metres (259.2 feet). There is no reason to believe that this is not a fairly conventional diesel boat with the normal complement of six 533-millimetre torpedo tubes. It should, therefore, have presented few construction problems to shipyards which already had over ten years' building experience of such boats. But only three appear to have been built. This suggests that the design was inadequate, and the result may well be that a new class will appear in the late 1980s.

The comparison between the length-to-beam ratios of 'Ming' and 'Han' are interesting – the diesel submarine has a ratio of ten to one, the SSN one of 9.1 to one. These are somewhat different from current Soviet ratios: the diesel-electric 'Kilo' has a ratio of 7.7 to one and the 'Akula' SSN one of 9.6 to one. The British 'Trafalgar' SSN has a ratio of 8.7 to one, and the American 'Los Angeles' SSN one of 10.9 to one. Of the larger submarines there is a not unexpected similarity between the SSBNs of the 'Xia' class of some 8,000 tons dived displacement and a ratio of twelve to one and the Soviet 'Yankees', with a displacement of 10,500 tons and a ratio of 11.8 to one.

In the early 1970s reports of a Chinese nuclear-propelled submarine were becoming more definite. A little earlier, in 1970, it was suggested that China had deployed liquid-fuelled medium-range ballistic missiles up to a total of about fifty, the deployment date later being amended to 1966. These were designated CSS-1 by Washington, and were followed, probably in 1971, by CSS-2. This is an intermediate missile with a range between 1,500 and 2,500 miles, and it may be similar to the liquid-fuelled first stage of the rocket used to launch China's first satellite in April 1970. After a very slow production period the CSS-3, an ICBM with a range of 4,400 miles, reached the point of deployment some time after 1975, and the conjunction of Chinese nuclear submarine and missile technologies then appeared probable. In fact the first 'Xia' class SSBN was almost certainly laid down between 1976 and 1978 and launched in 1981. On 30 April 1980 a test launch of what was later designated CSS-NX-3 took place from a submerged pontoon near Huludao in the Yellow Sea. This achieved a range of 1,800 miles, as did a later test flight on 12 October 1982. It was an interesting coincidence that only two days later the Soviet Navy achieved its first multiple missile launch from their first 'Typhoon' class boat. This juxtaposition clearly illustrates the great lead in such submarine operations possessed by the Soviet fleet, while emphasising the comparatively slow build-up of China's missile armoury, both on shore and afloat.

In 1964 a ballistic-missile submarine to the Soviet diesel-propelled 'Golf' class design had been completed at Luda by the Chinese, long before any suitable missile was available. This immediately raises several questions. Had the USSR intended to assist the Chinese construction of ballistic-missile submarines and their weapons at a time when they had only recently introduced them to the Soviet fleet, and was this prevented by the split between the countries? Did the Chinese build this submarine to assist in their eventual development of an SSBN? Was the whole programme halted by the Cultural Revolution? The answers to these queries will probably never be known, but it does seem feasible that, before the era of détente, it might have been to the Soviet advantage to have her Pacific ally suitably armed to threaten the west coast of the USA. This plan would have come unstuck as China became progressively disillusioned with Soviet policies. She was therefore left with her single 'Golf', useless without missiles. The fact that in 1959 the USSR had refused to provide nuclear weapons to the Chinese does not necessarily invalidate this item of speculation, which is an attempt to make sense of an apparently inexplicable piece in the Chinese naval jigsaw puzzle. The plans for 'Golf' and her missiles were available at least by 1953.

It is impossible to review the Chinese submarine force as a separate entity, divorced from the remainder of a navy that has become formidable in numbers if not in modernity. In the early days of the People's Republic the Nationalist forces were entrenched in Taiwan, and had obtained some forty destroyer/frigate/escort type ships, as well as a considerable number of minesweepers, landing ships and craft and patrol craft. The chances of conflict between this fleet and the hotch-potch of ships which made up the navy of the People's Republic remained fairly high for some time. Occasional air attacks by Chiang Kai-shek's forces caused some damage, while in Taiwan there was an expectation of invasion from the mainland. This never materialised, but in 1958 fierce bombardments of the 'off-shore islands', Quemoy and Matsu, where the Nationalists maintained a foothold within sight of the Chinese coastline, kept tension high and apprehension alive. As the years passed and the level of strife remained low except in these small outposts, the centres of tension were swinging to the north. The Sino–Soviet squabbles took on a more sinister aspect with border engagements on the Ussuri River, while Chinese diplomatic advances to countries in Africa and the Middle East were designed, in the words of a Chinese diplomat, to 'forestall or delay Soviet infiltration'.

Despite this latter aim, the only vessels in a short-range navy which had pretensions to anything but a purely coastal defence role were the eight destroyers and frigates from the USSR, and the submarines. In the 1960s, when Lin Piao was minister of defence, this philosophy underwent a change. The first of a new class of frigate, 'Jiangnan', was laid down at Shanghai in 1965, her design being based on the Soviet 'Riga' class. In all, twenty-seven of this and two similar classes were built over the next twenty years.

By mid-1960, the time of the final split between China and the USSR, the large group (possibly as many as 2,000) of Soviet naval advisers had all been withdrawn and China was on her own. At that time her navy had managed a minor miracle of construction and training and had produced the largest home-based navy in eastern Asia. Despite this improvement the fleet was in no shape to carry out deep-water operations, and the naval command was well aware of the fact that a superior naval power, the USA, had prevented direct action against Taiwan in 1950 and had played a vital part in the Korean War of 1950–3. This foreign fleet was assessed as a possible threat, and strategic thinking now centred on maritime defence – by submarines as an outer screen and fast attack craft operating off the coast. China was primarily a land power, and the unexpected ability which the US Navy conferred on politicians in Washington to negotiate treaties with states close to the Chinese sea and land frontiers most certainly promoted an impression of encirclement to the leaders in Beijing. However, the only fighting which occurred arose out of the continuing conflict with the Nationalists from Taiwan. This reached a peak in 1954–5 in the island groups off Taichow Bay, half-way between Shanghai and Taiwan, and again, further south, in 1958.

Incident at Quemoy
During the 1958 engagement, which took place around the island of Quemoy (Jinmen), the Chinese Navy at first succeeded in blockading the Nationalist forces on the island, but the blockade was broken by the intervention of the US Seventh Fleet operating a minimum of four aircraft carriers in the vicinity. Whether this considerable American force might have been attacked by Chinese submarines, had they been available, will probably never be known. But this is, again, a matter of speculation – in 1958 the only submarines in the Chinese Navy were four ex-Soviet 'SI' class and four 'M5' class, and it was only five years since the foundation of the submarine arm of the service. The first 'Whiskey' class were still being assembled from sections provided by the USSR, and training had possibly not reached the stage where an attack on elements of the largest and one of the most experienced navies in the world could be considered. A disastrous outcome would have resulted in a slump in morale and a severe loss of face. Success might have been equally disastrous, bringing heavy retaliation from an incensed USA.

By 1962 the last of the twenty-one 'Whiskey' class was completed and construction was then concentrated on the 'Romeo' design. The plans for this class were available some time before the schism, and though these boats are believed to have had certain Chinese modifications they were basically similar to their Soviet counterparts. The items of modernisation of the 'Whiskey' class in the late 1960s were probably a reflection of these modifications, and the whole submarine programme benefited from the major increases in defence expenditure which began in 1962 and continued until the death of Lin Piao, minister of defence, after his attempted coup in September 1971. After over five years when the defence budget rose by an annual ten per cent, it was cut by twenty per cent in 1972, and over the next ten years the annual increase was only in the region of one per cent. Despite these swingeing cuts, the submarine programme survived – to the detriment of the major surface ships. 'Romeos' were built at the rate of about five a year, and plans for their replacement by the somewhat larger 'Mings' went ahead. The construction of the first of the nuclear-propelled 'Han' class had moved slowly forward to her launching in 1972, and it is clear that this branch of the navy was being given much the same preference that was accorded to the fast missile craft.

This attitude may possibly be traced back to the early training of the Chinese Navy, begun in 1950 by Soviet advisers. At that time a huge submarine building programme was under way in Soviet yards. This philosophy of defence in depth by submarines may well have influenced future Chinese thinking, and the actions of the growing and hostile Soviet Pacific Fleet would have confirmed its relevance to China. In 1973, at a time when there was a lessening of tension between China and the USA and a US liaison office was established in Beijing, the first Soviet foray around Taiwan took place. Two years later, in May 1975, Mao decreed an expansion and development of the Chinese fleet – his announcement followed closely in the wake of the Soviet Okean 75 exercise (14–21 April), in which the Pacific Fleet based at Vladivostok took a major part. At a time when China's foreign trade was expanding rapidly and oil exploration was being added to the age-old fishing industry as an essential off-shore requirement, these operations by her powerful neighbour posed a very clear threat to Chinese interests. The Sino–Soviet engagements on the Ussuri River were only six years in the past, and could well be used to support the 'intention' element in the definition of a threat as being a combination of capability and intention.

Over the next ten years Chinese suspicion of Soviet aspirations was steadily increased. After the armed exchanges on the Sino–Vietnam border in 1979 and the latter's occupation of the Khmer Republic (Cambodia), Soviet forces established themselves in the old American bases at Cam Ranh Bay and Danang. This has resulted in a strong Soviet naval and air force, as well as a rejuvenated Vietnamese navy, being based only about 500 miles from China's most southerly extension, Hainan Island. Any force operating eastwards from Cam Ranh Bay will very soon pass only some 300 miles to the south of the

Paracel Islands and Macclesfield Bank, and very close to the northern-most of the Spratly Islands, all of which are claimed by a far-sighted Chinese government. It is also through this area that China's burgeoning trade passes en route to and from the Malacca Straits. Any interruption of the free passage of this vital waterway would cause serious harm to China's economy.

When one discusses the roles and tasks of the Chinese Navy today with its senior officers there is nothing enigmatic in their replies. The most general emphasis is on the use of submarines to interdict Soviet supply routes to their forces in the South China Sea, and to counter any incursions into Chinese northern waters. To carry out these tasks a highly professional and modern navy is needed. The blight of the Cultural Revolution has delayed the necessary education and training, as well as the research into new technology, needed for a modern fleet. But the most abiding memories of a recent visit to China are the energy, enthusiasm, ability and dedication which is being brought to bear upon this huge gulf. The current fleet of two SSBNs and three SSNs (with more of both types building) and about a hundred diesel submarines may not appear of impressive proportions, but the next ten years will see a very major improvement in all areas.[1]

10

The Menace of the Midgets

Attention is necessarily concentrated today on the giant nuclear attack submarines which master the seas. But at the other end of the size scale, where anti-submarine detection is very difficult, the extraordinarily successful midgets of the Second World War have largely been forgotten: defences against X-craft and the like have, almost everywhere, fallen into disrepair and have been neglected.

Numerous alarms and exursions in Scandinavian – mainly Swedish – waters since 1962 are a sharp reminder that very small submersibles can penetrate harbours and inlets where their bigger brethren cannot, or dare not, go. Late in 1985 there was an unconfirmed report of unidentified midget activity off Brazil; and despite official denials Japan has probably also been a target on several occasions.

Speculation about Soviet midget incursions into other nations' territorial waters is supported by remarkably few hard facts; or, rather, not much information has been made public and that usually means that not much is known. Midget submarines are relatively easy to keep secret and hidden, and it could well be that the best way of gauging the possibilities of underwater warfare in midgets today and tomorrow is to examine the practicalities and achievements of the past, updating them in the light of modern technology and the known unclassified capabilities of commercial mini-subs. It would certainly be prudent to try to determine what underwater sneak craft could accomplish nowadays – perhaps all too easily in the face of inadequate opposition.

During the last war there were three distinct kind of mini-submersibles, all of which would be suitable for development today: human torpedoes, small transportable submersibles, and more or less independent midget submarines.

Except in Japan, where the craft were virtually suicidal, human torpedoes were misnamed. In their most successful Italian and British form they were indeed modelled on torpedoes, but they were not suicide craft: the warheads were detachable and were fastened to target hulls – the targets, of course, being moored or anchored in harbour.

The concept first bore fruit in 1918 at the northern end of the Adriatic, where the Italian Navy had made a number of daring raids with small, fast torpedo-armed motor boats (MAS) against the Austrian Navy. The Austrian reaction to the destruction of the old coastal defence battleship *Wien* by *MAS–9* in the principal Austrian port of Trieste on the night of 9–10 December 1917, followed by the sinking of the new dreadnought *Szent Istvan* by *MAS–15* in the open Adriatic on 10 June 1918, was to bottle up its remaining battleships in the heavily fortified port of Pola. Here the harbour defences were deemed to be impenetrable and the Austrian Navy felt safe. It was soon to be disillusioned.

Human Torpedoes

During the night of 31 October/1 November 1918 a revolutionary little device, based on an old fourteen-inch B–57 bronze torpedo with two men astride it, struggled through the Pola barriers and was not discovered until a delayed-action mine had been attached to the Austrian flagship *Viribus Unitis*. The 'infernal machine', styled the *S–1* or *Mignatta* (Leech), unmanned while the operators dealt with the battleship, motored on to collide with the Transatlantic Austrian-Lloyd *Wien* (not to be confused with the battleship of that name which had gone down earlier) upon which the second of the two warheads detonated and sank the luckless liner. The clockwork mechanism on the first mine ticked away while the two Italian inventor–operators, Major Raffaele Rossetti (from the Naval Constructor Corps) and Surgeon Lieutenant Raffaele Paolucci, were seized and taken on board the battleship, where confusion reigned. At 0644 there came, according to Paolucci, 'a dull noise – a deep roaring, not loud or terrible but rather light. A high column of water followed.' A few minutes later the *Viribus Unitis*, the pride of the Austrian fleet, turned turtle and sank.

Unknown to the gallant Italian frogmen, the Austro-Hungarian Empire had collapsed on the previous day, and Austria was in a state of revolution. A Yugoslavian crew had taken over the ship, expelling all German and German-Austrian officers and locking up others below decks. The new crew had spent the night carousing, and this partly explained how Rossetti and Paolucci were able to force their way into the harbour unseen.

The *Mignatta* was not capable of submerging, but lay very low in the water; the operators camouflaged their heads to look like floating wine-casks. Before setting out Rossetti had coolly calculated that the

A Soviet Mod 'Golf 1' (ex-SSB) fitted with extensive facilities as a relatively secure command and control/communications vessel for amphibious or other co-ordinated operations. The pillar-box aft contains raising gear for the associated radio mast.

Anti-submarine netlaying is a cumbersome business, as this wartime photograph suggests. Few experts remain who know how to go about it, but nets may well be necessary again.

(ABOVE) Even quite moderate-sized submarines can embark a significant number of troops. USS *Perch*, 1,526 tons (APSS-313), was converted for this purpose in about 1948 (although she was taken out of service later) and could carry 160 troops. The large cylinder was for amphibious landing equipment.(*US Navy*) (BELOW LEFT) Periscopes have come a very long way from the 'optical tubes', 'hyposcopes' and 'cleptoscopes' of the early days. They can now incorporate a laser rangefinder, stabilizer, artificial sextant, image-intensifier (thermal imager) for a day and night capability, ESM and a camera. Remote viewing on a TV screen (with recording for subsequent analysis) is now usual. The photograph shows a Barr & Stroud CK34 search periscope with most modern extras. (BELOW RIGHT) Soviet submariners by no means normally enjoy a diet of roast suckling pig, but that became the traditional reward for (supposedly) successful patrols in 1943. Here, Captain Third Rank Fisanovich (*M-172*) displays anticipatory enjoyment of the prize. (OPPOSITE PAGE ABOVE) The idea of putting mine-chutes in external ballast tanks was conceived in the First World War and there is no reason why it should not, for double-hulled boats, be continued today. This picture of HMS *E-51*, taken in 1917, shows how difficult it might be, except at very close range, to determine that a boat is carrying external mines – which does not necessarily detract from the torpedo and missile load in many types of submarine. (OPPOSITE PAGE BELOW) Correct ballasting is, of course, crucial. Here, HMS *Resolution* (SSBN) is carrying out basin trials at Rosyth after a refit in October 1984.

(ABOVE) Senior Political Officer E. V. Gusarov reading out political information in the Soviet *D-3* during the Great Patriotic War. The uniforms have changed a little, but the Party doctrine has not. (BELOW) SSBNs carry torpedoes for defensive purposes. The rapid reloading gear shown here in HMS *Resolution* is noisy – the need to use it would not arise in the normal course of events, but the torpedo system would give an SSBN formidable anti-submarine and anti-ship firepower if the deterrent mission were to be changed for some reason to standard offensive patrolling or surveillance. Three of the older US Navy SSBNs have so far been redesignated SSNs, two of them being converted to amphibious transports.

(ABOVE) A Soviet 'Whiskey' SSK: there are still about fifty of these 1951–57 boats (Type V) at sea, though they rarely operate out of area, with seventy-five in reserve. Owing a good deal to German influence stemming from the 'Type XXI' (but not following that design to the extent sometimes suggested), these 1,080/1,350-ton boats can make eighteen knots on the surface and fourteen knots submerged, although they can only maintain the latter speed dived for a relatively short period – probably less than one hour. This is the most popular export model and several boats are still in service in the navies of Albania (three), Cuba (one), Egypt (five), North Korea (four) and Poland (four). This was the type – number 137 – which ran aground near the Swedish naval base at Karlskrona on 28 October 1981: the commanding officer, Captain Second Rank A. A. Gushchin, was apparently exonerated, because it has been reported that he has since been given a new command. Presumably the division commander and the *zampolit*, also on board, carried the can. (BELOW) A Soviet 'Foxtrot' 1,950/2,500-ton SSK – a most successful class of which sixty-two were built in 1958–71 for the Soviet Navy. Production continued for export to Cuba (three), India (eight) and Libya (six). Three diesel-electric systems drive three shafts giving eighteen knots on the surface and sixteen knots dived. There are six twenty-one-inch bow tubes and four sixteen-inch stern tubes; twenty-two torpedoes (or mines) can be carried.

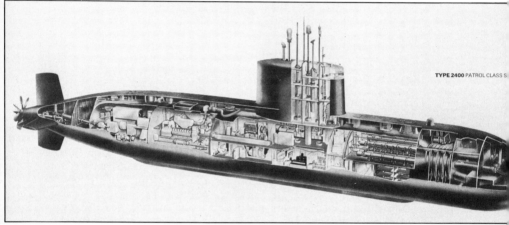

TYPE 2400 PATROL CLASS S

(TOP LEFT) A Soviet 'Kilo' SSK, the type now being transferred to India. Intended to replace ageing boats, these 2,500/3,100-ton diesel-electric submarines do not have many marked improvements over their predecessors, but their shape suggests that they are very manoeuverable and they may well have an extended underwater performance – at an estimated maximum speed of sixteen knots. They can probably snorkel at ten to twelve knots. Eight bow twenty-one-inch torpedo tubes are fitted and the crew totals about fifty-five. (TOP CENTRE) The Dutch *Walrus*, the first of six planned diesel-electric boats, commissioned in 1986. Displacing 2,800 tons dived, *Walrus* is very well proportioned, with a length-to-beam ratio of eight to one and a submerged speed of twenty knots. The diving depth approaches 1,000 feet. Four bow torpedo tubes can discharge Mark 48 torpedoes, Sub Harpoon or mines. The Royal Netherlands Navy has always produced good and often innovative submarines; and Dutch submariners are outstanding. (TOP RIGHT) The small but effective 450/498-ton West German *U-26*, one of eighteen 'Type 206' diesel-electric SSKs commissioned between 1973 and 1975. Built, very wisely, with high-tensile non-magnetic steel, these boats can make seventeen knots dived and need a crew of only four officers and eighteen men. There are six bow torpedo tubes (no reloads) – loading is accomplished through the bow caps while trimmed by the stern; and twelve mines can be carried on each side externally, held in GRP containers, in addition to the sixteen mines which can be embarked instead of torpedoes. The Krupp Atlas DBQS-21D sonar is excellent, and the West German U-boat arm is run with extreme efficiency, as befits the successors to Doenitz and his men. (ABOVE) A drawing of HMS *Upholder*, first of the new Royal Navy 'Type 2400' SSKs, hoped to be commissioned in late 1987. The diesel-electric machinery will consist of two Paxman Valenta 1600 RPA-200 S diesels, two GEC alternators, and one GEC electric motor driving a seven-bladed propellor for speeds of up to about twenty knots submerged. The fire-control system will be the Ferranti-Gresham-Lion DCC, with six bow tubes, type 2040 bow sonar, type 2024 towed array, and Micropuffs ranging. The crew will be relatively small, with seven officers, thirteen senior ratings and twenty-four junior ratings. (*VSEL*)

(ABOVE) A Soviet 'Tango' 3,000/3,900-ton SSK, one of eighteen diesel-electric two-shaft patrol submarines of this class, successor to the 'Foxtrots' from 1972 and with a comparable performance. They have eight twenty-one inch bow tubes, but no stern tubes.

(ABOVE) HMCS *Onandaga*, first commissioned in June 1967, basically similar to the British O class SSKs but equipped with KA CSU3-41 active/passive and type 2007 long-range passive sonar. American Mark 37C anti-submarine torpedoes are carried. Fire-control and sonar are now being updated and will include Sperry Micropuffs for passive ranging. (BELOW) One of Australia's six 'Oberon' class SSKs surfacing. The Royal Australian Navy, wisely shopping around, has equipped its submarines extremely well with Type 2007 long-range passive sonar, Sperry Micropuffs for passive ranging, Krupp Atlas (West German) CSU3-41 attack sonar, a fire-control system from Singer Librascope USA, American Mark 48 Mod 8 torpedoes and Sub Harpoon missiles. Australia has every reason to be proud of its submarine force which, with some debt to the Royal Navy, is very efficient and well trained.

chances of returning safely were six to four against. As things turned out the war was effectively over when the attack was made, and after four days of captivity aboard the hospital ship *Hapsburg* the successful operators returned to a wildly enthusiastic reception at Venice. Rossetti, the senior partner, was given 650,000 lira prize money: it was typical of the chivalrous spirit common to Italian human torpedo operators, then and later, that the prize money was handed over, unostentatiously, to families bereaved by the attack.

The sinking of the *Viribus Unitis* came too late to have any effect on the war and, from a strictly strategic point of view, it was a wasted effort attended by a considerable loss of life. But the success of the little Leech had far-reaching results: it inspired a whole new generation of frogmen and laid solid foundations for a powerful and effective Italian harbour penetration force in the Second World War.

Mussolini's navy was not notable for sound tactics, expertise or, in Nelsonian terms, engaging the enemy more closely – save for the heroic and devastating exploits of the Tenth (formerly the First) Light Flotilla of assault craft, whose Special Weapons Department was detached and formed into two divisions, one underwater and one surface, in March 1941. Until the Armistice in September 1943, when most Italian forces came under the control of the Allies, the Department was responsible for sinking or damaging four warships and twenty-seven merchant ships totalling 265,352 tons. The Tenth was, fortunately, commanded by the Duke of Aosta, who was able to use his considerable personal influence in acquiring stores and supplies when these were very short elsewhere; and he also knew how to lead men. The Special Assault Units therefore enjoyed a degree of logistical support and leadership which the surface navy and many submarines lacked.

The reasons for good or bad morale are always difficult to quantify. Why was it so excellent in the Special Weapons Department when it declined so rapidly and so markedly throughout almost all of the remainder of Mussolini's forces? So far as the surface fleet was concerned, poor logistics were a root cause of the decline: capital ships were kept in harbour not only because Il Duce desperately wanted to maintain his fleet intact, but also, more importantly, because there was insufficient fuel for offensive operations.

The intolerable restrictions on active service were undoubtedly detrimental to morale, and the blame lay with Mussolini and his avowed belief that the war would be short. Oil stocks were not maximised when opportunities still existed, and 212 out of 786 Italian merchant ships (larger than 500 tons gross) were cut off from the Mediterranean or locked in enemy ports at the commencement of hostilities on 10 June 1940. During the thirty-nine months of war that followed a total of 983 cargo vessels and tankers were, or became, available to Italy; 565 losses were incurred. Many of the merchantmen, inadequately protected by the oil-starved navy, fell victim to the extremely efficient British and Allied submarines operating from Gibraltar, Malta, Alexandria, Beirut and, in the later stages, Algiers.

Paradoxically, while officers in the fleet distanced themselves from the men – and this was common even in submarines where officers enjoyed exceptional privileges and, in some, even had their own galley – the Special Weapons Department officers, who included in their number several of high birth, enjoyed close relationships with their men, who often came from humble rural backgrounds. Loyalty was absolute upwards and downwards, and if this stemmed in part from *noblesse oblige* there was never any sense of inverted snobbery. So long as there was a worthwhile job to do (and that is always the foundation of good morale), class differences worked for, and not against, team spirit amongst the crews.

There was another influence that favoured small compact units in the Italian Navy, and it could also be seen to work in crack army units like the *Folgore* paratroopers. Not easily defined, it was concerned with the Latin temperament. The Italians, singly or in small numbers, were courageous – glad and willing to volunteer for dangerous duty provided that individual prowess could stand out. They were not, on the other hand, so happy about being small cogs in a large wheel.

Special Assault Weapons, economical in terms of men and fuel and bold in execution, were thus ideally suited to the Supermarina's dire need. But it was actually the Abyssinian campaign launched in 1935, rather than the entry of Italy into the Second World War in 1940, that led to the development of manned torpedoes. The threat posed by the superior British Fleet (which, in the event, did not actively oppose the Italian march on East Africa) prompted the formation of a new corps with a secret weapon which could be cheaply and quickly produced to attack naval targets in harbour, and thereby reduce Italy's naval disadvantage. Covert underwater warfare was the answer for a weaker power, just as it had been in 1776 when David Bushnell's tiny *Turtle* – 'an effort of genius' in General George Washington's words – attempted the first midget submersible attack on Admiral Lord Howe's fleet in New York harbour.[1]

In October 1935 two young submarine engineers, Sub Lieutenants

Tesei and Toschi, submitted plans for a much-improved version of the *Mignatta* to Admiral Cavagnari, Chief of the Italian Naval Staff, who immediately seized on the idea and put thirty technicians from the La Spezia Submarine Weapons Works on to the project. Speed was the essence and improvisation the method: the first engine came from an elevator in a dockyard block which was being demolished. Two prototypes were ready in January 1936 – less than three months after the design left the drawing board. Toschi described the beast that emerged as very similar to a torpedo, but '... in reality a miniature submarine with entirely novel features, electrical propulsion and a steering wheel similar to that of an aeroplane ... The crew (pilot and assistant), instead of remaining enclosed and more or less helpless in the interior, keep outside the structure. The two men, true fliers of the sea-depths astride their little underwater "aeroplane", are protected by a curved screen of plastic glass ... At night, under cover of darkness and steering by luminous instruments, they will be able to attack their objective while remaining invisible to the enemy ... They will be able to cut nets and remove obstacles with compressed air tools and reach any target ... with long-endurance breathing sets they can operate at depths down to thirty metres[2] and can carry a powerful explosive charge into an enemy harbour. Invisible and undetectable by the most sensitive acoustic detectors, the operator will be able to operate inside the harbour until they find the keel of a large ship, attach the charge to it and ensure an explosion which will sink the vessel.'[3]

That was as good a description of the manned torpedo idea as any.

The production weapons which followed, 6.7. metres long with 300 kilos of explosives in a detachable head, were formally styled SLC (the Italian initials for Slow Speed Torpedoes) but they were usually called *Maiale* (Pigs or Swine) because when, during early trials, Tesei had to abandon a sinking craft he came out of the water complaining 'That swine got away again!' The name stuck.

As it happened, the Ethiopian campaign did not call for special weapons and the Department was dissolved. But in July 1939, with war in Europe imminent, the Supermarina gave orders for the training of special weapons personnel to recommence, and this started in earnest, albeit on a part-time basis, at the beginning of 1940. Operational exercises, initially with three 'Maiale' lashed to the deck of the submarine *Ametista* in the Gulf of La Spezia, were starkly realistic and reasonably successful. But despite the perceptive support of Admiral Cavagnari, the new weapons were generally distrusted at high level, and no plans were agreed for a mass attack at the beginning of hostilities. Judging by results later, with 'Pigs' that were far from perfected, such an attack against unalerted British capital ships might at least have resulted in a temporary reversal of naval strength in favour of the Italians. As it was, when three 'Maiale' crippled the 30,000-ton British battleships *Valiant* and *Queen Elizabeth* (together with a valuable tanker and a destroyer) in Alexandria Harbour on 21 December 1941, the balance of naval power in the Mediterranean was upset by six brave men in the space of a few minutes. And that was by no means the only quick success: three months earlier, before dawn on the morning of 19 September, two tankers and a 10,900-ton cargo vessel had been shattered by explosions at Gibraltar – one of them inside the seemingly secure harbour itself.

Prime Minister Winston Churchill, justifiably annoyed by these onslaughts from a navy which British propaganda insisted was weak and cowardly, spurred the Admiralty on 18 January 1942: 'Please report what is being done to emulate the exploits of the Italians . . . One would have thought we should have been in the lead?'

It took only a bare three months to produce the first flock of British-manned torpedoes; they were christened Chariots, but were sometimes known as 'Jeeps', after the rodent-like creature which emitted a series of 'Jeep-Jeeps' in the *Popeye* strip cartoon. Chariots achieved some notable triumphs in the Mediterranean, sinking the 8,500-ton troop transport *Viminale* and the new cruiser *Ulpio Traiano* at Palermo in January 1943; and in June 1944 forces were joined with the post-armistice Italian frogmen, now allies, to attack the German-controlled Italian cruisers *Bolzano* and *Gorizia* at La Spezia, an operation which destroyed the *Bolzano* and prevented the cruiser from being used as a block ship in the port of Spezia itself.

Chariots could, incidentally, be transported by specially adapted Short Sunderland flying boats. 'Operation Large Lumps', as it was quaintly called, was not put into effect, but small submersibles could easily be airlifted now.

All this is history, and baldly stated it shows little more than that manned torpedoes could achieve striking results against ships in well-defended harbours, even when enemy intelligence was aware of the threat. But behind the bare bones of these stories there are some interesting and apposite conclusions to be drawn.

Firstly, the men who took part in 'Maiale' and Chariot operations – forerunners of the SBS[4] and similar organisations – were imbued with a spirit of their own which was unique to an elite corps and which could not, perhaps, have been predicted from a knowledge of the pre-war Italian and British navies as a whole. Secondly, although it was possible to develop these weapons very quickly, training took longer. Thirdly, determined men working in pairs could breach strong harbour defences. And fourthly, a very small vehicle could carry a devastating quantity of explosive. All of these factors are highly relevant today in relation to both large and small naval powers who may see clandestine operations as the way to achieving certain important objectives in peace, crisis and war.

Submarines were the ideal transporters for 'Maiale', but the attacks on Gibraltar, mounted from purportedly neutral Spain, involved the use of a curious kind of base which deserves to be remembered because the concept could very well be revived: indeed, a variant has probably been used recently off Sweden.

The Italian merchant ship *Olterra* had been scuttled in shallow Spanish territorial waters close to Gibraltar on the day that Italy entered the war. Eighteen months passed and the engines and boilers rotted; but then an idea began to take shape at the Tenth Light Flotilla headquarters. Under the pretext of the owner wanting to refit his ship before handing it over to a Spanish company, the vessel was salvaged and brought into Algeçiras harbour. Here, under the windows of the British Consulate – well staffed by Intelligence officers – and with Spanish sentries on deck and on the quayside, 'Maiale' men and technicians replaced the regular crew and constructed workshop and support facilities in the hold for craft that were to be sent piecemeal from Italy.

A large square hole was cut low down in the hull while listing the ship for pretended careening; the workmen were protected from the sun – and observation – by a canvas screen. The adjacent section of the hull was then deliberately flooded to provide an underwater dock for Pigs setting out on missions against Gibraltar a few miles across the bay. Nothing could have been simpler or more secure.

There is no reason why some of the numerous Soviet merchant ships which ply their legitimate trade around the world – all under naval-political control – should not be equipped with hatches below the waterline and facilities for miniature submersibles of one kind or another. Large trawlers would be ideal, but they have become so notorious as intelligence gatherers that the GRU might prefer to adapt more overtly innocent cargo vessels – although the latter, too, are apt to bristle with antennae. Nor would a ship necessarily have to anchor or go alongside to discharge and recover submerged craft. It would not be too difficult to devise arrangements for doing so under way at slow speed on the Ro-ro ferry principle. It would seem sensible to regard any Soviet vessel with suspicion when at or near a port of interest, or if manoeuvring slowly off an unguarded coastline.

The particular characteristics of manned torpedoes, as distinct from miniature submarines, is that the operators have to wear breathing sets and are exposed to water pressure. At first sight they are not very suitable for the Soviets because, as the British discovered on Norwegian operations, cold water and bad weather are emphatically not conducive to success. Nevertheless, Yugoslavia has sold a number of one-man R–1 and two-men R–2 Mala (perspex-hooded but free-flood) types to the USSR, and at least two have gone to Libya. Sweden has also acquired a couple of these Yugoslavian craft, presumably (and ironically) for use in the 'loyal opposition' role to practise attacks against Soviet invaders. Soviet usage is more likely to be for basic training and probing defences rather than serious warlike operations, but realistic training for the latter could certainly be extended to surrogates like Libya. The range of an R–2 is only eighteen nautical miles at 4.4 knots or twenty-three nautical miles at 3.7 knots, while the R–1 has a top speed of three knots and a range of eight nautical miles at 2.5 knots; but silver-zinc rather than lead-acid batteries would improve performance considerably.

An R–2 can carry 550 pounds of limpet mines or equipment – a formidable load. It is quite possible that, released from a submerged submarine or parent surface vessel close to shore, the Soviets are using Mala for some of their Baltic intrusions, but one would think that vehicles with a rather greater capability, as suggested later, are needed for important clandestine missions. Rumour has it that the Yugoslavs themselves are not keen on the craft; but in May 1985 the Yugoslavian Navy commissioned the first of a new eighty- to ninety-ton, four-man Una type, which looks quite impressive, and is a proper miniature submarine.

Manned torpedoes of whatever kind cannot lightly be dismissed today, as evidenced by Vickers proposed 134/150-ton *Piranha* submarine, which, for one of its roles, is designed to carry a pair of them secured amidships below the surface waterline: the craft will be manned through a lock-out chamber while the boat is submerged. There would be no way of telling from the surface if a Soviet or surrogate submarine was similarly equipped. Chariots slung externally would be a considerable hindrance to the operations of a modern Soviet submarine, but would not inhibit an ageing, noisy 'Whiskey' or 'Romeo' overmuch.

Manned torpedoes would certainly suit small Mediterranean navies, and there is said to be considerable interest in them along the North African coast. Algeria with her two 'Romeos' is an obvious candidate, as is Libya with her 'Foxtrots'; but there is no need to transport manned torpedoes by submarine or even a converted merchant ship in areas where no particular watch is being kept. A small fishing vessel could conceal one or more under tarpaulins on deck and hoist them out by derrick, or one could be slung underneath the keel. It has all been done before.[5]

The Japanese version of a human torpedo, *Kaiten*, was entirely different. Built around the surface-ship, high-performance Type 93 Long Lance oxygen torpedo, but fatter and lengthened from thirty to fifty-four feet, *Kaiten* looked like being what its name implied – a 'heaven-shaker', which would make a tremendous difference to the way things were going (on the whole, badly for the Japanese fleet after the Battle of Midway in June 1942). It was really a cross between a midget submarine and a giant torpedo. The single, fully enclosed and dry pilot was provided with controls, a small handcranked periscope and a gyro compass. There were no ballast or trim tanks – with slight positive buoyancy (and a self-destruct switch in the event of coming to the surface, stopped, in the presence of the enemy), depth-keeping relied entirely on the horizontal rudders aft, and it was far from easy to maintain an accurate depth. Every craft had its own idiosyncrasies: the controls were often stiff; rust was a continual problem; and scarce maintenance men were unable to keep pace with the adjustments and tuning needed at the training base, let alone with the defects which were prone to occur when the weapons were embarked on ocean-going submarines – which could carry three, four or six of them.

The *Kaiten* design was hatched, like the Italian *Maiale*, by two young officers – Lieutenant (jg) Hiroski Kuroki and Ensign Sekio Nishina, who were pilots of torpedo-armed midget submarines at the time of Midway. Working with Hiroshi Suzukawa, a civilian employee at the Kure naval dockyard, they produced completed plans for the new craft by January 1943. The aim was to attack crowded American anchorages in the atolls that would be used for bases when American amphibious forces started to advance westwards across the Pacific.

The Naval General Staff were not interested in the plan: it was too fantastic. So Kuroki and Nishina resorted to a traditional Japanese strategem and submitted the proposal written in their own blood. (It would be interesting to see the effect of such a sanguinary petition from junior officers to the MoD or Pentagon today.) This device worked, although it took eight months before approval for a prototype was given, and even then the Staff insisted that it must not be a suicide weapon – the pilot must be able to get out. This was patently absurd, but the escape hatch below the cockpit became very convenient for linking to a carrier submarine by means of a flexible tube. When the first operation was eventually mounted Admiral Miwa presented each pilot with a ceremonial short sword. This meant that the pilot's life was pledged to the emperor and empire: he must either seek death in battle or atone for failure with disembowelment by committing *seppuku*. So much for not being suicide weapons!

The first (thirty-eight-foot) model was ready in October 1944, by which time kamikaze exploits were widespread and there was no shortage of volunteers (often trainee naval aviators) for a submerged suicide craft. The final types, capable of forty knots for fourteen nautical miles and fifty at half that speed, carried 1,550 to 1,800 kilos of explosive in the head – about four times the weight of a normal torpedo warhead and enough to sink or inflict crippling damage on the largest ships.

Although some surface vessels (for instance, the cruiser *Kitaknami*) were able to slide *Kaiten* into the sea, the best carriers were obviously submarines. The pilot entered his craft from the parent boat through the flexible tube when a target presented itself, or when near the anchorage to be attacked; he remained in telephone contact with the submarine captain, who provided final bearings and course instructions up to the moment of release. The weapons were used either like ordinary torpedoes (at high speed), or they were launched to make their own way at moderate speed into the midst of an enemy assembly. When a few hundred metres from the target and on a collision course it was intended that the pilot should go to a depth of four metres, lock the controls, and prepare to meet his ancestors.

Several hundred *Kaiten* were built, but only about fifty saw action and their achievements were negligible. The tanker *Mississinewa* and the destroyer *Underhill* were the only certain victims. *Kaiten* may also have been responsible for damage to three or four American auxiliaries and destroyers, according to the most reliable reference[6] (records are scant), but mere damage to lightly built vessels sounds improbable from such a heavy warhead; perhaps the pilots missed their targets and self-destructed nearby, or maybe the damaged vessels were hit by standard torpedoes fired by parent submarines after *Kaiten* had been launched.

Whatever the truth may be, *Kaiten* were difficult to operate and the essential intensive training for their pilots was too seldom available. They were usually visible and open to counterattack; and they did nothing to bring about a great change in the empire's fortunes – which went from bad to worse, with eight parent submarines being sunk or damaged and some 900 Japanese lives being lost as a direct or indirect result of human torpedo operations.

Suicidal volunteers could readily be found amongst certain Middle Eastern political groups today, but the degree of technology required to reintroduce *Kaiten* would preclude its use by small bands of fanatics; and with history decisively against a sophisticated weapon it is improbable that larger organisations would wish to revive the idea. Having said that, it would be quite easy and inexpensive to adapt, crudely, an off-the-shelf torpedo with a standard warhead for a bareback rider to control and steer straight into a target. A simple kamikaze weapon would appeal to Muslim death-and-glory extremists and be more exciting than an explosive car: a hit on an infidel Sixth Fleet ship – a tanker would be tempting – would be bound to result in the perpetrator going straight to paradise.

Miniature submarines proper were built in a wide variety of shapes and sizes for the navies of Japan, Germany and Italy between 1939 and 1945, but it is the score or so of British 'X-craft' and (very similar) 'XE-craft' which call for most attention in retrospect, because they were more independent, they carried more powerful weapons, and they were more adaptable to a wide variety of operations than any other kind of midget. As a broad basis for a new design they would seem, in most major respects, to meet conjectural Soviet operational requirements.

On 13 February 1943 Prime Minister Winston Churchill, ill with pneumonia in North Africa, dictated another irritable minute to the Chiefs of Staff in London about a German battleship which he usually called 'The Beast':

> Have you given up all plans for doing anything to *Tirpitz* while she is in Trondhjem? We heard a lot of talk about it five months ago, which all petered out. At least four or five plans were under consideration. It seems very discreditable that the Italians should show themselves so much better at attacking ships in harbour than we do . . . It is a terrible thing to think that this prize should be waiting and no one be able to think of a way of winning it.

In fact, a handful of submariners had been devising ways of winning this particular prize for two years or more, but so secret – necessarily – were their efforts that people at the top knew little if anything about them. Ignorance or lack of understanding, which we said at the beginning has weighed against logical submarine development and employment throughout underwater history, was to be the particular bugbear of midget submariners and, eventually, the prime cause of their demise in the Royal Navy a dozen years after the war.

What the thirty-ton X-craft accomplished is well documented[7] but seldom recognised. They were originally designed in 1941 to deal with the German battleship *Tirpitz*, holed up in a Norwegian fjord where no other units could reach her. The Beast was much on Churchill's mind. He summed up its nuisance value to the enemy, out of all proportion to its actual capacity, in one of his milder asides in August 1941: 'It exercises a vague general fear and menaces all points at once. It appears and disappears causing immediate reactions and perturbations in the other side.' So long as *Tirpitz* threatened vital Russian convoys (vital politically as well as militarily), capital ships of the Home Fleet had to stand guard against her coming out, and two new American battleships had to be retained in the eastern Atlantic. Those ships were desperately needed elsewhere, especially in the Far East: something had to be done about The Beast.

On 11 and 12 September 1943 six 'X-craft', towed by 'T' and 'S' class submarines, set off for Kaa Fjord from Loch Cairnbawn in northern Scotland. Operation Source was under way. Two towing lines parted en route; one craft was lost, and another, with faulty explosive charge mechanisms, had to be scuttled.

For the want of a nail . . .

Parsimony prevented all the craft from being given 600-foot nylon tow ropes, each of which could have supplied the material for 20,000 pairs of black nylon stockings – a highly prized commodity in wartime England. Hemp ropes were much cheaper, but Lieutenant Donald Cameron (commanding officer of *X–6*) demanded nylon, rightly believing that hemp would be liable to break and that its weight would drag a craft to the bottom: he duly got nylon for his own craft, but the captains of *X–8* and *X–9* whose tows parted, did not. For the want of a nail the shoe was lost, for the want of a shoe . . .

To cut an exciting story short,[8] two craft (*X–6* and *X–7*) made their way through Soroy Sound across a declared German minefield, up Alten Fjord and into Kaa Fjord at the head, some sixty miles from the positions where they had been slipped from their parent submarines. Fortune favoured the brave and they penetrated the outer boom and the anti-torpedo nets to release four two-ton 'side-cargoes' – delayed action mines – beneath the huge target. At 0812 on 22 September 1943 the charges detonated: eight men in two fragile craft with half-inch pressure hulls had disabled a 42,000-ton battleship sheathed in fifteen-inch armour with a crew of 2,500 officers and men behind supposedly impregnable defences. The menace was eliminated. The Beast never put out to sea again; and rather more than a year later on 12 November 1944 the *Tirpitz* was finally destroyed in a new berth off Haakoy Island by RAF 'Tallboy' bombs. Six men from the two four-man crews survived to be taken prisoner. Both successful commanding officers, Cameron and Place, were awarded the Victoria Cross.

The charges they had used were not quite powerful enough but that could easily be remedied today. With the relatively high chances of failure and loss, a nuclear charge would not be suitable for a job of this kind, but it is certainly conceivable that an 'X-craft' type could lay nuclear, or indeed high-explosive, mines for remotely controlled detonation at some future time. Determination, risk and long, exceedingly thorough and authentic training were the keys to this important strategic success.

Taking command of an 'X-craft' was rather like being given a toy train set for Christmas. It was a perfect submarine in miniature – fifty-one feet and six inches long, five feet and nine inches in diameter, and displacing about thirty tons submerged without charges. Everything was reduced in size – main-vent hand-levers, valve wheels, high-pressure air bottles, battery cells, gauges and indicators, electrical switches and the main periscope – a masterpiece of miniaturisation by Barr and Stroud. The diesel engine which drove it on the surface and recharged the battery belonged, properly speaking, to a London omnibus – and it proved just as reliable rumbling throatily up the Norwegian fjords as on the streets of the metropolis. Simplicity and ruggedness underlay design and construction, and anything in the least complex was prone to breakdowns – the electric periscope hoist system in particular – so most of the controls were handraulic. In the main, 'X-craft' were robust and reliable. They could (and did) thump the bottom and run full tilt into solid obstructions without damage; their resistance to shock was comparable to that of large submarines; and the safe diving depth was 300 feet, giving a healthy safety margin over the collapse depth of about 600 feet.

A craft was divided into four distinct areas for the battery, 'Wet and Dry' diving lock, control room, and engine room. It could be parted into two or three bolted sections when lifted on board or hauled up on a slipway for maintenance. The battery was housed forward in its own compartment, and the 112 sixty-three-pound lead-acid cells were laid in two sections of fifty-six cells each. The sections could be electrically grouped at the control room switchboard to supply the main motor with a nominal 112 volts or 224 volts DC. The auxiliary circuits were fed from either of the two sections in turn. The top speed submerged was about five knots, but this could be maintained for only one hour at best before the battery was flattened. At the more usual economical speed of two knots a craft could go for eighty miles without recharging, provided that the auxiliary load was kept to a minimum. (Depending on the space made available, modern batteries could double or triple submerged performance.)

The four-cylinder Gardner diesel engine, aft, was rated at forty-two horsepower at 1,800 rpm for continuous running, and sufficient fuel was carried to give a range of 1,320 miles at a surface cruising speed of four knots, and proportionally less at the top speed of 6.5 knots. The engine, motor and propeller were mounted on a common shaft: the motor drove the single propeller through a clutch and reduction gearing, and the engine drove the motor as a generator when charging or floating the load – exactly the same system as in most large submarines of the period. The engine was started by the motor.

It would, in theory, have been possible to snorkel through the induction mast which was used on the surface, but no head valve was fitted. A valve-equipped induction mast and a longer telescopic periscope (as fitted in post-war 'X-craft') would allow a craft to snorkel, given an engine that could cope with back pressure, but the top of the casing would not be more than five feet below the surface. It would therefore be very difficult to control a craft in anything more than a low to moderate sea, and it might have to zig-zag to keep sea and swell more or less abeam. However, in heavier weather it would probably escape detection on the surface – at the probable price of acute sea-sickness for the crew.

Initially, there were only three men in the X-craft crew – captain, first lieutenant and engineer room artificer, but it became clear during early training that these men were too fully occupied for one of them to take time off to swim outside the craft to cut nets or place limpets (which were the alternative weapons to the big 'side-cargo' mines). A diver, recruited from Chariots, was therefore added to each crew when the craft were working up for Operation Source.

Today a second diver could be accommodated – just – in a craft of this size, and he might be needed for certain tasks. Carbon dioxide scrubbers and oxygen generators ought to be able to purify the air for two or three days fully submerged. Some degree of automation for steering and depth-keeping would not be unduly complex, but the very sensible Soviet view is to keep things simple whenever possible, so automation would not necessarily feature in a modern craft. A crew of four or five, including a couple of divers, is predictable if the Soviet Navy has something on these lines in its armoury.

Although excellent commercial and sports diving sets are available nowadays when scuba diving is a common hobby, they are far from ideal for covert operations because they release bubbles to the surface – acceptable off-shore, perhaps, but not in tricky harbour situations. A closed-circuit oxygen re-breathing set is necessary to avoid detection, but this imposes severe limitations on the user, a point which hunters will want to note. A depth of eight to ten metres is the limit for light work for up to seventy-five minutes – tolerance to oxygen is drastically reduced by the build-up of carbon dioxide when working hard and breathing heavily. Brief excursions to deeper depths can be made, and divers have frequently exceeded the advisory limits and got away with it down to thirty metres and more – but oxygen tolerance is impossible to predict with confidence for any one person on any particular day, and a moribund diver is the last thing that the Soviets would want to be discovered floating on the surface. One answer to that, of course, is to ensure that a diver cannot get rid of negative buoyancy (by cutting loose his weights), but that seems a little ruthless, even for the GRU.

Living conditions inside an 'X-craft' were abominable. A crew could not possibly be in a fit state to undertake a skilled and hazardous operation after a long tow, so a passage crew acted as caretakers en route and turned over to the operational team when nearing the objective.

Ranges in the Baltic are not too great to prevent an operational crew, working watch and watch, manning a midget throughout a passage to and from an operation. If longer distances are involved, one or two midgets, comparable in size to an 'X-craft', could be carried on the deck of an SSN or SSK, with connecting hatches like the *Kaiten* arrangements. The 4,000-ton 'India' class diesel submarines (one in the Northern Fleet and one in the Pacific) already carry two deep sea rescue vehicles and could presumably embark military midgets instead. Come to that, with fairly minor modifications, so could US and British submarines equipped to take or receive DSRVs for escape.

The US Navy has reportedly converted two SSBNs (one for each coast) with a drydock shelter which fits on top of the submarine and mates with a hatch. Swimmer Delivery Vehicles (SDVs) can thereby be accommodated and transported over long ranges for covert deployment by these former SSBNs; and it is understood that the SDVs themselves have been modernised to include better weapons and offer a longer independent range than the early models. Little is known about the capabilities of this submarine-SDV package, but the midget concept has certainly been revived in the US Navy which was singularly unenthusiastic about it during the war. However, it seems probable that SDVs are intended primarily for 'inserting' special forces (which would presumably be invaluable in the context of anti-terrorist operations amongst other uses), but nothing has apparently been said about plans for strategic operations along the lines of those carried out in the Second World War.

When slipped and on its own an 'X-craft' was so self-contained – a complete weapon system in itself – so handy, so manoeuvrable and so difficult for an enemy to detect by any means that the captain could take calculated risks with confidence. Skill and meticulous attention to detail as well, obviously, as courage were mandatory, but properly handled a craft could insinuate itself into and out of the tightest corners. A good first lieutenant at the pump, hydroplane and motor controls could hover, change depth vertically without way on, or go astern with precision, although the trim was so delicate that plates of potmess passed forward, from the carpenter's glue-pot which served as a double-boiler galley, could alter the pitch angle.

The dangers were inevitably great in action because a craft had to make physical contact with its target, or at least come within feet of it, while the captain positioned it in exactly the right place for the charges to have maximum effect. It was, incidentally, memories of this exactitude in 'X-craft' command that prompted the captain of one of the first SSKs which went far under the Arctic icecap[9] to propose stopping and surfacing – without automated aids – in *polynyas* only just large enough to take the boat's length.

In order to place limpets, which were stowed in an otherwise empty 'side-cargo' and under the casing, three short masts, with springy buffers at their extremities, were raised: with slight positive buoyancy, the craft rested on these beneath the target's hull like a fly on the ceiling. The diver, sitting gloomily on the WC in the Wet and Dry chamber, then pumped up water from an internal tank (to avoid upsetting the trim) and knew, all too well, when the lock was full by the incompressible water squeezing suddenly and hard on his compressible breathing bag and person: it was never a pleasant experience.

The diver could also cut through nets (although this never had to be done in war) with a hydraulic cutter on a long lead. For this operation the captain, watching through a stubby fixed periscope, put the bow into the net at minimum speed to stem the tide. Nets could not be cut *with* the tidal stream or current because the craft was then swept broadside on, making the task too long and laborious to be practicable – a point worth remembering when manning net defences.

Much encouraged by Operation Source, 'X-craft' went on to deal blows at Bergen and Singapore; but other, non-attacking jobs illustrate the versatility of the midgets. In January 1944, on Operation Postage Able, *X–20* sent swimmers ashore to reconnoitre a proposed Normandy invasion beach, and in June she and *X–23* preceded the invasion fleet to mark Sword and Juno beaches accurately for the incoming amphibious forces. In July 1945 two craft cut the seabed telephone cables linking Hong Kong, Saigon and Singapore, forcing the Japanese to revert to radio communication which the code-breakers could intercept.

A mere midget

Amongst a number of failures or semi-failures, there was one striking success by a Japanese torpedo-firing midget.

On 30 May 1942, sixteen months before the British attack on the *Tirpitz*, a Type A 'fly' commanded by Lieutenant Saburo Akieda was floated off the large submarine *I–20* ten miles north of Diego Suarez at the northern tip of Madagascar. Other 'flies' released at the same time from a group of three submarines broke down or lost their way; but Akieda, with crewman Petty Officer Masami Takamoto, was by far the most experienced operator, and he successfully navigated the long, treacherous channel leading to the inner anchorage used by the British fleet.

At 2025 a torpedo struck the battleship HMS *Ramillies* on the port anti-torpedo bulge just forward of 'A' turret. The bulge plating was holed for thirty feet by thirty feet and the outer bottom for twenty feet by sixteen feet. The damage assessment was that 'fighting efficiency was seriously impaired', and the battleship was out of action for nearly a year – another strategic triumph by a mere midget.

A few minutes after *Ramillies* was hit, the 6,993-ton tanker *British Loyalty* went down to Akieda's second torpedo.

The term 'cost effectiveness' was not coined until long after the war, but 'Maiale', 'Chariots', 'X-craft' and at least one 'Type A' were arguably the most cost-effective submersible craft ever built.

The Germans, on the other hand, achieved very little with the many assorted midgets which they flung hastily into battle towards the end of the war, mainly against invasion forces. Lack of training was their weakness.

After the war the British continued to exercise with 'XE-craft', and in 1954–5 four craft of a new type were built – but they were not as handy as their predecessors. The X-craft unit was finally disbanded in 1958, one craft, *Stickleback*, going to Sweden where she became *Spiggen*. It was rumoured that Flag Officer Submarines had been invited to cut his flotilla by four hulls, and that this was the least painful way of achieving the reduction. But the truth was that midget submarines simply did not fit into the peacetime navy: the crews took wartime risks – and enjoyed taking them – but they worried the Staff, and that is always the most dangerous thing a submariner can do. And at high level 'X-craft' were clearly considered to be not quite nice. The Whitehall attitude was exemplified by a top secret message in response to a suggestion that a couple of craft should be flown out to destroy Egyptian blockships before they could be moved into position to seal the Suez Canal at the beginning of the abortive Anglo-French operation in 1956: 'too much like real war' were the immortal words used on this occasion, while French and British aircraft were bombing Egyptian airfields from 31 October and dropping airborne troops five days later.

The US Navy, apparently on a private whim, built the solitary but advanced peroxide-diesel craft USS *X–1*, which was accepted in May 1956. She was soon placed, thankfully, 'Out-of-Service in Reserve' in December 1957, after an explosion eight months earlier. USS *X–1* was subsequently re-equipped with the ordinary diesel-battery configuration, which she ought to have had in the first place, and used as a test vehicle.

Important lessons were learned from midget operations. Brought up to date and summarised, they are:

a. Thorough, realistic training lasting months rather than weeks is mandatory: this may be a truism, but it must be borne in mind when intelligence indicates that a particular navy has acquired midgets of one kind or another.

b. Midget submarines, Chariots and basic human torpedoes can be built quickly, cheaply and secretly.

c. Practically any submarine or merchant vessel can be adapted to carry miniature submersibles without that necessarily being obvious.

d. No anti-submarine or anti-torpedo defences have ever defeated determined, trained midget operators: they have been a hindrance, sometimes a severe impediment, but no more than that.

e. A very special kind of man is required to crew miniature submersibles, and he is not likely to be the type who will succeed in a normal, peacetime naval career.

f. One man, by himself, will lose heart: there must be at least two in a crew.

g. Covert attack units must be allowed to develop their own team spirit in their own way, and this will, very probably, fly in the face of naval custom and tradition. Risks are implied in peacetime, and these must be accepted if craft are to be ready for war.

h. Kamikaze tactics worked with aircraft because the pilots attacked at exhilarating speed in hot blood. Long, cold-blooded submerged operations, involving meticulous navigation and fire-control, will not succeed if certain death lies ahead. Nevertheless, a dedicated extremist riding a suicidal human torpedo over a short distance could experience more than enough exhilaration to ram his weapon into an important target.

i. Any navy, however small, can afford midgets, and their inclusion should be suspected if it appears that objectives – which are by no means confined to overtly warlike aims – are not being achieved by more conventional means.

One other kind of midget, the German amphibious *Seeteufel*, calls for especially close attention. The *Sea Devil* was only an experimental model at the end of the war, and its existence was thought to be a well-kept secret. Admiral Heye (wartime commander of the *Kleinkampfmittel* Small Battle Unit Force) was quoted in 1949[10] as saying that the type was 'strongly believed to be unknown to the Soviets', but that belief must, with regret, be discounted, since tracks photographed on the seabed in Sweden and reported off Brazil match the amphibian's caterpillar traction.

The *Sea Devil* was designed with an engine that could be coupled either to a propeller or to a caterpillar undercarriage adopted from a tank. It had a crew of two and could carry torpedoes or mines, a machine-gun, and a rocket or flame-thrower. In Heye's words:

I consider the *Sea Devil* a promising weapon for use in commando raids. It is independent of mother craft and base personnel, can land on foreign shores, commit acts of sabotage, and evade pursuit ashore or afloat. It can be taken to site by a mother ship equipped with a large crane. With an engine of higher output than that of the experimental boat, a speed of 8 to 10 knots can be obtained. Speed and radius of action could be further increased by installation of a closed-cycle engine. Intended for use in coastal waters if weather is not too rough, and on rivers, lakes and artificial lakes.

A *Sea Devil* today would not necessarily need to climb completely out of the water: from a shelving beach, frogmen could haul ashore heavy packages of equipment and explosives which swimmers could not carry from further out. When hounded by helicopters and patrol boats the craft could rest securely on the bottom until the furore died down. Hydrographic and sonar conditions in the Baltic favour intruders of this kind.

Divers and midget submarines have been spotted at a number of locations along the Swedish coast, and there can be no real doubt about where they come from – although Sweden has been careful not to name the obvious suspect. Foreign frogmen have been seen using measuring lines around the defensive minefields blocking the entrances to the Stockholm archipelago; and one was sighted climbing ashore on an island off Karlskrona before disappearing into the water on the other side.[11]

The indications are that Soviet midget operations in Swedish waters are being conducted on quite a large scale, and there is every likelihood that they are going on in other areas which have not yet fully woken up to these clandestine activities. The Swedish Navy – alone it seems – is taking the threat seriously: light aircraft, helicopters, patrol boats and coastal corvettes are being equipped with suitable sonobuoys and bottom-scanning sonars; submarines are attached to anti-submarine groups; and magnetic detection systems are being installed across key entrances. It remains to be seen how effective these defences will prove. Deterrence rather than total prevention would seem to be the right aim: that is, it will be sufficient in peacetime to make the capture of a craft or frogmen a distinct possibility – a risk that would be deemed intolerable to the USSR.

Why, one asks, are these incursions aimed, primarily as it appears, at Sweden? The answer is surely that Sweden is the route to south Norway where, with the Norwegian Sea in the main well guarded by NATO submarines, the Soviet Navy must establish a base if a sudden offensive is to be launched against Europe. In the meantime, one might suppose that the Kremlin must be very interested in the chatter on those secret NATO communication lines which could have been tapped by Spetsnaz units. In a crisis, Spetsnaz teams working with Osnaz signal-interception experts can also be expected to feed false messages into marine and underground cables.

The Baltic Fleet's independent intelligence service (RU) is headed by a rear admiral who reports to the chief of staff[12] and thence to the fleet commander.[13] However, the head of the RU is also responsible – more importantly – to the chief of the Fifth Directorate of the GRU, which in turn is controlled by the head of the Department of Administrative

Organs of the Central Committee of the Communist Party[14] and, above that, the Politburo and the Defence Council. The Baltic RU is scarcely independent save in name: the structure is so rigidly controlled, and there are so many cross-checks, that security is absolute and defection is very improbable.

It is Department Three of the Baltic RU which recruits and operates men and women in the Spetsnaz organisation; but Department One, which has an officer on board every naval and merchant vessel (the captain's first assistant in the latter), would organise transport for midget submersibles.

Armed with some notions of what will and will not work in midget submarine warfare, we can speculate about the sort of craft that would suit the opposition today. We have not been privileged to scan a Soviet Staff Requirement, but, first initiated perhaps in 1972[15] by the commander-in-chief Baltic Fleet, it might look something like this:

MINIATURE SUBMERSIBLES

OBJECTIVES

Consequent upon Polit directives the head of GRU has formulated requirements to infiltrate special units into Scandinavia and to intercept marine communication lines. Concurrently, a requirement is foreseen, in the event of war, for neutralising important ships, submarines and facilities in naval ports and anchorages where defences are strong against attacks from the air.

Taking into account the wartime experience of all navies concerned (which removes the need for a tentative Staff Target) and adhering to the War Principles of Offence, Economy of Force, Manoeuvre and Initiative, Combined Aims, Surprise and Deception[16] the Staff Appreciation is that miniature submersibles of three types will best meet the stated objectives.

OPERATING AREAS

The Baltic will be the primary operating area but provision must be made for worldwide operations.

BASES

Operational and training bases must be secret and well removed from normal naval bases.

RANGE

Only exceptionally are midgets expected to transit to and from a target zone independently. Some merchant vessels and submarines must be adapted for covert transport, launching and recovery. This is the subject of a separate Staff Requirement.

Hence the independent range of any midget is not a governing factor in design.

WEAPON SYSTEMS

Although great advantages can be seen in constructing very small torpedo-firing submarines on the lines of the German Type (1944) XXVIIB 'Seehund' 13.7-ton U-boats, no practical way can be devised for sending them into action in sufficiently large numbers to swamp enemy anti-submarine escorting forces at sea as intended by the Nazi U-boat arm: this concept has therefore not been added to the objectives. Nor is it considered that torpedoes fired into well-defended harbours would be significantly effective.

Ground mines (nuclear and high explosive) with variable delays and capable of being triggered remotely at any time after being laid are therefore selected as primary weapons with limpet mines as the secondary system.

However, the principal purpose is to deploy special assault forces and sufficient space must be allocated for personnel with their equipment and personal weapons in the two operational types of craft proposed.

TYPE 1 – GENERAL PURPOSE

ARMAMENT

Two ground mines (released from inside the craft) carrying at least two tons of high explosive each or up to five kilotons of nuclear explosive plus twelve standard limpets.

HULL

Non-magnetic. Glass-reinforced plastic acceptable. Control room forward. Hull to be faired with minimal projections. Periscope housing but no conning tower as such.

DIMENSIONS

No greater than fifteen metres by two metres (not including external mines).

DENSITY RANGE

Standard saltwater range (Baltic), but must also be capable of operating in freshwater and compensating instantly for fresh or low density patches: 1,000 litre rapid flood/blow safety tank in addition to standard negative tank.

CREW

Four including a diver. (GRU to recruit and train in co-operation with Seventh Submarine Brigade Commander.)

ASSAULT SWIMMERS/SPECIAL FORCES

Space for two additional to crew.

EXIT AND RE-ENTRY LOCK

Standard but with additional hatch below for parent submarine connection.

RANGE AND ENDURANCE

a.   1,000 miles snorkel or surface at eight knots or better. Standard diesel.
b.   150 miles at five knots submerged on battery or 300 miles at three knots.
c.   Burst speed fifteen knots submerged for forty-five minutes (to no less than fifty per cent battery capacity).

HABITABILITY

Unimportant, but special forces embarked must not be unduly cramped. Chemical WC.

AIR PURIFICATION

Oxygen generator and carbon dioxide scrubber sufficient for sixty hours total submergence with six personnel on board.

NAVIGATION AND CONTROLS

Automated or semi-automated with immediate reversion to direct physical control when required. Hover-assist trimming. NATO radio navigational aids (from commercial sources). Secure echo-sounder (standard).

COMPASSES

Aircraft/helicopter type – electrical gyro and one precision air-blast (thirty-minute duration) with a plus or minus five degrees magnetic compass for emergency use.

SHOCK RESISTANCE AND DIVING DEPTH

Compatible with standard diesel submarines. Minimum safe depth of 250 metres. 1.5 safety factor.

NOISE REDUCTION

No cavitation at periscope depth (propeller/propulsor at three metres) below 3.5 knots. Resilient mountings for all machinery with particular attention to air purification. Anti-sonar coating over the whole hull; sound insulating tiles around main machinery space.

SELF-DEFENCE

No weapons, but two mobile decoys (standard external launchers) and internal discharge tube for chemical decoys.

NET-CUTTING

Diver-portable net-cutting gun to be stowed externally. Guards around propeller/propulsor.

VIEWING

a. Main periscope telescopic/periscopic: head diameter less than three centimetres; monocular; selectable magnification six or 1.5; ranging by graticule only. Image intensification desirable but not at the expense of top-optics head diameter. (Note: comparatively low speed should permit periscope and associated fairing to be forward rather than amidships without affecting handling characteristics.)

b.   Non-raisable wide-angle image-intensified periscope fifty centimetres above casing level for night viewing on the surface and for use underwater when submerged.

c.   Non-raisable, protected faired periscope right forward for conning through nets and obstructions when submerged.

d.   Scuttles (with deadlights) for side and upward viewing by commanding officer in control room forward. Laminated glass suitable for relaying and amplifying external diver's speech without a direct link; capable of withstanding shock as for hull.

SONAR

Passive listening in low kH_2 range. Directivity plus or minus one degree.

COMMUNICATIONS

a.   HF transmitter (voice and CW) with raisable elbow-joint whip antenna.

b.   VLF/LF receiver with antenna incorporated in hull.

c.   Underwater telephone (standard).

SELF-DESTRUCT

Internal charge with time delay up to one hour.

ADDITIONAL

To be fitted for but not with:

a.   Taut wire measuring gear.

b.   Bottom contour navigation equipment.

c.   Grapnel for locating cables.

d.   Underwater searchlight.

e.   Bacteriological/chemical warfare dissemination equipment.

TYPE 2 – AMPHIBIAN

All requirements as for TYPE 1 except:

a.   Caterpillar traction (non-metallic) additional to propeller/propulsor.

b. Closed-cycle diesel, plus battery. Four knots bottom-crawling, eight knots on propeller/propulsor, twelve knots burst speed.
c. Diving depth can be reduced to 100 metres if necessary.
d. Breadth up to three metres.
e. No connecting hatch for parent submarine: craft will be transported only by adapted trawlers/merchant vessels.
f. Two-man diving lock.
g. Trainable underwater searchlights (two).
h. Magnetic cable-detection equipment.
i. Three-cubic-metre stowage compartment (internal).
j. Internal-operated excavating, cutting and handling arms (standard commercial) capable of dealing with mines and buried armoured cables.
k. Acoustic telemetry for co-ordinated operations.
l. Seabed navigation (computerised) to within plus or minus two metres.

ADDITIONAL

To be fitted for but not with:
a. Minelaying or mine neutralising equipment.
b. Limpet mines.

TYPE 3 – TRAINING

Very simple one- or two-man craft, on the human torpedo principle, are required for basic training to accustom operators to the environment and, under favourable conditions, to undertake preliminary reconnaissance operations.

It is anybody's guess what the Soviet Staff Requirements actually were or when they were put forward, but those listed above are realistic and achievable. They could be bettered in the future.

The probability of increasing midget submersible operations in many areas of Western concern not excluding the United States is high. The prospects for preventing intrusions, agent-infiltration, eavesdropping, sabotage and actual attacks on harbours, anchorages and naval bases appear, at present, to be low. And there is a conceivable risk to ships in the Mediterranean from suicide craft. To make the picture gloomier, it is not impossible, as suggested above, that biological and chemical warfare agents will feature amongst midget weapon systems.

The Soviet system demands tight control of all units so it may be expected that, apart from the need to transport midgets, a mother ship or submarine will be lying somewhere close by an area of activity, with a senior GRU officer and a political officer embarked: this could be a useful clue to clandestine activities.

Defences against sneak submerged attacks have never been adequate and, by and large, they are now woefully lacking. Modern anti-submarine warfare is not designed to cater for pint-sized gate-crashers, and most standard anti-submarine equipment performs poorly in shallow water; but it seems advisable, to say the least, to pay more attention to actual and potential midget operations. The Swedish Navy is doing its best, but it may be that we shall all have to revert to booms across harbour entrances, to small patrol craft for seaward defence along vulnerable coastlines, and even to net protection for vulnerable ships at sea and in harbour in parts of the Mediterranean.

These old-fashioned methods of protection are not likely to be popular, but, regrettably, they might have to be considered once again. Meanwhile, there is one little trick which nobody seems to have remembered. Conservationists will hate it, but if an attack is suspected oil pumped on to the harbour surface will blind a small periscope, and no midget submariner can do his job if he cannot see where he is going. It sounds laughable against a background of complex anti-submarine systems, but as a last-ditch measure it will work. Midgets are uncomplicated craft, and the best defences against them may be equally simple.[17]

11

Strategic Underwater Missile Systems

A noted professor of war studies recently remarked that he was beginning to think that there was something fishy about the concept of nuclear deterrence. The professor was making a good point. So far as the average citizen is concerned the idea is quite simple: if you hit me I'll hit you, and the counter-blow will be so hard that you won't be able to bear it. That was plain and straightforward in the 1950s under Eisenhower's 'Massive Retaliation Doctrine'. Any attack would receive an immediate and devastating response. In the 1960s, in the face of a rapidly growing Soviet nuclear armoury, Robert McNamara, President Kennedy's defence secretary, coined the phrase 'Mutual Assured Destruction', which sounded all too realistic and, with the apt acronym MAD, subtly modified the original concept.

Thereafter, while ordinary people were encouraged to cling to the basic deterrent theory, the issue at top military and political levels started to lose much of its clarity. Expressions such as 'damage limitation' crept into military usage, and it began to look very much as if American militarists were planning not simply to make a single immediate response, but to *win* a nuclear war that might last for months rather than hours or days.

Nixon made the first declared change in the early 1970s with his doctrine of 'Sufficiency and Controlled Response' (flexible response), but it was President Carter's 'Countervailing Strategy' which finally broke away from the Mutual Assured Destruction concept of nuclear deterrence by specifically demanding that American forces should plan to 'endure' a long nuclear war. Latterly, President Reagan cemented this new attitude towards nuclear warfare by adding that the United States must prevail in the fighting. In other words, while the world at large firmly believed, with simple logic that is hard to fault, that there could be no winners in a nuclear conflict, Reagan was saying that a nuclear war *could* be won. Navy Secretary John Lehman put it this way: 'You have to have a war-winning capability if you are to succeed.'[1] And from Principal Under Secretary of Defence James Wade came this remark:

'We don't want to fight a nuclear war, or a conventional one either, but we must be prepared to do so if such a battle is to be deterred, as we must also be prepared to carry the battle to our adversary's homeland. We must not fear war.'

Chilling remarks of this kind, which must surely have been really intended to strengthen the deterrent posture, were later to be corrected by Defense Secretary Weinberger, who proclaimed that the Reagan team did not in fact believe that there could be any winners and that the policy of deterrence remained unaltered.

Weinberger went on to say that the deterrent policy had been 'approved through the political processes of the democratic nations it protects, since at least 1950'. From a strictly legal point of view Weinberger might get away with that – because heads of government are indeed elected in the Western democracies – but it was really less than the truth. In the United States, United Kingdom and France the respective nuclear deterrent policies were conceived in secrecy; and the subsequent modifications in the United States, summarised above, were not debated publicly. In Britain's case when it came to the nuclear ballistic-missile submarines with which we are specifically concerned, the political act of conception was discreetly private, casual almost.

The whole purpose of deterrence at all levels is to convince a potential aggressor that the risks involved in (military) aggression are greater than the possible benefits. At the top end of the scale, where the aim is to prevent global nuclear warfare, the potential aggressor must be certain of receiving an unbearable nuclear counter-strike, even if he has endeavoured to disarm his chosen victim(s) by a first strike against opposing forces. To achieve that certainty in Kremlin minds, the West must have the ability to launch a second strike. SSBNs are the only missile platforms that can be virtually guaranteed, for a long time yet, to retain that capability convincingly because they enjoy – given certain conditions – a high degree of security.

If politicians vacillate and do not proclaim an unambiguous and consistent policy the Kremlin will scent uncertainty and the ultimate deterrent will lose the credibility on which its effectiveness absolutely depends. To the layman, the whole business of deterrence is becoming fuzzier and further removed from the real world as time passes, the more so as a result of new issues concerning anti-missile defences. But it is vital, in the literal sense of the word, that the Soviet leaders, who have no deterrence in their vocabulary, are in no doubt whatever about the Western nuclear deterrent: it must not be kept secret in any respect of its effectiveness if it is to continue working. It is the other side's perception of deterrence that matters; but ordinary people in the free world also need to understand it because never before in history has anything been so critical to the survival of nations as a whole; citizens must be solidly behind deterrence and play their full part in decision-making if the Kremlin is to be convinced that the Western nuclear deterrent is still a reality, and that massive retaliation is not becoming just a shadowy or receding threat.

Statements implying that the United States aims to win a nuclear war detract from credibility, simply because the notion is utterly incredible. There can only be losers after a global nuclear exchange.

We have not, in fact, been able to discover a definition of 'winning' in the nuclear context during the past thirty years. Chief of Naval Operations Admiral James D. Watkins has avoided mention of winning in stating a realistic wartime goal for US Navy overall maritime strategy[1]: '. . . to use maritime power, in combination with the efforts of our sister services and the forces of our allies, to bring about war termination on favourable terms'.

Submarines, most of which can confidently be expected to survive nuclear warfare at whatever level, are bound to be a principal, if not *the* principal, means of achieving this goal, even if conflicts are traditionally decided on land at the end of the day. So long as Western SSBNs are on patrol in sufficient numbers in secure areas, a second strike will be assured whatever first strike damage is inflicted on land-based missile silos and air bases. Hence, given that communications with SSBNs can be maintained and that presidential decision-making is not affected – both, of course, being major provisos – it is not mandatory for full-scale retaliation launch-on-warning to be initiated at the very instant that signs of a first strike are perceived: there is no compelling need to shoot off the rattlesnake's head the moment its tail begins to rattle. SSBNs are a true reserve and are fully capable of inflicting unacceptable damage in their own right.

An adequate SSBN force ('adequate' will be defined later) has an inbuilt and variable length of fuse which land-based nuclear ICBMs do not. It is an invaluable attribute: the underwater button does not have to be pressed in a (possibly mistaken) moment of panic. Time, meaning delay, is to be sought above all else in a nuclear crisis.

For that reason alone, SSBNs could be considered superior to any other deterrent forces – with the possible exception of airborne units, which also have a delay-factor but which, even with stealth technology, will be increasingly vulnerable, in our time-scale, to destruction before their bombs or missiles can be released. But there is an even greater advantage in mounting the nuclear deterrent in submarines: they do not attract first-strike counter-force bombardment of populated areas.

The facts are highly classified, but one can infer one supposed disadvantage in employing SSBNs. Until now, with the advent of the terminally accurate Trident II missile which may well change the situation, it seems that submarine-launched ballistic missiles have not been expected to have sufficient accuracy to write off Soviet missile bases. But so what? A second strike would be too late for counter-force targeting to have any significance. Nuclear deterrence, as opposed to war-fighting or the absurd idea of war-winning after a nuclear exchange, must be aimed – regrettably – at centres of population. So the fact that land-based missiles are – or have been – inherently more accurate is irrelevant.

In the light of all this, are the comparatively vulnerable land and air components of the US nuclear Triad under the Single Integrated Operational Plan (SIOP) viable, justified, or even desirable for the future? In passing, it is noted that the Command, Control, Communications and Intelligence (C^3I) programme supporting all three legs of the Triad has been running at more than thirty billion dollars a year under the Reagan administration without taking into account the cost of weaponry. A single undersea leg would bring about huge savings.

There is nothing new about the submarine being regarded as a strategic weapon. Although submarines have achieved very numerous tactical successes, underwater warfare has generally been linked with strategy on a grand scale. In both world wars it was used extensively to blockade the enemy, to deny him food, fuel, supplies and military reinforcements in the hope of forcing him to surrender. Twice Germany nearly succeeded in bringing Great Britain to her knees in this way, and there is good cause for claiming that American submarines, apart from sinking a significant proportion of the Imperial Japanese Navy, brought the island nation of Japan to a standstill by virtually destroying the Merchant Marine upon which its livelihood and war-making potential depended. That was evident weeks before the two atomic bombs were dropped in August 1945 on Hiroshima and Nagasaki – 'the greatest event', according to Senator McMahon, 'in world history since the birth of Jesus Christ'.

Only spasmodic attempts were made by submarines to inflict damage on enemy territory by occasional shore bombardment and landing armed agents, although the Japanese made two bombing raids by submarine-launched float-planes on the American west coast. However, in the closing stages of the Second World War furious thought was given in Germany and, later, in America to using missiles from submarines against shore targets. Like so many of the ideas and improvements that emerged towards the end of the war, the missiles came too late to see active service; but the way in which strategic missiles started to develop is interesting because it was the early experiments that showed the way to go – or, more often, not to go.

Not invented here

The possibility of launching missiles from a submarine was first seriously considered by the Germans. Feasibility studies were started in the late 1930s, but the technical difficulties seemed insuperable. However, by chance a brilliant young engineer and pilot, Ernst Steinhoff, working at the Peenemunde Rocket Research Centre, had a brother, Fritz, commanding the 'Type IXC' *U–511*, which was completing at Hamburg at the end of 1941. The two brothers frequently exchanged ideas and the U-boat commander suggested that, since existing rockets could be ignited underwater, a very simple arrangement using launching racks mounted on the deck of a U-boat – obviating all the problems connected with an integrated system – might easily succeed. Naturally, *U–511* was selected for the experiment: the boat was a good choice anyway, because she was destined to patrol off Venezuela and the bombardment of oil tanks along the coastline was an attractive possibility.

Army technicians from Peenemunde duly installed an outfit of six thirty-centimetre Wurfkorpfer 42 Spreng rockets in racks, connected together as a battery and angled to starboard at forty-five degrees from the horizontal, abaft the conning tower. The rockets themselves were made watertight with candle wax, but they were not capable of withstanding pressure at any great depth. It was a simple matter to pass a cable through the hull to a multiple-firing switch inside the U-boat.

With only a couple of minor mishaps, trials at sea in the summer of 1942 were almost completely successful. With the U-boat submerged at normal periscope depth of about fourteen metres, putting the rockets some eight metres below the surface, the weapons, each one and a half metres long, planed smoothly up to the surface in succession and soared into the sky on their predicted trajectory for three kilometres before striking the water. The results were thoroughly encouraging, but unfortunately inter-service rivalry put an end to the project. Peenemunde was predominantly an army establishment, and when Major General Dornberger offered his conclusions to the Naval Weapons Department the navy flatly refused to accept an army idea. It was the first, but by no means the last, 'NIH' (Not Invented Here) reaction in the growing missile field, and a promising proposal, years ahead of its time, came to nought: the rocket racks were removed, and in 1943 *U–511* was transferred to the Japanese Navy, where she became the *RO–500*. Despite the cold water that had been poured on the scheme, the navy tried to repeat the experiments privately; but they failed, and evidently nothing was said about them.

On 6 September 1944, a huge object hurtled down from the sky, literally out of the blue, and exploded violently on Paris. It was the world's first operational ballistic missile, the V–2 (German designation A–4) and it revolutionised warfare thereafter.

Missiles at sea

The first successful A–4 test firing, to a range of 190 kilometres, took place on 3 October 1942, but it was not until early 1943 that Hitler could be persuaded to order the new, top secret weapon into full production. At this point, the navy revised its opinion of the army's activities at Peenemunde and research was started into the possibility of U-boats towing submersible containers for the missiles – mobile launching platforms – which could be brought to the surface off the American coast, well outside shore radar coverage.

There were hazards inherent in the proposed system: it would take three experts up to half an hour to prepare a missile (there might be three on a tow line), and the U-boat, as well as the containers, would be vulnerable to patrolling aircraft. Sea conditions would have to be calm, even though each platform was gyro-stabilised. But the missiles would have surprise on their side, and there was absolutely no defence against them once they had been launched. The system was undeniably attractive, and it was perfectly practicable to mount the liquid-oxygen and alcohol-fuelled rockets in the containers as designed.

Construction was begun in August 1944, but the first three platforms were only two-thirds complete when Peenemunde had to be evacuated in the face of the Russian advance in February 1945. The Russians, of course, took careful note of all that they found there.

Meanwhile, credit for the first submarine-launched rocket attack on enemy territory went to USS *Barb* (SS–220): Commander Eugene Fluckey, patrolling off Hokkaido and the Kuriles, fired, from the surface, about seventy five-inch rockets from a deck-mounted launcher into Japanese coastal towns and harbours in June and July 1945 from two- and three-mile ranges. They were not particularly significant attacks and did not come into the strategic category, but they shook the local population and did a fair amount of damage. Rocket delivery was a great deal quicker than gun action: each affair was over in moments and it would have been difficult to pinpoint the submarine's position.

The V–2 towed-container scheme would not have suited the US Navy, but the ballistic missile's predecessor, the Luftwaffe's V–1 pilotless aircraft-bomb, looked like being an acceptable interim answer to the need for a medium-range weapon, for use against land targets, when a number of the 'buzz bombs' fell into American hands towards the end of the war. The vehicles were thoroughly tested in the United States, and if the war had continued into 1946 the American copy, called the Loon, would probably have been used against the Japanese mainland. The United States Army and Navy were both enthusiastic, and submariners immediately appreciated the potential. The two fleet submarines *Cusk* (SS–348) and *Carbonero* (SS–337) were equipped with launching ramps abaft the conning tower, and *Cusk* was given a small hangar to house the twenty-six-foot 'bird'. The Loons were a considerable improvement on the original V–1 in that they could be guided in flight by radio-controlled guidance systems.

USS *Cusk*, now SSG–348, launched the first submarine-guided missile on 12 February 1947, off the coast of California, to a range of rather more than fifty miles. More launches followed during February and March, with ranges out to nearly one hundred miles. One Loon exploded during countdown on the launcher, but there were no casualties because the upper deck was invariably cleared of personnel during launch operations. There were other problems, but *Cusk* and *Carbonero* provided a solid background of experience, and enough technical data was amassed in a couple of years for the US Navy to initiate a series of submarine missile programmes. Strategic attacks by submarines against enemy territory were now feasible, and the US Submarine Force prepared to take its place, with the Strategic Air Command and carrier-based aircraft, in the show of force which would fulfil the Massive Retaliation Doctrine.

The first step was to design a successor to the Loon, one which could fly faster, further and deliver a nuclear warhead. At the same time a limited number of submarines had to be adapted to carry the new weapons. Development was accomplished very quickly – not least because of inter-service competition – and Regulus I (SSM–N–8), which was intended for use from surface ships and shore installations as well as submarines, was the product.

The thirty-three-foot missile had swept wings, folded when in its cylindrical, pressure-tight hangar, and flew at a relatively slow speed – little more than 400 knots – out to about 400 miles on a pre-set flight profile which usually took it to 35,000 feet before dropping low when approaching the target area to avoid enemy radar detection. The SSG, whose own position was known with no great accuracy – within, say, one mile by Loran radio or Astro navigation – guided the missile by radio from periscope depth. The nuclear warhead weighed 4,000 pounds but had a comparatively low yield which, combined with navigational inaccuracies, made the weapon less than effective. USS *Tunny* (SSG–282) and *Barbero* (SSG–317) were converted to carry two Regulus I missiles each in 1952 and 1955 respectively.

In the meantime, a totally new missile, the SSM–N–9 (called Regulus II to ease its passage through the funding system – an old trick) was being developed with a larger nuclear warhead, a speed well in excess of mach two, and a range of more than 1,000 miles. This was, for its time, a superb cruise weapon and it had an excellent inertial guidance system; but it was awkwardly long at fifty-seven feet and six inches, and it weighed more than ten tons.

USS *Grayback* (SSG–574) fired the first Regulus II on 16 September 1958. Three months later production was stopped by the navy's pronouncement that 'the ballistic missile has greater growth potential in overall military effectiveness than have air-breathing missiles'. The two types of weapon could not be afforded in parallel, but existing Regulus I missiles were fitted in *Grayback*, *Growler* and the US Navy's only purpose-built SSGN *Halibut*. From 1960 to 1964 two submarines were kept on patrol in the western Pacific with missiles targeted on Siberia.

The abandoning of Regulus II lost valuable time for America in the cruise-missile field, but the Soviet Navy seized on the idea (and doubtless appropriated details of the design) although their purpose was initially different: Soviet submarine-launched cruise missiles were to be used not primarily against territory, but to destroy important surface targets at long range. 'Whiskey' diesel boats were converted to 'Twin Cylinder' for trials of SS–N–3 (Shaddock) cruise missiles in 1958–60, and the 'Long Bin' version with four Shaddocks came in 1960–3: the GRU had been working overtime.

The significant thing about these developments in the US and Soviet navies is the speed with which submarines could be converted to take cruise missiles. This is relevant when considering the large Chinese submarine force and smaller navies which may seek to acquire, rapidly, a submarine-launched strategic delivery system. Indeed, there are arguments, which will be advanced later, for Britain – if she insists on remaining a nuclear power – adapting attack submarines to carry a limited number of cruise missiles rather than pursuing the Trident project. The problem with a cheap *ad hoc* conversion is that it would require a submarine to surface for perhaps fifteen minutes with obvious attendant dangers. And an integrated submerged launch system would deny the Royal Navy a proportion of its current underwater attack capability – although that might be thought acceptable, as it evidently is in the US Navy. UK strategic submarines (SSBNs) are at present funded separately, and are supposed not to detract from the cost of other submarine building programmes – but whether that situation will continue remains to be seen. Trident boats will, anyway, reduce the availability of British SSN building resources.

The last nuclear deterrent patrol conducted by a Western submarine carrying cruise missiles was made in 1964, by which time the US Navy had some thirty nuclear-powered fleet ballistic-missile submarines in commission or nearing completion; the Soviet Navy was catching up fast, and the Royal Navy was laying down four SSBN hulls.

The creation of the US Navy's FBM Polaris force was a triumph from start to finish, although there were traditionalist submariners who would have been content to see it founder. It made sense – for the United States – in every way, and the imaginative idea of cutting the *Skipjack* SSN hull (originally intended for *Scorpion*) in two, then inserting the missile and control sections between the halves, was a great time-saver. The Polaris programme was formally approved on 1 January 1957, and Rear Admiral William E. Raborn Jr, an aviator with a forceful but pleasant personality, was appointed as director of special projects:[1] his very talented technical team was to be led by Captain Levering Smith.

'Red' Raborn took a bold decision that deserves to be remembered. Liquid fuel for the rockets, like the army's 1,500-mile Jupiter project, had several disadvantages, not least the fact that it obliged them to be very large; solid fuel was much to be preferred for size and safety, particularly in a submarine system, but the state of the art had not reached the point where it could be employed in 1957. Raborn took the risk, fully justified in the event, of the art developing while the programme was actually under way over the next six years. At the same time a launching system had to be devised, and both the SLBM and its launching submarine would need extremely accurate navigational systems. These were some of the major problems which confronted Raborn and his team: they were all overcome speedily and effectively. Raborn was also responsible for an extremely sensible demand that an extra twenty-five feet of ship length should be afforded for future growth in the *Ethan Allen* (SSBN–608) and subsequent classes – hence the ability to progress to A2, A3 and Poseidon missiles.

On 4 October 1957 the Soviet Union placed a 184-pound satellite in orbit around the earth. President Eisenhower dismissed Sputnik I as having 'no military significance', but nobody with a grain of common sense could believe that. America's missile forces shifted into top gear, while the administration blandly assured the world that Sputniks made 'not one iota' of difference to Western security. That scarcely equated with the demand to bring forward the completion of the Polaris project from 1963 to 1960. Incredibly, the new time scale was achieved. USS *George Washington* (SSBN–598) was launched on 9 June 1959 and commissioned on the last day of the year. She was the first submarine to be built around a weapon system.

The first Polaris missile was fired from submerged at 1239 on 19 July 1960. Armed with sixteen A–1 missiles with a range of 1,200 nautical miles, *George Washington* (Commander James B. Osborn) sailed for the first American strategic patrol on 15 November, one year after completion. By any standards, it was a remarkable achievement: in the strategic deterrent business it put the United States far ahead of the Soviet Union – but not for long.

In September 1955 the world's first SLBM launch had taken place from a modified Soviet 'Zulu V' submarine whose sail had been modified to take two tubes. Three years later the 'Golf' class appeared with three tubes in the sail, carrying the same SS–N–4 missiles (with a range of 300 nautical miles) requiring a surface launch. While the 'Golf' class was being completed between 1958 and 1962 (one for China in 1964), so were the nuclear-propelled 'Hotel' class with three surface-launch tubes in the sail. This was a poor payload for a 5,500-ton submarine; but in 1967 the first 'Yankee' class was commissioned, a great advance. Sixteen tubes were fitted for SS–N–6 missiles (with a range of 1,300 nautical miles) in the 9,500-ton hull, and the whole boat bore a marked resemblance to the 'Ethan Allen' class of the US Navy. USS *Ethan Allen* (SSBN–608) had been laid down in September 1959 and commissioned in August 1961, so there was ample time for the Soviet design to be matched. On the other hand, given the ubiquitous and comprehensive activities of the KGB and GRU, the Soviet Union was only about six years astern of the United States. As usual, thoroughly efficient espionage (to say nothing of commercial leaks) saved the Kremlin a huge amount of research and development. Worse, for the West, Russian scientists, naval architects, engineers and technicians were (and are) freed thereby to build upon proven systems, improve illicitly acquired plans and originate entirely new concepts. Agreed, some of the differences in Soviet boats, when compared with American equivalents, might not seem advantageous to Western observers. For example, built-in redundancy – two nuclear reactors, two steam turbines and two shafts in the Soviet 'Yankee' reproduction – made this class much noisier than the US Navy's 'Ethan Allen'.

Most successive Soviet SSBNs are generally not up to the standard of those of the US Navy, although their SLBM nuclear strike capability is more than powerful enough. The modified SS–N–20 ('Typhoon') and SS–NX–23 MIRVed missiles (for the 'Delta IV' class and probably to be back-fitted in 'Delta IIIs') are likely to be more accurate than their predecessors out to about 4,500 nautical miles, and have six or nine and possibly nine plus re-entry vehicles respectively. These compare with the Poseidon C–3 SLBM's 2,500-nautical-mile range with ten to fourteen MIRVs, and Trident C–4's 4,350-nautical-mile range with eight MIRVs of higher explosive yield, quoted as 100 kilotons each. Trident II (D–5) missiles will have a range of 6,000 nautical miles, although this has been questioned.

By February 1964, when the first of four British Polaris submarines – HMS *Resolution* – was laid down at Vickers, the US Navy had forty-one SSBNs in service or about to be commissioned: the Soviet Navy had about forty 'Zulu' and 'Golf' SSBs and ten 'Hotel' class SSBNs. France entered the field only one month later than Britain: *Le Redoutable* (SNLE–611), the first of five in the initial *Force de Dissuasion* or *Force de Frappe*, was laid down at Cherbourg on 30 March 1964: the five SSBNs were commissioned between 1971 and 1980, and a sixth, *L'Inflexible* (SNLE–615), was operational in March 1985. The Royal Navy's boats, *Resolution, Repulse, Renown* and *Revenge*, were completed much more quickly at Vickers and Cammell Lairds, all commissioning between 1967 and 1969.

The method of firing missiles from submerged is assumed to be broadly similar for the SSBNs of all the navies concerned, and a very general description based upon US Navy procedures will suffice.

The aim, in a sixteen-missile 'Boomer' ('Bomber' in the Royal Navy), is believed to be to maintain at least fifteen missiles ready for launch fifteen minutes after the command for ninety-nine per cent of the time. Readiness is monitored and, so to speak, audited: a commanding officer cannot bluff about his state of preparedness.

A Poseidon missile is thirty-two feet long, six feet in diameter and weighs thirty-four tons. The dozen or so MIRVs carrying W–76 warheads (the number reportedly varies) are independently targeted. Targets are recorded on magnetic discs and fed into fire-control computers, which constantly revise trajectories on the basis of the submarine's own movements. The targets attacked by one missile's MIRVs would presumably not be all that far apart as distances go in the Soviet Union. Some missiles might be held in reserve for a later attack, but the firing submarine's position can be pinpointed remarkably quickly after launch and a submariner would doubtless prefer to get rid of the lot at twenty-second intervals and clear the area as quickly as possible.

Before the missiles are launched the submarine slows to a very low speed or starts to hover with automated or semi-automated trimming/compensating arrangements to maintain depth – no mean feat for a boat displacing 8,250 tons submerged ('Lafayette' class) or 18,700 tons ('Ohio' class) with, during each launching sequence, something in the order of three tons of additional seawater weight to compensate for (a larger scale version of the torpedo firing problem) as well as the downward thrust that occurs as each missile is launched. Ejection is often by gas and steam, but compressed air is used in certain systems; for Poseidon and Trident, a small fixed rocket is ignited, and its exhaust is directed through cooling water to the base of the tube. Firing depth, having equalised external/internal pressure in the tubes, is apparently not critical within broad limits for most systems.

If the submarine is below the Arctic icecap there will be some delay while it breaks through the ice above, or preferably, surfaces in a *polynya* (pool) or rift: it is likely, in fact, to keep close to weak patches in the ice, but these are so changeable that they are probably not, at present, much of a guide to anti-submarine hunting units. Freezing of topside equipment and missile-tube doors could present problems after surfacing.

Secure, reliable, immediate communications from shore are essential to effective SSBN operations wherever they may be. VLF frequencies, for all, are the baseline link with ELF coming on line in the USSR and, less comprehensively, in the USA. Received mainly through a buoyant cable (trailing wire) or an antenna buoy deployed a few metres below the surface, there is more or less continuous traffic – sometimes meaningless and even frivolous – to cloak messages of real significance. Thus, the weekly forty-word Familygrams permitted to each Western crewman from his loved ones (or, on occasion, unloved ones, when the vetting officer at base or the commanding officer on board may have to exercise discretion in favour of morale) are actually helpful to the communications plan.

If VLF/ELF transmissions cease the implications are clear. US SSBN alternative communications from shore (presumably with similar arrangements for the UK and French forces) are provided – expensively – by an airborne fleet of VLF/LF antenna-trailing C–130 TACAMO (Take Charge and Move Out) aircraft. The latter are ageing, overweight and have little room for equipment expansion: the navy has proposed that Boeing E6A variants replace a proportion of them. If trials are successful, the first E6A should be operational shortly and by 1993 the TACAMO fleet is scheduled to consist of fifteen E6As and ten updated C–130s (EC–130Qs).[3]

The widest possible range of communication paths and frequencies is required to ensure message delivery and convince the Kremlin that signals will *always* get through – ELF, VLF, LF, TACAMO, HF, FLEETSAT (UHF), SHF satellites, forthcoming EHF and lasers are all in use or envisaged. No wonder that a modern US Navy SSBN's radio room has three times as many receivers as earlier 'Boomers' and costs twice as much as a complete Second World War fleet submarine! Nevertheless, it is probable that communications costs could be cut dramatically if pure deterrence, rather than the ability to fight and win a protracted nuclear war, was the aim.

As in so many other areas, adequacy is a great deal less expensive than the best. But, in any event, SSBNs offer the best value for money in mounting the ballistic deterrent. The question is, who should exercise nuclear deterrence? We will look for an answer to that a little further on.

Communications are dominant in the C^3I package and the Soviet Navy has given high priority to systems featuring automated, frequency-agile, high data-rate, increasingly digitized techniques for battle management. With several (low data-rate) ELF stations in operation from 1986 onwards Soviet SSBNs will be able to receive messages at great depths. Admiral Gorshkov pointed out, before his retirement, that if his C^3I organisation were to be disrupted it would be equal to the destruction of Soviet naval forces in combat. The same, of course, is true of NATO forces.

The recent appointment of General of the Army Maksimov as commander-in-chief of strategic rocket forces (RSVN), together with Gorshkov's departure from the scene, indicate the complete integration of all Soviet nuclear weapons under a single command. Secure C^3I will assume even greater importance for the Soviets with centralised control: presumably NATO has contingency plans for disrupting it to fulfil Gorshkov's prediction.

In an SSBN on patrol the order to fire would come in a coded message whose authenticity must be checked: there are foolproof and absolute safeguards against wrongful launch. However, it might be fairly easy for an ordinary crew member to *abort* a launch.

Obviously, warhead accuracy depends not only on precise trajectories under inertial or stellar-inertial guidance with updated meteorological corrections along the path (an input that requires considerable effort and communications), but also on a very exact knowledge of the SSBN's position. Accurate navigation, presumably to within yards rather than hundreds of yards if hardened sites are targeted, is a prime requisite, and there is no reason to think that this requirement, nowadays, is not met by both East and West.

Two, and in some SSBN's three, SINS systems are installed: a continuous positional read-out is given, corrected and backed up by radio navigational aids, principally LORAN (insufficiently exact), and navigation satellites (better and possibly within 100 metres for the Soviets soon, but still not good enough). The most accurate method of determining position is by bottom-contour navigation, using a secure echo-sounder whose transmissions are, for all practical purposes, undetectable; but that is only possible if bottom contours are precisely charted for the areas required.

The Soviets have devoted far more resources than the West to oceanography in all its aspects, which includes mapping the seabed; and with seventy-six oceanographic research vessels (possibly more if other ships have been converted in fact but not in name) and 148 survey ships in the Soviet fleet working over widely diverse areas, it must be difficult for Western intelligence to determine the places of particular Soviet SSBN interest, and hence where Soviet submarines are most likely to be operating or what tracks they follow by bottom-contour methods. The Royal Navy, on the other hand, has allowed its hydrographic surveying and oceanographic capabilities to become seriously deficient, with only nine survey ships (six coastal/inshore), despite the well-reasoned recommendations made by the Hydrographic Studies Group established in 1975. France is no better supplied. The US Navy has a dozen oceanographic research (AGOR) vessels fitted with instrumentation and laboratories to measure gravity and magnetism, water temperature, density and sound transmission in water – increasingly important factors in anti-submarine warfare – and nine surveying ships (AGS); by 1987 there will also be about eighteen (twelve in 1985) ocean surveillance ships (AGOS) designed to deploy SURTASS (towed array) sonar and transmit data to shore for evaluation.

The contrast between efforts in the East and West to learn the nature of the oceans and chart the profile of the ocean floor is self-evident, and must surely be reflected in submarine operational capabilities – particularly, in the context of this chapter, Soviet SSBN navigational facilities. It is also assumed that bottom-contour charts have been produced for the Arctic Ocean by specially adapted Soviet SSBNs or SSNs – or perhaps that is a purpose of the two small nuclear research submarines (AGSSN) which were first seen in 1982 (designated 'Uniform') and 1983. How much do Western navies know about the topography, overhead and below, of the under-ice world and ice-edges? Or about radio communications, sonar conditions, torpedo performance, the effect of explosives? One would guess quite a lot by now, but probably nothing approaching the Soviet store of data. With the Soviets using the Arctic Ocean as the strongest of SSBN bastions, it will be interesting to see what is known or can be conjectured about under-ice operations.[4] Deploying in the Arctic, the fourth largest of the world's oceans and nearly landlocked, Soviet SSBNs and supporting SSNs have no need to transit through choke points, and their Arctic operating areas are necessarily much more familiar to them than to opposing NATO boats: in April the edge of the (then maximum) Marginal Sea Ice Zone (MIZ) is less than 300 miles from the Kola Peninsula.

Conversely, Western submarines – SSBNs (which might conceivably seek ice-cover) or anti-SSBN SSNs – have to make their long passage through the choke points of the Davis, Denmark or Bering Straits, the latter shallow and dangerous. There is a real danger of hitting the bottom or colliding with the ice projecting downwards, in places down to 200 feet and sometimes touching the bottom in the Bering Strait: reliable but detectable ice-detection active sonar has to be used. Bottom-contour navigation is probably impossible with any great degree of accuracy; radio aids – Omega and Loran C – are not good enough for SSBNs above eighty degrees north; and satellite navigation (if an antenna can be raised) is degraded by the high elevation angles of the existing US polar-orbiting satellite system. SINS, in its polar mode, is also less reliable because of the paucity of geodetic and gravitational information for calculating vertical deflection forces, a prime source of error. It has to be checked more often than usual – but a sufficiently accurate means of making those checks for missile-launching seems to be lacking in the US and Royal Navies at present, although technology can surely provide them if the need is indeed there. US, British and probably French SSNs can, however, navigate perfectly well for anti-submarine warfare purposes throughout the Arctic Ocean.

The Soviets must long ago have appreciated the requirements for accurate SSBN positional firing data beneath the ice, and it is reasonable to assume that they have been met – at least in some, possibly quite limited, areas under the icefield proper, and over much wider areas at the fringes.

For anti-submarine hunters, non-acoustic sensors are largely (although not entirely) negated by ice, but sonar conditions are excellent except in the shifting, grinding, noisy margin. Target classification is easy: a contact can be nothing but a submarine! Attacking is more of a problem: reflections from ice keels may confuse solutions; targets are likely to be too quiet for passive weapons; active-homing torpedoes will experience reverberations, and may even home on an ice keel or strike one on the way to the target; and if the target is resting, like a fly on the ceiling, with slight positive buoyancy under a slab, or if it actually surfaces to launch missiles, it will be invulnerable – a predictably frustrating experience for the would-be attacker at the very moment of truth. It presumably remains to be seen how Mark 48 ADCAP, Tigerfish and Spearfish torpedoes will perform in this environment.

For the Soviet SSBN on station, there are also problems. ELF and VLF (trailing wire) communications from transmitters much closer to the area of operations than Western stations should be reliable; but signals may be upset from time to time, for several days, by the ionic polarcap disturbance (PCD) which is prevalent during high sunspot activity. It could be that SSBNs will move out from under the ice and become more detectable – and vulnerable – during these periods.

It is not difficult to find a thinnish patch of ice and 'lean' upwards against it, ready to break through; but *polynyas* can vanish or change shape rapidly, so an SSBN must be prepared, and be very strongly constructed, to force its way upwards through several feet of solid ice if necessary. This is practicable, but it takes a little time if serious damage is to be avoided. Then, ice blocks – enormously heavy – may have to be shifted off the missile tube doors or the protective casing above them: perhaps heavy deliberate listing would help, but it would be a Herculean task to move the blocks by hand. The 'Typhoon' is well configured for surfacing through ice, with its high, rounded freeboard and no hydroplanes on the sail. The 'Deltas' and 'Yankees', judging from appearances, would have more difficulty, although they are better designed for the purpose than Western submarines, provided that they can rotate their sail-planes vertically.

In short, one of the latest Soviet SSBNs on station is very well sheltered beneath Arctice ice: the 'Typhoons', if not the rest, should be able to launch missiles within fifteen minutes or so of the command from shore. At a guess, the 'Deltas', 'Yankees' and others will prefer to patrol, during the winter months, at the margin, where they too are quite well protected; but if *polynyas* are plentiful at any time of the year they may equally well operate in the deep field. In other words, they could be anywhere – which is not very helpful to our anti-submarine forces – but aerial or satellite reconnaissance over the pack could give some faint clues to the most likely operating areas, although it would not reveal the submarines themselves.

In all the vastness of the open oceans SSBNs are even more difficult to find – which is just as well if the deterrent theory is to hold together. So far as is known, there has been no detection by Soviet forces of our boats on deterrent patrol. Submarine hunting, unless a submarine discloses its presence, is still akin to finding a needle in a haystack. Nevertheless, an SSBN is not totally immune to detection and attack (especially if security has been breached by espionage) nor to sabotage before sailing – conceivably by biological warfare. Mining, too, is a threat. A really massive effort might discover one on station, and trailing a boat when it sails for patrol is not, theoretically, impossible – particularly if personnel 'in the know' are not properly screened for loyalty. A single loss in a near-crisis situation might have a considerable effect on policy-makers when it came to be realised what had happened: it is just possible that the Politburo would judge the effort – and the risk – worthwhile, in certain circumstances short of war. But for the foreseeable future submarines are easily the most secure and survivable missile-platforms available to both sides, and they are also capable of effective self-defence if hard pressed. Despite spectacular inventions in the press, there are positively no new technologies in existence today which threaten the SSBN as a vehicle and no threshold of a breakthrough in anti-submarine warfare is yet visible for tomorrow. The oceans are not becoming 'transparent', and they are not being made to 'ring like a bell' – to quote two popular prognostications.

Against this solid background favouring the SSBN as the most effective nuclear-missile launcher, there can be no rational argument against the United States mounting about half of its strategic warheads in submarines for so long as an East–West nuclear balance is sought. Indeed, for the reasons we have given, there is a strong case for putting the nuclear deterrent entirely underwater. But what are Britain and France doing in the business?

Shorn of rhetoric, France acquired her *Force de Frappe* (striking force) or, a more acceptable phrase today, her *Force de Dissuasion*, because General de Gaulle wanted to claim leadership of a *Europe des Patries* with Chancellor Adenauer's West German support and without British competition for the title; and he saw his nuclear ambitions as a supplement, or even a successor, to what he believed was a waning American guarantee. America invited France to accept Polaris on the same terms as Britain, but on 14 January 1963 de Gaulle rejected this offer. At the same time he vetoed British membership of the EEC: France would join with West Germany in an *entente nucléaire* and, with her own nuclear weaponry, would lead Europe.

In the event the *entente* was a non-starter so far as nuclear forces went, but the prospect of it led to a proposal in Washington – horrified by the thought of apocalyptic weapons in German hands – for a multilateral force (MLF) as a safer alternative which, it was suggested, would give West Germans the equal status which they demanded and satisfy the French at the same time. In fact, fears of German nuclear ambitions were probably groundless; and anyway, the mixed-manned, jointly financed and jointly controlled MLF fleet of twenty-five surface ships was not supported in a group of countries pursuing their own courses and alliances. The MLF was ungraciously regarded as another misguided American proposal, and the concept was abandoned at the end of 1964, being replaced, in effect, by the establishment of NATO's Nuclear Planning Group, which gave everybody some participation.

The spectre of a national German nuclear force was finally laid to rest when West Germany signed the Non-Proliferation Treaty in 1969; but later in the year Chancellor Willy Brandt showed his determination to pursue a wholly independent foreign policy towards the Eastern bloc – *Ostpolitik* – which convinced de Gaulle that the time had come to seek much closer co-operation with Britain, the traditional rival, *La Perfide Albion* herself. Gaullist France, with General Ailleret as its most aggressive spokesman, had earlier declared a provocative strategy *à tous azimuts*, and France had withdrawn from NATO in 1966. Now it was at last recognised that the threat came not from all round, but from the East.

De Gaulle's successor, Georges Pompidou, reversed the former opposition to Britain's EEC membership in 1970 (more's the pity, some in the UK would say) and set about restoring Franco-American relations with President Nixon in the face of concern about Willy Brandt's *Ostpolitik*. Bilateral discussions at military staff level were arranged, and it was believed that, *inter alia*, the French said privately where and how their nuclear missiles would be employed.

Regrettably, the 'when and how' has never been made public, and there have since been contradictory currents in French defence policy. France has lost pre-eminence in the EEC and, so far as valid dialogue with Moscow goes, she has largely given way to the West German and UK governments. It is difficult to see exactly how France now stands: she is not militarily in NATO (thereby losing invaluable training opportunities), but maintains the Atlantic alliance. Giscard d'Estaing acknowledged in 1976 that the security of Western Europe as a whole was essential to France, but she contributes no share to NATO defences. What is the Kremlin to make of this ambivalent attitude? If uncertainty about SSBN targeting and trigger-pulling is a deterrent in itself – and uncertainty is often quoted as being an important factor in the deterrence game – France certainly provides that quality.

One distinguished French author[5] has suggested that 'it is possible for a nuclear exchange to be interrupted – along the lines foreseen by the American flexible response or by a final warning of an independent deterrent like the French Force de Frappe, for example'. Frankly, that sounds suspiciously like a pious hope; the lack of a more positive dissuasion attitude could lead one to suspect that France, equipped with Gaullist thunder, is stuck with an exceedingly expensive, albeit powerful, force – six SSBNs (SNLEs) with two or even three constantly on patrol – which she is having some difficulty in justifying to herself, let alone to the outside world. Having said that, however, France has suffered invasions in the recent past – unlike England, which has not been seriously invaded since 1066 – and the acquisition of a nuclear capability may have comforted French citizens with long memories.

One might speculate not only about the purpose of the force, but about its security and real effectiveness. France does not have communications facilities or test-firing ranges approaching those available to the USA, UK and USSR. The 1,500-nautical-mile MSBS M–20 missiles (sixteen tubes in each boat) with megaton single heads hardened against ABM explosions are now being replaced by 2,500–3,000-nautical-mile M–4 missiles carrying six 150-kiloton heads (possibly MRV rather than MIRV), but even the latter ranges are becoming a little restrictive in terms of sea-room and patrol areas – which is why, by 1994, it is planned to have the first of a new SSBN class at sea with 6,000-nautical-mile M–5 missiles.

Some (but not all) of the considerations leading to France's present nuclear posture have been sketched, as well as some rather uncharitable remarks about substance and intent, to exemplify the blurred and shifting images that a European national nuclear submarine deterrent force can present to a Soviet observer. French nuclear policies are not illustrative of the logic for which pragmatic French philosophers are famed; and resolve – the backbone of deterrence at all levels – is not readily apparent despite the nuclear *matériel*.

There have been some hints that France is considering a new approach for her SSBNs – either by intensifying her missile-penetration aids programme or by building a new unspecified (cruise?) weapon system to bypass future defences (along SDI lines) against ballistic missiles.[6] She wants to be seen in the nuclear forefront.

Bonn has welcomed French and British nuclear forces, but only so long as they are additions to, and not substitutes for, American forces. It is relevant to note, incidentally, that West Germany, with no nuclear bargaining power of her own, achieved parity with nuclear France and nuclear Britain at the top table towards the end of the 1970s. A Bonn-appointed deputy SACEUR NATO general alongside the standard UK post, along with Chancellor Helmut Schmidt's presence at the Guadaloupe summit conference with President Giscard d'Estaing and Prime Minister Callaghan, were clear evidence of West Germany's accepted and vital role in European (and hence American) defence affairs: wealth – industrial muscle with high-quality conventional forces to defend it in consort with the alliance – was the reason for the Federal Republic being invited to join the elite. Her geographical position in the front line, host to NATO armies, certainly promoted Bonn's revalued role of East–West communicator and interpreter; but West Germany's real strength lay in the Deutschmark – which was not being squandered on fantastic weaponry – and on political, economic and military efficiency, which was neither confused nor over-stretched by unrealistic national nuclear demands.

Doubt must therefore be cast on the claim, which has frequently been voiced in Britain, that a nation needs nuclear arms to qualify for a respected place at the conference tables of the world. There are other considerations: a thoroughly sound economy is foremost among them.

In Britain the Admiralty watched the US Polaris project closely from 1956. In 1958 an additional staff officer for the Royal Navy Staff in Washington was appointed, by agreement between Admiral Mountbatten (First Sea Lord) and Admiral Arleigh Burke (CNO), for liaison with Raborn's Special Project Team; and the Board of Admiralty initiated a kind of contingency study to see what would have to be done if – as then seemed rather unlikely – Polaris was chosen for Britain's nuclear arm, instead of the Blue Streak land-based missile (which was to be cancelled in 1960), or the alternative US Skybolt air-to-surface missile. Although a good deal of conditional staff work was undertaken, the Royal Navy was not very enthusiastic about Polaris, and was unwilling to sacrifice a 'balanced' fleet, with new aircraft carriers, for a seaborne nuclear force; and the RAF certainly did not wish to see the deterrent task shifted to the navy.

In the event, Skybolt foundered in America at the end of 1962, and the UK could not possibly go it alone, since US trials so far had been unsuccessful. Despite continuing misgivings in the Admiralty, notably about the prospective manpower drain and the cost effect on the established fleet, the navy was to be made responsible for the provision of a deterrent force to replace the V-bombers. President Kennedy met Prime Minister Macmillan at Nassau on 20–21 December and agreed to transfer Polaris missiles to Britain.

The value of the US Navy's trust and generosity in allowing the Royal Navy to observe, formally and informally, Polaris's progress was now apparent. Britain's Polaris development and construction programme got under way almost immediately after the Nassau meeting: the Polaris Executive was established just four days later on Christmas Eve of 1962.

Reactions in the submarine service were mixed. The decision came as a complete surprise to most officers, including the staff of Flag Officer Submarines (FOSM), although a select few were aware of the background. FOSM himself saw Polaris and SSBNs as the way towards an expanded SSN programme, and he welcomed the responsibility for a new force. Manpower was going to be a problem, but there was to be separate funding for Polaris and that relieved many minds. The Conservative government, anticipating future anti-nuclear moves by Labour, if and when it came to power, sewed up the contracts so tightly that it was thought they could not be cancelled without unacceptable financial penalties. At a lower level, one or two prospective SSBN commanding officers very privately expressed doubts about their forthcoming role, but the offer of a large and important command overcame any qualms they may have had.

When Harold Wilson's Labour government did come to power in late 1964 it was supposedly faced with a *fait-accompli*, although it has been argued[7] that cancellation was still, in fact, a fiscally viable option. At any rate, Wilson's cabinet felt that the point of no return had been passed, and satisfied itself by cancelling the fifth SSBN, thus definitely limiting the seaborne deterrent to only one submarine on patrol.

British warhead development proceeded smoothly for the chosen US

A–3 missile, and like the American system each head carried three 200–250-kiloton MRVs.

HMS *Resolution* sailed for the first deterrent patrol in June 1962, less than six years after the Nassau agreement was signed, but it was not until the third SSBN, *Renown*, went on patrol in August 1969 that RAF Strike Command formally handed over responsibility for the strategic nuclear deterrent to Flag Officer Submarines.

The costs, of course, were enormous, and there was serious questioning within the Ministry of Defence and elsewhere about the value of Polaris. In 1966–7 there began to be some savage and dramatic cuts in all three fighting services, but it was denied, politically, that Polaris was the cause. Whether that was true or not, save for those directly profiting by the programme there was neither public nor service rejoicing when Polaris was announced. But a navy does what its government tells it, so there was virtually no open resistance to the purely political decision.

Nevertheless, there was a compromise solution which, if it had been properly aired, might have been thought acceptable for the UK at the time while saving enough money to obviate a great many of the defence cuts. It involved abandoning regular deterrent patrols and employing the SSBNs as SSNs, while maintaining missile training for the crews; cutting the latter to one for each boat instead of two; and extending missile readiness to a given notice unless and until the world situation gave rise to particular anxiety. The British Polaris force would still have been able to get back into business quite quickly if the political climate chilled.

The suggestion was made at too low a level to have any great impact, although it did spark considerable interest in higher echelons for a while; and it was plain that a sizeable number of senior officers and permanent Ministry of Defence officials had serious – but largely unexpressed – reservations, both about the expense of British Polaris and its questionable contribution to national, NATO and world security.

The costs mounted with improvements to defeat defences but were not as high as they might have been. In 1969–70 intelligence about Soviet anti-ballistic missiles (ABMs) concluded that the Galosh system was designed for exo-atmospheric interception. Previous assessments had been that Soviet ABMs were intended for close-in interception so Poseidon multiple independently targetable re-entry vehicles (MIRVs) would be needed. Now the UK decided that a combination of decoys and less expensive non-independently targetable multiple re-entry vehicles (MRVs) could replace the original warheads.

The result was Project Chevaline. Initiated under the Heath government in 1973, development continued under successive Labour and Conservative administrations. There was evidently a serious breakdown in cost management between 1974 and 1977, and British Aerospace were called in by the Ministry of Defence to put Chevaline back on track. It seems probable that the original estimate of £1 billion was doubled by the time that Chevaline reportedly reached operational status in 1982. Rocket motors also had to be replaced at an estimated £300 million. However, Chevaline is said to be a good system 'with MIRV qualities':[8] presumably these refer to the reported payload of 'marginally either side of six' forty-kiloton RVs, with penetration aids, capable of separation between impact points to a maximum of forty to forty-five statute miles.[9]

The building price of each SSBN in 1964–8 (before inflation started to grip) approached £40 million, but the costs of research and development, infrastructure and support, training and communications, missiles and US liaison (including test-range facilities) are difficult to determine, and it is not known whether all these factors were taken into account in the various announced costings of the total package: it is suspected that they were not. It has been insisted that everything has been accounted for in the replacement Trident cost announcements, but questions linger because a good many costs are wrapped up, inextricably, with other activities which, to some extent, share them – for example, the design sections at the Ministry of Defence in Bath, the Faslane base, VLF broadcasts and basic submarine training facilities.

ABM defences have now assumed much greater significance with the future proposed American Strategic Defence Initiative – SDI or 'Star Wars' – but it will be best to look first at missiles and defences as they are today.

The USA has claimed that the Soviet Union has already violated the 1972 ABM treaty in several ways. Be that as it may, the ABM launchers around Moscow have recently been increased from sixty-four to the 100 permitted by the treaty, with one reload per silo. Several of the older Galosh silos have been modernised to launch the new quick-reaction SAH–80 ABM, armed with a low-yield nuclear head designed to destroy incoming warheads inside the atomosphere. Road-mobile SA–12 missiles, linked to the new phased array early warning radar at Krasnoyarsk (to be completed in 1986–7), will be used to defend SS–18 ICBM silo complexes against 'Trident' attacks from the Pacific and whatever, one day, may come winging in from China; and there are

(ABOVE) A Spearfish being prepared for sea trials in Scotland. This fast (about sixty knots) new heavyweight anti-submarine British submarine torpedo, expected to be in service fairly soon, is wire-guided out to long ranges and the wire will exchange data between the torpedo and firing submarine as well as conveying guidance commands. The engine burns OTTO fuel and the warhead, with a directed energy high explosive device, is designed to penetrate the outer skin of a double-hulled submarine and concentrate the explosion against the pressure hull. (BELOW) A Tigerfish (Mark 24) torpedo being loaded into a 'Churchill' class SSN. This dual-purpose (MOD I) anti-submarine and anti-surface wire-guided twenty-one-inch British weapon has had a long and chequered history, but earlier faults now appear to have been rectified. Electrically driven, with two speeds available, Tigerfish has an active/passive three-dimensional acoustic homing system and an impact/proximity fuze. Long delays in producing a reliable weapon, particularly against surface ships, have probably resulted in its being at least partially outdated by modern Soviet surface and submarine capabilities. (*Marconi Underwater Systems*)

(ABOVE) The Ikara anti-submarine weapon was initiated by the Australian government and has been widely fitted in the Royal Australian Navy, Royal Navy and Brazilian Navy. It carries an anti-submarine torpedo (US Mark 44 or 46, Swedish type 42, Italian A244/5 or UK Stingray) and releases it over the submarine target's position. It can be used in any weather conditions out to the usual maximum range of a surface ships's active sonar. In a boxed version it can be mounted in merchant vessels, when the system is controlled by a nearby escort. (*British Aerospace*) (BELOW LEFT) Sub Harpoon at launch. The nosecap and tail of its capsule, in which it was ejected from the torpedo tube, have just blown off and the booster motor has ignited just before the missile's main engine starts. This exceptionally reliable anti-ship sea-skimming weapon, employed by the US, Royal Australian and Royal Navies, has a range of about fifty nautical miles. (*US Navy*) (BELOW RIGHT) Ballistic missile re-entry vehicles passing through clouds over the Kwajalein Pacific Missile Range after a 4,130-nautical-mile flight from Vandenburg Air Force Base, California. This was an MX land-based missile test, but it illustrates well the re-entry vehicle concept for SLBMs. (US Air Force via *Jane's Defence Weekly*)

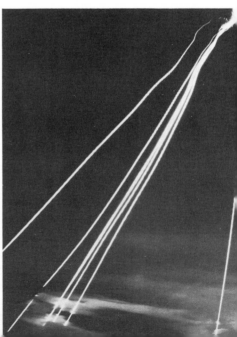

A Subskimmer submersible transporter for divers and combat frogmen. Based on a rigid hull inflatable and powered by an eighty hp outboard engine, the craft can carry four men or two with stores. With a maximum (total) range of 100 nautical miles at speeds up to twenty-eight knots on the surface, it can dive in less than one minute and is very manoeuverable submerged for up to six nautical miles. If necessary, Subskimmer can be 'parked' underwater and retrieved when the crew's mission is completed. Although ideally launched from a beach or river bank, it could be deployed by a helicopter or, better for covert military tasks perhaps, it could be hoisted out from an innocent looking fishing vessel or merchant ship. Equally, it could be 'garaged' in a clip-on cylinder on a submarine's casing, where its pressurisation system could, if necessary, be supplied from the mother submarine's air system. (*Submarine Products Ltd, Hexham, Northumberland*)

(ABOVE) Charioteers about to cut their way through an anti-submarine net. Some nets, particularly those designed to stop torpedoes, were much tougher than this, especially those made after the war; but trials proved that no net protection – at least up until 1957 when the last known tests were conducted – were proof against divers armed with suitable tools. (BELOW) Italian *maiale* at St Andrea, Venice, probably in 1944 after the armistice, but while the city was still under German control. (*IWM*).

(ABOVE) XE-craft (slightly modified X-craft) ready for operations on the deck of HMS *Bonaventure* in the Far East in 1945. The one on the left has standard two-ton 'side cargoes' fitted and the other two are equipped with limpet-mine carriers. (BELOW) This collection of five-man Japanese *Koryu* at Kure in 1945 shows the importance which the Imperial Japanese Navy attached to midget submersibles. The two torpedo tubes were muzzle loaded. It is odd that Western powers paid so little attention to this excellent design after the war; but the Soviet Union undoubtedly took note of their potential, with a range of 1,380 miles on the surface and a maximum submerged speed of fifteen knots.

(RIGHT) A reconnaisance photograph of the German battleship *Tirpitz* (top right) at the time of Operation Source, September 1943. The nets and boat gap can be clearly seen.

(BELOW) Post-war X-craft HMS *Minnow* in 1956 with author Compton-Hall behind Commander-in-Chief Home Fleet, Admiral Sir John Eccles.

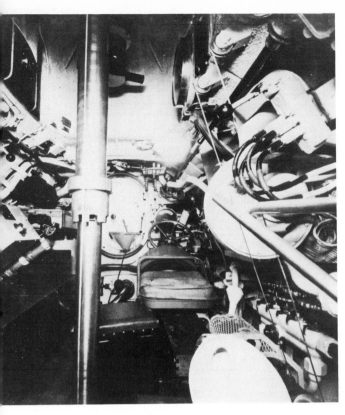

(LEFT) The control room of post-war X-craft HMS *Stickleback* looking forward, past the lowered periscope, to the wet and dry compartment, which also contained the WC.

(BELOW) A wartime wooden mock-up of a German amphibious midget, probably the basis for *Seeteufel*, and hence certain Soviet *Spetsnaz* craft with caterpillar traction.

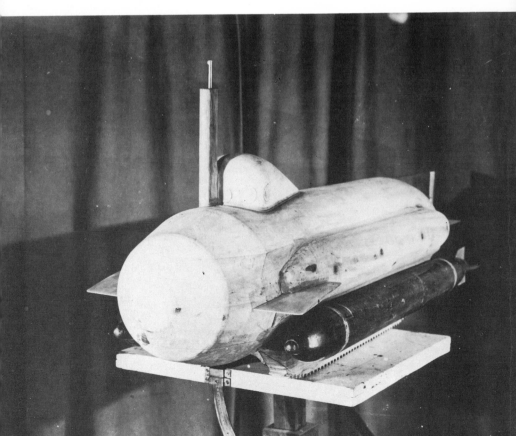

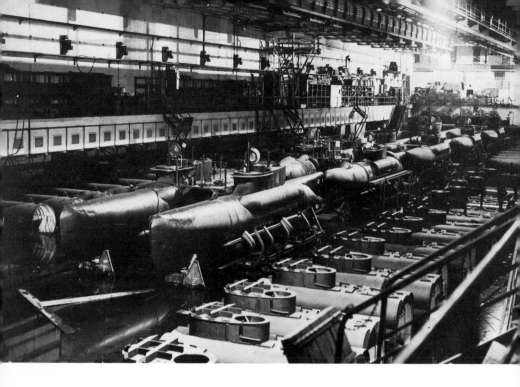

(ABOVE) The US Navy's midget *X-1* launched at Jacobson's Shipyard, Long Island on 7 September 1955. An open cycle oxygen-diesel reciprocating engine powered the thirty-six ton craft submerged, but the system proved hazardous and the project was soon abandoned. As Richard Boyle, the engineer officer and officer-in-charge, remarked: 'High concentration unstabilized hydrogen peroxide has no place in a fighting ship.' (*US Navy*).
(BELOW) German *Seehund* type XXVIIB two-man miniature U-boats at Kiel. Between January and May 1945 these very good craft sank or damaged about 100,000 tons of Allied shipping with the torpedoes, one on each side, which they carried. Anti-submarine defences would have been swamped if large groups had been able to make co-ordinated attacks and, anyway, they were — and still would be — very hard to detect.

numerous ABMs, some transportable, in other areas. For control, ABM battle management systems are being hardened against electromagnetic pulse effect.

At present, in round figures, the 3,000 nuclear warheads capable of delivery by US Navy SSBNs alone (without 'surging' boats in harbour) would wipe out the Soviet Union as a nation, without any land-based missiles or bombs being used, even if no more than a fair percentage followed accurate trajectories and exploded on or near a guesstimated 600 cities – which are presumed to be the principal targets for a second, retaliatory strike because the prospect of 'city-busting' provokes the greatest fear in the deterrent concept. It is assumed (justifiably, it is hoped) that the United States would never, in any circumstances, initiate a first pre-emptive nuclear strike: a power that does so would be bound to target missiles primarily on enemy airfields and missile-launching sites – which would not include relatively invulnerable submarine platforms in the foreseeable future.

It is almost beyond belief that the solitary British SSBN patrol would ever be ordered to fire in independent, unilateral, retaliation for some fell deed by the enemy. What prime minister would give the order? On what pretext? When? As part, a tiny part, of a general East–West exchange, maybe; but surely not alone. Nevertheless, it has to be admitted that the impossible occasionally proves possible, so we ought to see what an existing SSBN, HMS *R......*, can deliver all by herself. With Chevaline and all but one of the missiles up (the commonly quoted readiness figure) she might be required to target fifteen large cities or populated areas (compared with thirty or forty potential targets for two or three French boats on patrol). The actual number of targets could be greater than that if the warheads do indeed have a MIRV similarity, but the relatively few RVs and decoys available would surely not saturate strong ABM defences in important zones. Some warheads would undoubtedly get through, but the total numerical quantity and megatonnage could scarcely be such as to threaten the vast Soviet landmass with unacceptable destruction. If the targets were military, some submarine bases and airfields would be destroyed; but, of course, Soviet submarines at sea would be unscathed.

Trident II missiles, if and when they come into service, might (from the information available) have the terminal accuracy necessary to hit a small proportion of the widespread hardened Soviet missile silos, but that is irrelevant in the context of second-strike deterrence. Three Trident submarines (out of a total four) in the operating cycle (seven- or eight-year commissions between refit/overhauls) with, hopefully, an equally long life for missiles in their tubes should make it possible to ensure that two boats are constantly on patrol, although there seem to be no public indications of that being the intention. But, again, it has to be expected (as the French have evidently recognised) that the still comparatively small number of missiles/RVs targeted will be subject in future to considerable attrition; and, in the nature of things, it cannot be hoped that all the missiles launched would follow the assigned paths. In fact, American, British and – probably to a greater extent – Soviet and French SSBNs must, to be realistic, expect missile failures: there have been enough malfunctions on very carefully prepared test and training firings to suggest that.

It has to be emphasised that some of the figures used above are open to question and argument. They are based on published data which may or may not be correct. Targeting, indeed everything about SSBN operations, is classified at the highest level. All that we can do is to try to put the relative values of the US, British and French submarine deterrent forces in perspective.

When missiles are targeted it is presumably taken into account that nuclear explosions on certain important complexes – the Leningrad base or the Kola Inlet, for instance – would have speedy and unpleasant effects on bordering countries. Perhaps, in whatever circumstances are contemplated, that would be reckoned as just too bad; but it raises an important and more far-reaching point.

No country in the world would entirely escape the appalling effects – sooner or later – of a nuclear exchange. And it would be an exchange, rather than a one-sided attack, if anybody launched ballistic missiles because that is how warning devices and computers are rigged to react, and that is why nuclear missiles are mounted in submarines. It is not the slightest use a country – or more absurdly a town – declaring itself a nuclear-free zone, however far it may think itself from the megatons. Such a gesture is mere wishful thinking. The entire planet will inevitably suffer the consequences from the moment that the first ballistic missile soars up into space, which is a good reason for limiting the nations that possess these weapons to two – the USA and USSR: fewer triggers mean fewer chances of a mistake. Global involvement is not, incidentally, the inevitable case with cruise missiles, which are much less susceptible to early warning, defensive and reaction systems. It is just conceivable that, used selectively and in small numbers, they would not automatically result in everybody letting loose their nuclear armouries; but even a few nuclear explosions, wherever they occur, would have terrible effects far beyond the target area.

We have, then, to ask whether the British (and French) SSBNs really are an effective deterrent in Soviet eyes. True, the Soviet foreign minister demanded that they be included in arms reduction negotiations, but his motives may not be what they appear. He would doubtless like to see the uncertainties about them removed; but it is more likely that he is just trying another approach towards his aim of driving a wedge between Europe and America – and America has generally supported British and French nuclear weapons, albeit with a rationale that has become less convincing over the years.

We have already questioned the political independence of the British deterrent policy in one respect – the possibility of a unilateral launch. It is hard to believe that the Kremlin envisages any real risk of that – and it is the Kremlin, not the British public, that has to be convinced. We have also suggested that the quantity of British warheads likely actually to explode on the USSR, in the remote event that the prime minister *does* give the word at some unspecified point, might not be seen as a definitive bar to Soviet military action. We now turn to the claim that the UK deterrent force is independent in the physical sense.

The Royal Navy's SSBNs, and the organisation which supports them, are very dependent indeed upon the closest co-operation with the USA for a host of operational and technical matters – missile procurement, demonstration and shakedown operations (DASO) and missile firings at Cape Canaveral, and perhaps for certain communication facilities. In part return the USA wants to retain cruise missiles on UK soil and its submarine base in the Holy Loch; and it is also an avid user of intelligence collected through British resources (such as the Cheltenham GCHQ). But that is beside the point: it is very doubtful whether the British strategic deterrent force could operate efficiently without continued wholehearted American co-operation; and certainly Britain will be wholly dependent for Trident missiles on the USA.

The effect of ballistic-missile defences (BMD) in future arising from the American Strategic Defence Initiative (SDI) and some kind of equivalent Soviet system well under way now has to be considered. The declared American aim is to shift from mutually assured destruction to mutually assured security.

Several alternative or complementary SDI sensors and weapons are proposed for what is eventually intended to be a four-layer system to detect and destroy missiles in all stages of flight. In the initial boost stage (very hot, infra-red signature); post-boost phase, while sequentially releasing RVs (small infra-red signature against cold space background); mid-course, while RVs are coasting as cold targets (no infra-red signature); and terminal stage, when RVs start to enter the atmosphere (extremely hot infra-red emissions).

The sensors proposed in space, high-altitude aircraft and remotely controlled drones include infra-red, imaging radars, laser radars (ladars) and laser-induced vibrometry systems with which a laser pulses an object to sense its responding vibration and measure its mass.

Kill-systems include particle beams (the USSR is in the lead with particle accelerators); X-ray lasers (possibly 'pumped' from a nuclear burst); gamma ray lasers (the ultimate in lasers); nuclear or non-nuclear microwave weapons which wreck missile-guidance systems with electronic pulses; hybrid laser/particle beam weapons which shoot particles through laser-ionised channels in near-earth space; kinetic energy weapons (KEW); electromagnetic guns firing projectiles with velocities in excess of 100 kilometres per second; and advanced ground-launched ABMs under guidance and/or infra-red homing.

SDI aims eventually for a seventy to eighty per cent missile-kill probability rather, not surprisingly, than 100 per cent; and nobody has any real idea of what can be achieved or whether the concept is viable in part or in whole. We guess that it will work at least in part, and that the USSR, regardless of the possibility of teaming up with the USA (which has been the subject of an American proposition), will certainly develop particle accelerators to the stage where they will, together with ABMs, destroy a fairly high proportion of incoming missiles if they do not arrive in large flocks. It is the number of missiles which have to be eliminated more or less at the same time (assuming multiple and virtually simultaneous launches) which appears to pose the biggest problem for both sides.

Hence, an SDI/BMD capability (if it becomes reality) is bound to encourage thoughts of a pre-emptive first strike by the possessor against missile bases and command posts, because it offers the chance of limiting damage to a degree from a weakened second-strike response. It is a matter of which side acquires the ability first; and it is therefore very desirable (leaving aside more high-minded declamations) for there to be full American–Soviet co-operation – bizarre though that sounds – so that developments will proceed at the same pace.

There are those who are for SDI and those who are against it; but the quaintest reason for supporting the programme, more and more loudly voiced by scientists and academics, is that invaluable high technology will spin off from the research and development. At the astronomical prices quoted, with humanity at stake and a two-trillion-dollar deficit in the USA (a stack of 1,000 dollar bills 126 miles high by rough calculation) it is a little incongruous to measure the benefits (or dangers) of SDI by its by-products. If SDI is essential to prevent human existence coming to an end, so be it; but it is madness to seek some other kind of justification in order to promote the arms industry in the United States, while the UK and other countries scramble to pick up the sub-contracting crumbs which fall from the rich man's table.

The consequences of a Soviet ballistic-missile defensive capability on SDI lines for the British and French nuclear deterrent forces are obvious. If there is already reason to question their effectiveness, future enhanced defences – probably much enhanced – which can reasonably be expected to combat *limited* numbers of ballistic missiles (if not missiles in hundreds and thousands) must go far to deny their credibility. France appears to have appreciated that already, but there has been no open comment from the UK government.

One of the opposing Soviet views of SDI is that it would destabilise the nuclear strategic balance. Morton H. Halperin, a pioneer in strategic nuclear thinking, has established criteria calculated to achieve stability, and according to his thesis this means doing nothing that would undermine the adversary's capability to retaliate successfully.[10] According to Halperin, 'good' weapons are invulnerable to attack, and there is thus no pressure to 'use 'em or lose 'em'. We earlier offered the argument in another way, and this logic reinforces the desirability of secure submarine-launched missiles. The other definition of 'good' is that such weapons should not be capable of destroying the enemy's retaliatory forces in a first strike – which is true of most current SSBN systems other than Trident II and probably the Soviet 'Typhoon'.

'Bad' weapons, on the other hand, are vulnerable and are capable of negating the probability of retaliation: the MX Peacemaker and other land-mounted missiles must come into that category. We have added to the thesis that 'bad' weapons also invite counterforce attacks on areas which are populated.

Nuclear disarmers would say that all nuclear weapons are bad and that none is good. They are right in the sense that they are more liable than other weapons to kill whole populations and, indeed, destroy the world. But it is intellectually unsound to separate nuclear weapons from warfare as a whole when high explosives and chemical and biological warfare disseminators bid fair to cause such widespread death, misery and disease that the unfortunate victims might well prefer, if given a choice, to be incinerated by a thermonuclear blast. Total disarmament – the prevention of all war – is the only rational objective.

Taking 'good' and 'bad' criteria a step further, if the Soviets threaten to use nuclear weapons at sea in a localised confrontation, it would not be a credible deterrent to base the response upon a massive attack on Soviet cities, because that would be suicidal. It follows that ballistic missiles, if intended for use in this situation against shore targets, are 'bad', although so long as they are reserved in submarines for ultimate deterrence at the top end of the scale they remain 'good'.

Submarine-launched cruise missiles (SLCMs), on the other hand, are 'good' in all nuclear situations up to a full nuclear exchange; and, in the light of predicted SDI/BMD capabilities, there is much to be said for securing them as a parallel nuclear deterrent.

SLCMs are 'good' because they are too slow and not sufficiently powerful for a first strike; they are not susceptible to SDI defences, although doubtless some means of intercepting them will be devised in due course; they can carry either conventional or nuclear warheads; they are flexible and can be used for measured response against seaborne or land targets in a way that is wholly credible; and they are relatively inexpensive ($3.1 million for Tomahawk as against $74 million for MX and $25 million for Trident D-5[11]) so that they could sensibly be afforded for fitting in the submarines of major or medium-sized naval powers. We noted earlier that they are not as liable as ballistic missiles to provoke a full-scale reaction on either side (that is, they are applicable to a graduated response if that philosophy is realistic).

The new Soviet SS–NX–21 and a predicted follow-on submarine-launched cruise missile are a clear indication that the USSR is posing another level of strategic threat. Major targets in the USA tend to be near the coast. Every level of violence must be countered – ideally like for like – if deterrence is going to be credible all the way up the scale. If that and the preceding points are agreed, it will be advantageous to equip a sizeable number of NATO submarines with cruise missiles to match the Soviet SLCMs.

Arguments against equipping NATO fleets with land-attack cruise missiles (such as Tomahawk) are mainly concerned with SLCMs furthering a nuclear war-fighting ability rather than strengthening the peace-keeping deterrent; and with the added danger that surface ships carrying nuclear Tomahawk cruise missiles make fleets a strategic target. The first objection, which at first sight aligns with the arguments we have put forward, is answered by the great desirability of deterring at all levels with the broadest possible spread of platforms; and the second is satisfied by confining Tomahawk to submarines. A third objection put forward has been that SLCMs would make arms-control reductions difficult to verify, because conventional and nuclear warheads are virtually indistinguishable on cruise missiles; but all kinds of nuclear warheads are difficult to verify numerically (how many MIRVs does a ballistic missile actually carry?), and this is a weak reason for not acquiring sea-launched cruise missiles. There is also a political faction which seems to think that SLCMs will be a substitute for SLBMs in the US Navy; but that is certainly not the US Navy's intention with Tomahawk. At any rate, nothing of the kind is envisaged today, although nobody knows what future arms-control agreements may bring about.

Terrain-hugging land-attack Tomahawk missiles are an excellent addition to the undersea leg of the nuclear deterrent Triad. Tomahawk could quadruple the number of submarine platforms that would have to be destroyed in order to neutralise the counter-threat; but very widespread fitting in SSNs could scarcely be justified while SSBNs remain relatively invulnerable. However it would certainly be advantageous to have an unspecified and unidentified number of SSNs (if arms talks allow) equipped with nuclear Tomahawk. The maximum range, which is presumably dependent on how much of the 550-knot flight is conducted at high altitude, has been quoted as 500–700 nautical miles and 1,300–1,400 nautical miles. Whatever the realistic range may be within these brackets, it is obviously great enough to satisfy the moneymen, because the US Navy's 1985 appropriation was for twenty-five conventional and seventy-five nuclear land-attack weapons. However, it has to be recognised that Tomahawk submarines must be stationed relatively close to the USSR, and are bound to be more vulnerable than SSBNs patrolling in the distant open ocean. On the other hand, SLCM boats off Norway, in the North Sea, Baltic, eastern Mediterranean and western Pacific could be well protected in bastions, along Soviet lines, by forces which already exist.

The latest '688 class' SSNs are getting fifteen vertical launch tubes, but Tomahawk can be discharged through a standard twenty-one-inch torpedo tube so its use (given the installation of fire-control equipment) is not confined to purpose-built submarines – nor even to SSNs.

Tomahawk (or some similar SLCM) would seem to be well suited not only as a complementary deterrent weapon for the US Navy, but also as a satisfactory, if not ideal, weapon for Britain, if she is indeed determined to retain a nuclear deterrent capability; and it would not be restricted to specifically strategic submarines. It is true that Tomahawk might not be able to strike at the Soviet heartland, but enough vital areas in the USSR and Warsaw Pact countries are within reach of the system to deter at a lesser, but still high, cost than Trident; and more missiles from more submarines might actually get through to their targets.

Moreover, a land-attack SLCM with an alternative conventional warhead is a highly desirable weapon for use in limited non-nuclear wars and skirmishes. Although the HE warhead obviously lacks the destructive power of a multi-kiloton nuclear head, Tomahawk's accuracy has been described as 'within several yards'[12]: this would make it effective for the deep interdiction of airfields, radar and communication facilities, HQs, bridges and rail junctions, as well as naval ports. And then, of course, there are substantial savings – in terms of equipment, training and maintenance – to be had by employing a weapon which is much the same whether it comes in the land-attack or the anti-ship version. The latter can target high-speed manoeuvring ships out to around 250 miles – a four- or five-fold improvement over Harpoon.

Tomahawk is a 'good' weapon, and despite its range limitations it could be thought adequate for the Royal Navy's strategic role. Eight missiles, say, could be carried in practically any modern submarine without unacceptably reducing the fairly generous standard torpedo load. It is perhaps taking the proposition too far to follow one suggestion that a couple of hundred cruise missiles could be accommodated in an old SSBN hull with SLBM tubes stripped out; but that idea, also, deserves more than a passing thought.

Britain examined the submarine cruise missile option in 1980–1[13] and the Defence Committee was against it. The reasoning, together with our comments, went thus:

> CMs have many attractions. They cost much less each than Trident missiles; they are even more accurate; they are a good deal smaller and easier to store. The fact that they would take hours rather than minutes to reach targets in the Soviet Union is not important, since Western deterrent concepts do not envisage trying to catch Soviet missiles in their silos.

It is assumed that Soviet cities are still the primary targets for deterrent purposes.

> There are however major factors on the other side. The United States judges that present Soviet air defences have little chance against CMs; but with advancing technology the defence problem is not insuperable given time and effort, and Soviet defences against CMs, unlike ABM defences, are not

limited by Treaty. It is impossible to put precise figures on what proportion of CMs Soviet air defences in the two decades from the early 1990s – roughly the timeframe we want for our new strategic system – might succeed in shooting down; but we must reckon with the possibility that it could progressively become very substantial, especially since we probably could not afford to re-equip with new and better CMs as often as the United States may well do to keep pace with defences in this new and rapidly changing field. We have to take into account also that whereas the United States ALCM [air-launched] force can plan to saturate the defences of key strategic targets, we could not operate on the same scale. In addition, the apparent advantage of CMs over BMs in cost per missile is misleading. Trident can carry up to eight separately targetable warheads; currently CMs carry only one (and SALT II would prohibit CMs carrying more).

ABM defences are advancing rapidly, but there is no known evidence that CM defences are keeping pace. At Tomahawk prices, even allowing for staged improvements, SLCMs are about one eighth the cost of Trident missiles and a large number could be kept at sea.

There are also considerations affecting the submarine. We, like the United States, have always judged it important that a strategic missile submarine should be able to fire its weapons within a short space of time, to avoid the risk that enemy action – by ASW forces or by 'counter-battery' fire from land-based ballistic missiles after the launch of our own missiles had perhaps revealed the submarine's position – might be brought to bear before all the missiles had been fired. Our Polaris boats accordingly can fire their full complement within a very few minutes. But this is much more difficult with CMs. With torpedo tubes – the only submarine-launch mode so far developed – repeated re-load would be necessary to launch a number of CMs anywhere equivalent in striking power to a boatload of Trident BMs. The process would take hours, during which the submarine would be at increasingly severe risk, and it might well not survive to complete the task. Alternative launch modes, such as vertical launch on the SLBM pattern, would require extensive new system development and submarine design.

We have already suggested that a single SSBN or a pair of SSBNs may not be a convincing deterrent in light of increasing ABM defences and the relatively small number of targets covered. We also question whether one or two ballistic-missile submarines can survive in the face of a determined effort to abort their mission. The US Navy has now developed vertical launch tubes for Tomahawk, but we see no reason for necessarily adopting this system for existing British SSNs and SSKs – although it seems desirable for future designs, when SLCMs could be carried for land-attack or anti-ship purposes. The risk when launching six or eight CMs from torpedo tubes is not that severe: there is no reason to try to cram SLCM striking power equal to the fifteen ready SLBMs into one submarine; it would be better for tactical reasons to spread (and perhaps even increase) the total fire-power by equipping several boats. CM launch will not be detected as rapidly as BM launch; and the launching process, for a few missiles per boat, would take minutes not hours.

> There is a further operational point. Certain CMs have much less range than BMs; moreover, at least with systems now in prospect, there is a limit on how far off-shore a land-attack CM can be launched, since beyond a certain distance cumulative inertial navigation errors may mean too high a risk that the missile will fail to make its landfall accurately enough to initiate the overland navigation phase successfully. The effective range of a CM launched from the North Atlantic would be significantly less than that of Polaris. The searoom available to the submarines, and their scope for evading improved Soviet ASW forces, would be restricted accordingly.

This overstates the navigational problems if a weapon like Tomahawk is employed; and we suggest that CM submarines would not, in practice, be unduly vulnerable if their launching zones are selected with an eye to poor anti-submarine (ASW) operating conditions (such as inshore waters), or if they can be afforded a degree of 'bastion' protection when in certain areas.

> The factors (above) relate essentially to a CM-launching submarine devoted entirely to the strategic role. We also considered the possibility of equipping each of our hunter-killer submarines with a small number of CMs, for launch through the torpedo tubes. But there are two difficulties about this. Firstly there is the problem of conflicting tasks ... Our non-strategic submarine force is already fully committed to its existing tasks, and the patterns of deployment and operation for the last-resort strategic role are very different from those for seeking out and attacking other submarines and surface ships.
>
> Secondly, it would not be possible to build up enough strike capability for strategic deterrence in 'penny-packet' numbers of CMs on non-strategic submarines.

Standard operational commitments most certainly militate against SSNs and SSKs devoting themselves wholly and uniquely to the strategic role with SLCMs. But many (assumed) wartime operating areas are probably not too far removed from potential CM launch points; and a second, retaliatory, strike does not have to be immediate. Indeed, instant reaction implies grave dangers of mistake, and a potential delay in launching any kind of missile could be no bad thing in some circumstances. It would be possible to spread about fifty SLCMs amongst half a dozen SSNs and SSKs; all things considered, including the area covered by each ballistic-missile's RVs and the attrition of missiles due to ballistic-missile defences, the CMs which penetrated could be as effective as the fifteen (ready) SLBMs (eight RVs apiece), which are less likely to penetrate, in one SSBN – where, incidentally, all the eggs are in one basket. Equally it would be possible to put twice that number in a dozen boats to make up – again very approximately – the effective striking power of two SSBNs. In these comparisons we have assumed that a considerably larger proportion of ballistic-missile RVs will be intercepted than cruise missiles: the assumption is reasonable because a terrain-hugging missile is extremely hard to intercept, as the Soviets clearly appreciate, and Soviet defences tend, strongly, to be concentrated against ballistic-missiles.

> All this means that CMs are not in fact a cheaper option than BMs. For a given weight of striking power and a given level of probability of delivering it successfully, CM-based forces are in fact much more expensive. For example, eleven boats each capable of carrying eighty CMs would give less assured deterrent capability than a force of five boats each with sixteen Trident BMs; and it would cost at least a third as much again to acquire and about twice as much to run. One of the major reasons for this, important to bear in mind in all evaluation of delivery system options, is that for almost any submarine force the boats are a much more costly element than the missiles.

The cost comparison is not valid and an alternative comparison in effectiveness has been suggested above. Four, not five, Trident SSBNs are planned, and of those one (or conceivably two) will be 'deterring' at any one time. Limiting the number of SLCMs in any one existing boat to, say, eight and installing fire-control equipment for torpedo-tube launch would cost, even if all SSNs and SSKs were equipped, much less than the Trident programme. If a future SSN has vertical launch tubes, so much the better, especially if a Tomahawk-type SLCM could be switched on board from the land-attack to the anti-ship role. In that case submarines should carry considerably more weapons than we have proposed – perhaps twice as many – with only, say, half of them fitted with nuclear warheads. It is very true that the boats are a more costly element than the missiles: that is why we have suggested adapting existing and future attack-type submarines. There would still be room for plenty of anti-submarine weapons.

Forces of these types could also require a much greater investment in manpower to operate. Any cruise missile alternative could in future be countered by enemy air defences. The necessary TERCOM (Terrain Contour Matching) guidance for cruise missiles could involve continual dependence on information from United States satellites and thus would reduce the operational independence available with an SSBN force. Inertial guidance could be provided independently but would not achieve the necessary accuracy. In addition there are a number of other objections relating to political, environmental and command problems.

On the first point, no significant additional manpower would be required for a quite sizeable response fitted in standard submarines. We doubt very much the assertion that future enemy air defences will be sufficient to detract from a cruise-missile deterrent posture in our timeframe. The indications are that inertial guidance would be sufficiently accurate and Tomahawk trials have demonstrated this. Dependence on US information would, so far as we can see, be no greater than for Trident; in fact it might be less. The other problems are not specified and the omission raises further doubts about these objections.

The above comments relate to an alternative cruise-missile strategy and they tend to suggest that, for the UK anyway, it would be preferable to a ballistic-missile strategy. But the real question is whether Britain needs a nuclear deterrent at all. If she does, there is a case for re- examining the cruise-missile option – the last published enquiry was begun in June 1980. In some important respects things have changed since then (notably Tomahawk's successful tests), while the government has opted for Trident. What has not changed, however, is Britain's dependence on America for technology, missiles, missile-servicing and trials.

There is another consideration besides cost which affects a medium maritime nation which has a so-called nuclear deterrent. It concerns effective naval power in the real everyday world in which we live, beset by terrorists and with minor conflagrations starting up all around.

Deterrence is crucially important at the lowest levels of violence: if minor conflagrations are not put out quickly the fire is bound to spread. If terrorists or relatively minor trouble-makers further extend their activities at sea, as they very probably will, they must be stopped before world trade is seriously affected. Already American citizens are cancelling European cruises following the *Achille Lauro* hijacking in 1985. Above all, a close watch must be kept on areas from where there is a danger of war arising. Early warning is the key to preventing conflagrations and confrontations.

While nuclear deterrence at the highest level prevents a global nuclear exchange, it certainly does not prevent fighting, invasions and skirmishing. Instead, it provides an umbrella under which these damaging activities can continue largely unchecked by the nuclear powers because the latter are inhibited, by fear of escalation, from interceding.

It happens that Britain is historically well equipped to deal with such activities. Pax Britannica worked pretty well in its time, and the Royal Navy was its instrument. Today, not only does the expense of a strategic nuclear deterrent rob the UK of sufficient naval power and influence to fight fires and police trouble spots, but its possession stifles the initiative to do so. Nor is enough cash left in the defence budget for the armed services to be equipped with a sufficient surveillance capability to give assured early warning – to detect a spark or sniff the first faint trace of smoke.

In other words, Britain cannot afford to prevent real war while mounting a deterrent against unreal war – which is how a nuclear exchange can be viewed for so long as the two superpowers maintain a nuclear balance.

The UK contribution to the nuclear deterrent is miniscule by comparison with that of the USA; but the trans-Atlantic link has been forged so strongly that, despite Soviet efforts, a break in the alliance is inconceivable. Britain could play an inestimably more valuable role in the alliance by deterring at the commonplace level, and watching for warning signs, using submarines for surveillance, than by adding marginally to America's massive retaliation capability. As for a national defence by one or two SSBNs against a 'bolt from the blue', we simply cannot think that this is necessary, realistic or credible.

Nevertheless, the British Conservative government, advised by the Royal Navy which is the servant of the government, is going flat out for Trident – flat out because the elderly Polaris fleet, whose hulls and equipment have a limited life, is becoming impossibly expensive to maintain and update. And for sea-room, security and penetration in the future with the least through-life expenditure, the longer range D–5 missiles and associated warheads are required.

The cost, for Britain, is impossible to specify exactly without changing sterling-dollar exchange rates, but it was hovering around the £10 billion mark in early 1986, with prices spread unevenly over a fifteen-year period. The submarines themselves account for thirty-five per cent, missiles seventeen per cent, weapon systems seventeen per cent and shore construction eight per cent. Seven per cent of the budget had been spent by the end of 1985. The procurement programme for four sixteen-tube Trident SSBNs and missiles is still open to debate.

One might secure good odds with a betting firm on a future Labour or

Liberal/SDP Alliance government vigorously opposing the Trident programme and bringing it to a halt. Nor is it impossible that the present Conservative government will endeavour to shake the weighty financial burden off its shoulders by offering to sacrifice Trident as the United Kingdom's voluntary contribution to nuclear arms limitation talks.

British politicians and strategists have repeatedly said that conventional forces are more expensive than the strategic nuclear deterrent, and that Trident is only a small percentage – three per cent has been quoted – of the annual defence budget. That is beside the point. A vast sum of money is involved, whatever the relative costs, and finding the manpower is not going to be easy either. Worse, by the middle of 1985 there were rumblings to the effect that any over-run on Trident would have to be paid for out of the total defence budget – meaning that other forces would suffer further. The defence secretary in 1985 was confident that the programme could be managed without adverse effects on Britain's defence capability, but the Defence Committee pointed out that the unitary nature of the Trident programme and its implications for the strategic deterrent will make it less susceptible to adjustment to match budgetary constraints than other programmes.[14] Too right!

Nuclear deterrence is not a contraceptive; it will not prevent the birth of a novel means of warfare or defence. History demonstrates that concepts like the Strategic Defence Initiative will continue to evolve. Only the two superpowers will be able to afford continually updated capabilities, and Britain is bound, like it or not, to rely more and more heavily on the alliance which the United States leads and upholds.

The French philosopher Voltaire[15] once remarked about the Hapsburg Holy Roman Empire that it was 'neither holy, nor Roman, nor Empire'. Today he might say of the British Independent Deterrent that it is neither British, nor independent, nor deterrent.

12

The Underwater Way Ahead

Examining war as a phenomenon a dismal reflection comes to mind: war has never, in recorded history, been eliminated by any kind of deterrent threat, from gunpowder to thermonuclear bombs. Like the poor, it will always be with us. It is an integral part of politics, not just a rude eructation at the table of civilisation. At the last count there were some twenty-six bloody battles going on around the world. New weapons simply establish, or limit for a while, the level of violence employed.

Quite apart from outright warfare, the underwater threat is now worldwide and, realised or unrealised, it ranges from trespassing, through something like piracy, to deterrence at all levels, and from the possibility of a restricted confrontation to all-out nuclear war. The underwater way ahead will need to take account of all these eventualities.

It is also obvious that the panoply of defences against undersea attack is much more expensive than the submarine force which poses the threat. It follows that the USSR, with whatever surrogates it encourages, is going to be in a more enviable position at sea than the free world for as long as the West is on the defensive and the Soviet Navy, controlled by the Defence Council, continues to give priority to offensive underwater warfare. Selective offence is cheaper than comprehensive defence, and there is ample opportunity, especially in submarine warfare, for an apparent threat of offensive moves to be increased by bluff.

The USSR perfectly appreciates the advantages of an aggressive posture going under the name of defence; and the attitude of Pentagon 'hawks' in the light of this is very understandable. Unfortunately, the latter tend to press their warlike recommendations a little too far, just as peace organisations go dangerously far in the other direction. As implied throughout this review, underwater warfare is particularly prone to descriptive exaggerations and superlatives – high and low – by supporters and detractors at extreme ends of the argument.

The ideal answer for the West would be to present a demonstrable threat to the Kremlin and anybody else who bids to disturb the peace such that the would-be aggressor has to occupy himself so much with defence that he is unable to embark on war at any level. This, of course, is simply deterrence in another light; but it does suggest seeking to take the initiative rather than merely responding to shows of force. That is why Mr Gorbachev is so anxious to halt the US Strategic Defence Initiative (SDI). Seen from his standpoint it carries the threat of weapons in space under the soubriquet of Star Wars, but above all it is a dangerous initiative – the first devised by the West since the Strike Fleet was assembled in the 1950s.

The Soviet Navy has continually taken the initiative with its submarines and weapons systems, as shown in the preceding chapters. War has not come any closer thereby, even if the threat has so dramatically increased. Why, then, should the West not follow the same policy? It involves, primarily, a new attitude of mind, a change in our way of thinking – but that does not mean engaging in brinkmanship. All it requires is to worry the Soviets rather than allowing them the privilege of worrying us all the time.

The immediate retort is that deterrence, to which the West is committed while the USSR is not, depends on the ability to retaliate in kind at all levels. But why should the deterrent theory, which is becoming confused with war-winning, be confined to retaliation alone? Why should we not oblige the USSR to devote its resources to true defence and hence weaken its ability to attack? Other than deploying the Strike Fleet (which arguably caused the Soviet submarine reaction), the West has been on the defensive for decades, struggling to meet each new challenge and never quite catching up. That is, of course, if the threat is realistic and interpreted correctly, which is not certain in each and every respect. A lot more expenditure on Western intelligence services, for pure intelligence gathering and analysis, ought to clarify matters, enable defence targets to be set more accurately in good time, and save money in the long run.

Attack-type submarines are exceptionally well suited to posing a threat to the USSR. They force the Soviet Navy to implement costly defences and deter the Politburo at a very realistic level. Submarine deterrence is emphatically not confined to a nuclear riposte. The effectiveness of a submarine threat was well illustrated in 1982 when it kept the Argentinian fleet in harbour during most of the Falklands conflict; and, when units did briefly venture out, the unfortunate *General Belgrano* was duly sunk, an event which amply proved that the deterrent was real – although the British had bluffed in the early stages to make the enemy think that the submarines were lying in wait, when in fact they were still hurrying south.

Taking the initiative, with innovation, has attractions – not least it would be accompanied by a resurgence of morale. Initiative would

THE UNDERWATER WAY AHEAD

allow objectives to be crystallised in a way that is very difficult with today's increasingly complex concepts of deterrence and defence, which seem no longer to be wholly comprehensive to most of us, nor very well defined.

If only because it is an initiative, SDI has advantages for the West. It will keep Soviet scientists occupied when they might be turning their minds to other things. Whether the entire business is practicable or affordable is another matter altogether; but parts of it, like the curate's egg, are excellent.[1] The trouble is that its greatest benefits are to the power which contemplates a first strike because it will be most effective against a reduced second strike. Europe has also to ask whether American SDI defences will eventually cover the West as a whole. If so, what might the Russians be tempted to do in the period between the USA gaining (partial) protection and the system being extended to shelter allies on the other side of the Atlantic? Only seven and a half per cent of the world's microtechnology expertise lies in Europe, so the European contribution – and consequent rewards – cannot be great. There are, by the way, only five people in the West who are reputedly capable of designing the SDI battle-management system; the USSR is probably ahead in this field, as well as with research and development for particle-beam accelerators and lasers, so in some respects the Soviet Union might feel encouraged to launch a first strike before the American plan is fully developed – if, in due course, research does lead to development. The Soviets are also believed to be actively engaged not only in producing anti-satellite weapons, but also in developing means for destroying SDI weapons in space.

Enormous problems lie ahead, but the strong probability is that both East and West will end up with much-enhanced anti-ballistic-missile defences of sundry kinds – not enough to prevent totally unacceptable devastation arising from a massive first strike, but very possibly sufficient to reduce the effect of retaliation with a small number of ballistic warheads (such as Britain's Polaris/Trident force) to a level that might be considered just bearable. But it will be a very long time indeed before American and Soviet defences are layered down to catch their opponents' huge arsenal of ballistic missiles, launched from submarines in virtually any ocean area, during the important boost phase; and it has to be repeated that cruise missiles are impervious to SDI weapons.

In other words, whatever develops from SDI on either side in the years ahead will tend to favour an aggressor unless both sides should develop the system simultaneously – a crazily logical notion; but at the same time such huge expenses will be incurred that economies and more conventional forces are bound to suffer.

In all this, SSBNs will remain by far the most secure launching platforms in the time-scale we are considering (up to the year 2025) – provided that there are enough of them constantly on patrol and that communications remain intact. But the British one, or perhaps two, boats at sea would seem altogether too vulnerable to a vigorous anti-SSBN campaign – which could be aimed at submarines in harbour and while sailing to or returning from patrol as well as in the open sea. In that respect, US SSBNs based on the Holy Loch in Scotland are geographically less secure than those on American seaboards. European communications systems, too, are more liable to disruption by sabotage or minor raids than are those based in America. There are dangers as well as operational advantages in being closer to the opposition.

In Chapter 11 arguments have been offered for scrapping British Trident plans; and France's *Force de Dissuasion* lacks the logic for which Frenchmen used to be famed. On the other hand, the arguments in favour of the US Navy's numerous SSBNs as America's nuclear deterrent, maintaining the balance for the entire free world, are simple and unassailable – although service prejudices and inter-service rivalries will doubtless result in continuing opposition to further strengthening the force and backing it with land-attack SLCMs for selected SSNs. It is hard to understand the case being made for more land-based missiles like the MX Peacemaker, to say nothing of airborne weapons: those are the legs of the Triad which are most liable to totter.

The argument advanced by British politicians that our so-called independent nuclear deterrent protects us from a 'bolt from the blue' is not persuasive. Europe depends on the United States for holding the Soviet Union at bay, and no delusions of national grandeur can alter the fact. It is right for Europe to contribute a fair share towards supporting American deterrent forces – and particularly the strongest, most dependable and convincing leg of the Triad, the SSBN fleet – but not by providing British or French SSBNs to augment it in such a small but expensive way.

There are practical, economical, cost-effective ways by which the UK – and maybe France in the fullness of time – could play an invaluable operational part in preventing war and making trans-Atlantic bonds even stronger without adding to the number of ballistic missiles at sea.

First, it has to be admitted that cancelling British Trident would not necessarily result in more funds being made available for Royal Navy attack-type submarines, although there is a current report to the effect that Vickers are sewing up the contract in such a way that money would be transferred for the construction of ten or a dozen hunter-killers should Trident be cancelled. If this report is not confirmed it is worth noting that the £900 million allocated for 1988–9 alone would pay for four new SSNs – a twenty per cent increase in the flotilla. But, either way, cancellation should prevent SSN and SSK forces, equipment and weapons being eroded by Trident, and release hundreds of highly experienced civilian and naval personnel (who represent some of the most disquieting, largely unquantified costs) for very gainful employment in other areas. The Royal Navy (which is doing very well, for a middling power, in ordering its nineteenth SSN including the original *Dreadnought*) could then expect to find its quite powerful submarine flotilla still better armed, equipped, manned and trained at no additional expense. The resources are available, and much could be accomplished if they are used wisely. Waste is certainly evident, but it has been said that the next generation of British SSNs, compared with the US Navy 'Seawolf' (SSN 21) class, will have eighty per cent of the capability for less than one third of the cost – a fact which the Treasury may care to note.

Meanwhile, because the US Navy managed to commission an SSBN fleet of thirty-one 'Benjamin Franklin' and 'Lafayette' sixteen-SLBM type boats in the space of four years (between April 1963 and April 1967) from four yards, these boats are now becoming obsolete in the same short time-span. The replacement twenty-four-SLBM 'Ohio' SSBNs (726–749) for the Trident programme were planned in 1974 to be built at a rate of three SSBNs every year for the first ten of the class. But the Department of Defense almost immediately revised this to 1–2–2–2–2–1, and in 1975 the planned reduction was further slowed to 1–2–1–2–1–2–1. In 1976 it was announced that continuing production after the first ten would also be at the rate of 1–2–1–2, consistent with SALT agreements. Yet again, in March 1978 it was agreed that planned building from fiscal year 1980 onwards would be retarded to 1–1–1–1–1–2–1–2, apparently to allow the sole contractor, General Dynamics Electric Boat Division, to catch up.

If Newport News shipyard becomes able to compete with Electric Boat for SSBN contracts fairly soon, as expected, the 'Ohio' building problem will be eased, although under the Reagan administration only one 'Ohio' is planned annually until fiscal year 1990.

Thus, at least until the early 1990s, it appears that the number of US Navy SLBMs at sea could be considerably reduced: the length of this period depends, presumably, on the longevity of the 'Benjamin Franklin' and 'Lafayette' boats, and on the success of the Trident I and II (D–5) missile programmes together with the Mark 500 MARV now being made compatible with Trident I. (A MARV – Manoeuvering Re-entry Vehicle – is intended to evade ABM interceptor missiles and, to increase its accuracy, is not terminally guided.)

Three SSBNs – USS *Robert E. Lee, Sam Houston* and *John Marshall* – have been converted, for about $400,000 a piece, to SSNs and re-designated SSN–601, 609 and 611 respectively. The latter two have become amphibious transports, and imaginative schemes have been proposed for converting other old SSBNs, when they become redundant, for various purposes, including fleet replenishment tasks.

One radical but economic solution to any future US Navy SSBN shortfall could be for America to buy the currently planned four Trident SSBNs from Vickers (UK). Although they would carry only sixteen D–5 missiles, the building costs at Vickers, Barrow-in-Furness (who have an extremely good track record and are now under private ownership), will be one third or less of those for the twenty-four-missile SSBNs being built at Electric Boat, Groton.

Without SSBNs of its own, the Royal Navy could give considerable support to the US Navy's 'Boomers'. Submarine escorts (which will become increasingly necessary) could be provided in critical eastern Atlantic areas, while logistical and certain communications facilities could be more widely shared.

In the Royal Navy itself, research and development for weapon systems, propulsion and hulls could be concentrated on attack boats; and training would be devoted entirely to them. The benefits could not be other than enormous if the cards were played correctly. Too great a proportion of our scant resources is currently being expended on Trident. And if the British government is irrevocably committed to keeping a nuclear deterrent at sea, for some valid reason that has escaped the authors, it could go into partnership with America for the Tomahawk (SLCM) cruise missile system with little or no detriment to the deterrent posture.

Irrespective of whether the British nuclear deterrent is given a new life by Trident or Tomahawk, NATO should not only provide effective national underwater warfare forces, but also give all possible assistance to American SSBNs and SSNs if the alliance is to look for the continued protection which only the United States can give to Europe and the rest of the free world. It is wrong, in every sense, for European media and peace organisations to criticise and attempt to denigrate American forces when they are vital to the safety of Europe: to do so is to play into the hands of the Soviet opposition and give encouragement to certain US media which, it has been remarked (perhaps not entirely in jest), are the only section of American society which seems to be working full time for the KGB. Above all, American taxpayers need to be convinced that they are getting value for money and that the Allies are tipping in a sensible contribution towards the huge US expenditure.

So where does the West go from here? How best can responsibilities be apportioned and costs be afforded? And what will be cost-effective in the future?

It should be possible, after the discussion of underwater warfare that has occupied previous chapters, to reach some objective conclusions and establish certain priorities without being unduly presumptuous or attempting to peer into classified matters.

THE UNDERWATER THREAT

Nuclear arms reduction talks may or may not succeed to some degree. The latest proposal by the Soviet Union to do away with all nuclear weapons by the year 2000 looks, on the face of it, hopeful. But no reduction in the Soviet underwater threat to Western naval and mercantile assets can be foreseen. Nor is it reasonable to think that while talks continue Soviet SSBNs will do other than increase their capabilities in the face of SDI. Nor will the USSR lessen its anti-ballistic-missile defences; quite the contrary. Meanwhile, it would be logical for the Kremlin to arrange for surrogates to do its dirty work wherever possible.

Second-guessing Moscow's long-term intention is a chancy business, but a glance at the globe suggests that the Politburo's prime target areas, having prepared to neutralise Sweden and walk into Norway, are now the Middle East and Africa. Mounting Soviet pressure can then be applied to South East Asia, whose geographical hub for the ASEAN organisation is Singapore, a thriving state despite stock exchange problems at the end of 1985. Significant units of the Soviet Navy are now based in Vietnam, but the ASEAN countries are singularly well defended by missile-craft against incursions. The answer for the Soviet fleet is to employ submarines, preceded by midget intruders, if force has to be used. The level of violence needed here, as seen by the outside world, could be quite low.

China, of course, might attempt to occupy the ASEAN position first, but the will to do so is not yet apparent, and Moscow must hope that Beijing will be fully occupied with its own internal affairs for a long time to come.

Either way, Australasia would be isolated, notably from fuel supplies coming from America and Japan: Australia is only half self-sufficient in oil, and New Zealand has none. Western Europe could be left stewing (as a detached and brutally frank American observer has put it) in its own juice, while the KGB applies itself wholeheartedly to destabilising and fomenting the North and South American continents. The KGB faces a tough assignment in the United States, which is strong in every way, but there is enough inflammable material there to blaze if the right matches are struck at the appropriate moment.

Shed of niceties, the Soviet Defence Council's submarine force objectives appear to be sixfold:

a. To mount a massive submarine-based missile force capable of launching a nuclear strike if non-military or conventional methods of achieving political goals fail. (The Russians may themselves perceive this as a monstrous bluff, but the capability is demonstrably real.)

b. To prevent the Strike and Amphibious Fleets from attacking the Soviet Union.

c. To project power and deploy submarine weapon systems in ways that will stretch Western anti-submarine resources to the limit or beyond in times of tension or crisis, thereby preventing the West from assembling a sufficiently concentrated offensive force to invade the Soviet Union.

d. To clear the way for the establishment of bases in Norway and a secure outlet to the Atlantic.

e. To maintain the ability of disrupting trans-Atlantic supply lines and preventing 'the safe and timely arrival'[2] of convoys.

f. To track down Western SSBNs.

These objectives fulfil all the Soviet Principles of War, and we can reasonably assume that they are the basis of Soviet maritime strategy. All but the first amount to 'denial of the sea', a policy by which Western navies are allowed progressively less space for manoeuvre in the oceans of the world. The Western objective might therefore be 'denial of sea denial'.[3] A clear-cut aim to counter Soviet policy now (as opposed to when war has been declared) has been notably absent from top level NATO strategical maritime aspirations. Something succinct, simple to grasp and interpret downstream, would be welcome and helpful.[4]

Taking this as a not unreasonable starting point, for lack of anything better (that we have found) offered by politicians or admirals, we propose looking at Western submarine force planning with regard to strategy, tactics and material to see if they match the Western Principles of War. In the past these Principles have indicated the way to success, and a failure to take note of them has almost always been attended by failure in practice. The Principles are not dogmatic and they do not constitute a kind of checklist; but neither are they simply academic, and there is nothing in present or future war considerations to outdate these basic, true and tested guidelines.

The British Principles of War are used for convenience, except when noted otherwise. It is understood that the US Naval War College no longer teaches Principles of War as such, but does emphasise the analysis of historical situations – which presumably comes to the same thing.

SELECTION AND MAINTENANCE OF THE AIM

Accepting 'the denial of sea denial' (until someone dreams up a better aim for the existing state of more or less permanent tension) SSBNs with Trident missiles can be confident of maintaining the aim by retaining their freedom of action. Anything much less than the range which the Trident missile affords could be inhibiting in the future.

On the Soviet side, a bastion strategy for their SSBNs – together with a long-range missile capability – goes some way to meeting the Soviet equivalent, the Principle of Advance and Consolidation. But doubtless it would be better served by establishing advance bases for submarines of all kinds in southern Norway and, indeed, much further afield – in the Pacific, the Indian Ocean and perhaps South America, if Cuba is deemed too close to the United States for comfort. It is certain that the Soviet Northern Fleet will do everything possible to avoid being contained in the Barents and Norwegian Seas, and is preparing for moves to gain more freedom now.

Soviet attack submarines are obviously bent on sea denial. But do NATO SSNs and SSKs have a clear, identifiable aim? It is not apparent – perhaps because of security implications – if they do although plenty of tasks are assigned to them. If repeated insistence on an aim seems to smack too much of staff academies, it can only be said that history has shown the great value of stating a simple governing objective which everybody – forces, politicians and taxpayers – can understand. Today there is almost always a suggestion of compromise in Western political speeches – and it spreads downwards. It is all very well to 'speak softly and carry a big stick',[5] but the Politburo bosses are deaf to whispers and have pachydermic skins. The West must speak loudly and pointedly if the message is to get through to Moscow.

One message might be that NATO submariners are ready, able and willing to fight – wherever and whenever – in order to keep the seas open, which is a more positive way of stating political intentions than saying (usually too late and too vaguely) that 'we will do so and so if you do such and such'. And submarines – unlike other forces – do not have to show their cards in this gigantic all-at-stake international game of poker, unless and until they reckon they will win the hand.

MAINTENANCE OF MORALE

Morale is hauled up from its classical position as the last Principle because so much depends on it – more so now than ever before. Morale is based upon a number of factors, but confidence in weapon systems and an unequivocal resolve to use them – albeit only in the last resort – lead the list.

Submariners might be more confident about their weapon systems if the spearhead was sharpened before polishing the shaft. If the analogy is not immediately obvious, the difference between a 'jolly good show' of submarine hulls and a flock of unseen submarine-fired warheads that are pretty sure of killing should be clear. The best submarine in the world is only as good as the weapon systems it embodies.

Weapon tests and training are more thorough and more realistic than they were, but they are still acknowledged (privately) by submariners to be less than adequate. Other commitments and shortage of money for this purpose prevent enough time and effort from being devoted to them – yet history (including the 1982 Falklands conflict) has repeatedly demonstrated that weapons will not work in war without exhaustive and often embarrassing trials, evaluations and exercises in peace. That means heavy expenditure; but even if another pocket has to be robbed – perhaps to the extent of forgoing two or three hulls (or, in Britain's case, uncoupling from the Trident train), the price has to be paid.

The Soviet system does not gladly tolerate the embarrassment of failure in tests, and if poor weapon performance is covered up this could give a significant advantage to the West.

From experience, the effectiveness of a weapon system is apt to vary inversely with its complexity. A distinguished British admiral[6] remarked after the Falklands war that performance 'was not nearly good enough, and some [weapons] obviously didn't work . . . The navy allowed itself to be taken in by sophistication. We sacrificed reliability and simplicity for highly complex weapons that were highly unreliable!'

The right weapon system must be selected, for an advanced time-scale, in the first place and the simpler they are the better. It cannot be emphasised too strongly that a submarine must be designed as a total integrated system which is easy to understand and operate in the most testing circumstances. However, a weapon should logically be conceived (to deal with a future enemy) before the vehicle that embodies it; thereafter the system, hull and propulsion will best move through the processes of design and construction together, anticipating technological advances when necessary. That is by no means how procurement works at present, although the US Navy has made great progress in the right direction. It would do better still – and so would the Royal Navy – if the moneymen fully understood the need for looking far ahead. Big strides are generally much more cost-effective, despite breathtaking cost-estimates, than continual modifications which extend 'down time' while increasing training and maintenance difficulties. Moreover, quantum jumps will certainly be needed if the West is to regain a lead over the Soviet submarine fleet's estimated capabilities.

Simplicity generally results in less expensive and more reliable equipment in the long run, but it can involve more work and cost in research and development. The French mathematician and physicist Blaise Pascal had a similar problem three centuries ago when he wrote, 'I have made this letter rather long only because I have not had time to make it shorter!'[7]

It may seem that these remarks have drifted away from the subject of morale, but a dependable weapon system is an important foundation for wartime spirit, whether or not that is apparent in peace. And if anybody thinks that ordinary sailors will not care or know about weapon-system effectiveness and that more highly educated officers will not display their doubts, we must hasten, as old salts, to disabuse them of these notions – although ignorance of such matters may be more prevalent amongst the unfortunate enlisted men in Soviet *podlodky*.

With respect to political resolve, and its corollary, political support, US Navy Secretary John Lehman looks after US Navy submarine interests well, boosts morale with perceptive messages, and displays resolution even when the White House wavers. Britain has, at present, a resolute leader, but resolve is less evident amongst her ministers and senior political advisers; and submariners, like anyone else, need to feel that their work is valued and their interests represented where it counts.

OFFENSIVE ACTION

Seizing the opportunity for offensive action is crucial to success; and offensive action does marvels for morale. Peacetime surveillance, and any operations which take submarines into close contact with the Soviet fleet, come as close to offensive action as can be without ever, on the Western side, infringing territorial rights. If and when a Soviet submarine breaks the rules and trespasses, there is no reason for hesitation on our part: it should be hammered, *pour encourager les autres*. Sweden was thoroughly – incomprehensibly – weak over the 'Whiskey on the Rocks' incident, and has been exposed to increasing incursions ever since.

Exercises and operations under the ice and on the high seas are not provocative. Western boats ought not to be detected in the normal course of events; but if they are, what amounts to a show of force can do nothing but good. It would be well, therefore, to accustom politicians to a rather more aggressive stance. They can be assured that their submariners – more highly professional than surface sailors by virtue of their constant fight against the sea – know exactly what they are doing; and the Soviet Navy can be convinced of that too.

Offensive action can, of course, only be undertaken with effective weapon systems and we have touched on those in relation to morale. But weapon systems depend, in turn, on effective detection equipment. Sonar will remain the primary sensor, but the question is whether passive or active sonar will be predominant in the future.

Fifteen or twenty years ago a submarine with passive sonar could be likened to somebody who was deaf wearing a couple of hearing aids: at a cocktail party he could hear, by turning in the right direction, what was being said in the room. Now, to continue the analogy, he can hear what is being said several streets away and he has a problem sorting out the sounds that reach him. Passive sonar (the deaf aid) has come a very long way, but we cannot expect it to progress at quite such a rapid rate from now on. Advances will probably be concerned mainly with detecting transient noises and providing the necessary computerisation to sort out the mass of incoming data.

Active sonar, meanwhile, will be increasingly important when at least some enemy submarines become virtually silent.

CONCENTRATION OF FORCE

A submarine is the perfect example of Concentration of Force at sea. Enough said.

ECONOMY OF EFFORT

A sensible submarine design is very cost-effective and, sensibly operated, a submarine is able to exert just so much force as is needed with a fair stock of weapons in reserve and without wasting effort. On the other hand, an over-designed submarine represents wasted resources. The new British 'Type 2400' is a very expensive example of a flexible diesel-electric submarine designed for a wide export market, which it is not likely to attract at £110–£120 million per boat – two thirds to one half of the price of the latest 'Trafalgar' class SSN, depending upon what figures at what time one cares to compare.

The 'Midnight' class, the obvious nickname for the Type 2400, has been dubbed a nuclear submarine propelled by a diesel engine – a fair enough description. It could, in fact, theoretically accommodate a reactor;[8] but the Royal Navy's infrastructure could not cope with any great increase in the planned number of SSNs – unless, of course, Trident is abandoned, which is another good reason for ditching that project.

The US 'SSN 21' design, twenty-five per cent larger than the '688' class, also seems open to criticism, although it has attracted remarkably little so far. Size will be discussed more fully, for convenience, under the heading of security, but for the moment, talking of economy, it looks as though something with a greater capability could be built at half the size for about half the cost if innovative ideas were introduced.

The most significant savings could be achieved by having fewer men in a crew. A submarine's crew is an enormously expensive item involving recruitment and training, accommodation, caring for dependents, the provision of pure air, food and water for long periods, waste removal and temperature control. Automation could substantially reduce the size of a crew (the technology is available but navies are slow to adopt it), as could cutting down the number of manned watch-keeping stations (each requiring three men on a normal watch-keeping roster).

A reduction in the number of stations implies a radical rearrangement of internal spaces. Again, a clean sheet of paper is required. Possibilities include amalgamating the control room with the weapon space, bearing in mind that television links can obviate the need for the control room to be situated around the periscopes (which must themselves remain not too far forward in a fast submarine). The weapon-reload area could be used (as it often was in the past) for part of the crew accommodation. Consideration might also be given to putting torpedoes aft, where they can 'swim out' quietly astern, rather than forward, where they interfere with sonar performance and usually necessitate angling tubes outwards abaft the array – and this presumably implies that 'fish' cannot be discharged at high speed. Alternatively, the sonar might be put aft; and certain weapons could be forward and others aft. There are several possible permutations and combinations if traditional arrangements do not mesmerise operators and designers.

A smaller crew would, of course, require major maintenance to be undertaken by shoreside personnel, so there might not be much of an overall reduction in numbers. However, shoreside personnel are much easier to recruit, and training can be confined to their particular task – they do not have to be submariners. Above all, taking men out of the submarine itself would achieve considerable economies in auxiliary machinery, living spaces and storage areas, all leading to a smaller, cheaper and less detectable boat.

A half-cost submarine would, of course, enable twice as many boats to be built for the same money, and sheer numbers are bound to count for more and more as submarines become quieter and detection ranges shorter.

Ashore, uneconomical effort is exemplified in non-operational Ministry of Defence departments. To take a mundane example, it is complained that drafts are commonly sent 400 miles to typists in Glasgow; hold-ups of three weeks in a typing pool are quite usual; and it is not unknown for frustrated officers to take material which is unclassified (they swear to that) home to their wives for typing. The mills of God grind slowly in Whitehall and, to continue the aphorism, they grind 'exceeding' small – achieving exceedingly petty economies thereby. Consequently, the huge amount of effort devoted to a project – at vast expense – is dissipated by delays.

Sheer inefficiency could easily be cured if a businessman of the right calibre were given a free hand; but the inertia which lies behind it is deep-rooted. Inertia is seldom due to sloth: it derives from the prolonged questioning and cross-questioning (arguably arising more often from pedantry than a sincere desire for rightness) which fills minute sheets and dockets until they pile so high that the original aim, right at the bottom, is lost to sight.

On the one hand the civil service (of any ministry) is quite right, if sincere, to probe and explore very thoroughly before consenting to expenditure; but on the other hand paperwork takes so absurdly long to circulate that the fruit is over-ripe or past its best before it reaches the customer. So far as the sincerity of civil service intentions (of any country) are concerned, some words from the British humorists

Flanders and Swann in the 1950s are apposite: 'Always be sincere even if you don't mean it.'

There are three ways in which inertia and delay – rather more notorious in the Royal Navy than the US Navy – could be overcome.

The first is to establish confidence between naval customers and civil service middle-men – and that requires the customers (operators) to prove their needs *quantitatively*, and in the right time-scale, so that they are trusted never to ask for more than they really require. Tentative extrapolation from experience of the system implies that trust would take five years to cement, but it would be well worth the wait.

Secondly, naval officers in procurement appointments (amongst which we would include intelligence posts) should remain at the same desk, without jeopardising promotion prospects, for several years and not just for a two or, exceptionally, a three year stint. We could follow the Soviet custom in this.

Thirdly, Staff Targets and Outline Staff Requirements should be handed to industry (including shipbuilders) to formulate detailed Staff Requirements with submarine operators acting as customer-consultants. When this procedure has been followed in principle the results have been encouraging. After all, commercial firms are going to produce the finished product; they advance their own technology for the best of reasons – profit – and they know their capabilities and limitations. Why attempt to dictate to the weapons industry or shipbuilders – especially when neither a transient staff officer nor a permanent civil servant understands, as a rule, what is practicable and what is not?

Trident or tax cuts?

In 1904, when submarines were first emerging, Admiral Jackie Fisher promised: 'My beloved submarines are not only going to make it damned hot for the enemy . . . but they are going to bring income tax down to threepence in the pound.' In this, unfortunately, the otherwise reliable prophet was wrong; but jettisoning the British Trident project (very recently re-estimated by some observers, one hopes wrongly, as likely to cost in the region of £14 billion – about £750 per family in the UK – rather than the quoted £9.87 billion) would certainly permit some tax cuts or, better still, the saving could be used to boost the economy and reduce the UK's current appallingly high unemployment figures.

Economy of effort originally advocated for strategy and tactics is a Principle which has to be applied long before going into battle.

FLEXIBILITY

Flexibility is better expressed in Soviet and French Principles as 'Manoeuvre and Initiative' and 'Liberty of Action' respectively.

Submarines are more flexible than other units, and hopefully they will remain so. War never turns out as predicted; the unexpected must be expected. Submarines of all types may well be required to undertake roles for which they are not primarily intended: SSNs may have to go close inshore, like it or not, for raids by frogmen or to survey a coastline; and it is not inconceivable that they will, on occasions, be required to transport troops. Minelaying may also be necessary at short notice, and it would seem prudent to maximise this capability in future designs by giving thought to external mine-chutes.

It seems desirable, too, for ballistic and cruise missile targeting by submarines on patrol (on orders from shore) to be as flexible as possible.

But, above all, flexibility in thought must be encouraged and rewarded, whatever the rank or status of a proposer, so that new ideas and innovations are not rejected out of hand simply because they are not orthodox.

CO-OPERATION

Submarine operations have usually, in war rather than peace, been degraded by attempts to co-operate with other forces. Submarines of all types work most efficiently as lone wolves. There is nothing foreseeable in the communications field that will markedly change that basic fact of life, although robotic siblings, either totally independent or controlled by underwater wire/fibre links, are an attractive possible way of increasing detection and attack opportunities.

Nevertheless, submarines can co-operate with air and surface units if some degradation of performance (such as maintaining the best sonar depth) is acceptable. They can also co-operate with their own kind, and the Soviets are probably bound, with the number of boats involved, to co-ordinate transits and attacks. History, in particular the success of German wolf-pack tactics, is on the side of co-ordination; but, again, individual performance is likely to be inhibited to some extent by the need to communicate. This does not, however, necessarily imply that submarines themselves will have to talk. SSGNs and SSGs firing at long range must rely on target data from external sources, and anti-submarine units might profitably seek to neutralise those sources at the outset.

In general, attack boats will perform best on the lightest possible rein, whether patrolling in assigned areas or acting in support of surface groups.

Upstream, much greater co-operation in procurement between NATO navies could save huge sums. Unilateral competitive developments will have to be avoided if the smaller navies are to get what they plainly need. However, experience has shown that it is very much better for one country alone to develop a piece of equipment to suit itself and others, rather than for two or more countries to work together on research and development. The actual production can subsequently be undertaken locally, thus providing the employment which is constantly cited as the reason for going it alone. Very little extra employment is involved at the investigative stage of a new system.

Practically every country has its own special expertise. Britain, for example, excels in computer software, nuclear power-plant design and quieting,[9] and she used to lead the way in sonar.

SECURITY

SSBN security has been discussed at length, but there remains the question of whether extensive ELF communications should be afforded. All in all, ELF looks like a luxury that could be omitted in our time-scale, whether for SSBNs – the primary stated requirement – or for SSNs. The Ministry of Defence has said that ELF feasibility studies (costing a modest £350,000 up to early 1985) are aimed at 'improving the operational effectiveness of Royal Navy submarines',[10] and that ELF could enable submarines to run deeper and faster with, thereby, an enhanced capability of remaining undetected,[11] and thus with greater security.

One advantage of ELF would be that SSBNs or SSNs transiting fast at depth, in the open ocean or under the ice, could be quickly pulled up to full alert status by a message from shore, thus making fuller use of available submarines. Expenditure on the systems might be justified for these operational benefits, especially if the UK and USA collaborated; but ELF, with antennae strung out over long distances, is unusually susceptible to sabotage or a first strike. On the whole, it looks as though it could be way down the list of priorities so far as security is concerned and, anticipating another Principle, it seems only marginally worthwhile for control.

With midget submersibles showing distinct signs of broadening their activities and with the omnipresent minelaying threat from all kinds of boats, the security of bases and their approach routes deserves to be moved up to top priority – perhaps it already has been. But at the same time it would be reassuring to know that Nato navies have plans and means for making non-nuclear attacks on enemy (not uniquely Soviet) ports, anchorages and communications facilities. If this is not so (and obviously such plans would be highly classified), they might also be considered for shifting up the schedule of priorities.

There are two optimum places to kill wasps. They can either be swatted while they buzz around a honey pot, or they can be destroyed in their nest. The first method is apt to be expensive, both in honey and effort; in terms of cost-effectiveness it is better to eliminate the nest. Incidentally, anybody who tries to hit wasps en route from nest to honey will soon discover that the attrition rate is low and the hunter is exposed to surprise flank attacks from his quarry.

The feasibility of carrying anti-submarine warfare into enemy harbours (other than by nuclear strike) has not, so far as is known, been investigated with enthusiasm in the West, although potential capabilities (such as the US Navy/Swimmer Delivery Vehicle/ex-SSBN combination) appear to be developing. The Soviet Navy is clearly very interested in harbour penetration. Midget submarines are thought to be attracting more attention now in Western navies and they could be advantageous weapon systems, especially for countries relatively close to Soviet bases. Some might, in the future, take the shape of robotic mini-subs (like Scicon's proposed SPUR – Scicon Patrolling Undersea Robot) or remotely operated vehicles. Midgets like these might be a good way of increasing the density of a barrier – a predictable need as Soviet submarines become quieter. Secure links over tens of miles between controlling submarines and remotely operated vehicles or robotic mini-subs are feasible.

Midgets would be a quite simple way of demonstrating a more offensive capability and giving the Politburo another headache. They also show great promise, in unmanned versions, for mine warfare work. Remotely controlled identification vehicles and remotely controlled mine-disposal system mini-subs should be in service soon. For inserting anti-terrorist teams and for covert offensive tasks (but not, probably, anything comparable to the strategic X-craft raids during the Second World War) the Subskimmer[12] sixteen-foot, two-man submersible rubber dinghy, capable of thirty knots on the surface, is promising, and doubtless better and better designs will evolve. Irrespective of anti-Soviet operations, mini-submersibles carrying special forces and a variety of weapons would be very suitable for neutralising, in harbour, the submarines and other weapon systems of pro-terrorist or piratical organised groups.

The forthcoming US submarine-launched mobile mine will go some way towards affording a harbour penetration capability, but it will hardly be selective.

It was noted in Chapter 10 that there is a fairly high risk of failure and loss in mini-submarine operations; but the greatest risk only occurs – if training is comprehensive and the vehicles are reliable – during the actual attack and, very probably, after the weapons have been planted. The chance of political embarrassment from failure can be acceptably small if the operators are determined and willing to destroy their craft. Recyclable (bite or swallow) cyanide capsules were issued to men involved in these kinds of operation in Japanese-controlled waters during the war, but that may be a trifle callous and out of place in the modern world. Special forces like the SBS, judging by what can be inferred of their performance in varied and tricky situations in the not too distant past, would like as not administer the poison capsules to the enemy in unequivocal fashion and vanish over the horizon with all guns blazing rather than go down with their craft. The wartime midget submariners were superb, but there is reason to be confident that worthy successors are ready to step into their shoes given the opportunity. On the Soviet side, Spetsnaz male and female midget submariners would probably swallow whatever pills they are given if failure loomed.

It might be sensible to put imagination to work on how Soviet sneak craft could launch an unconventional attack to penetrate NATO security. Despite comforting words from the doctors, germ warfare is a distinct possibility, and one which the Soviets are known to be researching. At the risk of being accused of looking for reds under beds, it is suggested that some of the minor, localised diseases which have mysteriously appeared (such as the Coxsackie B epidemic diagnosed since 1978 amongst inhabitants of Helensburgh near the submarine base on the Clyde) could have resulted from germ dissemination experiments. A midget submersible is not the ideal vehicle for dissemination, but Spetsnaz agents landed from it could do this job easily enough. How about infecting water supplies for a start? Submarines from the Clyde, or anywhere else, are not going to sail with sick crews.

At sea, anti-sonar and anti-torpedo decoys, acoustic countermeasures and counter-countermeasures call for more research. Soviet submarines are well equipped with devices of various kinds, and the latest boats are shaped to offer the smallest possible reflecting area to active sonar. Western navies, by contrast, seem very reluctant to consider untraditional outlines for their boats, even though a submarine is the one kind of vessel where appearances do not matter. There is current debate about what the large nacelle at the stern of certain Soviet SSNs contains: *Jane's* suggests the possibility of MHD propulsion (and this theory is strengthening), while Norwegian intelligence reckons that it houses a decoy system and the rest of NATO seems convinced it is for a towed array. It might combine both the latter functions if the pod is not in fact for auxiliary propulsion as seems likely.

As submarines become quieter, active sonar – perhaps with transmissions sounding like random noise – will have to be used more frequently to find them. Smaller boats will then be less detectable than monsters: big is not necessarily better in the submarine world.

Size is a vexed question and nuclear submariners are apt to become apoplectic when large (expensive) boats are criticised. Their argument is that weapon systems and equipment take up so much space that they cannot do with less and that Archimedes must have his say: sheer weight demands a large pressure hull, which is in any case required for a powerful reactor to achieve high speed.

One way of solving this problem could be to have two hulls with much of the equipment and weaponry that can withstand pressure and is naturally buoyant housed in the outer (light) hull. And there could be a third (light) hull aft for housing the kind of AC synchronous electrical motor, with permanent magnets that do not require excitation, that can run immersed in seawater. The technology is believed to be proven, and the only supplies from the reactor and generator(s) (which must remain within the pressure hull) would be carried by a simple three-phase connection. The avoidance of a propulsor shaft penetrating the pressure hull would greatly simplify construction of a deep-diving submarine.

Auxiliary machinery could be made smaller without undue effort (especially if there were fewer crew requirements to supply), and liquid air containers could replace bulky high-pressure air bottles. Waste heat transfer to the sea from reactor energy is also thought to be possible with less weight and space than at present.

It is not correct to say that a nuclear plant itself has to be large. At the bottom end of the scale the US Navy's 400-ton ocean engineering and research submarine NR–1, in service since 1969, is 136.4 feet long with a 12.4-foot beam. It is powered (albeit modestly) by a pressurised-water cooled reactor. Only a naval architect can say whether a reduction in hull size with a smaller reactor generating proportionally less shaft horsepower could attain the same speed as a large hull with a large reactor, but it seems sensible to enquire. Certainly boats can be made more slippery to give higher speed for no more power.

In any event, it would surely be worthwhile making large submarines more difficult to sink (for instance, by adopting double-hull design). At the same time consideration might be given to designing lighter boats, more difficult to detect, for the sort of work that traditional cruisers and destroyers used to undertake.

Is it really right, operationally and in terms of cost-effectiveness, to allow submarines to become bigger and bigger?[13]

Another vexed question concerns the diesel SSK. Is it sufficiently secure in a wartime environment? Or is it obsolescent by reason of the SSNs and the anti-submarine opposition it will encounter?

When a diesel-electric boat (SSK) is quiet, it is very quiet indeed; but it is claimed that SSN reactor coolant pumps are becoming very much quieter at all frequencies, and that natural circulation is possible up to a certain power level – which is especially desirable for SSBNs. The noise-gap between an SSN and an SSK – at low and moderate speeds – is narrowing rapidly in the US and British fleets.

Quietness is no longer the dominant factor in favour of using SSKs for specific tasks that once it was. Nor would it seem right, with huge distances to cover, for the US Navy to embark on a new SSK programme. However, SSKs are invaluable for NATO inshore work – and they need not cost anything like the British 'Type 2400'[14] if their operations are limited to what they can do best. They can be small, like the excellent German 450/498-ton 'Type 206', or its still quite modest successor the 'Type 211' of 1,500 tons; and, if thought really necessary, closed-cycle diesels are now available together with high-performance batteries (with a quoted capacity of 11,000 ampere-hours at the 100 hour rate) for extended, fully submerged operations. It is believed that a German hybrid boat incorporating a fuel-cell system is now being tested, and that its performance is hoped to be seven knots for twenty-four days. The '206's, by the way, can carry twenty-four external mines in GRP containers – an excellent feature.

It might be a mistake, however, to consider SSKs as second-class SSNs and invite them to operate in heavily patrolled open sea areas – necessary in peacetime exercises, but a trifle hazardous in war.

The idea of using submarines as secure troop transports, tankers or merchant vessels has often been mooted. Sizes up to 300,000 tons have been considered. Another suggestion has been to use a small nuclear submarine as a tug, for towing a string of sausage-like containers, primarily for oil.

The concept has its attractions, but it does not appear to be commercially viable in peace, and in war it raises a very important issue which is, again, related to the size problem. While it is true that submarines are much more secure than surface vessels, the comparison is relative, not absolute. It is not logical to talk about submarine security in one breath, and in the next to make claims for the effectiveness of anti-submarine warfare. Very large submarine transports, or a train of submersible barges, might prove all too easy to detect, and there could scarcely be any hope of survivors if they were attacked.

Security cannot be discussed without looking at the implications of classified material passing into Soviet hands. The danger arises, in part, from a tendency to over-classify documents. If a document which by its nature has to circulate widely is given a needlessly high security classification, that classification tends to be degraded, and keeping track of the documents of genuine secrecy becomes a problem – and one which Soviet agents exploit to the full. It is at least worth considering whether broad characteristics and capabilities should not be classified because, if well founded, they contribute, as has already been suggested, to deterrence. This would make it a great deal easier to keep secret the operational details which are crucial to security – submarine operating areas, times of sailing, radio and EW frequencies, and so on.

SURPRISE

Surprise has always been the submarine's main reason for success. There may be some slight danger, after long decades of peace, that submariners and designers are tending to forget that the enemy ought only to be surprised when he is hit – and not, if all goes well, before. Long-range missile-firing is not compatible with total surprise – which is fortunate for the West. But there may be no warning of torpedoes and short-to-medium-range missiles until it is too late.

Exercises, where war-shots are only simulated, do not always reveal detectable weaknesses caused by the possibly noisy opening of bow caps, torpedo discharge and so on. Observing that weapons are nowadays usually fired from comparatively long range (not least to avoid counter-detection of the attacking submarine), there could be something to be said, as previously mentioned, for letting wire-guided fish swim out astern: displacing tubes well away from the principal sonar would be advantageous anyway. It is not known if designers have this in mind for the future, although it is said that the possibility has been explored and, for some reason, rejected. Perhaps it could stand another look. In the meantime it is reported that the new US Navy SSN 21 ('Seawolf') class may have eight thirty-inch swim-out tubes in the mid-section and wide aperture array sonar at the bow, amidships and at the stern on each side – providing a precise base line for target localisation.

Speed is associated both with surprise and detectability. Nuclear submariners are adamant that high speed, though very expensive, is essential. So be it, but although they say the specific requirement does not lend itself to mathematical modelling, common sense insists that it ought to be quantifiable. The majority do seem to agree, however, that quietness at moderate speeds comes first. Again, peacetime exercise results can be misleading: high speed towards (or away from) a target which the commanding officer reckons is the only one around – from studying his exercise orders – is fine, but in war he may be exposing himself to an undetected submarine lurking silently in the shadows. Not that he can be too cautious: stealth cannot be allowed to override the risk of allowing a target to slip past. Submarines are intended, borrowing the words of John Paul Jones, to go in harm's way. Similarly, the use of active sonar, sacrificing stealth thereby, cannot be avoided if that is the only way to find and nail the enemy.

Speed can be increased without higher power or greater noise by a variety of means which will be applied soon if they are not already employed – as some undoubtedly are on Soviet boats, and presumably on certain US and British classes too. Shape is important, but unless sacrifices are made in other directions it will be difficult to return to the ideal fish-like Albacore hull, although a double-hull design could help. Turbulence can be dampened by synthetic hull coatings. Drag can be lessened by ejecting drag-reducing additives around the hull or applying them directly as a paint; or by covering the hull surface with gases; or by aviation flow techniques. One coating[15] is claimed to reduce frictional drag by more than fifty per cent. A great deal can be learned by studying fish and sea-mammals; Soviet researchers have been aware of this since soon after the war, and are probably way ahead of the West. It is assumed that anti-drag and turbulence coverings can be combined with sonar-absorbent anechoic coatings.

Propellers are being, or have been, superseded by propulsors (pump jets or something similar), which will probably progress by stages to pure underwater jet engines.

Electromagnetic (EMT) ram jet engines or magnetohydrodynamic (MHD) generators, with what amounts to jet propulsion, are on the horizon; but it seems doubtful whether they will appear outside the Soviet Navy (which has had a capability for EMT and/or MHD, possibly for auxiliary propulsion, for several years) or in the next generation of US SSNs, even if it is now agreed to be desirable. Enthusiasm may be moderated by the reportedly exceptional detectability of an MHD system by magnetic sensors, the huge amount of electrical power required (in the order of two to four megawatts at five knots) and the fact that it may not be as quiet as first suggested. Submarine technological advances must obviously not reduce one signature while raising the level of another. But the supposed advantages of water jet propulsion by some means seem such that magnetic detectability would be a relatively minor consideration, given that a system is otherwise practicable.

Surprise naturally involves weapons, and they in turn need to be fast and – up to the point where evasion is impossible – ideally undetectable. Soviet submarine speeds could reach the fifty to sixty knot mark in the next decade. The US Mark 48 torpedo in its ADCAP version should, hopefully, deal with current Soviet boats; and the British Spearfish, for which Staff Target 7525 was formulated in 1976 with broadly similar characteristics to ADCAP, is on its way now.[16] However, a partial air-flight weapon is probably the only real answer to very fast, distant targets, and it is to be hoped that Britain will bid for the forthcoming US anti-submarine stand-off weapon ('Sea Lance') when it goes into production in about 1990. A replacement for the ASW-SOW ought to be on the drawing board by then if we are to keep pace with Soviet underwater capabilities in the years 2000–25. If submariners agree to settle for mission kills (severe damage), rather than destruction, the problem should be simplified.

Finally, the mine has to be remembered: it could cause some very nasty surprises on both sides if submarines are not designed or equipped to negate its various sensing mechanisms. Incidentally, by September 1940 – one year in to the last war – the Royal Navy needed 698 minesweepers; today it has about fifty in service or ordered.

CONTROL

Control (which goes under the somewhat dowdy name of Administration in the list of British Principles) is a subject that has recurred throughout this review, but one point needs underlining again. Control depends upon communications; and communication links, including satellites, are liable to be jammed, interrupted or destroyed. Communications are also notorious for plain old-fashioned malfunctioning in times of emergency. They are governed by Murphy's Law: anything that can go wrong *will* go wrong. From all experience it would be extremely unwise to put submarine commanding officers (other than captains of boats with strategic missile systems) in a position of absolute dependence on external control: they must know how to proceed if everything shuts down. Since the Soviet system is inherently against independence, it follows that the disruption of Soviet submarine communication facilities would go a long way towards gaining the upper hand in a future anti-submarine battle.

So far as SSBNs are concerned, no expense can be spared in providing secure communications with adequate stand-by systems. In recommending approval for more TACAMO aircraft, the US House-Senate committee's report stated that 'the United States' sea-based deterrent can be no more effective or reliable than the communication relay capability to our SSBNs'. Amen to that!

It is not expected for one moment that there will be general or even widespread agreement with what has been criticised or proposed in this examination of submarine warfare. We think it has been reasonable – and reasonably rational; but if it can be proved wrong – in any respect – no matter. The intention is to stimulate informed debate about the most powerful and least understood fighting units in the whole history of war. If facts and arguments are contested or refined, and if seemingly better answers are produced thereby, the review's purpose will have been served.

Notes

CHAPTER 1

1. Admiral H. Moineville (French Navy, retired) gives this succinct definition in his strongly recommended book *Naval Warfare Today and Tomorrow* translated by Richard Compton-Hall (Basil Blackwell, 1983).
2. G. Jackson, *The Spanish Republic and the Civil War, 1931–1936*, page 424 (Princeton University Press, 1965).
3. 'The Nyon Arrangement', *League of Nations Treaties Series*, 181 (1937), pages 137–140, 149–153.
4. In 1940 Admiral Horton, with memories of his own 1914–17 exploits in the Baltic in the handy *E.9*, sent the large minelayer *Seal* to the shallows of the Kattegat against the strong advice of his staff, one of whom resigned over the issue. *Seal* was captured on her second mission.
5. In 1943, USS *Argonaut*, a cumbersome 4,164-ton minelayer (never employed as such), was ordered by Admiral Fife to carry out a standard submarine patrol in the hazardous area between New Britain and Bougainville. She was totally unsuited to the task and went to the bottom, under Japanese attacks, taking 105 officers and men with her. Submariners might say it was a needless loss.
6. The thoroughly professional quarterly *Submarine Review* published by the (US) Naval Submarine League performs an outstanding service for the US Navy submarine force, seconded by the United States Naval Institute *Proceedings*. Both publications include contributions from overseas writers.
7. Rear Admiral A. T. Mahan, *Influence of Sea Power on History*. Chapter 1 Part VI, page 58 of 1889 edition.

CHAPTER 2

1. Admiral Vladimir Chernavin relieved Admiral Sergei Gorshkov in December 1985. Earlier in his career he was the first commanding officer to launch missiles submerged and he was a pioneer in under-ice work.
2. The authors are indebted to the Defence Radiological Protection Service, RN Institute of Naval Medicine, and to Surgeon Commander Chris

Kalman in particular, for this section, which is probably the most complete and objective summary of nuclear reactor risks, safety precautions and countermeasures ever published for general readership. It has been authorised by the Ministry of Defence. Professor (and Surgeon Commander) Roger Berry, Honorary Consultant to the Department of Oncology, Middlesex Hospital, offered the comparison of radiation received from a constant and faithful partner sharing a double bed.

3. Admiral James D. Watkins, USN, CNO, to the House appropriations defence subcommittee, quoted in *Jane's Defence Weekly* 14 September 1985. It is not known how many accidents had a nuclear reactor connection.

4. *Ibid.*

5. *Ibid.*

6. A favourite remark of John Jorrocks in *Handley Cross* (1843) by R. S. Surtees.

7. *With the Red Fleet*, translated by Peter Broomfield and published by Putnam, London, 1965. To be read in conjunction with *Submarines in Arctic Waters* by I. Kolyshkin, first translated and published by Progress Publishers, Moscow in 1966, and subsequently republished by Bantam Books in 1985. Both books are out-and-out propaganda so far as claimed results are concerned; but cross-checked with British and German sources they provide an illuminating insight into Soviet methods.

8. *Handbook for U-boat Commanders*, 1942. Translation held in RN Submarine Museum library.

9. Nevertheless, the *Typhoon* captain in Tom Clancy's first-rate novel *The Hunt for Red October* (USNIP 1984) is a believable character.

CHAPTER 4

1. The accepted view of Bill Sanders, MoD Director General Submarines, quoted in December 1985.

2. Their views are respected, but history sides with the authors.

3. Quoted in *Doenitz' Memoirs* (Weidenfeld & Nicolson, 1958).

4. Quotes and references from *The Underwater War 1939–1945* by Richard Compton-Hall (Blandford Press, UK, and Stirling Publishing Company, USA).

5. VADM N. R. Thurman USN to the Seapower Subcommittee of the Senate Armed Services Committee on Submarine Warfare, 5 March 1985.

6. House Armed Services Committee in their mark-up of the 1986 Defence Bill, reported in the *Submarine Review*, July 1985.

7. BBC TV 'Defence gives Offence' (John Knox), 7 July 1985.

8. House of Representatives Select Committee under House Resolution 288, hearings beginning 9 March 1908.

9. *Parkinson's Law* by C. Northcote Parkinson (John Murray, 1958).

10. This is the figure generally quoted but, unlike the others below, it has not been calculated by the authors. Nor are the latter figures likely to be

absolutely correct. They are now being refined and analysed by the MoD to determine their relevance today.
11. Author's research, cross-checking British and German statistics with Soviet claims.

CHAPTER 5

1. The historic message flashed by lamp when USS *Nautilus* (SSN–571) got under way in the River Thames shortly after 1100 on 17 January 1955.
2. Lieutenant (later Captain) G. E. Hunt DSO*, DSC* RN.
3. Morton was Lord Chancellor to Henry VII from 1487: he extorted gifts to the exchequer from men who lived handsomely on the grounds that their wealth was manifest, and from those who lived plainly on the plea that economy had made them wealthy. In other words, Morton got what he wanted either way!

CHAPTER 7

1. Captain F. J. Walker's description from HMS *Starling* during the Battle of the Atlantic.
2. *Sink 'em All* by V. A. Charles Lockwood USN (Retd) (E. P. Dutton & Co Inc., New York, 1951).
3. By Rear Admiral J. R. Hill in his *Anti-Submarine Warfare* (Ian Allen Ltd, 1984). This is the best general readership book on ASW produced so far.
4. An eminently practical suggestion offered to the author by Cdr J. B. Bryant USN, lately executive officer of USS *Haddock* (SSN–621).
5. Reported in *Jane's Defence Weekly*, 25 January 1986.
6. Quoted by Rear Admiral Hill (see note 3).
7. See the article 'Should NATO be Fustest with the Mostest' by Cdr E. J. Ortleib USN (Retd) in USNIP October 1985. This gives a very useful summary of possible situations and probabilities based on sound reasoning.
8. *Ibid.*
9. A succinct and credible analysis of missile requirements against Soviet units was given in the article on 'Cruise Missile Warfare' by Captain H. M. Hura USN and Lcdr D. Miller USN in USNIP October 1985. We have by no means done their excellent work justice by following up the implications of a few of their pointers here.
10. *Ibid.*

CHAPTER 8

1. Commander Boris Karnicki, Polish submarine *Sokol*.

CHAPTER 9

1. For further reading, see *China as a Maritime Power* by David G. Muller (Westview Press, Boulder, Colorado, 1983).

CHAPTER 10

1. The story of *Turtle*'s attack is largely mythical, but George Washington's remark was justified by the seeds which Bushnell sowed.
2. The safe limit for neat oxygen is now known to be eight to ten metres, according to work and temperature.
3. *Escape over the Himalayas* by Elios Toschi (Ed. Eur Milan).
4. British Special Boat Squadron.
5. In October 1942 the forty-five-foot Norwegian fishing boat *Arthur* took two 'Chariots' to Norway. Bad weather foiled the attempt and the 'Chariots' broke loose – but only because of poor British workmanship on the securing bolts.
6. *Axis Submarine Successes* by Jurgen Rohwer (English Language Edition by USNIP, 1983, published in the UK by Patrick Stephens Ltd).
7. *Submarine Warfare Monsters and Midgets* by Richard Compton-Hall (Blandford Press, UK and Sterling Publishing Company, USA, 1985). Also the first authoritative account in *Above us the Waves* by Warren and Benson (Harrap, 1953); *Sink the Tirpitz* by Leonce Peillard (Jonathan Cape, 1965) and *Against all Odds* by Thomas Gallagher (Macdonald, 1971).
8. *Ibid.*
9. HMS *Grampus* (then Lt Cdr Compton-Hall) on Operation Skua, 1963.
10. ONI publication *Small Battle Units* (March, 1949).
11. The article by Carl Bildt in *Jane's Naval Review* 1985 titled 'Submarine Incursions: Sweden fights back' gives a very useful summary of sightings and reports by the Swedish Submarine Defence Commission, together with sources.
12. Vice Admiral K. V. Makarov in 1985.
13. Vice Admiral I. M. Kapitanets in 1985.
14. N. I. Savinkin in 1985.
15. Soviet defector Arkady Shevenko revealed in 1984 that '... the ruling Politburo had empowered the Soviet military in the early 1970s systematically to survey the Scandinavian coastline ...' and that 'Moscow had plans to hide its nuclear submarines in the fjords of Norway and Sweden in an international crisis.'
16. These are five of the ten Soviet Principles of War. The others are Advance and Consolidation; Concentration; Adequate Reserves; Morale; and Annihilation.
17. There is also the suggestion of using gunnery with delay-fused rounds to substitute for the depth-charges and rocket-thrown depth bombs which are no longer fitted in many modern ASW vessels.

CHAPTER 11

1. Notably in his article 'The Maritime Strategy' included with the January 1986 issue of USNIP.
2. Unfortunately Raborn's subsequent appointment as Director of the CIA was not considered a success.
3. Report in *Jane's Defence Weekly*, 16 November 1985.
4. The authors are greatly indebted to a comprehensive review of 'Under Ice Operations' by Captain T. M. LeMarchand RN first published in the *Naval War College Review*, March-April 1985.
5. Contre-Amiral Hubert Moineville in his book *Naval Warfare Today and Tomorrow* (Basil Blackwell, 1983. Translated from the French by Richard Compton-Hall).
6. Interview with French Defence Minister Paul Quilès reported by Jean de Galard in *Jane's Defence Weekly*, 14 December 1985.
7. Professor Lawrence Freedman in his *Britain and Nuclear Weapons*, p. 38 (Macmillan, 1981).
8. This expression is used by Peter Malone, derived from interviews, in his comprehensive book *The British Nuclear Deterrent* (Croom Helm and St Martin's Press, USA, 1984).
9. *Jane's Weapon Systems.*
10. An excellent summary of the arguments, with an appreciation of SLCM pros and cons, was given in 'An Uncontrollable Tomahawk?' by Russell S. Hibbs (USNIP, January 1985). We are not doing full justice to the reasoning and to the quoted strategists here because there is insufficient space; but we hope that we have picked out the salient points.
11. These estimated 1985 figures, taken or extrapolated from the best available published sources, give some idea of comparative costs; but even if reasonably correct, they are not absolute. RDT & E has to be taken into account: the latter was running at $2077.5 million in 1985 for Trident II in the USA. If the UK buys the weapons at 'retail' price it is getting a bargain.
12. Apparently from test results described by RADM Walter Locke, USN, a former head of the Tomahawk Project Office.
13. Fourth Report from the Defence Committee, Session 1980–1, 'Strategic Nuclear Weapon Policy' (HMSO).
14. Sixth Report from Defence Committee, Session 1984–5, 'The Trident Programme' (HMSO).
15. Pseudonym of François Marie Arouet (1694–1778): *Essay on the Morals of the Holy Empire of the Hapsburgs.*

CHAPTER 12

1. From the famous *Punch* cartoon of 1902. Bishop to curate at breakfast: 'I'm afraid you've got a bad egg, Mr Jones.' 'Oh no, my Lord, I assure you! Parts of it are excellent.'
2. The traditional convoy phraseology.

3. Lt Cdr G. D. Noble RN coined the phrase in 1985 at the Naval Staff College, where a tutor described it as clumsy. We disagree with the tutor and can find no better expression.

4. Admiral Watkins' goal '. . . to use maritime power . . . to bring about war termination on favourable terms . . .' (quoted in Chapter 10) satisfies the war aim, but does not address the situation from the start.

5. Quoted by Theodore Roosevelt in an address at the Minnesota State Fair, 2 September 1901. The source is uncertain, but Roosevelt said it was a West African proverb!

6. Admiral Sir James Eberle, reported as criticising weapon systems during the British Defence Committee's 1984 examination of performance in the Falklands conflict.

7. Pascal, *Lettres Provinciales*, 14 December 1656.

8. At the present advanced production stage this is probably no longer feasible.

9. Rolls-Royce and Associates, Derby, are arguably unrivalled, but it is suspected that they may not always be given the chance to show what they can do, possibly because they may not always be asked the right questions.

10. MoD PE statement, 4 June 1985.

11. Letter (paraphrased) from John Lee MP, Parliamentary Under Secretary of State for Defence Procurement, to Rt Hon Donald Stewart MP, 4 June 1985.

12. Submarine Products Limited, Hexham, Northumberland.

13. The limited technical research which the authors have been able to do in this field has been partly initiated by an imaginative and far-sighted article, 'Don't Make It Bigger – Please' by Harold C. Hemond in the *Naval Engineers Journal*, March 1985.

14. First of class, HMS *Upholder*, due to complete towards the end of 1987 at an estimated £110–120 million.

15. Reported to be invented by the German scientist Max O. Kramer, now living in America. Details have not been published. More recently, in 1983, a fluorocarbon-base liquid has been developed by Fluorocarbon Technologies Inc., and tested with encouraging results in China. Doubtless other points are also being evaluated.

16. Marconi Underwater Systems have managed to develop Spearfish more quickly than has been usual in Britain; but it will still be more than ten years from Staff Target to service availability.

Glossary of Acronyms

GENERAL

AA	anti-aircraft
ADP	automatic data processing
ASUW	anti-surface warfare
ASW	anti-submarine warfare
BW	Biological/bacteriological warfare
CW	chemical warfare
DoD	Department of Defense (US)
ELF	extremely low frequency (radio)
EMP	electromagnetic pulse (nuclear)
EMT	electromagnetic (propulsion)
Fin	conning tower/bridge/masts streamlining (RN); 'sail' in US Navy
FY	fiscal year (US) 1 October to 30 September (i.e. FY 1988 begins on 1 October 1987)
GPS	global position system (NAVSTAR)
GRU	*Glavnoye Razvedyvatelnoye Upravleniye* Chief Intelligence Directorate of Soviet General Staff
HF	high frequency
HF/DF	high frequency direction finding (radio)
hp	horsepower (see also shp)
HTP	high test peroxide (fuel)
HY	high yield (steels)
IFF	identification friend or foe (automatic response to radar-type interrogation)
KGB	*Komitet Gosudarstvennoy Bezopasnosti* Soviet security/intelligence service.
LAMPS	light airborne (helicopter) multi-purpose system
LF	low frequency
MHD	magnetohydrodynamic (propulsion)
MoD	Ministry of Defence (UK and others)
NATO	North Atlantic Treaty Organisation
NAVSTAR	navigation satellite timing and ranging (see GPS)
Politburo	Supreme policy-making body of the Soviet Communist Party, renamed in 1952 the Praesidium of the Central Committee but reverting to the old title (abbreviation of Russian for Political Bureau) in 1966

PWR	pressurised water reactor (nuclear)
R & D	research and development
RDT & E	research, development, test and evaluation
RN	Royal Navy (UK)
RPV	reactor pressure vessel (nuclear)
Ro-Ro	roll on-roll off (ferry)
Sail	*see* Fin
SALT	Strategic Arms Limitation Treaty
SDI	Strategic Defense Initiative
SHF	super high frequency (radio)
shp	shaft horsepower
SINS	ship inertial navigation system
Snorkel	pipe for drawing air from the surface to run diesel(s) at periscope depth (US) *Schnorchel* (i.e. shnozzle – vulg. for 'nose') was the original German word.
Snort	RN term for US Navy snorkel
SOA	speed of advance
TERCOM	terrain contour matching navigation system (cruise missiles)
VHF	very high frequency (radio)
VLF	very low frequency (radio)
UHF	ultra high frequency (radio)
USN	United States Navy

SUBMARINES

AGSS	auxiliary submarine (e.g. for rescue or oceanological work)
APSS	auxiliary transport submarine
ASSA	auxiliary cargo submarine
ASSO	auxiliary oiler submarine
DSRV	deep submergence rescue vehicle
DSSV	deep submergence search vehicle
DSV	deep submergence vehicle
FBM	fleet ballistic-missile submarine (see also SSBN)
Guppy	greater underwater propulsive power (the name given to the fast US Navy diesel-electric submarines converted and stream-lined from standard fleet boats after the Second World War)
HTV	hull test vehicle (formerly NR–2) (nuclear propulsion)
IXSS	miscellaneous unclassified submarine (alongside harbour training)
LPSS	amphibious transport submarine
NR	submersible research vehicle (nuclear propulsion)
SDV	swimmer delivery vehicle
SNLE	*sous-marin nucléaire lance-engins* (French) SSBN
SPUR	Scicon's patrolling underwater robot
SS	submarine (usually implying diesel-electric propulsion)
SSA	cargo submarine

SSB   ballistic-missile submarine (diesel-electric)
SSBN   ballistic-missile submarine (nuclear propulsion)
SSG   guided-missile submarine (diesel-electric)
SSGN   guided-missile submarine (nuclear propulsion)
SSK   patrol submarine (diesel-electric)
SSM   Submarine minelayer
SSN   fleet attack submarine (nuclear propulsion) – 'hunter-killer' and
              colloquially in the Royal Navy 'Fighter' (as opposed to SSBN
              'Bomber' in the Royal Navy and 'Boomer' in the US Navy)
SSO   submarine oiler
SSP   submarine transport
SSR   radar picket submarine
SSRN   radar picket submarine (nuclear propulsion)
SST   target and training submarine

SENSORS AND WEAPONS

ABM   anti-ballistic missile
ADCAP   advanced capability (specifically applied to Mark 48 torpedo)
ALCM   air-launched cruise missile
ALWT   advanced lightweight torpedo (US)
ASAT   anti-satellite (weapon or system)
ASCM   anti-ship cruise missile
ASROC   anti-submarine rocket
CM   cruise missile
COMINT   communications intelligence
ECCM   electronic counter-countermeasures
ECM   electronic countermeasures
ELINT   electronic intelligence
ESM   electronic support measures
FRAS   free rocket, anti-submarine
Hz   Herz – formerly cycle(s) per second
ICBM   intercontinental ballistic missile
IR   infra-red
MAD   magnetic anomaly detector/detection (*also*, mutually assured
              destruction)
MIRV   multiple independently targetable re-entry vehicle
MRV   multiple re-entry vehicle
SLBM   submarine-launched ballistic missile
SLCM   submarine- (or sea-) launched cruise missile
SLOC   sea line of communication
SOSUS   sound surveillance system (sonar ground array)
SUBROC   submarine-launched rocket (tactical nuclear weapon)
SURTASS   surveillance towed array sensor system
TACTAS   tactical towed array sonar
USGW   undersea guided weapon

Acknowledgements

We have such a large number of people to thank for help of one kind and another that the following list is bound to be incomplete. There are also many who – for political, service or personal reasons – have offered contributions or opinion off the record and do not wish to be acknowledged.

First and foremost we are grateful to Jane's Publishing Company without whose unique publications – notably *Jane's Fighting Ships*, *Weapon Systems*, and *Defence Weekly* – it would be difficult for anybody to learn much about the world's navies.

The monthly *United States Naval Institute Proceedings* (US Naval Institute, 2062 Generals Highway, Annapolis, Maryland 21401) has also been a fruitful source of information and ideas; and the excellent *Submarine Review* (published quarterly by the Naval Submarine League, Box 1148, Annandale, Virginia 22003) has been a positive inspiration. Both publications are strongly recommended for continued reading, particularly the latter in the submarine context. Membership of the Institute and League can be applied for outside, as well as within, the USA.

For the most part we have used published books and articles as signposts for our own research; but where factual information or informed opinion has been extracted – without, we trust, being guilty of plagiarism – we have endeavoured to credit authors and ideas in our notes, if not in the text itself.

Where photographs have not specifically been credited they come either from the Jane's library or from the RN Submarine Museum (by kind permission of the Trustees) or from the authors' collections. It has sometimes been impossible, regrettably, to trace the origin of a particular picture, but we have done our best to acknowledge sources.

For his customary excellent drawings we are grateful to David Hill, whose skill in producing simple and meaningful illustrations from complex information is probably unequalled.

For various documents, photographs and attributable advice our particular thanks go, amongst numerous others, to:

Australia	Lt Cdr Barry Evans RAN
France	Direction des Constructions et Armes Navales, Marine Nationale, Cherbourg
Germany	Kapitän Zur See H. Ewerth

302 ACKNOWLEDGEMENTS

Japan   Admiral Kazuo Ueda (Retd)

Netherlands Captain J. Kleijn RNLN

UK   Jane's Publishing Company
               The Trustees of the Royal Navy Submarine Museum
               Captain G. R. Villar DSC, FBIM RN(Retd)
               Captain R. H. S. Thompson RN
               Captain A. E. Thomson RN
               Captain R. J. F. Turner RN(Retd)
               Lt Cdr G. D. Noble BA (Hons) RN
               Lt Cdr C. H. Donnithorne RN
               Cdr J. F. Perowne OBE, RN
               Lt Cdr A. P. Johnson MBE, RN
               Captain J. O. Coote RN(Retd)
               Cdr M. P. Gilbert RN
               Cdr R. P. Stevens RN
               D. K. Brown RCNC
               Professor (and Surgeon Cdr) R. J. Berry
               Surgeon Captain R. R. Pearson RN
               Surgeon Cdr C. J. Kalman RN
               Lt Cdr M. R. Wilson RN(Retd), Naval Historical Branch
               Colin James
               Vickers Shipbuilding and Engineering Ltd
               Scicon Consultancy International Ltd
               Marconi Underwater Systems
               Submarine Products Ltd
               Rolls-Royce and Associates (RRA) Ltd
               Chloride Power Storage (division of Chloride Industrial
                   Batteries Ltd)
               Bryan Heeps, National Westminster Bank, Gosport

USA   Vice Admiral R. Y. Kaufman USN(Retd) (Yogi Inc.)
               Vice Admiral James Calvert USN(Retd)
               Cdr J. B. Bryant USN
               Dr R. C. Olson (Engineering & Science Associates Inc,
                   Rockville MD)
               Dr W. A. Von Winkle (Naval Underwater Systems Center)
               MMCS (SS) R. Zollars, Director Submarine Force Library
                   and Museum
               Professor Richard K. Morris
               The General Dynamics Electric Boat Division
                   Naval Ocean Systems Center, San Diego
               Richard J. Boyle
               Norman Polmar and USNIP

Index